Statistical Symbol | Meaning

Statistical Symbol	Meaning
s^2	sample variance
z	z-score
ρ	Spearman rank-difference correlation coe
r	Pearson product-movement correlation coefficient
r^2	coefficient of determination
H_0	null hypothesis
H_1	alternative hypothesis
df	degrees of freedom
n	number of scores in a group
k	number of independent groups
grand ΣX	sum of all scores in all groups
grand ΣX^2	sum of the square in all scores in all groups
SS_T	total sum of squares
SS_W	sum of squares within groups
SS_B	sum of squares between groups
MS_W	mean square for the sum of squares within groups
MS_B	mean square for the sum of squares between groups
F distribution	table value required to reject null hypothesis
$N - k$	degrees of freedom within groups
$k - 1$	degrees of freedom between groups

Measurement by the Physical Educator

Why and How

Eighth Edition

David K. Miller

University of North Carolina Wilmington (retired)

Mc
Graw
Hill
Education

MEASUREMENT BY THE PHYSICAL EDUCATOR: WHY AND HOW, EIGHTH EDITION

Published by McGraw-Hill Education, 2 Penn Plaza, New York, NY 10121. Copyright ©2020 by McGraw-Hill Education. All rights reserved. Printed in the United States of America. Previous editions ©2014, 2010, and 2006. No part of this publication may be reproduced or distributed in any form or by any means, or stored in a database or retrieval system, without the prior written consent of McGraw-Hill Education, including, but not limited to, in any network or other electronic storage or transmission, or broadcast for distance learning.

Some ancillaries, including electronic and print components, may not be available to customers outside the United States.

This book is printed on acid-free paper.

1 2 3 4 5 6 7 8 9 LCR 21 20 19

ISBN 978-1-259-92242-8 (bound edition)
MHID 1-259-92242-1 (bound edition)

ISBN 978-1-260-39778-9 (loose-leaf edition)
MHID 1-260-39778-5 (loose-leaf edition)

Product Developer: *Francesca King*
Marketing Manager: *Meredith Leo*
Content Project Manager: *Lisa Bruflodt, Emily Windelborn*
Buyer: *Laura Fuller*
Designer: *Beth Blech*
Content Licensing Specialist: *Jacob Sullivan*
Compositor: *Lumina Datamatics, Inc.*

All credits appearing on page or at the end of the book are considered to be an extension of the copyright page.

Library of Congress Cataloging-in-Publication Data

Names: Miller, David K. (David Keith) author.
Title: Measurement by the physical educator : why and how / David K. Miller,
    University of North Carolina Wilmington (retired).
Description: Eighth edition. | New York, NY : McGraw-Hill Education, [2020] |
    Includes bibliographical references and index.
Identifiers: LCCN 2018051298| ISBN 9781259922428 (hardback) | ISBN 1259922421
    (bound edition) | ISBN 9781260397789 (loose-leaf edition) | ISBN
    1260397785 (loose-leaf edition)
Subjects: LCSH: Physical fitness—Testing. | Physical
    fitness—Testing—Statistics. | BISAC: SPORTS & RECREATION / General.
Classification: LCC GV436 .M54 2020 | DDC 613.7—dc23
LC record available at https://lccn.loc.gov/2018051298

The Internet addresses listed in the text were accurate at the time of publication. The inclusion of a website does not indicate an endorsement by the authors or McGraw-Hill Education, and McGraw-Hill Education does not guarantee the accuracy of the information presented at these sites.

mheducation.com/highered

Dedicated to my wife, Sandra, for your love and support.
You are the joy of my life.

CONTENTS

PREFACE

Purpose and Content

Students in measurement and evaluation classes often are bombarded with an abundance of information. Regrettably, some students complete the class with a little knowledge in many areas but no confidence or skills to perform the procedures and techniques presented in the class. As professionals in school or nonschool settings, these same students often do not measure and assess knowledge, and physical performance, in the proper way.

The purpose of this text is to help the physical education, exercise science, or kinesiology major develop the necessary confidence and skills to conduct measurement techniques properly and effectively. However, more than just measurement techniques are presented. Emphasis is placed upon the reasons for the measurement and the responsibilities after measurement is completed. These inclusions should help the student develop an appreciation of the need for measurement in a variety of settings. In addition, every effort has been made to present all the material in an uncomplicated way, and only practical measurement techniques are included.

Upon successful completion of the chapter objectives, the user of this text should be able to

1. Understand, explain, and use the professional terminology presented in the text.
2. Use and interpret fundamental statistical techniques.
3. Select appropriate knowledge and psychomotor tests.
4. Construct good psychomotor tests.
5. Construct good objective and subjective knowledge tests.
6. Objectively assess and grade students who participate in a physical education class.
7. Administer psychomotor and sports skills tests, interpret the results, and prescribe activities for the development of psychomotor and sports skills.
8. Administer body structure and composition tests, interpret the results, and prescribe scientifically sound methods for attainment of a healthy percentage of body fat.
9. Administer functional fitness tests to older adults, interpret the results, and prescribe activities for the development of functional fitness.
10. Administer psychomotor tests to special-needs populations, interpret the results, and prescribe activities for the development of psychomotor skills.

Audience

At one time, most undergraduate physical education majors planned to teach in grades K through 12. Today many majors in physical education, exercise science, kinesiology, and other similar subject areas anticipate a career in the nonschool environment. This book is designed for use by majors preparing for either environment—school or nonschool. With the exceptions of the construction of knowledge tests and grading skills, all of the competencies presented in this book will be expected in a variety of professional settings.

Additionally, the term *physical educator* is used throughout the text to refer to individuals who perform the professional responsibilities presented in the chapters. When working through the physical attributes to better the lives of others, we all are physical educators.

Organization

The text is organized so that the student will develop fundamental statistics skills early in the course (chapters 1–4). These skills are to be demonstrated throughout the text. Chapter 5, "What Is a Good Test?" describes the criteria of a good test. Since these criteria and related terms are used throughout the text, it is recommended that this chapter be covered before the chapters that follow. Chapter 6, "Construction of Knowledge Tests," and chapter 7, "Assessment and Grading," may be covered in the sequence presented or later in the course. It is recommended that chapter 8, "Construction and Administration of Psychomotor Tests," be presented before any discussion of psychomotor testing. The components of health-related physical fitness and skill-related physical fitness (chapters 9–14) are described before the presentation of health-related and skill-related physical fitness tests (chapter 15, "Physical Fitness") so that the student will better understand these components. Many practical tests are included in chapters 9–15. These chapters may be presented in a different sequence if the instructor wishes to do so. Chapter 16 on functional fitness of "Older Adults"; chapter 17, "Special-Needs Populations"; and chapter 18, "Sports Skills" also may be presented in a different sequence by the instructor.

Approach

The statistics information is presented in a friendly and simplified manner so that it is nonintimidating. In addition, although the text information is sometimes presented in a "nuts-and-bolts" style, it is comprehensive as well as straightforward, accurate, and practical.

This book and related assignments can be completed without the use of a microcomputer, but the microcomputer can be applied in a variety of ways. No instruction for the use of a statistical software program is provided. A variety of such programs are available, however, and the program of choice may be used by the instructor and students. The psychomotor tests presented in chapters 9–15 are practical, inexpensive, and satisfactory for both sexes. They require little, if any, special equipment, and norms are included with many tests. The lack of norms should not limit the use of any test, however. Upon completion of chapter 2, the student should have the ability to construct norms.

Pedagogy

The following features of this book will assist the student in mastering the material:

- The text is readable and understandable.
- Specific objectives are stated at the beginning of each chapter.
- Key words are in bold print.
- Statistical procedures are provided in steps, or cookbook format, and examples related to physical performance are provided.
- Reminders of chapter objectives are placed in the text in the form of "Are you able to do the following?" questions.
- A Point of Emphasis box is used to reinforce particular concepts or practices.
- Review problems to reinforce the chapter objectives are provided at the conclusion of most chapters.
- Review questions are provided at the conclusion of all chapters.

New to This Edition

All chapters in the previous edition have been retained. Included in this edition are the following:

- Description of teacher self-assessment
- Revision and updating of some tables
- Updating of health-related physical fitness tests

Users of edition 7 also will find that minor changes have been made in several chapters.

Instructor Resources

Online ancillaries that accompany this text include PowerPoint slides and test bank questions. These resources are available through Connect.

Acknowledgments

I am grateful to the many students and colleagues who contributed to the development of the eight editions of this text. The production of this text is possible because of your support. To the publishers who permitted use of their materials and to the McGraw-Hill Higher Education staff members who contributed to eight edition, I say thanks. To Kayci Wyatt, Stacey Lutkoski, Jacob Sullivan, Francesca King, and Nikhil Rajender Kumar Meena I express appreciation for your patience, skill, and guidance.

Eighth Edition Reviewers

Kay Daigle
Southeastern Oklahoma State University

Glenn Steimling
William Penn University

Shelia Lucyle Jackson
Arkansas Tech University

Kristin Heumann
Colorado Mesa University

Brian Brabham
University of Mary Hardin-Baylor

Julie M Knutson
Minnesota State University-Moorhead

Melissa A. Parks
Louisiana State University of Alexandria

Lauri Hauck
California Baptist University

® | Students—study more efficiently, retain more and achieve better outcomes. Instructors—focus on what you love—teaching.

SUCCESSFUL SEMESTERS INCLUDE CONNECT

FOR INSTRUCTORS

You're in the driver's seat.

Want to build your own course? No problem. Prefer to use our turnkey, prebuilt course? Easy. Want to make changes throughout the semester? Sure. And you'll save time with Connect's auto-grading too.

65%
Less Time Grading

They'll thank you for it.

Adaptive study resources like SmartBook® help your students be better prepared in less time. You can transform your class time from dull definitions to dynamic debates. Hear from your peers about the benefits of Connect at **www.mheducation.com/highered/connect**

Make it simple, make it affordable.

Connect makes it easy with seamless integration using any of the major Learning Management Systems—Blackboard®, Canvas, and D2L, among others—to let you organize your course in one convenient location. Give your students access to digital materials at a discount with our inclusive access program. Ask your McGraw-Hill representative for more information.

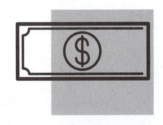

©Hill Street Studios/Tobin Rogers/Blend Images LLC

Solutions for your challenges.

A product isn't a solution. Real solutions are affordable, reliable, and come with training and ongoing support when you need it and how you want it. Our Customer Experience Group can also help you troubleshoot tech problems—although Connect's 99% uptime means you might not need to call them. See for yourself at **status.mheducation.com**

Effective, efficient studying.

Connect helps you be more productive with your study time and get better grades using tools like SmartBook, which highlights key concepts and creates a personalized study plan. Connect sets you up for success, so you walk into class with confidence and walk out with better grades.

" I really liked this app—it made it easy to study when you don't have your text-book in front of you. "

- Jordan Cunningham,
Eastern Washington University

Study anytime, anywhere.

Download the free ReadAnywhere app and access your online eBook when it's convenient, even if you're offline. And since the app automatically syncs with your eBook in Connect, all of your notes are available every time you open it. Find out more at **www.mheducation.com/readanywhere**

No surprises.

The Connect Calendar and Reports tools keep you on track with the work you need to get done and your assignment scores. Life gets busy; Connect tools help you keep learning through it all.

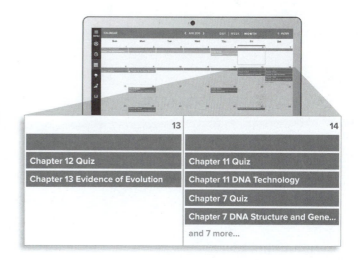

13	14
Chapter 12 Quiz	Chapter 11 Quiz
Chapter 13 Evidence of Evolution	Chapter 11 DNA Technology
	Chapter 7 Quiz
	Chapter 7 DNA Structure and Gene...
	and 7 more...

Learning for everyone.

McGraw-Hill works directly with Accessibility Services Departments and faculty to meet the learning needs of all students. Please contact your Accessibility Services office and ask them to email accessibility@mheducation.com, or visit **www.mheducation.com/about/accessibility.html** for more information.

Measurement, Evaluation, Assessment, and Statistics

1

After completing this chapter, you should be able to

1. Define the term *statistics*.

2. Define the terms *test*, *measurement*, *evaluation*, and *assessment*, and give examples of each.

3. List and describe the reasons for measurement, evaluation, and assessment by the physical educator.

4. State why the ability to use statistics is important for the physical educator.

"Why statistics? I don't need statistics to be a good teacher." "I don't need statistics. I plan to work in a health fitness center."

Perhaps you have made comments similar to these or have heard some of your classmates make them. If you do not plan to perform your responsibilities as they should be performed, and you do not plan to continue your professional growth, you are correct in believing that you do not need statistics. However, if you want to perform your professional responsibilities in exemplary fashion, the study of statistics should be included in your preparation.

Statistics involves the collection, organization, and analysis of numerical data. Statistical methods require the use of symbols, terminology, and techniques that may be new to you, but you should not fear these methods. The idea that statistics is a form of higher mathematics is incorrect. To successfully perform the statistics presented in this book, you need only a basic knowledge of arithmetic and some simple algebra. The most complex formula in statistics can be reduced to a series of logical steps involving adding, subtracting, multiplying, and dividing. If you are willing to study the statistical concepts and perform the provided exercises, you will master the statistics presented to you.

Before finding an answer to "Why statistics?" you should understand the meaning of measurement and evaluation and the reasons for measurement by the physical educator. Measurement is not a new concept to you. You measured your height and weight throughout your growing years. You have read how fast athletes have run, how high some have jumped, and how far a baseball or a golf ball has been hit. All of these are examples of measurement. When you assume a position as a physical educator in the private, public, teaching, or nonteaching sector, you will perform measurement tasks. On many occasions, this measurement will be administered in the form of a test, resulting in a score. For our purposes, a **test** is an instrument or a tool used to make a particular measurement. The tool may be written, oral, mechanical, or another variation. Examples of such tests are cardiorespiratory fitness tests, flexibility tests, and strength tests. On other occasions, measurement may not involve a performance by a person but will consist of the measurement of a particular attribute. Heart rate, blood pressure, and body fat measurements are such examples. You should recognize that in all of the preceding examples, numbers are obtained. So we can say that **measurement** is usually thought of as quantitative; it is the process of assigning a number to a performance or an attribute of a person. Sometimes when you measure, the score is a term or a phrase, but usually measurement will involve the use of numbers. Of course, objects are measured too, but as a physical educator you will be concerned primarily with people.

Once you have completed the measurement of a particular attribute of an individual, you must give meaning to it. For instance, if you administer a cardiorespiratory fitness test to participants of an adult fitness group, they will immediately want to know the status of their cardiorespiratory fitness. Without an interpretation of the quality of the test scores, the test has no meaning to the group. If you perform skinfold measurements in a physical education class, on athletes, or on members of a health club, the individuals will want to know what the sum of the measurements means in relation to body fat; otherwise, the measurements will have no meaning. The same can be said for written tests. There must be an interpretation of the test scores if they are to have meaning. This interpretation of measurement is **evaluation:** that is, a judgment about the measurement. For measurement to be effective, it must be followed by evaluation.

It is at this point that some physical educators stop. They measure an attribute, interpret the results to individuals, and go no further. They fail to use the results of their measurement and evaluation to identify performance and behavior problems and to prescribe how the problems can be corrected. This process—measure, evaluate, identify, and prescribe—is referred to as **assessment.** Let's again use the example of skinfold measurements. Assume that several individuals in the group that you measure are diagnosed as overfat as a result of your measurements. You should attempt to determine the eating and activity habits of the individuals and prescribe the proper diet and exercise program. This process is followed by exercise prescription specialists and athletic trainers. Individuals do not all begin an exercise program at the same level. The prescription level for an individual is determined through measurement, evaluation, and identification of the strengths and weaknesses or needs of the individual. Likewise, athletic trainers follow the same process with injured athletes. The extent of the athlete's injury is determined through measurement and evaluation and then a rehabilitation program is prescribed. Additionally, the athlete usually is not permitted to return to competition until certain tasks or tests can be performed successfully. In the school environment, the concept of authentic assessment is emphasized. This concept will be discussed in a later chapter.

- Define the term *statistics*.

- Define the terms *test, measurement, evaluation,* and *assessment,* and give examples of measurement, evaluation, and assessment.

Reasons for Measurement, Evaluation, and Assessment by the Physical Educator

Now that you know what is meant by the terms *measurement, evaluation,* and *assessment,* let's look at ways you will use them in your profession.

Motivation

If used correctly, measurement can highly motivate most individuals. In anticipation of a test, students usually study the material or practice the physical tasks that are to be measured. This study or practice should improve performance. Skinfold measures might encourage overfat individuals in health fitness programs to lose body fat. Older individuals may be motivated to improve their flexibility through the administration of flexibility tests. A sports skills test administered to inform individuals of their ability in the sport might motivate them to improve their skills. This motivation is more likely to occur, however, if you as the instructor provide positive feedback. Always try to keep your evaluation and assessment positive rather than negative.

Finally, most everyone enjoys comparing past performances with current ones. Knowing that a second measurement will take place, students and adults often work to improve on the original score.

Diagnosis

Through measurement you can assess the weaknesses (needs) and strengths of a group or individuals. Measurement before the teaching of a sports skill, physical fitness session, or other events you teach as a physical educator may cause you to alter your initial approach to what you are teaching. For example, you may discover that, before you do anything else in a softball class, you need to teach the students how to throw properly. You also may find that some individuals need more or less attention than others in the group. Identifying those students who can throw with accuracy and good form will enable you to devote more time to the students who cannot perform the skill. If you serve as an adult fitness leader, the identification of individuals with a higher level of fitness than the rest of the group will enable you to begin their program at a different level.

In certain settings, you may be able to prescribe personal exercises or programs to correct the diagnosed weaknesses. *Exercise prescription* is a popular term in fitness programs, but appropriate activities may be prescribed in other programs as well. Diagnostic measurement is valuable also after a group has participated in a class for several weeks. If some individuals are not progressing as you feel they should, testing may help you determine why they are not.

Classification

There may be occasions when you would like to classify individuals into similar groups for ease of instruction. In addition, people usually feel more comfortable when performing with others of similar skill. Sometimes, even in so-called noncontact sports, homogeneous grouping should be done for safety reasons. Also, homogeneous grouping is occasionally necessary in aerobic and fitness classes so that individuals with a low level of fitness will not attempt to perform at the same intensity as individuals with a high level of fitness.

Achievement

The most common reason for measurement and assessment is to determine the degree of achievement of program objectives and personal goals. Most people like to know how far they have progressed in a given period of time. Participants in diet modification and exercise programs like to know their changes in body fat percentage and muscle strength. Students like to know how far they have progressed in sports skills development in a given period of time. You too will need to know the achievement of participants to better evaluate the effectiveness of your instruction. If participants are failing to achieve their stated goals, you may need to revise their program or your method of instruction.

Achievement often is used to determine grades in physical education. If administered properly, performance tests and knowledge tests are appropriate for grading, and they decrease the need for subjective grading of the students. Many physical education teachers, however, mistakenly use tests only for determining grades. The assigning of grades will be discussed at length in chapter 7.

Evaluation of Instruction and Programs

With any responsibility you assume as a physical educator, occasionally you will have to justify the effectiveness of your instruction or program to your employer. For instance, when budget cuts are anticipated in the public schools, physical education and the arts are often the first programs considered for elimination. It is also necessary to justify a program when budget increases are requested. Furthermore, school accreditation studies require assessment of instruction and programs. If measurement and evaluation identify instructional or program problems, correctional procedures are stated. Standardized forms are available for program evaluation, but if program content is professionally sound, the success and effectiveness of instruction and programs are best determined by how well the participants fulfill program objectives. This statement is true for school programs, fitness and wellness programs, and all other professional programs in which you may have responsibilities. You must be able to measure and assess instruction and programs.

Assessment of each student's skill at the beginning of an activity unit helps you determine the effectiveness of previous instruction and programs and at what point you should begin your instruction. If the students do not know basic rules and cannot demonstrate the elementary playing skills of an activity, it will be necessary to begin instruction at that level. In addition, there may be times when you want to compare different methods of teaching sports skills or fitness. If you can be confident that the different groups are of equal initial ability, it is possible to compare the results of test scores at the conclusion of instruction and determine if one method of teaching is better than another. This procedure will be discussed in greater detail in chapter 4.

Prediction

Measurement to predict future performance in sports has increased in popularity, but this type of testing usually requires expertise in exercise physiology and psychology. Maximum oxygen uptake, muscle biopsies, and anxiety level are examples of tests that are used to predict future performance in sports.

Research

Research is used to find meaningful solutions to problems and as a means to expand a body of knowledge. It is of value for program evaluation, instructor evaluation, and improvement in performance, as well as other areas related to physical education. Many opportunities exist for physical educators who wish to perform research.

Now that you are aware of the primary reasons for measurement, evaluation, and assessment in physical education, you are ready to answer the question "Why statistics?"

▰▰ ARE YOU ABLE TO DO THE FOLLOWING?

- List and describe the reasons for measurement, evaluation, and assessment by the physical educator.

Why Statistics?

Whether you teach, instruct in a fitness center, administrate, or have responsibilities in a corporate setting, the ability to use statistics will be of value to you. Although no attempt will be made in this book to provide an extensive coverage of statistics, after you have completed chapters 2, 3, and 4, you should have the skill to do the following.

Analyze and Interpret Data

The data gathered for any of the measurement reasons described should be statistically analyzed and interpreted. It is a mistake to gather data and make important decisions about individuals without this analysis. Decisions regarding improvement in group performance and differences in teaching methodology should not be made without statistical analysis. Also, if you are willing to statistically analyze and interpret test scores, you can better inform all participants of the test results than you can with a routine analysis of the scores. So, using statistical analysis and interpretation, you can provide a more meaningful evaluation of your measurement.

Interpret Research

As a physical educator you should read research published in professional journals. After completion of this book you will not understand all statistical concepts, but you will understand enough to accurately interpret the results and conclusions of many studies. This ability will enable you to put into practice the conclusions of research. Too many physical educators fail to use research findings because they do not understand them. If you are to continue your professional growth, it is essential that you be able to interpret research related to your professional responsibilities.

Standardized Test Scores

Many measurements performed by the physical educator will be in different units—for example, feet, seconds, and numbers. To compare such measurements, it is best to convert the scores to standardized scores. A popular form of standardized scores is percentile scores (such as reported SAT scores).

Determine the Worth (Validity and Reliability) of a Test

Validity refers to the degree to which a test measures what it claims to measure. *Reliability* refers to the consistency of a test (i.e., the test obtains approximately the same results each time it is administered). These topics may not mean much to you now, but by knowing how to interpret statements about these characteristics, you are more likely to select the appropriate tests to administer to your students, clients, or customers. In addition, you will be able to estimate the validity and reliability of tests that you construct.

▰▰ ARE YOU ABLE TO DO THE FOLLOWING?

- State why the ability to use statistics is important to the physical educator.

Chapter Review Questions

1. What does the term *statistics* mean?

2. What do the terms *test, measurement, evaluation,* and *assessment* mean? Can you provide an example of a professional role where you might administer a test and perform all assessment responsibilities?

3. Imagine that you are now a professional in your chosen field. Can you provide examples of how you would use measurement, evaluation, and assessment in your field?

4. How might statistics be used in your chosen profession?

2 Describing and Presenting a Distribution of Scores

Regardless of your employment site, as a physical educator you often will test individuals. You may test for health fitness, sport fitness or skills, subject knowledge, or other areas. After the administration of a test, you will be expected to analyze the test scores and present your analysis to the test takers. The analysis of a set of test scores is referred to as descriptive statistics.

After completing this chapter, you should be able to

1. Define all statistical terms that are presented.

2. Describe the four scales of measurement, and give examples of each.

3. Describe a normal distribution and four curves for distributions that are not normal.

4. Define the terms measures of *central tendency* and *measures of variability*.

5. Define the three measures of central tendency, identify the symbols used to represent them, describe their characteristics, calculate them with ungrouped data, and state how they can be used to interpret data.

6. Define the three measures of variability, identify the symbols used to represent them, describe their characteristics, calculate them with ungrouped data, and state how they can be used to interpret data.

7. Describe the relationship of the standard deviation and the normal curve.

8. Define *percentile* and *percentile rank,* identify the symbols used to represent them, calculate them with ungrouped data, and state how they can be used to interpret data.

9. Define standard scores, calculate z-scores and T-scores, and interpret their meanings.

Statistical Terms

Before you begin to develop the skills to use descriptive statistics, become familiar with the following terms. Understanding these terms will be valuable to you in chapters 3 and 4 also.

Data   The result of measurement is called data. The term *data* usually means the numerical result of measurement but can also mean verbal information.

Variable   A variable is a trait or characteristic of something that can assume more than one value. Examples of variables are cardiovascular endurance, percentage of body fat, flexibility, and muscular strength. Their values will vary from one person to another, and they may not always be the same for one individual.

Population   A population includes all subjects (members) within a defined group. All subjects of the group have some measurable or observable characteristic. For example, if you wanted to determine the physical fitness of twelfth-grade students in a particular high school, the population would be all students in the twelfth grade.

Sample   A sample is a part or subgroup of the population from which the measurements are actually obtained. Rather than collect physical fitness data on all students in the twelfth grade, you could choose a smaller number to represent the population.

Random sample   A random sample is one in which every subject in the population has an equal chance of being included in the sample. A sample could be formed by randomly selecting a group to represent all twelfth graders. The selection could be done by placing the names of all twelfth-grade students in a container and randomly drawing the names out of it or by using a table of random numbers.

Parameter   A parameter is a value, a measurable characteristic, that refers to a population. The population mean (the average) is a parameter.

Statistic   A statistic is a value, a measurable characteristic, that refers to a sample. The sample mean is a statistic. Statistics are used to estimate the parameters of a defined population. (*Note:* When used in this manner the word *statistics* is plural. If used to denote a subject or a body of knowledge, the word *statistics* is singular.)

Descriptive statistics   When every member of a group is measured and no attempt is made to generalize to a larger group, the methods used to describe the group are called descriptive statistics. Conclusions are reached only about the group being studied.

Inferential statistics   When a random sample is measured and projections or generalizations are made about a larger group, inferential statistics are used. The correct use of inferential statistics permits you to use the data generated from a sample to make inferences about the entire population. Suppose you were in charge of a physical fitness program at a wellness center and wanted to estimate the physical fitness of all three hundred female adults in the program. You could randomly select thirty of the females, test them, and through the use of inferential statistics, estimate the physical fitness of the three hundred females.

Discrete data   Discrete data are measures that can have only separate values. The values are limited to certain numbers, usually whole numbers, and cannot be reported as fractions. Examples of discrete data are the sex of the individual, the number of

team members, the number of shots made, and the number of hits in a softball game.

Continuous data   Continuous data are measures that can have any value within a certain range. The values can be reported as fractions. Running and swimming events (time) and throwing events (distance) are examples of continuous data.

Ungrouped data   Ungrouped data are measures not arranged in any meaningful manner. The raw scores as recorded are used for calculations.

Grouped data   Grouped data are measures arranged in some meaningful manner to facilitate calculations.

▬▬ ARE YOU ABLE TO DO THE FOLLOWING?

- Define statistical terms.

- Provide an example of a study performed with a random sample and generalizations made about a population.

- Provide an example in which you might use descriptive statistics in professional responsibilities.

Scales of Measurement

Variables may be grouped into four categories of scales depending on the amount of information given by the data. Different rules apply at each scale of measurement, and each scale dictates certain types of statistical procedures. As measurement moves from the lowest to the highest scale, the result of measurement is closer to a pure measure of a count of quantity or amount. The lower the level of the data, the less information the data provide.

Nominal Scale

The **nominal scale,** also called categorical, is the lowest and most elementary scale. A naming level only, this scale is used to identify and report the frequency of objects or persons. Names are given to the variables, and categories are exclusive of each other; no comparisons of the categories can be made, and each category is assumed to be as valuable as the others. Some nominal scales have only two categories, but others may have more. Positions on sports teams, level of education, and state of residence are examples of the nominal scale. Numbers may be used to represent the variables, but the numbers do not have numerical value or relationship. For example, 0 may be used to represent the male classification and 1 the female classification.

Ordinal Scale

The **ordinal scale** provides some information about the order or rank of the variables, but it does not indicate how much better one score is than another. No determination can be made of the relative differences from rank to rank. For example, the order of finish in a 10-kilometer race provides information about who is fastest, but it does not indicate how much faster the person who finished in first position is than the person who came in second, or any of the other runners. Examples of the ordinal scale are the ranking of tennis team members from best to worst, class rank in a high school graduating class, team standings in an athletic conference, body frames (large, medium, small), and body fat (lean, normal, overfat).

Interval Scale

An **interval scale** provides information about the order of the variables, using equal units of measurement. The distance between divisions of the scale is always the same, so it is possible to say how much better one number is than another. However, the interval scale has no true zero point.

A good example of an interval scale is temperature. It is possible to say that 90°F is 10° warmer than 80°F and that 55°F is 10° warmer than 45°F, but it cannot be said that 90° is twice as hot as 45°. Since 0°F does not mean the complete absence of heat, there is no true zero point. Many measurements in physical education are in the interval scale. Surveys regarding sportsmanship and attitude toward physical activity are examples of the interval scale. In surveys of these types, a zero score does not mean that a person has absolutely no sportsmanship or no attitude toward activity.

Ratio Scale

A **ratio scale** possesses all the characteristics of the interval scale and has a true zero point. Examples of ratio scales are height, weight, time, and distance. Ten feet is twice as long as 5 feet; 9 minutes is three times as long as 3 minutes; and 20 pounds is four times as heavy as 5 pounds.

In most statistical studies or analyses, interval and ratio measurements are analyzed in the same way. Table 2.1 summarizes the major differences among the four scales of measurement.

▶ ARE YOU ABLE TO DO THE FOLLOWING?

- Define the four scales of measurement, and give examples of each.

TABLE 2.1   Scales of Measurement

Scales	Characteristics	Examples
Nominal	Numbers represent categories. Numbers do not distinguish groups and do not reflect differences in magnitude.	Divisions by gender, race, eye color, or political party
Ordinal	Numbers indicate rank order of measurements, but they do not indicate the magnitude of the interval between the measures.	Order of finish in races, grades for achievement
Interval	Numbers represent equal units between measurements. It is possible to say how much better one measure is than another, but there is no true zero point.	Temperature, year, IQ
Ratio	Numbers represent equal units between measurements, and there is an absolute zero point.	Height, weight, distance, time, heart rate, blood pressure, blood cholesterol

Normal Distribution

Most of the statistical methods used in descriptive and inferential statistics are based on the assumptions that a distribution of scores is normal and that the distribution can be graphically represented by the normal (bell-shaped) curve, as shown in figure 2.1. For example, the distribution of the college entrance test scores of all test takers nationally would be normal. The test scores for a particular high school or group of students, however, may not have a normal distribution. Individuals in the school or group may score exceptionally high or low, causing the curve to be skewed. This concept will be discussed later in the chapter. As they are on all graphic representations of frequency distributions, the score values are placed on the horizontal axis, and the frequency of each score is plotted with reference to the vertical axis. The two ends of the curve are symmetrical and represent the scores at the extremes of the distribution.

The normal distribution is theoretical and is based on the assumption that the distribution contains an infinite number of scores. You will not measure groups of infinite size, so you should not be surprised when distributions do not conform to the normal curve. If the distribution is

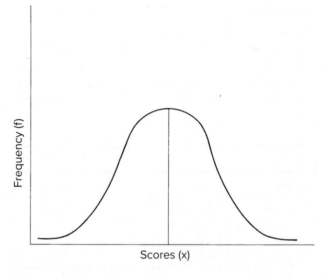

FIGURE 2.1 Normal curve.

based on a large number of scores, however, it will be close to normal distribution. You can have a large number of scores if you administer the same test to several groups or if you combine your test scores from several years of

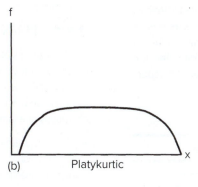

(a) Leptokurtic

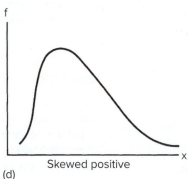

(b) Platykurtic

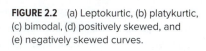

FIGURE 2.2 (a) Leptokurtic, (b) platykurtic, (c) bimodal, (d) positively skewed, and (e) negatively skewed curves.

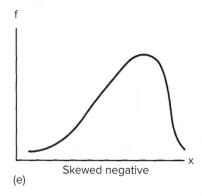

(c) Bimodal

(d) Skewed positive

(e) Skewed negative

testing into one distribution. A normal distribution has the following characteristics:

1. A bell-shaped curve.

2. Symmetrical distribution about the vertical axis of the curve; whatever happens on one side of the curve is mirrored on the other.

3. Greatest number of scores found in the middle of the curve, with fewer and fewer found toward the ends of the curve.

4. All measures of central tendency (mean, median, mode) at the vertical axis.

Note: Occasionally, a distribution of scores will produce a curve that is different from the normal curve (see figure 2.2). These curves are very possible in work with small groups. If a group consists of individuals who are very similar in ability (referred to as a homogeneous group), the curve is pointed and is called **leptokurtic.** If the group consists of individuals with a wide range of ability (referred to as a heterogeneous group), the curve is flat and is called **platykurtic.** If a group of scores has two modes, the curve has two high points and is called **bimodal.** Some distributions of scores may have more than two modes, producing a curve with more than two high points. A curve in which the scores are clustered at one end is **skewed.** Skewed curves will be described in greater detail later in this chapter.

ARE YOU ABLE TO DO THE FOLLOWING?

- Describe a normal distribution and four curves for distributions that are not normal.

Analysis of Ungrouped Data

Imagine that you have given a volleyball knowledge test to a group of 30 seventh-grade students, and you want to have a better understanding of the test results as well as interpret the scores to the students. With the aid of an inexpensive calculator, you can fulfill both of those objectives. This portion of the chapter shows you how to use descriptive statistics to analyze and interpret the volleyball knowledge test scores as well as other ungrouped data. A test with high scores has intentionally been selected as an example to demonstrate that the procedures are not difficult. Tables 2.2, 2.3, and 2.4 report the results of the volleyball knowledge test analysis.

TABLE 2.2   Rank of Volleyball Knowledge Test Scores

Rank		Score
1		96
2		95
3		93
4	4.5	92
5		92
6	6.5	91
7		91
8		90
9	9	90
10		90
11		89
12	12	89
13		89
14		88
15		88
16	16	88
17		88
18		88
19		87
20	20	87
21		87
22	22.5	86
23		86
24	24.5	85
25		85
26	26.5	84
27		84
28		83
29		82
30		81

Score Rank

Although you can perform statistical analysis without putting the scores in rank order, you may first want to carry out this procedure, which provides you with information about each person's rank in the score distribution. Be careful how you use the rank of scores. Sometimes, all the scores will be above what you consider a satisfactory score. Because someone has to be at the bottom when scores are ranked, you may not want to share this information with the group. Do not create alarm or embarrassment when there is no need. Table 2.2 shows the ranking of the thirty volleyball knowledge test scores. The steps for ranking the scores are as follows:

1. List the scores in descending order.

2. Number the scores. The highest score is number 1, and the last score is the number of the total number of scores. (Table 2.2 has thirty scores, so the last score is number 30.)

3. Because identical scores should have the same rank, average the rank, or determine the midpoint, and assign them the same rank.

Measures of Central Tendency

Measures of central tendency are descriptive statistics that describe the middle characteristics of a distribution of scores. The most widely used statistics, they represent

TABLE 2.3 Measures of Central Tendency and Variability and Percentiles (Deciles) Computed from Ungrouped Volleyball Knowledge Test Scores (N = 30)

Score	X^2	cf	Percentile
96	9,216	30	
95	9,025	29	
93	8,649	28	
92	8,464	27	90
92	8,464	26	
91	8,281	25	
91	8,281	24	80
90	8,100	23	
90	8,100	22	
90	8,100	21	70
89	7,921	20	
89	7,921	19	
89	7,921	18	60
88	7,744	17	
88	7,744	16	
88	7,744	15	50
88	7,744	14	
88	7,744	13	
87	7,569	12	40
87	7,569	11	
87	7,569	10	
86	7,396	9	30
86	7,396	8	
85	7,225	7	
85	7,225	6	20
84	7,056	5	
84	7,056	4	
83	6,889	3	10
82	6,724	2	
81	6,561	1	
$\sum X = 2{,}644$	$\sum X^2 = 233{,}398$		

$$R = 96 - 81 = 15$$

$$\bar{X} = \frac{\sum X}{N} = \frac{2{,}644}{30} = 88.1 \qquad Q = \frac{Q_3 - Q_1}{2} = \frac{90 - 85.5}{2} = 2.25$$

$$P_{50} = 88 \qquad s = \sqrt{\frac{N\sum X^2 - (\sum X)^2}{N(N-1)}} = \sqrt{\frac{30(233{,}398) - (2{,}644)^2}{30(30-1)}}$$

$$Mo = 88 \qquad s = 3.6$$

TABLE 2.4 Standard Deviation Computed from Volleyball Knowledge Test Scores, Deviations, and Squared Deviations (N = 30)

Score	d	d²	Score	d	d²
96	7.9	62.41	88	−0.1	0.01
95	6.9	47.61	87	−1.1	1.21
93	4.9	24.01	87	−1.1	1.21
92	3.9	15.21	87	−1.1	1.21
92	3.9	15.21	86	−2.1	4.41
91	2.9	8.41	86	−2.1	4.41
91	2.9	8.41	85	−3.1	9.61
90	1.9	3.61	85	−3.1	9.61
90	1.9	3.61	84	−4.1	16.81
90	1.9	3.61	84	−4.1	16.81
89	0.9	0.81	83	−5.1	26.01
89	0.9	0.81	82	−6.1	37.21
89	0.9	0.81	81	−7.1	50.41
88	−0.1	0.01	$\sum X = 2{,}644$		$\sum d^2 = 373.50$
88	−0.1	0.01			
88	−0.1	0.01			
88	−0.1	0.01			

$$\sum d^2 = 373.5$$

$\bar{X} = 88.1$

$$s = \sqrt{\frac{\sum d^2}{N-1}} = \sqrt{\frac{373.5}{29}} = 3.6$$

scores in a distribution around which other scores seem to center. Measures of central tendency are the mean, median, and mode.

The Mean

With any test, the first question usually asked by the students upon knowing their individual score is "What is the class average?" The **mean,** the most generally used measure of central tendency, is the arithmetic average of a distribution of scores. It is calculated by summing all the scores and dividing by the total number of scores. The following are some important characteristics of the mean:

1. It is the most sensitive of all the measures of central tendency. It will always reflect any change within a distribution of scores.

2. It is the most appropriate measure of central tendency to use for ratio data and may be used on interval data.

3. It considers all information about the data and is used to perform other important statistical calculations.

4. It is influenced by extreme scores, especially if the distribution is small. For example, when one or more scores are high or low in relation to the other scores, the mean is pulled in that direction. (See number 1 in characteristics of Median.) This characteristic is the chief disadvantage of the mean.

The symbols used to calculate the mean and other statistics are as follows:

$\overline{X}$ = the mean (called X-bar)

Σ (Greek letter sigma) = "the sum of"

X = individual score

N = the total number of scores in a distribution

The formula for calculating the mean is

$$\overline{X} = \frac{\Sigma X}{N}$$

Simply, to calculate the mean, you add all the scores in a distribution and divide by the number of scores you have. The calculation of $\overline{X}$ from the distribution in table 2.3 is

$$\overline{X} = \frac{2,644}{30} = 88.1$$

You probably would report the scores to the students in whole numbers, so you should round the mean to 88.

■ ARE YOU ABLE TO DO THE FOLLOWING?

- Define the term *measures of central tendency*.

- Identify the symbol for the mean.

- Define the mean.

- Describe the characteristics of the mean.

- Calculate the mean with ungrouped data and use it to interpret the data.

The Median

The **median** is the score that represents the exact middle in the distribution. It is the fiftieth percentile, the score that 50% of the scores are above and 50% of the scores are below. The following are some important characteristics of the median:

1. It is not affected by extreme scores; it is a more representative measure of central tendency than the mean when extreme scores are in the distribution. As an example, consider the height of five individuals. If the heights are 71", 72", 73", 74", and 75", the mean (average) height of the five people is 73", and the median (middle score) height is 73". Now imagine that we exchange the individual who is 75" in height for an individual who is 85" in height. The mean is now 75", but the median remains at 73".

2. It is a measure of position; it is determined by the number of scores and their rank order. It is appropriately used on ordinal or interval data.

3. It is not used for additional statistical calculations.

The median may be represented by Mdn or P_{50}. The steps for calculation of P_{50} are as follows:

1. Arrange the scores in ascending or descending order.

2. Multiply N by .50 to find 50% of the distribution.

3. If the number of scores is odd, P_{50} is the middle score of the distribution.

4. If the number of scores is even, P_{50} is the arithmetic average of the two middle scores of the distribution.

The calculation of P_{50} from the distribution in table 2.3 is as follows:

1. $.50(30) = 15$

2. The fifteenth and sixteenth scores (middle scores of distribution) are 88.

3. $P_{50} = 88$

Because you will be using this same procedure to calculate any percentile, you may want to place a cumulative frequency (cf) column with the ordered listing of scores. The cumulative frequency is an accumulation of frequencies beginning with the bottom score. In the cf column, the highest score will have the same number as N.

■ ARE YOU ABLE TO DO THE FOLLOWING?

- Identify the symbol for the median.

- Define the median.

- Describe the characteristics of the median.

- Calculate the median with ungrouped data and use it to interpret the data.

The Mode

The **mode** is the score that occurs most frequently. In a normal distribution, the mode is representative of the middle scores. In some distributions, however, the mode may be an extreme score. If a distribution has two modes, it is bimodal, and it is possible for a distribution to be multimodal or to have no mode at all. Because no symbol is used to represent the mode, Mo is sometimes used. Some characteristics of the mode are as follows:

1. It is the least used measure of central tendency. It indicates the score attained by the largest number of subjects. It also is used to indicate such things as the most popular item or product used by a group.

2. It is not used for additional statistical calculations.

3. It is not affected by extreme scores, the total number of scores, or their distance from the center of the distribution.

The mode of the distribution in table 2.3 is 88.

▰▰ ARE YOU ABLE TO DO THE FOLLOWING?

- Define the mode.

- Describe the characteristics of the mode.

- Calculate the mode with ungrouped data and use it to interpret the data.

Which Measure of Central Tendency Is Best for Interpretation of Test Results?

You have studied the definitions of the three measures of central tendency, calculation procedures, and some characteristics of each. Do you know which of the three is best for interpreting test results to any group that you might be testing? In making your decision, you should consider the following:

1. The mean, median, and mode are the same for a normal distribution (symmetrical curve), but you often will not have a normal curve.

2. The farther away from the mean and median the mode is, the less normal the distribution (i.e., the curve is skewed). Figure 2.3 shows the relationship of these measures to a symmetrical curve, a positively skewed curve, and a negatively skewed curve. In a positively skewed curve the scores are clustered at the lower end of the scale; the longer tail of the curve is to the right, and the mean is higher than the median. In a negatively skewed curve the scores are clustered at the upper end of the scale; the longer tail of the curve is to the left, and the mean is lower than the median. An extremely difficult test, on which most of the scores are low but a few high scores increase the mean, often results in a positively skewed curve. An easy test, on which most of the scores are high but a few low scores decrease the mean, usually results in a negatively skewed curve.

3. The mean and median are both useful measures. If the curve is badly skewed with extreme scores, you may want to use only the median. You must decide how important the extreme scores are. If the curve is approximately normal, use the mean and median.

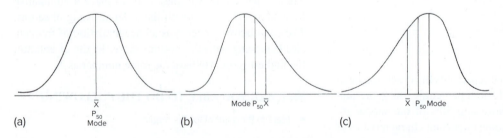

(a)   (b)   (c)

FIGURE 2.3 (a) Normal curve, (b) positively skewed curve, and (c) negatively skewed curve.

- Although the mean is considered the most reliable measure of central tendency and is also used for other statistical calculations, the following is an example of an important use of the median. Suppose that upon your graduation you apply for a job with a small company. The company employs 30 people. You are told that the average salary is $50,000. You ask, "What is the median salary?" You are told that the median salary is $30,000. What does this mean to you?

4. In most testing, the mean is the most reliable and useful measure of central tendency. It also is used in many other statistical procedures.

ARE YOU ABLE TO DO THE FOLLOWING?

- Use the three measures of central tendency to interpret test results to a group.

- Provide an example of a distribution of scores in which the mean is higher than the median.

- Provide an example of a distribution of scores in which the median is higher than the mean.

Measures of Variability

You now are prepared to use the mean, median, and mode to interpret data in relation to a central grouping of scores. However, to provide a more meaningful interpretation you also need to know how the scores spread, or scatter. For example, it is possible for two classes to have the same mean on a skills test, but the spread of the scores can be entirely different. To illustrate this point, consider the following two sets of scores:

Group A: 80, 82, 83, 84, 86 $\bar{X} = 83$
Group B: 65, 75, 90, 90, 95 $\bar{X} = 83$

Both groups have a mean of 83, but the spreads of the scores are very different. The spread, or scatter, of scores is referred to as **variability.** The terms *dispersion* and *deviation* are often used to refer to variability. When groups of scores are compared, measures of variability should be considered as well as measures of central tendency. By knowing the measures of variability, you can determine the amount that the scores spread, or deviate, from the measures of central tendency. The measures of variability are the range, quartile deviation, and standard deviation.

The Range

The **range** is determined by subtracting the lowest score from the highest score. It is the easiest measure of variability to compute, but because it represents only the extreme scores and provides no distribution information, it is also the least useful. Two groups of data may have the same range but have very different distributions. Consider the following scores:

Group A: 97, 95, 89, 87, 86, 85, 83, 80, 75, 72
Group B: 81, 77, 75, 73, 70, 68, 64, 61, 58, 56

Both groups have a range of 25, but the distributions are not similar. It is possible for you to have completely different distributions when you administer the same knowledge or physical performance test to different groups.

Some characteristics of the range are as follows:

1. It is dependent on the two extreme scores.

2. Because it indicates nothing about the variability of the scores between the two extreme scores, it is the least useful measure of variability.

The formula for determining the range (R) is

$$R = \text{High score} - \text{Low score}$$

You may see this formula also:

$$R = H_x - L_x$$

The range for the distribution in table 2.3 is $R = 96 - 81 = 15$.

ARE YOU ABLE TO DO THE FOLLOWING?

- Define the term *measures of variability*.

- Identify the letter used to represent the range.

- Define the range.

- Describe the characteristics of the range.

- Calculate the range with ungrouped data and use it to interpret the data.

The Quartile Deviation

Sometimes called the semi-quartile range, the **quartile deviation** is the spread of the middle 50% of the scores around the median. The quartile deviation is not reported often, but it is of value if the distribution is on the ordinal scale. The extreme scores will not affect the quartile deviation; thus, it is more stable than the range. Much like the other measures of variability, the quartile deviation is useful when comparing groups. Additionally, to determine the quartile deviation, the twenty-fifth and seventy-fifth percentiles must be calculated. These values will help you determine if the distribution is symmetrical about the median within the quartile deviation.

The following are some characteristics of the quartile deviation:

1. It uses the seventy-fifth percentile and twenty-fifth percentile to determine the deviation. The difference between these two percentiles is referred to as the interquartile range.

2. It indicates the amount that needs to be added to, and subtracted from, the median to include the middle 50% of the scores.

3. It usually is not used in additional statistical calculations.

The symbols used to calculate the quartile deviation are

Q = quartile deviation

Q_1 = twenty-fifth percentile or first quartile (P_{25} may be used also) = score in which 25% of the scores are below and 75% of the scores are above

Q_3 = seventy-fifth percentile, or third quartile (P_{75} may be used also) = score in which 75% of the scores are below and 25% of the scores are above

The steps for calculation of Q_3 are as follows:

1. Arrange the scores in ascending order.

2. Multiply N by .75 to find 75% of the distribution.

3. Count up from the bottom score to the number determined in step 2. Approximation and interpolation may be required to calculate Q_3 and Q_1 as well as other percentiles. Interpolation is necessary in the calculation of Q_1 from the distribution in table 2.3.

The steps for calculation of Q_1 are as follows:

1. Multiply N by .25 to find 25% of the distribution.

2. Again count up from the bottom score to the number determined in step 1.

To calculate Q, substitute the values in the formula

$$Q = \frac{Q_3 - Q_1}{2}$$

The calculation of Q from the distribution in table 2.3 is as follows:

1. .75(30) = 22.5
The twenty-second score from the bottom is 90, and the twenty-third score is 90. Midway between these two scores would be the same score, so the score of 90 is at the 75%.

2. .25(30) = 7.5
The seventh score from the bottom is 85, and the eighth score is 86. Since 7.5 is midway between these two scores, the score of 85.5 is at the 25%. Calculating the average of 85 and 86 would serve the same purpose.

3. $Q = \frac{90 - 85.5}{2} = \frac{4.5}{2} = 2.25$

Now what does 2.25 mean? Remember we said that the quartile deviation is used with the median. So now add 2.25 to 88 (the median in table 2.3) and subtract 2.25 from 88.

$$88 + 2.25 = 90.25$$
$$88 - 2.25 = 85.75$$

Theoretically, the middle 50% of the scores in the distribution should fall between the values 85.75 and 90.25. With thirty scores there should be fifteen scores between 85.75 and 90.25, but you will discover that sixteen scores fall between these two values. The difference is explained by the fact that the distribution in table 2.3 does not fulfill all requirements of normalcy. However, it is similar enough to use Q for interpretation purposes. Most of the test distributions you will use in your professional responsibilities will be similar enough to normalcy.

▬▬ ARE YOU ABLE TO DO THE FOLLOWING?

- Identify the symbol for the quartile deviation.

- Define the quartile deviation.

- Describe the characteristics of the quartile deviation.

- Calculate the quartile deviation with ungrouped data and use it to interpret the data.

The Standard Deviation

The **standard deviation** is the most useful and sophisticated measure of variability. It describes the scatter of scores around the mean. The standard deviation is a more stable measure of variability than the range or quartile deviation because it depends on the weight of each score in the distribution.

The lowercase Greek letter sigma (σ) is used to indicate the standard deviation of a population, and the letter *s* is used to indicate the standard deviation of a sample. Because you generally will be working with small groups (or samples), the formula for determining the standard deviation will include (N − 1) rather than N. This adjustment produces a standard deviation that is closer to the population standard deviation.

Some characteristics of the standard deviation are as follows:

1. It is the square root of the variance, which is the average of the squared deviations from the mean. The variance is used in other statistical procedures. The population variance is represented as σ^2 and the sample variance is represented as s^2.

2. It is applicable to interval and ratio level data, includes all scores, and is the most reliable measure of variability.

3. It is used with the mean. In a normal distribution, one standard deviation added to the mean and one standard deviation subtracted from the mean include the middle 68.26% of the scores.

4. With most data, a relatively small standard deviation indicates that the group being tested has little variability; it has performed homogeneously. A relatively large standard deviation indicates the group has much variability; it has performed heterogeneously.

5. It is used to perform other statistical calculations. The standard deviation is especially important for comparing differences between means. Techniques for making these comparisons will be presented later in this chapter.

The symbols used to determine the standard deviation are as follows:

$$s = \text{standard deviation}$$
$$\bar{X} = \text{mean}$$
$$\Sigma = \text{sum of}$$
$$d = \text{deviation score } (X - \bar{X})$$
$$X = \text{individual score}$$
$$N = \text{number of scores}$$

Two methods for determining the standard deviation will be presented. The first method requires only the use of the individual scores and a calculator that can compute the square root of a number. The second method requires the use of the squared deviations. The two methods obtain the same results.

Calculation with ΣX^2

1. Arrange the scores into a series.

2. Find ΣX.

3. Square each of the scores and add to determine the ΣX^2.

4. Insert the values into the formula

$$s = \sqrt{\frac{N\Sigma X^2 - (\Sigma X)^2}{N(N-1)}}$$

The calculation of s from the distribution in table 2.3 is as follows:

1. Scores are in a series.

2. $\Sigma X = 2,644$

3. $\Sigma X^2 = 233,398$

4.
$$s = \sqrt{\frac{30(233,398) - (2,644)^2}{30(30-1)}}$$
$$= \sqrt{\frac{7,001,940 - 6,990,736}{30(29)}}$$
$$= \sqrt{\frac{11,204}{870}}$$
$$= \sqrt{12.8781}$$
$$= 3.59$$
$$s = 3.6$$

Calculation with Σd^2

1. Arrange the scores into a series.

2. Calculate $\bar{X}$.

3. Determine d and d^2 for each score; then calculate Σd^2.

4. Insert the values into the formula

$$s = \sqrt{\frac{\Sigma d^2}{N-1}}$$

The calculation of s from the distribution in table 2.4 is as follows:

1. Scores are in a series.

2. $\bar{X} = 88.1$

3. $\Sigma d^2 = 373.5$

4.
$$s = \sqrt{\frac{373.5}{30-1}}$$
$$= \sqrt{\frac{373.5}{29}}$$
$$= \sqrt{12.8793}$$
$$s = 3.6$$

Note: The s value should be the same value as found in the ΣX^2 method, but owing to the rounding off of $\bar{X}$, there is a slight difference.

To determine the middle 68.26% of the scores, you now add 3.6 to $\bar{X}$ and subtract 3.6 from $\bar{X}$.

$$\bar{X} + 3.6 = 88.1 + 3.6 = 91.7$$
$$\bar{X} - 3.6 = 88.1 - 3.6 = 84.5$$

If the distribution were normal, the middle 68.26% of the scores would be between the values 84.5 and 91.7.

Because each score must be subtracted from the mean, and the mean is often not a whole number, this method can be time-consuming.

Relationship of Standard Deviation and Normal Curve

The use of the standard deviation has more meaning when it is related to the normal curve. On the basis of the probability of a normal distribution, there is an exact relationship between the standard deviation and the proportion of area and scores under the curve. The standard deviation marks off points along the base of the curve. An equal percentage of the curve will be found between the mean plus one standard deviation and the mean minus one standard deviation. The same is true for plus and minus 2.0 or 3.0 standard deviations.

The following observations can be made about the standard deviation and the areas under a normal curve:

1. 68.26% of the scores will fall between $+1.0$ and -1.0 standard deviations.

2. 95.44% of the scores will fall between $+2.0$ and -2.0 standard deviations.

3. 99.73% of the scores will fall between $+3.0$ and -3.0 standard deviations. Generally, scores will not exceed $+3.0$ and -3.0 standard deviations from the mean. Figure 2.4 shows these observations.

The relationship of the standard deviation and the normal curve provides you a meaningful and consistent way to compare the performance of different groups using the same test and to compare the performance of one individual with the group. In addition, by knowing the value of the mean and of the standard deviation, you can express the percentile rank of the scores. To illustrate how these procedures can be done, consider the following example.

As part of a physical fitness test, a fitness instructor administered a 60-second sit-up test to two fitness classes. She found the mean and the standard deviation for each class to be as follows:

Class 1	*Class 2*
$\bar{X} = 32$	$\bar{X} = 28$
$s = 2$	$s = 4$

Figure 2.5 compares the spread of the two distributions. The spread of scores in class 1 (± 3 standard deviations from the mean) is much less than the spread of scores for class 2. Class 1 is more homogeneous.

Now consider individual A in class 1, who completed thirty-four sit-ups, and individual B in class 2, who also completed thirty-four sit-ups. Though the two individuals have the same score, figure 2.6 shows that they do not have the same relationship to their respective class means and standard deviations. Individual A is 1 standard deviation above the class 1 mean, and individual B is 1.5 standard deviations above the class 2 mean. Table 2.5 shows that $+1$ standard deviation above the mean includes approximately 84% of the curve and that $+1.5$ standard deviations above the mean include approximately 93% of the curve. Though the two scores are the same, they do not have the same percentile score.

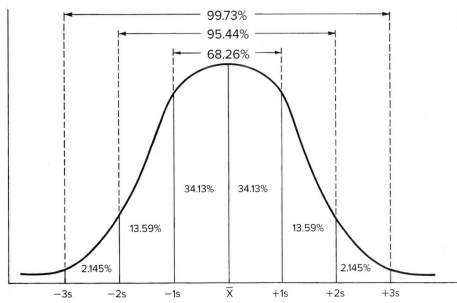

FIGURE 2.4 Characteristics of normal curve.

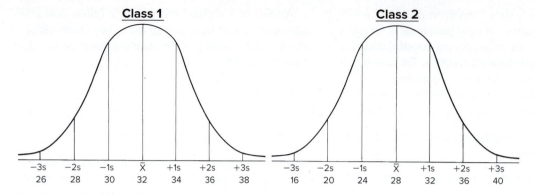

FIGURE 2.5 Comparison of X̄ and s for sit-up test.

The steps for calculating the percentile rank through use of the mean and the standard deviation are as follows:

1. Calculate the deviation of the score from the mean:

$$d = (X - \bar{X})$$

2. Calculate the number of standard deviation units the score is from the mean. Some textbooks refer to these units as z-scores. The use and interpretation of z-scores are described later in this chapter.

$$\text{No. of standard deviation units from the mean} = \frac{d}{s}$$

3. Use table 2.5 to determine where the percentile rank of the score is on the curve. On occasions it may be necessary to approximate the percentile rank.

Note: If a negative value is found in step 1, the percentile rank will always be less than 50. If a positive value is found in step 1, the percentile rank will always be more than 50.

ARE YOU ABLE TO DO THE FOLLOWING?

- Identify the symbol for the standard deviation.

- Define the standard deviation.

- Describe the characteristics of the standard deviation.

- Calculate the standard deviation with ungrouped data and use it to interpret the data.

- Describe the normal curve and the relationship of the standard deviation and the normal curve.

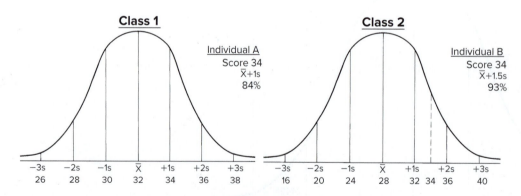

FIGURE 2.6 Comparison of individual performances for sit-up test.

TABLE 2.5 Percentile Scores Based on the Mean and Standard Deviation Units

X̄ and s Units	Percentile Rank	T-score	X̄ and s Units	Percentile Rank	T-score
X̄ + 3.0s	99.87	80	X̄ − 0.1s	46.02	49
X̄ + 2.9s	99.81	79	X̄ − 0.2s	42.07	48
X̄ + 2.8s	99.74	78	X̄ − 0.3s	38.21	47
X̄ + 2.7s	99.65	77	X̄ − 0.4s	34.46	46
X̄ + 2.6s	99.53	76	X̄ − 0.5s	30.85	45
X̄ + 2.5s	99.38	75	X̄ − 0.6s	27.43	44
X̄ + 2.4s	99.18	74	X̄ − 0.7s	24.20	43
X̄ + 2.3s	98.93	73	X̄ − 0.8s	21.19	42
X̄ + 2.2s	98.61	72	X̄ − 0.9s	18.41	41
X̄ + 2.1s	98.21	71	X̄ − 1.0s	15.87	40
X̄ + 2.0s	97.72	70	X̄ − 1.1s	13.57	39
X̄ + 1.9s	97.13	69	X̄ − 1.2s	11.51	38
X̄ + 1.8s	96.41	68	X̄ − 1.3s	9.68	37
X̄ + 1.7s	95.54	67	X̄ − 1.4s	8.08	36
X̄ + 1.6s	94.52	66	X̄ − 1.5s	6.68	35
X̄ + 1.5s	93.32	65	X̄ − 1.6s	5.48	34
X̄ + 1.4s	91.92	64	X̄ − 1.7s	4.46	33
X̄ + 1.3s	90.32	63	X̄ − 1.8s	3.59	32
X̄ + 1.2s	88.49	62	X̄ − 1.9s	2.87	31
X̄ + 1.1s	86.43	61	X̄ − 2.0s	2.28	30
X̄ + 1.0s	84.13	60	X̄ − 2.1s	1.79	29
X̄ + 0.9s	81.59	59	X̄ − 2.2s	1.39	28
X̄ + 0.8s	78.81	58	X̄ − 2.3s	1.07	27
X̄ + 0.7s	75.80	57	X̄ − 2.4s	0.82	26
X̄ + 0.6s	72.57	56	X̄ − 2.5s	0.62	25
X̄ + 0.5s	69.15	55	X̄ − 2.6s	0.47	24
X̄ + 0.4s	65.54	54	X̄ − 2.7s	0.35	23
X̄ + 0.3s	61.79	53	X̄ − 2.8s	0.26	22
X̄ + 0.2s	57.93	52	X̄ − 2.9s	0.19	21
X̄ + 0.1s	53.98	51	X̄ − 3.0s	0.13	20
X̄ + 0.0s	50.00	50			

Which Measure of Variability Is Best for Interpretation of Test Results?

You have studied the definitions of the three measures of variability, how to calculate them, and some characteristics of each. In deciding which of the three is best for interpreting test results of a group you might be testing, you should consider the following:

1. The range is the least reliable of the three, but it is used when a fast method is needed. It does not take into account all the scores and may not represent the true variability of the scores.

2. The quartile deviation is more meaningful than the range, but it considers only the middle 50% of the

scores. Thus, it too is limited in its ability to represent the true variability of the scores.

3. The standard deviation considers every score, is the most reliable, and is the most commonly used measure of variability.

■ ARE YOU ABLE TO DO THE FOLLOWING?

- Properly use the three measures of variability to interpret test results to a group.

- State why the standard deviation is the most often reported measure of variability.

Percentiles and Percentile Ranks

Though you have learned to calculate percentiles and percentile rank, it will be beneficial to discuss them in greater detail. **Percentile** refers to a point in a distribution of scores below which a given percentage of the scores fall. For example, the sixtieth percentile is the point where 60% of the scores in a distribution are below and 40% of the scores are above. To calculate a percentile, you first multiply N by the desired percentage. You then determine the score that is at that percentile in a distribution. In table 2.3, the sixtieth percentile score is 89.

The **percentile rank** of a given score in a distribution is the percentage of the total scores that fall below the given score. A percentile rank, then, indicates the position of a score in a distribution in percentage terms. Percentile ranks are determined by beginning with the raw scores and calculating the percentile ranks for the scores. In table 2.3, the score of 89 has a percentile rank of 60.

Although percentiles are of value for interpretation of data, they do have weaknesses. The relative distances between percentile scores are the same, but the relative distances between the observed scores are not. Because percentiles are based on the number of scores in a distribution rather than on the size of the raw score obtained, it is sometimes more difficult to increase a percentile score at the ends of the scale than in the middle. The average performers, whose raw scores are found in the middle of the scale, need only a small change in their raw scores to produce a large change in their percentile scores. However, the below-average and above-average performers, whose raw scores are found at the ends of the scale, need a large change in their raw scores to produce even a small change in their percentile scores. This weakness is usually found in all percentile scores.

If you do not remember how to calculate percentiles, you should refer to the sections on the median and quartile deviation. In table 2.3, the percentile scale is divided into deciles (ten equal parts). Deciles are represented as D_1 (tenth percentile), D_2 (twentieth percentile), D_3 (thirtieth percentile), on up to D_9 (ninetieth percentile).

Frequency Distribution

Statistics software programs will group data into frequency distributions. In such a distribution all scores are listed in ascending or descending order, and the number of times each individual score occurs is indicated in a frequency column. The percentage of times that each score occurs and the cumulative percentage (the percentage of scores below a given score) are also presented. Table 2.6 shows the frequency distribution for 100 push-up scores.

◆◆◆ POINTS OF EMPHASIS ◆◆◆

- The difficulty in describing and analyzing data or test scores is not calculating the statistics, but knowing why you wish to perform the calculations. You should know the questions for which you are seeking answers. Descriptive statistics will enable you to compare groups or compare the performances of members in the same group after the administration of different tests.

TABLE 2.6	Frequency Distribution of Push-Up Scores		
Score	Frequency	Percent	Cumulative Percent
27	1	1.0	1.0
28	1	1.0	2.0
29	1	1.0	3.0
30	2	2.0	5.0
31	3	3.0	8.0
32	3	3.0	11.0
33	4	4.0	15.0
34	3	3.0	18.0
35	5	5.0	23.0
36	6	6.0	29.0
37	6	6.0	35.0
38	5	5.0	40.0
39	6	6.0	46.0
40	8	8.0	54.0
41	6	6.0	60.0
42	6	6.0	66.0
43	7	7.0	73.0
44	6	6.0	79.0
45	5	5.0	84.0
46	4	4.0	88.0
47	4	4.0	92.0
48	3	3.0	95.0
49	2	2.0	97.0
50	2	2.0	99.0
51	1	1.0	100.0
	100		

■■■ **ARE YOU ABLE TO DO THE FOLLOWING?**

- Identify the symbols for percentiles, quartiles, and deciles.

- Define *percentile* and *percentile rank*.

- Calculate percentiles and use them to interpret the data.

Graphs

Data are often presented in graphic form. Well-prepared graphs enable individuals to interpret data without reading the raw data or tables. SPSS and other computer programs can create column, bar, line, pie, area, and other types of graphs. In your future professional responsibilities, you may be asked to provide reports that include much data. If you have the opportunity to develop the knowledge and skill needed to use such computer programs, you should do so.

Figure 2.7 is a histogram (bar graph) of 75 tennis serve scores. For graphing purposes, computer programs will group a large number of scores into groups and plot the midpoint of each group. In figure 2.7, there may be three possible scores in each interval. In the first interval, the score of 49 represents the midpoint of scores 48–50. The frequency column shows that one score occurred in this interval. The next interval is 51–53, and two scores occurred in this interval. The highest number of scores, 10, occurred in the interval 72–74. Figure 2.8 is a frequency polygon (line graph) of the same scores. With these graphs, it is easy to observe the frequency of the serve scores.

Figures 2.9 and 2.10 are a pie chart and a bar chart, respectively, of causes of deaths in the year 2005. These charts show the percentage of each type of death in relation to all deaths. Each chart enables the reader to interpret the data quickly.

Standard Scores

After collecting scores for different performances, you may want to combine or compare scores; but because the scores have no similarities, you cannot perform these functions. For example, suppose you are teaching a physical fitness unit to a high school class, and at the conclusion of the unit you administer a 1-minute sit-up test, the sit and reach test, a 2-mile run, and a physical fitness knowledge test. How do you average the scores of the four tests? You certainly cannot add the scores and divide by four. How do you compare a student's performance on the sit-up test with her performance on the 2-mile run? You cannot tell her that forty sit-ups is a better score than a time of 15:10— unless you have a procedure to convert the raw scores into standard scores. *The conversion of unlike raw scores to standard scores enables you to compare different types of scoring.* Procedures to make such conversions follow.

z-Scores

A **z-score** represents the number of standard deviations by which a raw score deviates from the mean. After calculation of the mean and standard deviation of a distribution, it is possible to determine the z-score for any raw score in the distribution through the use of this formula:

$$z = \frac{X - \overline{X}}{s}$$

Consider the example of the 75 tennis serve scores represented in figures 2.7 and 2.8. The actual scores are as follows:

88 83 75 81 56 82 86 62 87 79 93 58 61 61 75

73 94 48 79 72 81 85 52 73 62 80 73 84 63 61

67 63 75 73 67 72 73 72 77 73 85 82 70 57 58

54 79 68 54 70 77 81 68 83 65 77 90 52 75 62

84 69 56 68 69 63 70 91 70 80 65 70 88 72 63

For these scores, $\overline{X} = 72.05$ and $s = 10.79$. To convert the tennis serve scores into z-scores, you substitute each individual score in the formula. For the scores of 88 and 54, the z-scores would be

$$z = \frac{88 - 72.1}{10.8} \qquad z = \frac{54 - 72.1}{10.8}$$

$$= \frac{15.9}{10.8} \qquad = \frac{-18.1}{10.8} \qquad \begin{array}{l}(\overline{X}\text{ and }s\text{ are rounded}\\ \text{to one decimal place})\end{array}$$

$$z = 1.47 \qquad z = -1.68$$

FIGURE 2.7   Histogram of tennis serve scores made by 75 students.

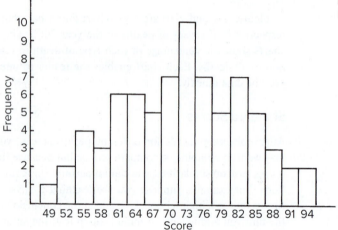

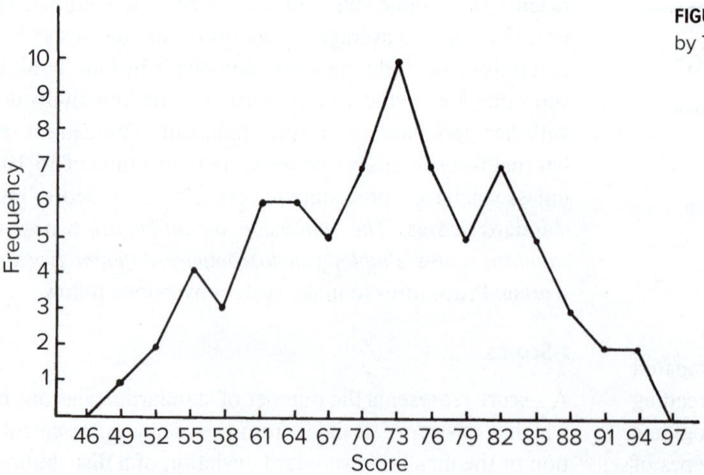

FIGURE 2.8   Frequency polygon of tennis serve scores made by 75 students.

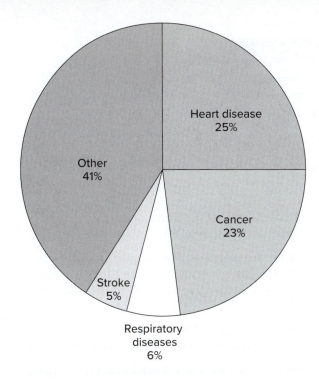

FIGURE 2.9 Pie chart of causes of death in 2009.

How are these z-scores interpreted? The z-scale has a mean of 0 and a standard deviation of 1, and it normally extends from −3 to +3 (plus and minus 3 standard deviations from the mean include 99.73% of the scores). In observing figure 2.11, you see that a z-score of 1.47 is approximately 1.5 standard deviations above the mean,

and a z-score of −1.68 is more than 1.5 standard deviations below the mean. Knowing the relationship of the standard deviation and the normal curve, we can state that 1.47 is an excellent z-score and −1.68 is a poor z-score. Also, by referring to table 2.5, we see that 1.5 standard deviations above the mean has a percentile rank of 93, and 1.7 deviations below the mean has a percentile rank of 4.

If other tennis skills tests (e.g., forehand, backhand, and lob tests) had been administered to the same 75 test takers, all scores could be converted to z-scores and averaged for one tennis skill score. Also, each individual's z-score for the four tests could be compared, and the strongest and weakest skills of each individual determined.

All standard scores are based on the z-score. Because z-scores are expressed in small numbers, involve decimals, and may be positive or negative, many testers do not use them.

T-Scores

The **T-scale** has a mean of 50 and a standard deviation of 10. T-scores may extend from 0 to 100, but it is unlikely that any T-score would be below 20 or above 80, since this range includes plus and minus 3 standard deviations. Figure 2.11 shows the relationship of z-scores, T-scores, and the normal curve. The z-score is part of the formula for conversion of raw scores into T-scores. The formula is

$$\text{T-score} = 50 + 10\left(\frac{\left(X - \overline{X}\right)}{s}\right) = 50 + 10\ z$$

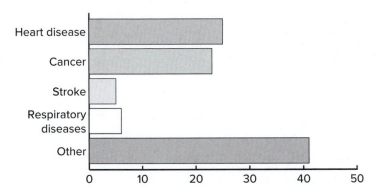

FIGURE 2.10 Bar graph of causes of death in 2009.

Again, consider the scores of 88 and 54 for the tennis serve test. The T-scores are

$T_{88} = 50 + 10(1.47)$ $T_{54} = 50 + 10(-1.68)$

     $= 50 + 14.7$ $= 50 + (-16.8)$

$T_{88} = 64.7 = 65$ $T_{54} = 33.2 = 33$

Note: T-scores are reported as whole numbers.

T-scores may be used in the same way as z-scores. However, because only positive whole numbers are reported and the range is 0 to 100, the T-scale is easier to interpret. However, it is sometimes confusing to the individuals being tested when they are told that a T-score of 60 or above is a good score. If you use T-scores, you should be prepared to fully explain their meanings. Table 2.5 shows the relationship of the mean and standard deviation, percentile rank, and T-scores.

You may prefer to convert the raw scores in a distribution to T-scores through the following procedure:

1. Number a column of T-scores from 20 to 80.

2. Place the mean of the distribution of the scores opposite the T-score of 50.

3. Divide the standard deviation of the distribution by 10. The standard deviation for the T-scale is 10, so each T-score from 0 to 100 is one-tenth of the standard deviation.

4. Add the value found in step 3 to the mean and each subsequent number until you reach the T-score of 80.

5. Subtract the value found in step 3 from the mean and each decreasing number until you reach the number 20.

6. Round off the scores to the nearest whole number.

Note: If a low score is better than a high score, subtract the T-values toward 80 and add the values toward 20. Table 2.7 shows the conversion of the 75 tennis serve scores to T-scores. For illustration purposes, only the T-scores 40 to 60 are included in the table. The value found in dividing the standard deviation by 10 (1.079) is rounded to 1.1.

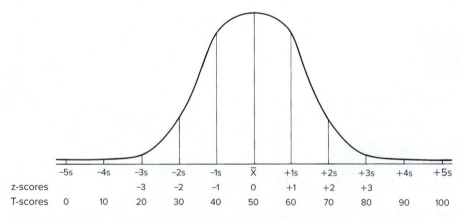

	-5s	-4s	-3s	-2s	-1s	X̄	+1s	+2s	+3s	+4s	+5s
z-scores			-3	-2	-1	0	+1	+2	+3		
T-scores	0	10	20	30	40	50	60	70	80	90	100

FIGURE 2.11   z-scores and T-scores plotted on a normal curve.

TABLE 2.7   Conversion of Tennis Serve Scores to T-Scores

T-Score	Observed Score
60	83.1 = 83
59	82.0 = 82
58	80.9 = 81
57	79.8 = 80
56	78.7 = 79
55	77.6 = 78
54	76.5 = 77
53	75.4 = 75
52	74.3 = 74
51	73.2 = 73
50	72.1 = 72
49	71.0 = 71
48	69.9 = 70
47	68.8 = 69
46	67.7 = 68
45	66.6 = 67
44	65.5 = 66
43	64.4 = 64
42	63.3 = 63
41	62.2 = 62
40	61.1 = 61

$\bar{X} = 72.1$

$s = 10.79$

$\dfrac{s}{10}\left(\begin{array}{l}\text{value added to and}\\ \text{subtracted from } \bar{X}\end{array}\right) = \dfrac{10.79}{10} = 1.079 = 1.1$

Percentiles

Percentile scores are also standard scores and may be used to compare scores of different measurements. Because they change at different rates (remember the comparison of low and high percentile scores with middle percentiles), they should not be averaged to determine one score for several different tests. For this reason, you may prefer to use the T-scale when converting raw scores to standard scores. The calculation of percentiles was previously described, so it will not be described here.

Statistics Software

Numerous statistics software programs—varying in cost, statistical procedures, computer requirements, and ease of use—may be purchased. In addition, student versions of many of these programs are available. Statistical Package for Social Science (SPSS) is one such program. It can be used to perform the statistical procedures presented in this chapter and chapters 3 and 4. Microsoft Excel also may be used to perform the descriptive statistics presented in this chapter. Additionally, Microsoft Excel provides supplemental statistical software programs that are used with the Excel spreadsheet to perform more complex statistical procedures.

You should become familiar with a statistical software program during your college experience. Use of the microcomputer and statistics software will significantly reduce the time needed to perform statistical procedures, and you will feel more confident in the results of your work than if you perform the calculations yourself. The use of statistics software will be especially helpful in regard to the statistics presented in chapters 3 and 4. Another reason for developing the ability to use statistics software is that potential employers may expect you to have this skill.

Information about statistics programs is available in campus computing centers or bookstores and from computer software retailers. In addition, most statistics software producers have a Web home page.

■ ARE YOU ABLE TO DO THE FOLLOWING?

- Describe the purposes of standard scores.

- Convert raw scores into z-scores, T-scores, and percentiles and interpret them.

Review Problems

1. Mrs. Block completed the volleyball unit with her 2 ninth-grade classes by administering the same volleyball skills test to both classes. One of the test items was the volleyball serve. Calculate the range, $\bar{X}$, P_{50}, mode, Q, s, and deciles for the two groups of scores. Were the performances of the classes different in any way? Was one class more homogeneous?

Class A

42, 50, 57, 45, 56, 69, 45, 43, 46, 51, 61, 55, 40, 47, 59, 47, 46, 30, 48, 53, 40, 40, 64, 48, 41

Class B

51, 43, 43, 37, 33, 53, 44, 44, 38, 34, 37, 51, 20, 24, 39, 34, 38, 50, 10, 37, 39, 27, 25, 29, 23

2. Prior to working with a group of twenty adults, ages forty to forty-nine, Mr. Fitness administered a sit and reach test (flexibility of lower back and posterior thighs). After a six-week flexibility program, Mr. Fitness tested the group again. Compare the medians, means, quartile deviations, and standard deviations of the two test administrations. Did the flexibility of the group change? If so, describe the changes.

Test Administration 1

10, 9, 11, 9, 10, 11, 12, 8, 9, 10, 8, 7, 9, 8, 10, 10, 7, 9, 11, 9

Test Administration 2

12, 11, 13, 11, 11, 14, 12, 12, 14, 12, 11, 11, 13, 12, 13, 14, 10, 11, 14, 12

3. Calculate the $\bar{X}$ and s for these 2-minute sit-up test scores:

42, 41, 53, 60, 84, 49, 57, 65, 61, 48, 33, 57, 55, 50, 65, 54, 55, 57, 65, 45, 58, 54, 52, 40, 55

4. Given the following information, use the normal curve and determine the percentile rank for the three observed scores:

$$\bar{X} = 33$$
$$s = 2$$
$$X_1 = 36$$
$$X_2 = 29$$
$$X_3 = 32$$

5. Mr. Bird administered a badminton clear test to sixty students. Determine the mean and standard deviation, and convert the scores into T-scores. The scores are as follows:

74 75 64 86 73 74 75 70 69 67

80 78 61 81 77 78 65 65 70 69

85 84 83 62 84 74 75 81 66 74

63 73 77 64 66 72 80 77 80 70

66 69 72 83 69 67 73 72 75 75

70 67 65 73 73 72 72 73 74 73

Chapter Review Questions

1. Which scales of measurement include how much the variables differ from each other?

2. Which scale of measurement has a true zero point?

3. If you ask other students to name their major, which scale of measure are you using?

4. What are the four characteristics of a normal distribution?

5. If you administered a performance test to a homogeneous group, what type of distribution curve probably would result? What curve probably would result if you administered the same test to a heterogeneous group?

6. What information is provided when you rank the scores in a distribution?

7. What information do measures of central tendency provide about a distribution of scores?

8. What is the average score in a distribution?

9. What score represents the exact middle in a distribution?

10. With the scores 3, 6, 9, 12, and 15, what are the mean and median values? If the score of 15 is changed to a score of 18, what are the mean and median values? Why will the median value be the same for both distributions?

11. What do the symbols $\bar{X}$, X, Σ, N, and P_{50} represent?

12. What is the most frequently occurring score in a distribution?

13. Which measure of central tendency is not influenced by extreme scores?

14. What can be said about the values of the mean, median, and mode in a normal distribution?

15. In what type of distribution is the mean lower than the median? When would the mean be higher than the median?

16. Which way is the tail of the curve pointed if a distribution of scores produces a negatively skewed curve? In a negatively skewed distribution, is the mean or median a higher value? If this type of curve is produced after the administration of a test, what can you say about the test?

17. What information do the measures of variability provide about a distribution of scores?

18. What do the symbols Q, Q_1, Q_2, Q_3, d, and s represent?

19. What is the weakness of the range measurement?

20. With which measure of central tendency is the quartile deviation used? Which percentage of scores is included in the quartile deviation?

21. With which measure of central tendency is the standard deviation used?

22. In a normal distribution, what percentage of the curve is found between the mean plus and minus one standard deviation, between the mean plus and minus two standard deviations, and the mean plus and minus three standard deviations?

23. In a normal distribution, what percentage of the curve is found between the mean plus one standard deviation?

24. In a normal distribution of scores, a score is one standard deviation above the mean. What percentage of scores is below the given score?

25. In a distribution of scores, the $\bar{X} = 30$ and the s $= 2$. What percentage of the scores is found between the scores 28 and 32? What percentage is found between the scores 26 and 34?

26. If two different groups are administered the same physical performance test, what can you say about the group that has the largest standard deviation?

27. Which measure of variability is the most reliable and most commonly used?

28. What does it mean if someone's test score is at the seventy-fifth percentile?

29. If your score for a test is one standard deviation above the mean, what is your percentile rank?

30. What is the purpose of standard scores?

31. With a z-scale, what is the value of the mean score? How many standard deviations above the mean is a z-score of 1? What is the percentile rank of a z-score of 1?

32. With a T-scale, what is the value of the mean score? Suppose you score one and one-half standard deviations above the mean on a test. What would be your T-score?

33. Normally, what are the highest and lowest z-scores and T-scores that will occur? Why?

Investigating the Relationship between Scores

After completing this chapter, you should be able to

1. Define *correlation* and *linear correlation*, interpret the correlation coefficient (statistical significance and coefficient of determination), and use the Spearman rank-difference and Pearson product-moment methods to determine the relationship between two variables.

2. Construct a scattergram and interpret it.

In chapter 2, we discussed descriptive statistics. Although it is important that you have the skills to use these statistics, your professional responsibilities will require that you be knowledgeable about other statistical procedures. You also should be able to demonstrate the relationship of scores. Skills in this procedure will enable you to better interpret professional literature and to conduct beneficial research.

Linear Correlation

Correlation is a statistical technique used to express the relationship between two sets of scores (two variables). In this chapter, we will discuss **linear correlation,** or the degree to which a straight line best describes the relationship between two variables. A relationship between two variables may be curvilinear, meaning that the relationship is best described with a curved line. Linear relationship is the simplest and most common correlation, however. In our profession, many opportunities exist for determining if there is a relationship between two variables. For example, is there a relationship between athletic participation and academic achievement? Do individuals with a high level of physical fitness earn higher academic grades? Is there a relationship between arm strength and golf driving distance? Is there a relationship between percentage of body fat and the ability to run 2 miles? Also, correlation

techniques are used to determine the validity, reliability, and objectivity of tests. These techniques will be described in chapter 5.

The number that represents the correlation is called the **correlation coefficient.** Two techniques for determining the correlation coefficient will be presented here. Regardless of the technique used, correlation coefficients have several common characteristics. (Statements 2 and 3 are general statements; the size and significance of the coefficient must be considered.)

1. The values of the coefficient will always range from $+1.00$ to -1.00. It is rare that the coefficients of $+1.00$, -1.00, and .00 are found, however.

2. A positive coefficient indicates direct relationship; for example, an individual who scores high on one variable is likely to score high on the second variable, and an individual who scores low on one variable is likely to score low on the second variable.

3. A negative coefficient indicates inverse relationship. The individual who scores low on one variable is likely to score high on the second variable, and the individual who scores high on the first variable is likely to score low on the second.

4. A correlation coefficient of, or very close to, .00 indicates no relationship. An individual who scores high or low on one variable may have any score on the second variable.

5. The number indicates the degree of *relationship,* and the sign indicates the type of relationship. The number +.88 indicates the same degree of relationship as the number −.88. The signs indicate that the directions of the relationship are different.

6. A correlation coefficient indicates relationship. After determining a correlation coefficient, you cannot infer that one variable causes something to happen to the other variable. If a high, positive correlation coefficient is found between participation in school sports and high academic grades, it cannot be said that participation in school sports causes a person to earn good grades. It can only be said that there is a high, positive relationship.

Scattergram

A **scattergram** is a graph used to illustrate the relationship between two variables. To prepare a scattergram, perform the following steps:

1. Determine the range for each variable.

2. Designate one variable as the X score and the other variable as the Y score.

3. Draw and label the axes. Represent the X scores on the horizontal axis and the Y scores on the vertical axis. Begin with the lower X scores at the left portion of the X axis and the lower Y scores at the lower portion of the Y axis.

4. Plot each pair of scores on the graph by placing a point at the intersection of the two scores.

Figure 3.1 is a scattergram of the relationship between isometric and isotonic strength scores.

The scattergram can indicate a positive relationship, a negative relationship, or a zero relationship. If a positive relationship exists, the points will tend to cluster along a diagonal line that runs from the lower left-hand corner of the scattergram to the upper right-hand corner. In a negative relationship, the points tend to do the opposite; they move from the upper left-hand corner to the lower right-hand corner. With a positive or negative line, the closer the points cluster along the diagonal line, the higher the correlation. In a zero relationship, the points are scattered throughout the scattergram. Figure 3.2 illustrates the three types of relationships.

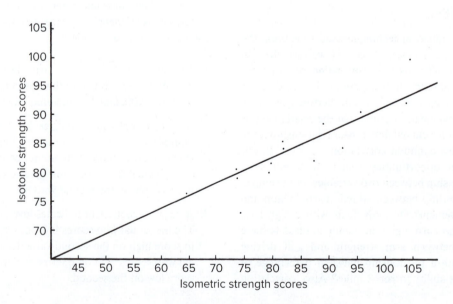

FIGURE 3.1 Scattergram of relationship between isometric and isotonic strength scores.

FIGURE 3.2   Scattergrams showing (a) positive, (b) negative, and (c) zero correlation between two variables.

Spearman Rank-Difference Correlation Coefficient

The **Spearman rank-difference correlation coefficient,** also called rank-order, is used when one or both variables are ranks or ordinal scales. The difference (D) between the ranks of the two sets of scores is used to determine the correlation coefficient. The following examples are relationships that could be determined through utilization of the rank-difference correlation coefficient:

- The ranking of participants in a badminton class and their order of finish in tournament play.

- The ability to serve well and the order of finish in a tennis tournament.

- Vertical jump scores and speed in the 100-meter run.

Of course, many other relationships can be determined with the rank-difference correlation coefficient.

The symbol for the rank-difference coefficient is the Greek rho (ρ) or $r_{\rho \eta o}$. To determine ρ, perform the following steps:

1. List each set of scores in a column.

2. Rank the two sets of scores.
   Note: This procedure was described in chapter 2 (see table 2.2).

3. Place the appropriate rank beside each score.

4. Head a column D and determine the difference in rank for each pair of scores.
   Note: The sum of the D column should always be 0. If it is not, check your work.

5. Square each number in the D column and sum the values (ΣD^2).

6. Calculate the correlation coefficient by substituting the values in the formula

$$\rho = 1.00 - \frac{6(\Sigma D^2)}{N(N^2 - 1)}$$

Table 3.1 illustrates the calculation of the rank-difference correlation coefficient for sit-up and push-up scores.

TABLE 3.1 Rank-Difference Correlation Coefficient for Sit-Up and Push-Up Scores

Student	Sit-Up Score	Rank of S-U Score	Push-Up Score	Rank of P-U Score	D	D²
A	28	19.5	19	18.0	1.5	2.25
B	31	16.5	22	15.5	1.0	1.00
C	32	13.5	25	11.0	2.5	6.25
D	35	7.0	23	13.5	−6.5	42.25
E	32	13.5	27	8.5	5.0	25.00
F	40	1.0	35	1.0	0.0	0.00
G	33	10.0	29	4.5	5.5	30.25
H	35	7.0	28	6.5	0.5	0.25
I	32	13.5	26	10.0	3.5	12.25
J	36	4.5	29	4.5	0.0	0.00
K	35	7.0	31	3.0	4.0	16.00
L	31	16.5	33	2.0	14.5	210.25
M	36	4.5	24	12.0	−7.5	56.25
N	30	18.0	21	17.0	1.00	1.00
O	37	2.5	18	19.0	−16.5	272.25
P	37	2.5	27	8.5	−6.0	36.00
Q	33	10.0	22	15.5	−5.5	30.25
R	28	19.5	17	20.0	−0.5	0.25
S	32	13.5	28	6.5	7.0	49.00
T	33	10.0	23	13.5	−3.5	12.25
						$\sum D^2 = 803.00$

$N = 20$

$$\rho = 1.00 - \frac{6(\sum D^2)}{N(N^2 - 1)}$$

$$= 1.00 - \frac{6(803)}{20(400 - 1)}$$

$$= 1.00 - \frac{4{,}818}{7{,}980}$$

$$= 1.00 - .60$$

$$\rho = .40$$

Pearson Product-Moment Correlation Coefficient

The **Pearson product-moment correlation coefficient,** also called Pearson r, is used when measurement results are reported in interval or ratio scale scores. The Spearman correlation coefficient actually is a Pearson r computed on the ranks. The Pearson r gives a more precise estimate of relationship because the actual scores, rather than the ranks of the scores, are taken into account. (This popular correlation coefficient has many variations, but only one method will be described.) The symbol for the product-moment correlation coefficient is r.

Observed scores are used with this calculation method of the product-moment correlation coefficient. The steps for calculation are as follows:

1. Label columns for name, X, X^2, Y, Y^2, and XY.

2. Designate one set of scores as X, designate the other set as Y, and place the appropriate paired scores by the individual's name.

3. Find the sums of the X and Y columns (ΣX and ΣY).

4. Square each X score, place squared scores in the X^2 column, and find the sum of the column (ΣX^2).

5. Square each Y score, place squared scores in the Y^2 column, and find the sum of the column (ΣY^2).

6. Multiply each X score by the Y score, place the product in the XY column, and find the sum of the column (ΣXY).

7. Substitute the values in the formula

$$r = \frac{N(\Sigma XY) - (\Sigma X)(\Sigma Y)}{\sqrt{N(\Sigma X^2) - (\Sigma X)^2}\sqrt{N(\Sigma Y^2) - (\Sigma Y)^2}}$$

Table 3.2 illustrates the calculation of the Pearson product-moment correlation coefficient for isometric and isotonic strength scores.

Interpretation of the Correlation Coefficient

After calculating the correlation coefficient, you must interpret it. This interpretation should be done with caution. For example, a correlation of .70 may be considered quite high in one analysis but low in another. Also, in your interpretation of the coefficient, you must remember that a high correlation does not indicate that one variable causes something to happen to another variable. Correlation is about the *relationship* of variables. The purpose for which the correlation coefficient is computed must be considered when making a decision about how high or low a coefficient is. Keeping the purpose of the correlation study in mind, use the following ranges as general guidelines for interpretation of the correlation coefficient. Note that negative values are considered in the same manner.

r = below .20 (extremely low relationship)

r = .20 to .39 (low relationship)

r = .40 to .59 (moderate relationship)

r = .60 to .79 (high relationship)

r = .80 to 1.00 (very high relationship)

Significance of the Correlation Coefficient

Your interpretation of a correlation coefficient should not be limited to the general interpretation described earlier. The **statistical significance,** or reliability, of the correlation coefficient should be considered also. In determining the coefficient significance, you are answering the following question: If the study were repeated, what is the probability of obtaining a similar relationship? You want to be sure that the relationship is real and did not result from a chance occurrence.

When r is calculated, the number of pairs of scores is important. With a small number of paired scores, it is possible that a high r value can occur by chance. For this reason, when a small number of paired scores is recorded, the r value must be large to be significant. On the other hand, if the number of scores is large, it is less likely that a high r value will occur by chance. Thus, a small r can be significant with a large number of paired scores.

A table of values is used to determine the statistical significance of a correlation coefficient. (In this discussion, .05 and .01 levels of significance and degrees of freedom are used. These terms will be explained in greater detail in the discussion of t-tests in chapter 4.) Before using the values table, you must first calculate the degrees of freedom (df) for the paired scores. The degrees of freedom equal $N - 2$ (N is the number of paired scores). In the calculation of r for isometric and isotonic strength scores in table 3.2, the degrees of freedom equal $N - 2 = 15 - 2 = 13$. To determine the statistical significance of r = .90, we will use the values in appendix A. Find the number 13 in the degrees of freedom column in appendix A. You see that a correlation of .514 is required for significance at the .05 level and .641 at the .01 level. These numbers indicate that, for 13 degrees of freedom, a correlation as high as .514 occurs only 5 in 100 times by chance, and a correlation as high as .641 occurs only 1 in 100 times by chance. Because the r value of .90 in table 3.2 is greater than both

TABLE 3.2 Product-Moment Correlation Coefficient for Isometric and Isotonic Strength Scores

Name	Isometric Score X	X^2	Isotonic Score Y	Y^2	XY
A	63	3,969	76	5,776	4,788
B	78	6,084	80	6,400	6,240
C	46	2,116	70	4,900	3,220
D	103	10,609	102	10,404	10,506
E	74	5,476	73	5,329	5,402
F	82	6,724	87	7,569	7,134
G	95	9,025	92	8,464	8,740
H	103	10,609	93	8,649	9,579
I	87	7,569	83	6,889	7,221
J	73	5,329	79	6,241	5,767
K	78	6,084	82	6,724	6,396
L	89	7,921	90	8,100	8,010
M	82	6,724	85	7,225	6,970
N	73	5,329	81	6,561	5,913
O	92	8,464	85	7,225	7,820
	1,218	102,032	1,258	106,456	103,706

$N = 15$

$$r = \frac{N(\Sigma XY) - (\Sigma X)(\Sigma Y)}{\sqrt{N(\Sigma X^2) - (\Sigma X)^2}\sqrt{N(\Sigma Y^2) - (\Sigma Y)^2}}$$

$$= \frac{15(103,706) - (1,218)(1,258)}{\sqrt{15(102,032) - (1,218)^2}\sqrt{15(106,456) - (1,258)^2}}$$

$$= \frac{1,555,590 - 1,532,244}{\sqrt{1,530,480 - 1,483,524}\sqrt{1,596,840 - 1,582,564}}$$

$$= \frac{23,346}{\sqrt{46,956}\sqrt{14,276}}$$

$$= \frac{23,346}{(216.69)(119.48)}$$

$$= \frac{23,346}{25,890.12}$$

$r = .90$

of these values, we conclude that the correlation is significant at the .01 level.

In summary, the obtained r is compared with the appropriate table values. If the obtained r is larger than the values found at the .05 and .01 level, r is significant at the .01 level. If the obtained r falls between these two table values, r is significant at the .05 level. If the obtained r is smaller than both table values, it is not significant. Significant correlation coefficients lower than .50 can be useful for indicating nonchance relationships among variables, but they probably are not large enough to be useful in predicting individual scores.

You should note that the correlation needed for significance decreases with the increased number of paired scores. Remember the earlier statement that a large number of scores decreases the likelihood that a high r will occur by chance. The table values reflect the influence of chance. You also should note that a higher correlation is needed for significance at the .01 level than at the .05 level. The reason is that we are reducing the odds that the correlation is due to chance (1 in 100 vs. 5 in 100).

Coefficient of Determination

The statistical significance of correlation is important, but to better determine the relationship of two variables, the **coefficient of determination** should be utilized. The coefficient of determination is the square of the correlation coefficient (r^2). It represents the common variance between two variables, or the proportion of variance in one variable that can be accounted for by the other variable. For example, imagine we administered a standing long jump test and a leg strength test to a group of male high school students, and we calculated a correlation coefficient of .85 between the two tests. We calculate that r^2 equals .72. We interpret this value to mean that 72% of the variability in the standing long jump scores is associated with leg strength. Or, we might say that 72% of both standing long jump ability and leg strength comes from common factors. We also can say that the two tests have common factors that influence the individuals' scores.

Using the coefficient of determination shows that a high correlation coefficient is needed to indicate a substantial to high relationship between two variables. In addition, coefficients of determination can be compared as ratios, whereas correlation coefficients cannot. For example, an r of .80 is not twice as large as an r of .40. By using the coefficient of determination, we see that an r of .80 is four times stronger than an r of .40 ($r = .80$, $r^2 = .64$; $r = .40$, $r^2 = .16$).

Negative Correlation Coefficients

There are occasions when a negative correlation coefficient is to be expected. When a smaller score that is considered to be a better score is correlated with a larger score that also is considered to be a better score, the correlation coefficient usually will be negative. The relationship between maximum oxygen consumption and the time required to run 2 miles is an example. In general, individuals with high values for maximum oxygen consumption will have lower times for the 2-mile run than individuals with low values for maximum oxygen consumption. In addition, a negative correlation will probably occur with performance that requires support of the body (weight correlated with pull-ups or dips).

Correlation, Regression, and Prediction

Recall that linear correlation refers to the relationship of two variables. It tells us how close the relationship between two variables is to a straight line. Once a relationship between two variables is found, if we have the score for one variable we can predict the score for the other variable. Consider the example provided in table 3.2. A correlation of .90 was found between isometric strength and isotonic strength. Through linear regression analysis, it is possible to predict an individual's isotonic score once the isometric score is known. Also consider the question asked at the beginning of the chapter about a possible relationship between physical fitness and academic grades. If a high relationship between these two variables were found, it would be possible to predict grades based on physical fitness scores. Rarely, however, will a predicted score be the actual score for an individual. Only if the correlation is -1 or $+1$ can we be confident that the predicted score will be the actual score. In correlation studies, we can determine the standard error of estimate (a numerical value that indicates the amount of error to expect in a predicted score) and how much confidence (referred to as *confidence limits*) we have in the prediction. To determine our confidence limits, we use the standard error of estimate in the same way as the standard deviation is used with a group of scores. Again, consider the isometric and isotonic scores in table 3.2. With linear regression analysis, an isotonic score may be predicted based upon an individual's isometric score. The standard error of estimate is then calculated to determine how much confidence we have in our predicted score. The standard error of estimate is added to and subtracted from the predicted score to determine the confidence limits. The confidence limits are:

68.26% of the time the predicted score is located ± 1 standard error of estimate from the predicted score

95.44% of the time the predicted score is located ± 2 standard error of estimates from the predicted score

99.73% of the time the predicted score is located ± 3 standard error of estimates from the predicted score

Correlation studies report these values.

Often correlation studies involve more than two variables. These studies, referred to as *multiple correlation-regression studies,* enable investigators to predict a score using several other scores. For example, many universities admit students based on their predicted freshman year grade point average. Values or scores for such variables as class rank, high school grade point average, and SAT or ACT score are used in a multiple regression equation to predict the freshman year grade point average. Also, many health-related or lifestyle studies involve multiple correlation-regression analysis. Such studies predict the health problems or diseases that may occur as a result of factors involved in a person's lifestyle.

Although linear and multiple correlation-regression techniques will not be presented in this text, you should be aware of their use and purpose. Your professional literature will include these studies.

■ ARE YOU ABLE TO DO THE FOLLOWING?

- Define *correlation, linear correlation, correlation coefficient,* and *coefficient of determination.*

- Interpret the correlation coefficient.

- Construct a scattergram and interpret it.

- Determine the Spearman rank-difference correlation coefficient and interpret it (statistical significance and coefficient of determination).

- Determine the Pearson product-moment correlation coefficient and interpret it (statistical significance and coefficient of determination).

Review Problems

1. Using the rank-difference correlation coefficient method, determine the relationship between the height (inches) and weight (pounds) measurements of twenty individuals. After you have determined r, calculate the coefficient of determination, interpret the obtained value, and use appendix A to interpret the significance of r.

Student	Height	Weight
A	68	170
B	68	160
C	66	140
D	67	150
E	69	155
F	65	145
G	70	168
H	71	182
I	74	208
J	65	144
K	68	165
L	67	160
M	71	195
N	71	190
O	70	195
P	66	150
Q	69	170
R	66	148
S	65	140
T	76	210

2. Using the product-moment correlation coefficient method, determine the relationship between a 2-minute sit-up test and physical fitness test scores. After you have determined r, calculate the coefficient of determination, interpret the obtained value, and use appendix A to interpret the significance of the correlation coefficient.

Student	Sit-Up Score	PF Score
A	45	81
B	51	94
C	30	91
D	55	75
E	32	65
F	42	82
G	41	85
H	52	65
I	61	73
J	39	85
K	38	93

L	37	51	E	6.6	147
M	41	65	F	7.2	188
N	42	73	G	6.5	140
O	42	74	H	7.1	178
P	43	79	I	6.9	164
Q	38	42	J	7.0	182
R	39	65	K	6.6	150
S	45	54	L	7.3	188
T	43	63	M	7.0	170

3. Using the product-moment correlation coefficient method, determine the relationship between the daily sodium intake and the systolic blood pressure of twenty-five individuals. After you have determined r, calculate the coefficient of determination, interpret the obtained value, and use appendix A to interpret the significance of r.

Individual	Sodium Intake	Blood Pressure
A	7.2	189
B	6.9	175
C	7.1	160
D	7.0	163

N	6.7	154
O	6.9	165
P	7.1	157
Q	7.4	193
R	6.5	139
S	7.1	176
T	7.0	180
U	6.8	164
V	6.9	159
W	6.7	151
X	6.8	163
Y	6.5	137

Chapter Review Questions

1. What is the purpose of a correlation study?

2. What are the two types of linear relationships that two variables may have?

3. What is another word that indicates a *direct* relationship?

4. A group of 100 adults, ages seventy-five to eighty, was tested for leg strength and balance while moving. A correlation coefficient of +.85 was found between the two variables. What can be said about the relationship of leg strength and balance? If a correlation coefficient of −.85 had been found, what would you say about the relationship?

5. When using the Spearman rank-difference correlation coefficient, which scales of measurement should be used?

6. When using the Pearson product-moment correlation coefficient, which scales of measurement should be used?

7. For the study described in question 4, use appendix A to determine the level of significance for the correlation coefficient. How do you interpret the significance of the correlation?

8. How do you obtain the coefficient of determination?

9. In question 4, what is the value of the coefficient of determination for the +.85 correlation coefficient, and how do you interpret it?

10. What is the purpose of linear regression analysis and multiple correlation-regression analysis?

4 Investigating the Difference in Scores

After completing this chapter, you should be able to

1. Define and give examples of *dependent variable, independent variable, null hypothesis, two-tailed test, one-tailed test, degrees of freedom, level of significance, standard error of the mean,* and *standard error of the difference between means.*

2. Define *Type I* and *Type II* errors.

3. Use and interpret the t-test for independent groups and the t-test for dependent groups.

4. Use and interpret analysis of variance for independent groups and analysis of variance for repeated measures.

5. Use Tukey's honestly significant difference test (HSD).

In your professional responsibilities, you may have occasions when you would like to determine if there is a significant difference in the performance of various groups (e.g., males and females, athletes and nonathletes). You also may wish to determine if there is a significant difference in methods of instruction, treatments of a particular injury, cardiorespiratory endurance programs, flexibility programs, or in other areas of interest or responsibilities that you have. To determine if a significant difference exists in the examples just provided, you must compare means. A discussion of all procedures that may be used to test for significant difference between means is beyond the scope of this textbook. However, two common procedures used by researchers, the t-test and analysis of variance (ANOVA), will be presented. Your understanding of these procedures will enable you to conduct beneficial research and better interpret professional research.

Testing for Significant Difference between Two Means

Imagine you are the instructor at a fitness center, and you initiate an aerobic fitness class for females, 25 to 30 years of age, who have a low level of fitness. Forty females select to participate in the class. Rather than have all forty individuals participate in the same program, you decide to randomly assign each person to one of two groups. One group will participate in aerobic dance, 3 times per week, for 8 weeks. The other group will participate in a running program, 3 times per week, for 8 weeks. There are other factors about the two programs that you would have to consider (e.g., intensity and duration of each session), but you want to know if one program will develop fitness better than the other.

At the conclusion of the 8 weeks, you administer the same cardiorespiratory fitness test to the two groups and note that the group means are different. Can you say that one program developed cardiorespiratory fitness better than the other? You cannot reach such a conclusion by merely observing the means. It is not unusual for the means to be different. In fact, if one thousand random samples were drawn from a population and administered the same test, the sample means would approximate a normal curve. The question you must answer is "Are the two sample means significantly different?" To answer this question you must statistically analyze the scores.

Dependent and Independent Variables

In experimental research, there are two important classes of variables. The response to the treatment (independent variable) is called the **dependent variable.** The dependent variable is the variable that researchers observe to see if it changes as a result of the treatment. It is the reason the researcher is conducting the study. The dependent variable also is called the *criterion variable.* Suppose a study is conducted to determine if change will occur in subjects' blood pressure after the reduction of salt intake. Blood pressure is the dependent variable. Blood pressure may or may not change as a result of a reduction in salt intake.

In experimental research, the **independent variable** also is a necessary component. This variable is the treatment in the study. It is controlled by the researcher. In the example included in the dependent variable definition, salt intake is the independent variable. The researcher controls the amount of salt and which participants consume the salt.

The Null Hypothesis

In statistics, a hypothesis is a prediction about the difference between two or more variables. The hypothesis that predicts there will be no statistical difference between the means of groups is the **null hypothesis.** The hypothesis that predicts there will be a difference is the **alternative hypothesis.** The hypotheses are written as

Null hypothesis $\qquad H_0 : \bar{X}_1 = \bar{X}_2$

Alternative hypothesis $\quad H_1 : \bar{X}_1 \neq \bar{X}_2$

This type of alternative hypothesis is used for a **two-tailed test,** meaning that the difference in means can be in either direction. The mean for group 1 can be either larger or smaller than the mean for group 2. If a statistical test of the null hypothesis presents no evidence that the hypothesis is false, you accept it and reject the alternative

hypothesis. If the statistical test presents evidence that the null hypothesis is false (the mean for group 1 is larger or smaller than the mean for group 2), you reject it and accept the alternative hypothesis.

It is acceptable to use an alternative hypothesis that is directional. With this hypothesis, the conductor of the study is predicting that one mean is either less or more than the other mean. This type of hypothesis is used for a **one-tailed test** and requires that the t distribution be used differently. The directional alternative hypothesis is written as

$$H_1 : \bar{X}_1 < \bar{X}_2$$

or

$$H_1 : \bar{X}_1 > \bar{X}_2$$

A one-tailed test is used when you are sure that the mean differences can occur only in one direction—that is, when one mean is either larger or smaller than the other mean. For most studies, the nondirectional alternative hypothesis (two-tailed) is sufficient.

Degrees of Freedom

The **degrees of freedom** (df) concept is used in all statistical tests. For the statistical procedures used in this chapter, the degrees of freedom are calculated by subtracting 1 from N ($N - 1$) for any set of scores. (The degrees of freedom are determined by the sample size.) The degrees of freedom indicate the number of scores in a distribution that are free to vary. For example, assume that you have determined the group mean for twenty scores. For this given mean, nineteen scores could vary. Once the nineteen scores are obtained, however, the twentieth score must assume a fixed value if the mean is to remain the same. To convince yourself of this concept, work with five scores that have a mean of 10 (the sum of the five numbers is 50). Assign four scores any value from 5 to 12. If the mean is to remain 10, you will see that the fifth score cannot be just any value. Its value is determined by the values that you assigned to the first four scores. In the case of a t-test where there are two groups, the degrees of freedom equal $(N_1 - 1) + (N_2 - 1) = N_1 + N_2 - 2$.

Level of Significance

The **level of significance** is the probability of rejecting a null hypothesis when it is true. The two most common levels of significance are .01 (p = .01) and .05 (p = .05). If you reject the null hypothesis at the .01 level of significance, there is 1 chance in 100 that you are rejecting the null hypothesis when it is actually true. At the .05 level, there are 5 chances in 100 that you are in error. Most investigators are not willing to accept a level of significance higher than .05, but some studies report a level of significance lower than .01. For example, a p = .001 means there is one chance in 1,000 that you are in error. Additionally, a study may report the level of significance as <.03, which means the significance is between .03 and .02.

Two types of error, **Type I** and **Type II,** can be committed when accepting and rejecting hypotheses. If you reject a hypothesis when it is true, you commit a Type I error. The Type II error occurs when the hypothesis is false and should be rejected, but the test results appear to make the hypothesis true; that is, you accept the hypothesis when it is not true. Using the .01 level of significance, rather than the .05 level, reduces the risk of making a Type I error but increases the probability of making a Type II error. Owing to the probability of making a Type I error, only in unusual studies is a level of significance above .05 used. In general, the best way for a researcher to decrease the probability of making a Type II error is to increase the sample size (the number of subjects in the groups). As the sample size increases, the probability of making a Type II error decreases.

The level of significance and the degrees of freedom are used together to determine the value that a statistical test must yield for you to reject the null hypothesis. Appendix B shows the values used to determine significance. To use the table in appendix B, go down the df column to the degrees of freedom that you have determined and then go across to the values (critical values) under the .05 and .01 columns. These values will determine whether you reject or accept the null hypothesis. Note that the greater the degrees of freedom, the smaller the value needed to reject the null hypothesis. Because the degrees of freedom are a result of the sample number, a large sample number is beneficial in terms of finding a significant difference.

Standard Error of the Mean

If a large number of equal-size samples were randomly drawn from the same population and their means formed into a distribution, we would have a sampling distribution of means. From the sampling distribution of means, we can compute the standard deviation of the sampling distribution called the **standard error of the mean** (SEM). When the means are in close agreement, the value of the SEM is small. Also, we are more confident that any one mean is near the value of the population mean.

Because it is not practical to calculate the SEM from a sampling distribution of means, a formula has been derived to provide an estimate of the standard error. The formula is

$$SEM = \frac{s}{\sqrt{N}} \quad (s = \text{standard deviation of sample scores})$$

Table 4.1 shows that, for the group running 3 days per week, the $\bar{X} = 80.9$ and the SEM = 0.38. The SEM value is added to and subtracted from the $\bar{X}(80.9 \pm 0.38)$ to demonstrate the distribution of the means. The resulting values indicate that if this study were repeated a large number of times, 68.26% of the time the means for the group running 3 days per week would be in the range of 80.52 to 81.28. For the group running 5 days per week, 68.26% of the time the means would be in the range of 90.51 to 92.09 (91.3 $\pm$ 0.79).

$\blacklozenge \blacklozenge \blacklozenge$ POINT OF EMPHASIS $\blacklozenge \blacklozenge \blacklozenge$

- The lower the probability, the higher the level of significance will be: p = .01 is a higher level of significance than p = .05.

This range is interpreted as the limits of the 68% confidence intervals for the mean. We also can establish the 95% and 99% confidence intervals for the mean. If, with the mean, we add and subtract two SEMs, we have 95% confidence that the true mean lies within the established range. If we do the same procedure with three SEMs, we have 99% confidence that the true mean lies within the established range. For the group running 3 days per week, the 95% confidence interval would be in the range of 80.14 to 81.66.

Standard Error of the Difference between Means

After calculating the SEM for each of the means, we can estimate the size difference to be expected between two sample means randomly drawn from the same population. To determine this value, called the **standard error of the difference,** we have to square the SEM of each group, add the results, and then find the square root of the sum. The standard error of the difference represents the standard deviation of all the observed differences between pairs of sample means. The formula is

$$s_{\bar{X}-\bar{X}} = \sqrt{SEM_1{}^2 + SEM_2{}^2}$$

In table 4.1, the difference between the means is 10.4 and $s_{\bar{X}-\bar{X}} = 0.87$. These values indicate that 68.26% of the time, the differences between the means would be in the range of 9.53 to 11.27 (10.4 ± 0.87). As was done with the SEM, we can use the same procedure to establish 95% and 99% confidence intervals for the range of differences between the means.

t-Test for Independent Groups

The **t-test for independent groups** may be used to determine the significance of the difference between two independent sample means. In a comparison of the means of two independent samples, the following assumptions are made:

1. Initially the two sample groups come from the same population.

2. The population is normally distributed.

3. The two groups are representative samples; that is, they have approximately equal variances.

To illustrate the steps involved in the use of the t-test for independent groups, suppose you wanted to determine if running 5 days a week would develop cardiorespiratory endurance better than running 3 days a week. Your null hypothesis is that there will be no difference in the means of the two programs ($\bar{X}_1 = \bar{X}_2$). After randomly selecting the individuals for each group, you prescribe the same running program (intensity and duration for each day) for both groups. After 12 weeks, you administer the Harvard Step Test to both groups in the running program. Table 4.1 shows the test scores and the necessary calculations for the t-test. (For convenience, only ten individuals will be in each group.) The steps for the calculations are as follows:

1. Calculate the mean and standard deviations for each group.

2. Calculate the SEM for each group.

3. Calculate the standard error of the difference between means ($s_{\bar{X}-\bar{X}}$).

4. Calculate the t-ratio by substituting the values in the formula

$$t = \frac{\bar{X}_1 - \bar{X}_2}{s_{\bar{X}-\bar{X}}}$$

TABLE 4.1 t-Test for Independent Groups: Harvard Step Test

Group Running 3 Days/Week		Group Running 5 Days/Week	
X_1	X_1^2	X_2	X_2^2
80	6,400	88	7,744
79	6,241	92	8,464
81	6,561	93	8,649
80	6,400	95	9,025
82	6,724	91	8,281
81	6,561	89	7,921
80	6,400	88	7,744
82	6,724	90	8,100
81	6,561	94	8,836
83	6,889	93	8,649
$\Sigma X_1 = 809$	$\Sigma X_1^2 = 65,461$	$\Sigma X_2 = 913$	$\Sigma X_2^2 = 83,413$

$\bar{X}_1 = 80.9$

$$s_1 = \sqrt{\frac{N\Sigma X^2 - (\Sigma X)^2}{N(N-1)}}$$

$$= \sqrt{\frac{10(65,461) - (809)^2}{10(9)}}$$

$$= \sqrt{\frac{654,610 - 654,481}{90}}$$

$$= \sqrt{\frac{129}{90}}$$

$s_1 = \sqrt{1.43} = 1.20$

$$SEM_1 = \frac{s_1}{\sqrt{N_1}} = \frac{1.20}{\sqrt{10}} = \frac{1.20}{3.16} = 0.38$$

$$s_{\bar{x} - \bar{x}} = \sqrt{SEM_1^2 + SEM_2^2}$$

$$= \sqrt{(0.38)^2 + (0.79)^2}$$

$$= \sqrt{0.1444 + 0.6241}$$

$$= \sqrt{0.7685}$$

$s_{\bar{x} - \bar{x}} = 0.87$

$\bar{X}_2 = 91.3$

$s_2 = 2.05$

$SEM_2 = .79$

$$t = \frac{\bar{X}_1 - \bar{X}_2}{s_{\bar{x} - \bar{x}}}$$

$$= \frac{80.9 - 91.3}{.87}$$

$t = -11.95$ (compare with t-values in appendix B)

5. Determine the degrees of freedom (df). For this comparison, the degrees of freedom = 10 + 10 − 2 = 18.

6. Refer to the t-values in appendix B. If the computed t-ratio is equal to or greater than the critical value in appendix B, reject the null hypothesis. If the t-ratio is less than the critical value, accept the null hypothesis. With 18 degrees of freedom, the t-ratio of 11.95 is greater than the t of 2.101 needed for significance at the .05 level and greater than the 2.878 needed for significance at the .01 level.

Note: The negative sign is ignored because it is the result of subtracting $\bar{X}_2$ from $\bar{X}_1$. If the group running 5 days a week had been designated as group 1, the result would have been positive. The important consideration is the size of t, not its sign.

7. Reject the null hypothesis: You may conclude that running 5 days a week develops cardiorespiratory endurance better than running 3 days a week.

t-Test for Dependent Groups

If two groups are not independent but are related to each other, the **t-test for dependent groups** should be used. This test is also called the t-test for paired, related, or correlated samples. The only changes in the assumptions for the t-test for dependent groups, as compared with those for the t-test for independent groups, are the following:

1. The paired differences are a random sample from a normal population.

2. The equal variances assumption is unnecessary, since you will be working with one group.

To illustrate the steps involved in the use of the t-test for dependent groups, imagine that you wish to determine if participation in a basketball class will improve the scores of ninth-grade girls on a speed spot shooting test. Your null hypothesis is that there will be no difference in the means of the speed spot shooting pre-test and post-test ($\bar{X}_1 = \bar{X}_2$). You administer the test the first day of the class and again at the conclusion of the basketball unit. Table 4.2 shows the pairs of scores and the necessary calculations for the t-test. (Again, for convenience, only ten pairs of scores will be used.) The steps for the calculations are as follows:

1. List the pairs of scores so that you can subtract one from the other.

2. Label a column D and determine the difference for each pair of scores.

3. Label a column D^2, square each D, and sum D^2 (ΣD^2).

4. Calculate the mean difference ($\bar{D}$).

5. Calculate the standard deviation of the difference. The formula is

TABLE 4.2   Test for Dependent Groups: Speed Spot Shooting Test

Pre-test Scores	Post-test Scores	D	D^2
10	12	2	4
12	15	3	9
9	10	1	1
11	10	−1	1
8	12	4	16
9	11	2	4
13	14	1	1
8	11	3	9
7	9	2	4
9	10	1	1
		$\Sigma D = 18$	$\Sigma D^2 = 50$

$$\bar{D} = 1.8$$

$$s_D = \sqrt{\frac{\Sigma D^2 - N(\bar{D}^2)}{N}}$$

$$= \sqrt{\frac{50 - 10(1.8^2)}{10}}$$

$$= \sqrt{\frac{50 - 10(3.24)}{10}}$$

$$= \sqrt{\frac{17.6}{10}}$$

$$s_D = \sqrt{1.76} = 1.33$$

$$s_{\bar{D}} = \frac{s_D}{\sqrt{N}}$$

$$= \frac{1.33}{\sqrt{10}}$$

$$s_{\bar{D}} = \frac{1.33}{3.16} = .42$$

$$t = \frac{\bar{D}}{s_{\bar{D}}}$$

$$t = \frac{1.8}{.42} = 4.29 \quad \text{(compare with t-values in appendix B)}$$

$$s_D = \sqrt{\frac{\Sigma D^2 - N(\bar{D}^2)}{N}}$$

6. Calculate the standard error of the difference ($s_{\bar{D}}$). The $s_{\bar{D}}$ is equivalent to the SEM and is obtained in a similar manner. The formula is

$$s_{\bar{D}} = \frac{s_D}{\sqrt{N}}$$

7. Calculate the t-ratio by substituting the values in the formula

$$t = \frac{\bar{D}}{s_{\bar{D}}}$$

8. Determine the degrees of freedom. For this comparison, the degrees of freedom = 10 − 1 = 9.

9. Refer to the t-values in appendix B. With 9 degrees of freedom, the t-ratio of 4.29 is greater than the t-value of 2.262 needed for significance at the .05 level of significance and greater than the t-value of 3.250 needed at the .01 level.

10. Reject the null hypothesis. You may conclude that participation in the basketball class improved performance on the speed spot shooting test.

▧ ARE YOU ABLE TO DO THE FOLLOWING?

▪ Define and give examples of *null hypothesis, degrees of freedom, level of significance, SEM,* and *standard error of the difference between means.*

▪ Define *Type I* and *Type II* errors.

▪ Determine if there is a significant difference between two means through use of the appropriate t-test.

Review Problems

1. An instructor used different methods to teach a health unit to two classes. Use the appropriate t-test to determine if the performances of the two classes on the knowledge test were significantly different.

Class 1					Class 2				
88	93	91	82	85	82	86	89	88	91
87	90	86	92	89	92	89	85	89	92
94	88	87	87	90	92	93	94	89	94

2. Use the appropriate t-test to determine if a group of twelve individuals experienced a significant change in percent body fat after participation in a 15-week exercise program.

Subject	Percent Body Fat before Exercise Program	Percent Body Fat after Exercise Program
A	26	21
B	17	15
C	18	16
D	20	16
E	21	18
F	25	21
G	19	16
H	21	18
I	27	23
J	21	17
K	20	18
L	24	22

3. After participation in an adult fitness program, the resting heart rates of twelve smokers and twelve nonsmokers were measured. Use the appropriate t-test to determine if there is a significant difference in the heart rates of the two groups.

Smokers	Nonsmokers
74	69
75	68
76	70
70	68
68	73
71	70
77	73
75	71
70	70
76	69
74	70
75	71

◆ ◆ ◆   POINT OF EMPHASIS   ◆ ◆ ◆

▪ The t-test for independent groups is used to determine differences between two groups of subjects taking the same test (the dependent variable). The t-test for dependent groups is used when a group of subjects is measured on two different occasions and usually involves administration of a pre-test and post-test (the dependent variable).

4. Fifteen males participated in a diet and exercise program for 6 months. Use the appropriate t-test to determine if the participants experienced a significant change in their serum cholesterol after the diet and exercise program.

Participant	Preprogram Cholesterol	Postprogram Cholesterol
A	230	210
B	205	200
C	195	190
D	210	195
E	233	212
F	240	202
G	195	190
H	220	200
I	225	198
J	211	200
K	221	199
L	225	220
M	203	195
N	240	220
O	207	198

Testing for Significant Difference among Three or More Means

The t-test is a method for testing hypotheses about two sample means, but there may be occasions that require the testing of hypotheses about more than two means. For example, you may elect to compare the effects of three or more methods of teaching, cardiorespiratory fitness programs, weight-training programs, or weight-reduction programs. **Analysis of variance** (ANOVA) is a method used to compare three or more means or even, at times, to compare two means. For these reasons, ANOVA is used in research more than any other statistical technique.

Special Terms and Symbols

Before attempting to perform the steps of the new techniques, you should have an understanding of these terms:

N = number of scores

n = the number of scores in a group (numbers in groups may be different)

k = the number of independent groups or the number of trials (measures) performed on the same subjects (repeated measures)

r = number of rows or subjects (repeated measures)

grand ΣX = sum of all scores in all groups

grand ΣX^2 = sum of the squares of all scores in all groups

total sum of squares (SS_T) = the sum of the squared deviations of every score from the grand $\overline{X}$; represents the variability of each score in all groups from the grand $\overline{X}$

sum of squares within groups (SS_W) = the sum of the squared deviations of each score from its group $\overline{X}$; also referred to as sum of squares for error

sum of squares between groups (SS_B) = the sum of the squared deviations of each group $\overline{X}$ from the grand $\overline{X}$; also referred to as treatment sum of squares

mean square for the sum of squares within groups (MS_W) = variance within the groups

mean square for the sum of squares between groups (MS_B) = variance between groups

F-distribution = table values required to reject null hypothesis

degrees of freedom within groups = $(N - k)$; total number of measures or scores (N) minus number of groups (k); degrees of freedom for denominator in F-distribution

degrees of freedom between groups = $(k - 1)$; number of groups (k) minus 1; degrees of freedom for numerator in F-distribution

$$\frac{\text{degrees of freedom between groups}}{\text{degrees of freedom within groups}} = \frac{k-1}{N-k}$$

Analysis of Variance for Independent Groups

The **analysis of variance for independent groups** is used when the sample groups are not related to each other. There are several assumptions for this ANOVA, but the basic assumptions are as follows:

1. The samples are randomly drawn from a normally distributed population.

2. The variances of the samples are approximately equal.

To illustrate the steps involved in the analysis of variance for independent groups, suppose that a fitness instructor wishes to determine if there is a difference in three programs designed to improve trunk extension. The null hypothesis is that there will be no difference in the means of the three programs ($\bar{X}_1 = \bar{X}_2 = \bar{X}_3$). The instructor randomly assigns the members of a fitness class to one of three groups, and each group participates for 10 weeks in a different program to improve trunk extension. At the conclusion of the training period, the groups are given the same trunk extension test. Table 4.3 shows the scores and the necessary calculations for the analysis of variance. As with previous illustrations, the total number of scores is intentionally small. The steps for the calculations are as follows:

1. Sum each group of scores to get ΣX_1, ΣX_2, and ΣX_3. Add the group sums to get a grand ΣX ($\Sigma X_1 + \Sigma X_2 + \Sigma X_3 = $ grand ΣX).

2. Square each score and sum the squared scores of each group (ΣX^2). Add the ΣX^2 for each group to get a grand ΣX^2 ($\Sigma X_1^2 + \Sigma X_2^2 + \Sigma X_3^2 = $ grand ΣX^2).

3. Calculate the correction factor (C). C is necessary because raw scores are used rather than deviations of the scores from the mean.

$$C = \frac{(\text{grand } \Sigma X)^2}{\text{total N}}$$

4. Calculate the total sum of squares (SS_T).

$$SS_T = \text{grand } \Sigma X^2 - C$$

5. Calculate the sum of squares between groups (SS_B).

$$SS_B = \frac{(\Sigma X_1)^2}{n_1} + \frac{(\Sigma X_2)^2}{n_2} + \frac{(\Sigma X_3)^2}{n_3} - C$$

6. Calculate the sum of squares within groups (SS_W).

$$S_W = SS_T - SS_B$$

7. Calculate the mean square for the sum of squares between groups.

$$MS_B = \frac{SS_B}{k-1}$$

8. Calculate the mean square for the sum of squares within groups.

$$MS_W = \frac{SS_W}{N-k}$$

9. Calculate the F-ratio.

$$F = \frac{MS_B}{MS_W}$$

10. Refer to the F-distribution in appendix C to determine if F is significant. To use the table in appendix C, locate the appropriate column for the numerator degrees of freedom (degrees of freedom between groups, k − 1). For the trunk extension study, there are 2 degrees of freedom between groups (3 − 1 = 2). We next find the row that corresponds to the degrees of freedom for the denominator (degrees of freedom within groups, N − k). We have 21 (24 − 3) degrees of freedom within groups. The F-ratio of 8.57 is greater than the 3.47 table value at the .05 level and the 5.78 value at the .01 level, so we reject the null hypothesis at both levels of significance. The F-ratio permits us to conclude that there is a significant difference in the three means, but it does not indicate which mean is significantly superior or if two means are significantly superior to one mean. A follow-up test must be performed to identify the means that are significantly different from one another. Table 4.4 shows a summary of the ANOVA as it is usually reported in research publications.

Post Hoc Test for Independent Groups

When the F-ratio indicates that there are significant differences between means, several tests may be used to identify which means are significantly different from each other. A test used for this purpose is referred to as a **post hoc test.** Only **Tukey's honestly significant difference test** (HSD) will be presented here.

The HSD calculates the minimum raw-score mean difference that must occur to declare a significant difference between any two means. The formula for computing the HSD value when the numbers of scores in the groups are equal is

$$HSD = q(\alpha, k, N-k)\sqrt{\frac{MS_W}{n}}$$

TABLE 4.3 ANOVA for Independent Groups: Trunk Extension Test

Group I		Group II		Group III	
X_1	X_1^2	X_2	X_2^2	X_3	X_3^2
22	484	20	400	18	324
23	529	19	361	19	361
21	441	18	324	17	289
22	484	19	361	22	484
19	361	18	324	18	324
21	441	21	441	19	361
22	484	20	400	20	400
21	441	19	361	19	361
$\Sigma X_1 = 171$	$\Sigma X_1^2 = 3{,}665$	$\Sigma X_2 = 154$	$\Sigma X_2^2 = 2{,}972$	$\Sigma X_3 = 152$	$\Sigma X_3^2 = 2{,}904$
$\bar{X}_1 = 21.38$		$\bar{X}_2 = 19.25$		$\bar{X}_3 = 19.00$	

$\Sigma X_1 = 171, \Sigma X_2 = 154, \Sigma X_3 = 152$

$\Sigma X_1^2 = 3{,}665, \Sigma X_2^2 = 2{,}972, \Sigma X_3^2 = 2{,}904$

grand $\Sigma X = 171 + 154 + 152 = 477$ (sum of all scores in all groups)

(sum of the square of all scores in all groups)

grand $\Sigma X^2 = 3{,}665 + 2{,}972 + 2{,}904 = 9{,}541$

correction factor $C = \dfrac{(\text{grand } \Sigma X)^2}{\text{total N}}$ (necessary because raw scores are used rather than deviations of the scores from the mean)

$$C = \frac{(477)^2}{24} = \frac{227{,}529}{24} = 9{,}480.38$$

(sum of the squared deviations of every score from the grand $\bar{X}$)

$SS_T = \text{grand } \Sigma X^2 - C$
$SS_T = 9{,}541 - 9{,}480.38 = 60.62$

$SS_B = \dfrac{(\Sigma X_1)^2}{n_1} + \dfrac{(\Sigma X_2)^2}{n_2} + \dfrac{(\Sigma X_3)^2}{n_3} - C$ (sum of the squared deviations of each group $\bar{X}$ from the grand $\bar{X}$)

$$= \frac{(171)^2}{8} + \frac{(154)^2}{8} + \frac{(152)^2}{8} - 9{,}480.38$$

$SS_B = 3{,}655.13 + 2{,}964.50 + 2{,}888 - 9{,}480.38 = 27.25$

$SS_W = SS_T - SS_B$ (sum of the squared deviations of each score from its group $\bar{X}$)
$SS_W = 60.62 - 27.25 = 33.37$

$MS_B = \dfrac{SS_B}{k-1} = \dfrac{27.25}{3-1} = 13.63$ (mean square for the sum of squares between groups; variance between groups)

$MS_W = \dfrac{SS_W}{N-k} = \dfrac{33.37}{24-3} = 1.59$ (mean square for the sum of squares within groups; variance within groups)

$F = \dfrac{MS_B}{MS_W} = \dfrac{13.63}{1.59} = 8.57$ (value required to reject null hypothesis; refer to appendix C)

TABLE 4.4 Summary of ANOVA for Trunk Extension Test

Source of Variation	Sum of Squares	df	Mean Square	F
Between groups	27.25	2	13.63	8.57*
Within groups	33.37	21	1.59	
Total	60.62	23		

*Significant at the .01 level.

where q = value obtained from the table in appendix D, α = significance level, k = number of groups, N = total number of observations, N − k = the degrees of freedom for the denominator in appendix D, MS_W = mean square for within-groups variance, and n = the number of scores in each group.

When the n's in any two groups are unequal, the formula is

$$HSD = q(\alpha, k, N - k)\sqrt{\frac{MS_W}{2}\left(\frac{1}{n_1} + \frac{1}{n_2}\right)}$$

Since the n's are equal in the example in table 4.3, the first equation will be used for our post hoc test. For the .01 level in the table in appendix D, we find that q is about 4.64 (k = 3 and N − k = 21, but since the table jumps from 20 to 24 for the denominator, we will use 3, 20). In table 4.3, MS_W is 1.59 and n = 8. Our equation is

$$HSD = 4.64\sqrt{\frac{1.59}{8}}$$
$$= 4.64\sqrt{0.19875}$$
$$= 4.64(0.446)$$
$$HSD = 2.069$$

This value (2.069) represents the minimum raw-score difference between any two means that may be declared significant. In table 4.3,

$$\overline{X}_1 - \overline{X}_2 = 21.38 - 19.25 = 2.13$$
$$\overline{X}_2 - \overline{X}_3 = 19.25 - 19.00 = 0.25$$
$$\overline{X}_1 - \overline{X}_3 = 21.38 - 19.00 = 2.38$$

If minus signs had occurred in our example, we would ignore them. We are interested only in absolute differences. We see that $\overline{X}_1 - \overline{X}_2$ and $\overline{X}_1 - \overline{X}_3$ are greater than 2.069. We thus conclude that there is a significant difference between these groups at the .01 level but not between groups 2 and 3.

Analysis of Variance for Repeated Measures

The **analysis of variance for repeated measures** is used when repeated measures are made on the same subjects. Basic assumptions are as follows:

1. The samples are randomly selected from a normal population.

2. The variances for all measurements are approximately equal.

To illustrate this technique, we will assume that a basketball coach wishes to determine if loudness of sound is a factor in the making of foul shots. He arranges for the ten members of the basketball team to shoot fifteen foul shots under three different sound conditions (no sound, medium sound, and loud sound). The null hypothesis is that the means of the three trials will be no different ($\overline{X}_1 = \overline{X}_2 = \overline{X}_3$). Table 4.5 shows the scores and the necessary calculations for the analysis of variance. (Note that in this technique, N refers to the total number of measurements.) Ten subjects

◆ ◆ ◆ POINT OF EMPHASIS ◆ ◆ ◆

■ If significant differences are found between means, a post hoc test must be conducted. You cannot conclude which means are significantly different without such a test.

TABLE 4.5 ANOVA for Repeated Measures: Foul Shooting While Exposed to Different Sound Levels

No Sound		Medium Sound		Loud Sound			
X_1	X_1^2	X_2	X_2^2	X_3	X_3^2	ΣRows	$(\Sigma$Rows$)^2$
11	121	12	144	10	100	33	1,089
9	81	10	100	9	81	28	784
10	100	12	144	9	81	31	961
8	64	10	100	9	81	27	729
12	144	12	144	10	100	34	1,156
10	100	11	121	9	81	30	900
12	144	13	169	11	121	36	1,296
9	81	9	81	9	81	27	729
10	100	11	121	8	64	29	841
9	81	10	100	10	100	29	841
$\Sigma X_1 = 100$	$\Sigma X_1^2 = 1{,}016$	$\Sigma X_2 = 110$	$\Sigma X_2^2 = 1{,}224$	$\Sigma X_3 = 94$	$\Sigma X_3^2 = 890$	grand $\Sigma X = 304$	$(\Sigma$rows$)^2 = 9{,}326$
$\bar{X}_1 = 10$		$\bar{X}_2 = 11$		$\bar{X}_3 = 9.4$			

grand $\Sigma X = 304$; grand $\Sigma X^2 = 3{,}130$

correction factor $C = \dfrac{(\text{grand } \Sigma X)^2}{\text{total N}} = \dfrac{(304)^2}{30} = \dfrac{92{,}416}{30} = 3{,}080.53$

$SS_T = \text{grand } \Sigma X^2 - C = 3{,}130 - 3{,}080.53 = 49.47$ (sum of the squared deviations of every score from the grand $\bar{X}$)

$SS_B = \dfrac{(\Sigma X_1)^2}{n_1} + \dfrac{(\Sigma X_2)^2}{n_2} + \dfrac{(\Sigma X_3)^2}{n_3} - C$ (sum of squares between trials; sum of squared deviations of each group $\bar{X}$ from grand $\bar{X}$)

$\quad = \dfrac{(100)^2}{10} + \dfrac{(110)^2}{10} + \dfrac{(94)^2}{10} - 3{,}080.53$

$SS_B = 3{,}093.60 - 3{,}080.53 = 13.07$

$SS_{\text{subjects}} = \dfrac{(\Sigma \text{rows})^2}{k} - C$ (sum of squares to determine the effects of test-retest)

$\quad = \dfrac{(11 + 12 + 10)^2 + (9 + 10 + 9)^2 + \ldots (9 + 10 + 10)^2}{3} - 3{,}080.53$

$SS_{\text{subjects}} = 3{,}108.67 - 3{,}080.53 = 28.14$

$SS_E = SS_T - SS_B - SS_{\text{subjects}}$ (sum of squares for error; sum of squared deviations of each score from its group $\bar{X}$)

$SS_E = 49.47 - 13.07 - 28.14 = 8.26$

$MS_B = \dfrac{SS_B}{k-1} = \dfrac{13.07}{2} = 6.54$ (mean square for the sum of squares between groups)

$MS_{\text{subjects}} = \dfrac{SS_{\text{subjects}}}{r-1} = \dfrac{28.14}{10-1} = 3.13$ (mean square for the sum of squares between subjects)

$MS_E = \dfrac{SS_E}{(k-1)(r-1)} = \dfrac{8.26}{(2)(9)} = 0.46$ (mean square for the sum of squares for error)

F-ratio $= \dfrac{MS_B}{MS_E} = \dfrac{6.54}{0.46} = 14.22$ (value required to reject null hypothesis; refer to appendix C)

were measured three times, so N = 30. Also, k refers to the number of times that the group is measured. The steps for the calculations are as follows:

1. Calculate the grand ΣX and grand ΣX^2 as in the ANOVA for independent groups.

$$\Sigma X_1 + \Sigma X_2 + \Sigma X_3 = \text{grand } \Sigma X$$
$$\Sigma X_1^2 + \Sigma X_2^2 + \Sigma X_3^2 = \text{grand } \Sigma X^2$$

2. Calculate the correction factor as before.

$$C = \frac{(\text{grand } \Sigma X)^2}{N}$$

3. Calculate the total sum of squares (SS_T) as before.

$$SS_T = \text{grand } \Sigma X^2 - C$$

4. Calculate the sum of squares between groups (SS_B) as before (actually, this is the sum of squares between trials).

$$SS_B = \frac{(\Sigma X_1)^2}{n_1} + \frac{(\Sigma X_2)^2}{n_2} + \frac{(\Sigma X_3)^2}{n_3} - C$$

5. Calculate the sum of squares to determine the effects of the test-retest ($SS_{subjects}$): Add the scores of the three trials for each subject, square the sum, and then add the squared sums for each subject. The sum of the squared sums for each subject is divided by k (the number of trials), and C is subtracted from the resulting value.

$$SS_{subjects} = \frac{(\Sigma \text{ rows})^2}{k} - C$$

6. Compute the sum of squares for error (also referred to as within-group sum of squares); this calculation represents the sum of the squared deviations of each score from its group $\overline{X}$. Since this sum of squares remains after SS_B and $SS_{subjects}$, it is easy to calculate.

$$SS_E = SS_T - SS_B - SS_{subjects}$$

7. Calculate the mean square for the sum of squares between groups (trials). k = number of independent groups.

$$MS_B = \frac{SS_B}{k - 1}$$

8. Calculate the mean square for the sum of squares between subjects. r = number of subjects.

$$MS_{subjects} = \frac{SS_{subjects}}{r - 1}$$

9. Calculate the mean square for the sum of squares for error.

$$MS_E = \frac{SS_E}{(k - 1)(r - 1)}$$

10. Calculate the F-ratio.

$$F = \frac{MS_B}{MS_E}$$

11. Refer to the F-distribution in appendix C. The degrees of freedom for the numerator are $(k - 1) = (3 - 1) = 2$. For the denominator, the degrees of freedom are $(k - 1)(r - 1) = (3 - 1)(10 - 1) = 18$. The F-ratio of 14.22 (6.54/0.46) is greater than the 6.01 value needed for significance at the .01 level, so we reject the null hypothesis. The HSD now should be used to determine which means are significantly different. Table 4.6 shows the analysis summary.

Post Hoc Test for Repeated Measures

For ANOVA for repeated measures, the formula for computing the HSD value is

$$HSD = q(\alpha, k, [k - 1][r - 1]) \sqrt{\frac{MS_E}{r}}$$

TABLE 4.6 Summary of ANOVA for Foul Shooting While Exposed to Different Sound Levels

Source of Variation	Sum of Squares	df	Mean Square	F
Subjects (rows)	28.14	9	3.13	14.22*
Between groups	13.07	2	6.54	
Error	8.26	18	0.46	
Total	49.47	29		

*Significant at the .01 level.

where q = value obtained from the table in appendix D, α = significance level, k = number of trials or measures performed on the same subjects, r = number of rows or number of subjects, (k − 1)(r − 1) = degrees of freedom for denominator in appendix D, and MS_E = mean square for the sum of squares for error.

At the .01 level, we find q is 4.70 (k = 3 and [3 − 1] [10 − 1] = 18). In table 4.6, MS_E = 0.46, so our equation is

$$HSD = 4.70 \sqrt{\frac{0.46}{10}}$$

$$= 4.70 \sqrt{0.046}$$

$$= 4.70(0.2145)$$

$$HSD = 1.008$$

$$\overline{X}_1 - \overline{X}_2 = 10 - 11 = -1$$

$$\overline{X}_2 - \overline{X}_3 = 11 - 9.4 = 1.6$$

$$\overline{X}_1 - \overline{X}_3 = 10 - 9.4 = 0.6$$

We see that $\overline{X}_2 - \overline{X}_3$ is greater than 1.008. There is a significant difference between medium sound and loud sound when shooting foul shouts. There is no significant difference between $\overline{X}_1$ (no sound) and $\overline{X}_2$ (medium sound) and between $\overline{X}_1$ (no sound) and $\overline{X}_3$ (loud sound). If we had tested at the .05 level, q would have been 3.61 and our HSD value would have been 0.774. We then would have found a significant difference between $\overline{X}_1$ (no sound) and $\overline{X}_2$ (medium sound) and between $\overline{X}_2$ (medium sound) and $\overline{X}_3$ (loud sound), but no significant difference between no sound and loud sound.

▨ ARE YOU ABLE TO DO THE FOLLOWING?

- Define *total sum of squares, sum of squares within groups, sum of squares between groups, mean square for the sum of squares within groups,* and *mean square for the sum of squares between groups.*

- Determine if there is a significant difference between two or more means through the appropriate one-way analysis of variance procedure.

- Use the HSD to determine which means are significantly different from each other.

Review Problems

1. An elementary physical education teacher typically used two different methods to improve the agility of the students in her classes. Trying to determine if one program developed agility better than the other, she randomly assigned the students to one of two groups. After the students had been in the programs for 12 weeks, she administered the same agility test to the two groups. Use the appropriate t-test to determine if the group means are significantly different.

Scores for Group I		Scores for Group II	
13	12	14	13
13	11	12	15
10	8	10	12
11	14	11	10
12	10	13	14

2. A high school teacher was interested in determining if mental practice would improve badminton serving ability. He randomly selected ten subjects from a population of students who had never played badminton, taught the correct way to serve, and administered a short-serve test to them. He gave the students instructions about mental practice and asked them to mentally practice the badminton short-serve 10 minutes/day for 7 days. They were instructed not to practice badminton in any other way. He then tested the group again. Use the appropriate t-test to determine if the group mean for the short-serve test improved after mental practice.

Subject	Pre-test Short-Serve Test Scores	Post-test Short-Serve Test Scores
A	37	43
B	42	46
C	36	38
D	50	55
E	34	32
F	44	51
G	51	53
H	42	48
I	45	43
J	52	55

3. A physical fitness instructor was interested in comparing three cardiovascular fitness programs. After three groups participated in the programs, she measured the oxygen uptake (ml/kg/min) of all the subjects. Use the appropriate ANOVA technique to determine if the group means are significantly different. If you find that there are significant differences in the group means, use the HSD to identify which means are significantly different.

Group I	Group II	Group III
46	47	49
46	50	51
48	50	50
47	48	49
50	49	52
48	47	53
47	51	49
51	50	52

4. A weight-training instructor was interested in determining the effects of external motivation on muscular strength. After a group of ten individuals had participated in a weight-training class for 15 weeks, the instructor tested the group for maximum strength on three different occasions. During one test, no external motivation was provided. During the second test, only the instructor shouted encouragement, and during the third test, he arranged for several spectators to shout encouragement. Use the appropriate ANOVA technique to determine if there is a significant difference in the group means of the tests. If you find that there are significant differences in the group means, use the HSD to identify which means are significantly different.

Subject	No External Motivation	Instructor Motivation	Spectator Motivation
A	81	84	88
B	88	89	93
C	92	94	97
D	83	85	88
E	81	83	85
F	79	80	85
G	84	84	87
H	87	86	93
I	88	90	94
J	84	86	88

5. A golf instructor used different instructional methods with three groups of females who were similar in age and golf experience. She then tested their ability to hit a golf ball for distance and accuracy with a 7-iron. Use the appropriate ANOVA technique to determine if there is a significant difference in the mean scores of the three groups. If you find there are significant differences in the group means, use the HSD to identify which means are significantly different.

Method I	Method II	Method III
110	105	115
115	112	120
112	105	118
98	100	110
120	118	126
90	93	110
119	115	124
125	120	130
111	112	118
102	113	115
116	113	125
118	108	130

6. The heart rate of twelve male college golfers was monitored during a golf match. Use the appropriate ANOVA technique to determine if their heart rates were significantly different when preparing to hit the drive, to hit approach shots to the green, and to putt. If you find that there are significant differences in the group means, use the HSD to identify which means are significantly different.

Player	Drive	Approach to Green	Putt
A	85	76	85
B	88	80	88
C	84	79	87
D	90	80	89
E	87	79	87
F	80	71	82
G	78	70	80
H	88	80	89
I	90	81	89
J	82	75	83
K	80	72	83
L	84	73	84

1. In a study testing for a significant difference in the effect of two medications on total cholesterol level, a .07 level of significance was found. What was the conclusion of the researchers about the significant difference in the medications and why did they reach the conclusion?

2. Suppose a manufacturer of exercise equipment conducted a study to determine if its abdominal exercise apparatus developed abdominal strength more quickly than similar equipment produced by a competitor. Subjects of similar age (N = 100) were randomly selected, comparable exercise programs (intensity and duration) with the two apparatuses were designed, and fifty subjects were randomly assigned to each of the two exercise programs. After participation in the two programs, the subjects were tested for abdominal strength. The group using the apparatus designed by the authors of the study had a better score on the strength test, and the analysis found a significant difference in the group means at the .05 level.

   a. What are the dependent and independent variables in the study?

   b. What is the null hypothesis?

   c. If a two-tailed test is used, what is the alternative hypothesis? If a one-tailed test is used, what is the alternative hypothesis?

   d. Which t-test should be used?

   e. What are the degrees of freedom (number)?

   f. How do you interpret the significant difference in the means?

3. Two groups of male college freshmen participated in a study to determine which training program best developed leg power as measured by the vertical jump. After participating in the training program, both groups were administered the vertical jump test. For group one, the $\bar{X} = 33$ and the SEM = 2; for group two, the $\bar{X} = 31$ and the SEM = 2.5.

   a. What are the limits of the 68% and 95% confidence intervals for the means of both groups?

   b. What are the limits of the 68% and 95% confidence intervals for the standard error of the difference between the means?

4. Suppose the same study described in review question 2 was done with three groups and three abdominal exercise apparatuses. All aspects of the study are the same except for the addition of the third group.

   a. Which statistical analysis should be used?

   b. If a significant difference is found in the three means, what must be done to determine which means are significantly different?

5 What Is a Good Test?

After completing this chapter, you should be able to

1. Describe criterion-referenced and norm-referenced measurement and state when it is appropriate to use each.

2. Define *validity* and *validity coefficient*, and describe how the validity coefficient is determined.

3. Describe how the criterion-referenced validity of a test can be determined through the use of behavioral objectives or testing before and after instruction.

4. Describe how domain-referenced validity and decision validity are used to determine criterion-referenced validity.

5. Define the three types of validity evidence for norm-referenced tests, provide examples of each type, and describe how each may be estimated.

6. Define *reliability* and describe the four methods for estimating the reliability of norm-referenced tests.

7. Define *objectivity* and describe how it may be estimated.

8. Describe the features of administrative feasibility that should be considered when selecting or constructing a test.

Note: Many of the testing examples in this chapter refer to the school environment, but the criteria for a good test also should be considered when testing in the nonschool environment.

As a physical educator you will often measure performances and attributes of individuals with a test, but it is irresponsible to select a test randomly. Before you select a test, or possibly construct your own test, consider (1) whether criterion-referenced measurement or norm-referenced measurement should be used and (2) the criteria for determining a good test—validity, reliability, objectivity, and administrative feasibility.

Criterion-Referenced Measurement

Criterion-referenced measurement is used when individuals are expected to perform at a specific level of achievement. In this type of measurement, one individual's performance is not compared with the performance of others; a minimum level of acceptable performance (referred to as **criterion behavior**) is described. Most health-related physical fitness tests use criterion-related measurement. In the teaching environment, criterion-referenced measurement involves the use of behavioral objectives that describe the expected level of performance of the individual. The following are examples of criterion-referenced standards:

- For successful completion of the running fitness class, the student must be able to run 2 miles in 14 minutes or less and correctly answer 80% or more of the fitness knowledge test questions.

- For successful completion of the badminton class, the student must correctly answer a minimum of thirty-five questions on the knowledge test.

- To meet the YMCA Physical Fitness Test "good" standard for the bench press, the 18- to 25-year-old female must perform twenty-eight to thirty-two repetitions.

- To meet the ACSM Fitness Test "average" standard for the sit and reach test, the 46- to 55-year-old male must score 13 to 14 inches.

Again, with this type of measurement, the individual's performance is not compared with the performances of other individuals.

In the medical profession, criterion-referenced standards are used for the classification of health risks. For example, individuals' blood cholesterol values place them in low-risk, moderate-risk, or high-risk levels for heart disease, and blood pressure values above normal determine stages of high blood pressure (hypertension).

Criterion-referenced measurement also can be used to determine grades. For example, in a running fitness class, the grading standards for males might be as follows:

A: Run 2 miles in 13 minutes or less. Correctly answer 90% or more of the fitness knowledge test questions.

B: Run 2 miles in 13:01 to 13:30. Correctly answer 80% to 89% of the fitness knowledge test questions.

C: Run 2 miles in 13:31 to 14:00. Correctly answer 70% to 79% of the fitness knowledge test questions.

Determining what performance earns an A or any other grade may be a problem. If you choose to use criterion-referenced measurement for grading purposes, the standards should be well planned.

Criterion-referenced measurement has some limitations. When a pass/fail standard is used, it does not show how good or how poor an individual's level of ability is. In addition, when criterion-referenced measurement is used by teachers, too often the standard for success is arbitrary. Remember, we know that measurement may be used for several reasons, so there will be occasions when criterion-referenced measurement is appropriate. For example, criterion-referenced measurement is used with the health-related physical fitness tests described in chapter 15.

Norm-Referenced Measurement

Norm-referenced measurement is used when you wish to interpret each individual's performance on a test in comparison with other individuals' performances. This comparison is done using norms that enable the test administrator to interpret an individual's score in relation to the scores of other individuals in the same population. Examples of norms are percentiles, z-scores, and T-scores. Very often norm-referenced measurement is used by teachers to determine grades, but it may be used for other reasons, such as to establish appropriate levels of achievement for criterion-referenced standards. Norms for tests in physical education are usually reported by gender, weight, height, age, or grade level. In selecting a test with norms, the following factors should be considered:

1. The sample size used to determine the norms—in general, more confidence can be placed in a large sample.

2. The population used to determine the norms—for example, if a basketball skills test has norms for tenth-grade students, only tenth-grade students should have been used to develop the norms. Varsity basketball players or students in other grades should not have been used.

3. The time the norms were established—norms should be updated periodically.

Both criterion-referenced measurement and norm-referenced measurement may be used in the measurement of skills and knowledge. In your professional responsibilities, you should recognize when it is appropriate to use each.

▓▓▓ ARE YOU ABLE TO DO THE FOLLOWING?

- Define *criterion-referenced* and *norm-referenced measurement*.

Validity

Validity is the most important criterion to consider when evaluating a test. Traditionally, validity is referred to as the degree to which a test actually measures what it claims to measure. For example, if a test is designed to measure cardiorespiratory fitness, you must be confident that it does so. Although the definition just given is commonly used, validity refers more to the agreement between what the test measures and the performance, skill, or behavior the test is designed to measure. This means validity is specific to a particular use and group. Consider cardiorespiratory fitness and tennis ability. Although cardiorespiratory fitness may be a factor in a long tennis match, a fitness test should not be used to determine tennis skill. Also, a test might be valid for one age group but not valid for a different age group.

Because the validity of tests varies, the selection of one test over another may depend on which test has the best evidence to support its validity. This evidence is reported as the **validity coefficient.** The validity coefficient is determined through correlation techniques. The coefficient may range from -1.00 to $+1.00$; the closer the coefficient is to $+1.00$, the more valid the test. A test being used as a substitute for another validated test should have a validity coefficient of about 0.80 or more. A test being used for predictive purposes may have a lower validity coefficient. Traditionally, predictive tests with validity coefficients of .60 have been accepted.

Validity of Criterion-Referenced Tests

Criterion-referenced validity is related directly to predetermined behavioral objectives. The objectives should be stated in a clear, exact manner and be limited to small segments of the unit of instruction. To estimate the validity of a knowledge test, you should construct the items to parallel the behavioral objectives and there should be several items for each objective. The validity of each group of items is subjectively estimated by how well they measure the behavioral objective.

A second method requires testing before and after instruction. Validity is accepted if there is significant improvement after instruction or if the behavioral objectives are mastered by an acceptable number of individuals. This method may be used for knowledge and physical performance tests.

The success of criterion-referenced testing depends on the predetermined standard for success. The standard for success should be realistic but high enough that the individuals are ready for the next level of instruction. If the individuals perform successfully at the next level, you can feel confident about the validity of a test.

Domain-referenced validity evidence and **decision validity evidence** are two techniques frequently used to establish validity evidence for criterion-referenced tests. The word *domain* is used to represent the criterion behavior. If the items, or tasks, on a test represent the criterion behavior, the test has logical validity evidence. This logical validity evidence is referred to as domain-referenced validity.

The following example shows how domain-referenced validity could be determined for a topspin tennis serve test:

1. The topspin tennis serve form (technique) is analyzed (see table 7.1).

2. The most important components of the serve form are selected to be included in the criterion behavior.

3. Successful performance is defined—for example, form, number of successful serves out of attempted serves, and placement and speed of serves.

If this procedure were followed for the tennis forehand or backhand strokes, court position would need to be determined as well as how the ball would be presented to the test taker. (Will someone throw the ball, or will someone hit it?) A similar procedure could be followed to establish domain-referenced validity for any skill test.

Decision validity evidence is used when a test's purpose is to classify individuals as proficient (masters) or nonproficient (nonmasters) of the criterion behavior. With mastery testing, a cutoff score is identified, and individuals scoring above the cutoff score are classified as proficient. Individuals scoring below the score are classified as nonproficient.

Baumgartner et al. (2007) describes procedures for estimating decision validity evidence. You may wish to refer to this source.

Validity of Norm-Referenced Tests

Remember, validity refers to the degree to which a test measures what it claims to measure. For norm-referenced tests, three types of validity evidence may be reported. The validity of a test is better accepted if more than one type of strong validity evidence is reported for the test. However, if different types of validity evidence are reported, it is unlikely that the validity coefficients will be the same. The three types of validity evidence for norm-referenced tests are **content validity, criterion validity,** and **construct validity.**

Content Validity.   Content validity evidence is related to how well a test measures all skills and subjects that have been presented to the test takers. To have content validity, a test must measure the objectives for which the test takers are held responsible. As the test administrator, you should administer tests that sample the subject matter or skills the test takers are expected to master. This means that regardless of how long or short the test is, it should measure stated objectives. More than likely you would have no problem constructing a test of 150 items that measures a group's knowledge of all the subject matter that has been presented, but such a test may be too long for the group to complete. To have content validity, the test must be reduced to a realistic number of items and still represent the total content of a longer test. Content validity evidence also is expected of performance tests. A performance test should measure the skills or abilities emphasized to a group.

Content validity evidence for most self-made tests is a subjective judgment, but asking yourself, "Does the test measure what the test takers have been taught?" will provide you with a good estimate of content validity. Content validity evidence also may be provided through the use of experts in the area that you are testing. For example, known tennis experts may be asked to identify tennis skills essential to tennis play and also determine test items to measure those skills.

Content validity evidence is sometimes called **logical,** or **face, validity evidence.** A test is considered to have logical validity evidence when it appears to measure a trait, skill, or ability logically. The developers of many physical performance tests have claimed logical validity evidence for their tests. In this textbook, you will observe logical validity evidence reported for agility, balance, flexibility, and muscular strength and endurance tests. For example, the sidestepping test (chapter 9), the sit and reach test (chapter 12), and the sit-ups test (chapter 13) are tests in which logical validity is reported.

When possible, it is best to use content validity evidence with other validity evidence. A written test may be based on unit objectives, but it may contain too few or too many questions related to one or two objectives. Also, an item may appear to measure a physical component but actually not do so. For example, the sit and reach test appears to measure hamstring and lower back flexibility, but some research has not supported this assumption.

Criterion Validity.   Criterion validity evidence is indicated by how well test scores correlate with a specific criterion (successful performance). As previously stated, the closer the correlation coefficient is to $+1.00$, the more valid the test. Criterion validity may be subdivided into predictive validity (future performance) and concurrent validity (current performance).

Predictive Validity.   When you wish to estimate future performance, you are concerned with **predictive validity evidence.** In general, predictive validity evidence is obtained by giving a predictor test and correlating the criterion measure (obtained at a later date). In the teaching environment, the later date is often after an instructional unit; in physical performance, the later time could be after years of development.

The predictor test is the instrument used to measure the trait or ability of individuals. A sport skills test, or some other type of physical performance, is an example. The criterion measure is the variable that has been defined as indicating successful performance of a skill. The definition of successful performance is an important factor or consideration in the establishment of predictive validity evidence. College entrance tests are used as predictor tests, with the criterion measure being success in college.

Concurrent Validity.   Concurrent validity evidence might be called immediate predictive validity. It indicates how well a test measures the current level of skill or knowledge of an individual. Concurrent validity evidence is determined by correlating test results with a current criterion measurement rather than future information; a test and the criterion measurement are administered at approximately the same time. This procedure is often used to estimate the validity of a test (how well the test measures what it claims to measure).

Criterion Measure.   An important consideration in the estimation of criterion validity evidence (predictive or concurrent) is the choice of the criterion measure. Three criterion measures are used most often.

1. Expert ratings: With this procedure, a panel of experts is asked to determine successful performance. A sport skills test is an example. Suppose a volleyball coach wishes to determine if a particular skills test can predict future performance of his or her players. He or she administers the test early in the season and asks a panel of volleyball experts to observe the team during games throughout the season and rank or rate the players' performances (the criterion measure). With the rank procedure, the players are ranked from the best to worst player. With the rating procedure, a point scale is used. Much as in diving and gymnastics competition, the players are assigned points based on their degree of success. (The use of a rating scale is described in chapter 7.) At the completion of the season, the coach then correlates the average of the experts' ranks or ratings with the skills test administered at the beginning of the season to estimate the predictive validity of the skills test. Expert ratings or rankings were used to estimate the criterion validity correlation coefficient for several tests described in this textbook—such as the Scott and French long-serve test, the racquetball skills test, and the McDonald soccer test (these tests are found in chapter 18).

2. Tournament play: If the test measures a sport skill, the scores can be correlated with tournament play. It is better to use a round-robin tournament because it provides the opportunity for the more skilled players to win. If the test is valid, the test takers who score well on the test will also place high in the tournament, and those who do poorly on the test will place low in the tournament. Tournament play was used to estimate the criterion validity correlation coefficient for several performance tests described in this textbook—such as the French short-serve test and the Poole forehand clear test (both tests are found in chapter 18).

3. Previously validated test: The scores on a new test can be correlated with the scores from a previously validated test. This procedure often is used to establish concurrent validity evidence for a test that requires less equipment and/or time than other tests. To illustrate, consider the following. Maximum oxygen consumption is best measured through expired gas analysis during performance on a treadmill (equipment and time). However, the 12-minute running test (chapter 11) is highly correlated with the treadmill test, so the run can be used to estimate the maximum oxygen of individuals. Also, we are able to use skinfold measurements to estimate body fat percentage because the sums of skinfold measurements correlate highly with the estimation of body fat percentage through under-water weighing. Previously validated tests were used to estimate the criterion validity correlation coefficient for several tests described in this textbook—such as the SEMO agility test (chapter 9) and the Queens College step test (chapter 11).

Construct Validity. Construct validity evidence refers to the degree that the individual possesses a trait (construct), presumed to be reflected in the test performance. Anxiety, intelligence, and motivation are constructs. These qualities cannot be seen with the human eye, yet an individual who possesses one of these characteristics is expected to behave in a certain way. Construct validity evidence applies to testing by the physical educator. The term *cardiorespiratory fitness* may be classified as a construct. Cardiorespiratory fitness tests are often based on the assumption that certain measures, such as differences in pulse rates or the ability to run a distance in a specified time, reflect cardiorespiratory fitness. That is, the individual with good cardiorespiratory fitness will have a lower pulse rate after physical exertion and will perform better on a running test than the individual with poor cardiorespiratory fitness. Construct validity evidence also applies to the measurement of sports skills. A tennis instructor assumes that when the individual learns the skills of the serve, the forehand and backhand, the overhead smash, and the volley, he or she will be able to put all the skills together and play tennis. These skills are measures of the overall construct of ability to play tennis. If a test includes items that measure these skills, it has construct validity evidence.

Construct validity evidence can be demonstrated by comparing higher-skilled individuals with lesser-skilled individuals. Again, consider a tennis skills test that is administered to both a tennis class and a varsity tennis team. With a test that has construct validity, the varsity players will most likely score higher than the members of the class.

Factors Affecting Validity

The validity of a test may be affected by several factors. Four of these factors are as follows:

1. The characteristics of the test takers: A test is valid only for individuals of age, gender, and experience similar to those on whom the test was validated.

2. The criterion measure selected: Several measures have been presented for estimating the validity evidence of a test. If all measures are correlated with the same set of scores, different correlation coefficients will be found.

3. Reliability: A test must be reliable to be valid. This concept is illustrated in the discussion of reliability later in this chapter.

4. Administrative procedures: If unclear directions are given, or if the test takers do not all perform the test in the same way, the validity will be affected. Environmental factors (e.g., heat and humidity) also may affect validity.

▰▰▰ ARE YOU ABLE TO DO THE FOLLOWING?

- Define *validity evidence* and *validity coefficient*, and describe how the validity coefficient is determined.

- Describe the procedures for determining criterion-referenced validity.

- Define the three types of validity evidence for norm-referenced tests, provide examples of each type, and describe how each may be estimated.

- List four factors that affect validity.

Reliability

Reliability refers to the consistency of a test. A reliable test should obtain approximately the same results regardless of the number of times it is given. A test given to a group of individuals on one day should yield the same results if it is given to the same group on another day. Of course, some individuals may not obtain the same score on the second administration of a test because fatigue, motivation, environmental conditions, and measurement error may affect the scores. However, the order of the scores will be approximately the same if the test has reliability.

For a test to have a high degree of validity, it must have a high degree of reliability. If test scores are not reliable, the validity of a test is limited. Imagine administering a test that measures the ability to hit the golf ball for distance to a beginning golf class. Many individuals will have a good score on one attempt but a poor score on another attempt. This lack of consistency influences the validity of the test, though high reliability does not necessarily mean high validity. A test may be consistent, but it may not measure what it claims to measure.

There are several methods to determine reliability, and all are reported in terms of a correlation coefficient that ranges from -1.00 to $+1.00$. The closer the coefficient value is to $+1.00$, the greater the reliability of a test. Some tests will have greater reliability than others. Physical performance tests of running, jumping, and throwing generally have high reliability coefficients, whereas tests such as the tennis serve, badminton serve, and chip shot (in golf) usually have lower reliability coefficients. The lower coefficients are due to subjective judgment when declaring if an object landed within the marked boundaries.

◆◆◆ POINT OF EMPHASIS ◆◆◆

- Validity is the single most important consideration in the selection of a test, and you should administer only tests for which you have confidence in the validity. However, no test is ever valid in all situations or circumstances. You must consider the purpose of the test and the population for which the test is to be used.

Reliability of Criterion-Referenced Tests

The reliability of criterion-referenced tests is defined as consistency of classification or how consistently the test classifies individuals as masters or nonmasters. Ebel (1979) states that the reliability of criterion-referenced tests can be determined in much the same way as the reliability of norm-referenced tests—that is, test-retest, parallel forms, split-half, or Kuder-Richardson formulas. One important difference, however, is that whereas norm-referenced reliability applies to the total test score, criterion-referenced reliability applies to a single cluster of items (each cluster is intended to measure the attainment of a different objective). In other words, several reliability coefficients, one for each cluster, will be estimated for a criterion-referenced test.

The reliability of criterion-referenced tests may also be estimated through the proportion of agreement coefficient. With this procedure, a test is administered to a group; on the basis of the results of the test scores, each individual is classified as a master or a nonmaster. On another day, the group is administered the same test, and again each individual is classified as master or nonmaster. The proportion of agreement is determined by how many group members are classified as masters on both test days and how many group members are classified as nonmasters on both test days. Some classifications during the two test days may occur because of chance. A statistical procedure is then used to correct for any chance agreement of masters and nonmasters.

Reliability of Norm-Referenced Tests

Four methods of estimating the reliability of norm-referenced tests are presented here: test-retest, parallel forms, split-half, and Kuder-Richardson Formula 21.

Test-Retest Method. The test-retest method requires two administrations of the same test to the same group of individuals, with the calculation of the correlation coefficient between the two sets of scores. The product-moment correlation method or analysis of variance (intraclass correlation coefficient) may be used to calculate the coefficient. In the school environment, the greatest source of error in the test-retest reliability estimate is changes in the students themselves. If knowledge tests are being administered, they are aware of the questions that will be asked on the retest and the answers they provided on the first test. The students also may have discussed the test. When a long interval of time elapses between the test and retest, maturational factors may influence the results of the retest, especially on physical performance tests. The appropriate time interval between administration of tests is sometimes difficult to determine. It could be as short as one day, or as long as several months, but if the test-retest method is used to estimate the reliability coefficient, the time interval must be considered.

Parallel Forms Method. The parallel forms method requires the administration of parallel or equivalent forms of a test to the same group and calculation of the correlation coefficient (product-moment or intraclass correlation coefficient) between the two sets of scores. Often, both forms are administered during the same test period or in two sessions separated by a short time period. The primary problem associated with this method of estimating reliability is the difficulty of constructing two tests that are parallel in content and item characteristics.

If the two tests are administered within a short time of each other, learning, motivation, and testing conditions do not influence the correlation coefficient. The reliability of most standardized tests in education is estimated through this method.

Split-Half Method. When the split-half method is used, a test is split into halves and the scores of the two halves are correlated. This method requires only one administration of the test and does not require construction of a second test. A common practice is to correlate the odd-numbered items with the even-numbered items. (This method assumes that all individuals being tested will have time to complete the test, so it is not appropriate when speed of completion is a factor in the test.)

The reliability coefficient calculated by this method is for a test of only half the length of the original test. Because reliability usually increases as a test increases in length, the reliability for the full test needs to be estimated. The Spearman-Brown formula is often used for this purpose. The formula is

$$\text{Reliability of full test} = \frac{2 \times \text{reliability on half test}}{1 + \text{reliability on half test}}$$

If the reliability between the two halves is found to be +.80, the reliability of the full test will be found as follows:

$$\text{Reliability of full test} = \frac{2 \times .80}{1 + .80} = \frac{1.60}{1.80} = .89$$

Though the split-half method may produce an inflated correlation coefficient, it is frequently used to estimate reliability coefficients for knowledge tests. It also can be used for some skills tests in which the odd and even trials are correlated.

Kuder-Richardson Formula 21. There are many ways to split a test to compute "half-test" scores for correlational purposes. For each split, however, a different reliability coefficient probably would be obtained. Kuder and Richardson developed a formula, K-R 20, that estimates the average correlation that might be obtained if all possible split-half combinations of a group of items were correlated. Two basic assumptions of the Kuder-Richardson formula are (1) the test items can be scored 1 for correct and 0 for wrong and (2) the total score is the sum of the item scores. As was indicated with the split-half method, the Kuder-Richardson formula should not be used with a test in which speed of completion is a factor. Since K-R 20 requires much computation, the simpler formula, K-R 21, is often used to provide a rough approximation of K-R 20. The K-R 21 formula is

$$r_{KR} = \frac{n}{n-1}\left(1 - \frac{\overline{X}(n - \overline{X})}{n(s^2)}\right)$$

n = number of items
$\overline{X}$ = test mean (average number of items correct)
s^2 = test variance (variance of items answered correctly)

To illustrate the use of this formula, assume that

$$n = 50, \overline{X} = 40, \text{ and } s^2 = 25$$
$$r_{KR} = \frac{50}{49}\left(1 - \frac{40(50 - 40)}{50(25)}\right)$$
$$= \frac{50}{49}\left(1 - \frac{40(10)}{1,000}\right)$$
$$= 1.02(1 - .40)$$
$$r_{KR} = 1.02(.60) = .61$$

Though K-R 21 is widely used, it gives a conservative estimate of reliability when the test items vary in difficulty, as they often do.

Factors Affecting Reliability

The reliability of a test may be affected by many factors, including the following:

1. The method of scoring: The more objective the test, the higher the reliability. A discussion of objectivity follows.

2. The heterogeneity of the group: Coefficients based on scores from fifteen-year-olds will probably be smaller than those based on a similar-sized group that includes fourteen-, fifteen-, and sixteen-year-olds. Therefore, when the reliability coefficient of a test is based on test scores from a group ranging in abilities, it will be overestimated. If you wish a test to measure a particular skill of fifteen-year-olds, the reliability coefficient of the test should be based on fifteen-year-old individuals. When you read background information about a standardized test, note the heterogeneity of the group on which the reliability was estimated.

3. The length of the test: The longer the test, the greater the reliability. This relation is true of physical performance and knowledge tests. Remember, we used the Spearman-Brown formula to demonstrate that the reliability coefficient for a whole test was larger than the reliability coefficient for one-half of the test.

4. Administrative procedures: The directions must be clear; all test takers should be ready to be tested, be motivated to do well, and perform the test in the same way; and the testing environment should be favorable to good performance.

■■■ **ARE YOU ABLE TO DO THE FOLLOWING?**

▪ Define *reliability.*

▪ Determine the reliability of a test through the test-retest, parallel forms, split-half, and Kuder-Richardson Formula 21 methods.

▪ List four factors that affect the reliability of a test.

Objectivity

A test has high objectivity when two or more persons can administer the same test to the same group and obtain approximately the same results. Objectivity is a specific form of reliability and can be determined by the test-retest (with different individuals administering the test) correlational procedure. Certain forms of measurement are more objective than others. True-false, multiple-choice, and matching tests have high objectivity when scoring keys are available, whereas essay tests have very low objectivity. Measurements of jumping ability, free-throw shooting, throwing for distance, and success in archery are objective, but judgments of the quality of performance in gymnastics, diving, and figure skating are not.

Objectivity is more likely when the following factors are present:

1. Complete and clear instructions for administration and scoring of the test are given.

2. Trained testers administer the test. All testers must administer the test in the same way.

3. Simple measurement procedures are followed. If the measurements are complicated, mistakes are more likely to occur.

4. Appropriate mechanical tools of measurement are used. Use of appropriate measurement tools decreases the chances for measurement errors.

5. Results are expressed as numerical scores. Scores expressed in phrases or terms are less likely to reflect objectivity.

ARE YOU ABLE TO DO THE FOLLOWING?

- Define *objectivity*.

- Determine the objectivity of a test.

- List the factors that provide for objectivity.

Administrative Feasibility

Administrative feasibility, along with validity, reliability, and objectivity, must be considered when selecting or constructing a test. In fact, if two tests are fairly equal in validity, reliability, and objectivity, the following administrative considerations may determine which test you should choose:

1. Cost: Does the test require expensive equipment that you do not have or cannot afford to purchase?

2. Time: Does the test take too much instructional time? Many authorities recommend that testing use no more than 10% of total instructional time. A test that requires several class or group meetings to administer may not be feasible to administer.

3. Ease of administration: (a) Do you need assistance to administer the test? If so, do you train assistants or ask other instructors to assist you? The training of student testers usually requires much time, but it is essential that whoever administers the test be qualified to do so. (b) Are the instructions easy to follow? The test takers should be able to understand the directions, and regardless of who administers the test, the results should be the same. (c) Is the test reasonable in the demands that are placed on the test takers? They should not be ill or sore after taking the test.

4. Scoring: Will the services of another individual affect the objectivity of the scoring? In an effort to duplicate the actual activity, some tests require the services of another individual (e.g., in some tennis tests, the ball is hit to the person being tested; in softball hitting, the ball is pitched to the hitter). Tests such as these have a place in the measurement of skill, but the helper should be qualified to perform the services. The scoring of the test should not hinder the differentiation among the levels of ability.

5. Norms: Are norms available to compare your test takers with others? If your test takers score well below published norms, you should attempt to determine the reason. When published test norms are used, the factors described in the discussion of norm-referenced measurement should be considered. As a teacher, you may wish to establish local norms to reflect the progress your students have made in a particular program.

One final comment about a good test: When selecting a sport skills test, try to find a test that is similar to game performance. Individuals enjoy taking this type of test more than taking one that has no resemblance to the game skill for which they are being tested. The use of this type of test is an important component of authentic assessment, which is described in chapter 7.

▬▬▬ ARE YOU ABLE TO DO THE FOLLOWING?

- Describe the administrative criteria that should be considered in the selection and construction of tests.

You should now feel capable of selecting good physical performance and knowledge tests. Complete the review problems, and then we'll begin to prepare you to construct knowledge tests.

Review Problems

1. Describe how you might use criterion-referenced measurement in a seventh-grade soccer class.

2. Select three sports skills tests and three other physical performance tests (e.g., agility, physical fitness, and balance) described in this book and determine how well they meet test selection criteria.

Chapter Review Questions

1. What is the difference between criterion-referenced measurement and norm-referenced measurement?

2. What are content validity, criterion validity, and construct validity?

3. What is meant when a test is described as having good reliability?

4. Can a test have a high degree of validity without a high degree of reliability?

5. Suppose you are employed as a fitness instructor and your responsibilities include the conduction of a program for fifty- to fifty-nine-year-old adults. After the participants have completed a 3-month exercise program, you administer the ACSM fitness test (chapter 15) to them. You advise the female participants that everyone who is able to perform nine to twelve push-ups will meet the average standard. Are you using criterion-referenced measurement or norm-referenced measurement?

6. In your job as a fitness instructor, you are told to select test items that will measure cardiorespiratory fitness, muscular strength and endurance, flexibility, and body fat percentage. What criteria should you consider in making your selection?

7. Which type of validity evidence would be used in the following examples?

   a. A teacher uses the unit objectives to develop a knowledge test.

   b. A company designs a new instrument for the measurement of body fat. How could the validity evidence be determined?

   c. A basketball coach develops a basketball skills test to help him determine who the best players are. How could the validity evidence be determined?

8. In review question 7b, how would the company determine the reliability and objectivity of the new instrument?

6 Construction of Knowledge Tests

After completing this chapter, you should be able to

   1. List and describe the steps for knowledge test construction.

   2. Construct a table of specifications and explain its use.

   3. State the purposes of item analysis.

   4. Define *item difficulty, index of discrimination*, and *response quality*.

   5. Conduct item analysis.

   6. Contrast the advantages and disadvantages of various test items.

   7. Construct true-false, multiple-choice, short-answer, completion, matching, and essay test items.

Because many good standardized psychomotor tests are available, you may construct only a few of these tests while performing your responsibilities as a physical educator. The same cannot be said of knowledge tests. (The term *knowledge test* refers to tests that measure the cognitive domain—that is, thought processes.) If you enter the teaching profession, you likely will construct many types of knowledge tests throughout your career. If your responsibilities are in a fitness or wellness club, there probably will be occasions when you will wish to determine the club members' knowledge of health-related matters. The information that you gather from the tests can help you determine the needs of the members and plan appropriate programs.

As you gain experience in constructing knowledge tests, it will be less difficult to complete the task. However, at no time should you feel that a test can be constructed within a few minutes or the night before it is to be administered. It takes time and planning to construct a good knowledge test. You can expect only problems from a haphazard test. In addition, a poorly constructed test will not adequately fulfill the reasons for measurement, as described in chapter 1.

Steps in Construction of a Test

There is more to test construction than writing the items. To construct a good test, you should follow these five steps: test planning, test item construction, test administration, item analysis, and item revision. Guidelines for these five steps, as well as construction of various types of objective items and essay items, are covered in this chapter.

Test Planning

The first step in planning test items is to consider content validity. The test should be representative of the instructional objectives and the content presented in the unit of instruction. The test should measure how well the students have fulfilled the objectives of the instructional unit.

With the unit objectives in mind, you should next develop a **table of test specifications,** which serves as an outline for construction of the test. Planning and adhering to a table of test specifications ensure that all material is covered and that the correct weight is given to each area. The table of test specifications indicates the following:

- Kinds and number of test items.

- Kinds of thought processes the items will present and number of each kind of task.

- Content area and number of items in each area.

(Some teachers also include an estimate of item difficulty.) Table 6.1 is an example of specifications for a volleyball test.

The most commonly used kinds of objective items are multiple-choice, true-false, matching, and completion. The total number of test items is usually determined by the length of the class period, the length of the items, the difficulty of the items, the conditions under which the test is to be administered, and the age of the students. Students should have time to attempt to answer all of the items when working at a normal rate. You might estimate that the slowest student will be able to answer multiple-choice items at the rate of one per minute and true-false items at the rate of two per minute. As you administer similar tests to similar groups, your ability to estimate the time needed to complete a test will improve.

Several thought processes may be included on a test. Bloom's classification (1956) of cognitive behavior remains the most popular system of delineating the types and levels of thought processes. The six levels of Bloom's classification, listed in table 6.2, vary in complexity from the simplest (knowledge) to the most complex (evaluation). You must decide if you only want a factual information test. Certainly it is easier to construct factual information items. If you attempt to construct the test items in a short period of time, you probably will put together this type of test. Though there is a need for items that measure knowledge, a good test will include various kinds of tasks. With adequate planning and practice, you can develop the skill to write a test with such variety. When you plan the test specifications, plan for different kinds of tasks and the number of items for each task.

TABLE 6.1 Specifications for a 50-Item Multiple-Choice Volleyball Test

Content Area	Task (Number of Questions and Percentages of Total)			
	Knowledge	Comprehension	Analysis	Application
History	2 (4%)			
Rules	5 (10%)	5 (10%)		5 (10%)
Technique	2 (4%)	5 (10%)	8 (16%)	
Offensive strategy	4 (8%)			5 (10%)
Defensive strategy	4 (8%)			5 (10%)

TABLE 6.2 Bloom's Classification of Thought Processes (Cognitive Behavior)

1. Knowledge (simplest): remember, recall facts.
2. Comprehension: lowest level of understanding; interpret and determine implications, consequences, and effects.
3. Application: use the knowledge and understanding in real situation.
4. Analysis: separate whole into parts; see their relationships and the way they are organized.
5. Synthesis: rearrange; put parts and elements together to arrange a new whole.
6. Evaluation (most advanced): make judgments about value of information and ideas.

The content area deals with the areas covered during instruction. In a physical activity class, content might include such things as history, terminology, rules, equipment, technique or mechanical analysis, strategy, and physiological benefits of participation. Before you begin construction of a test, plan the content areas and the number of items for each area. Too often physical education instructors spend only part of one class period describing the history of an activity and later administer a test that includes many historical questions. A good physical activity class test will include items dealing with rules, equipment, technique, and strategy.

Item difficulty, which is determined by the proportion of students who pass the item, should be related to the purpose of the test. It can be determined only after a test has been administered, and the ability to estimate it improves with experience. (Item difficulty will be discussed later in the section on item analysis.)

Observe table 6.1 again. Note that fifteen items are related to the rules of volleyball, but only five of the fifteen items are concerned directly with knowledge. The other ten items cover comprehension and application of the rules.

Test Item Construction

Regardless of the type of test items you construct, observe the following general guidelines:

1. Allow enough time to complete the test construction. Put it aside after a few hours and work with it again a day or two later. It is rare that anyone is able to construct a good test without time to revise the items.

2. No item should be included on a test unless it covers an important fact, concept, principle, or skill. Ask yourself three questions before you write the item: Why is the student responsible for this? What is the value of this point? What future benefit will it have?

3. Items should be independent of each other. This means that you should avoid items that provide answers to other items; correctly answering one item should not depend on correctly answering a previous item.

4. Write simply and clearly. Using correct grammar is essential, but try using terms and examples that the students understand. Avoid obvious, meaningless, and ambiguous terms. Textbook wording should be used rarely. The item should test the students' ability as related to the subject matter, not their ability to interpret the item.

5. Be flexible. As a general rule, the test should include more than one type of item. No one item is best for all situations or all types of material. Also, some students can better demonstrate their ability on certain types of items. (When using more than one type of item, place all items of a particular type together.)

6. If easy items are to be part of the test, place them at the beginning. When students have difficulty with the first few questions, they often are unable to concentrate on the remainder of the test. Easier items will build the students' confidence.

◆ ◆ ◆ POINT OF EMPHASIS ◆ ◆ ◆

- It is important to develop a table of specifications before you begin construction of your test items. It is your road map. It will aid you in reaching your destination, which is to prepare a good test.

---

7. As you construct the items, record the test number of each item in the table of test specifications. (For example, the numbers of the items that cover knowledge of history, application of rules, analysis of technique, and other content areas and tasks are recorded in the appropriate row and column of the table.) You may find that you want to change some of the specifications, but remember to monitor the content area and task of each item.

8. Prepare clear, concise, and complete directions. Leave no doubt as to how the items are to be answered.

9. Ask other instructors to review the test. If they have problems with the wording of an item, it is likely the students will have problems also.

Test Administration

If you have correctly followed the preceding guidelines and also observe the following ones, you likely will have few problems during test administration:

1. Provide a typed copy of the test. It is annoying to have to interpret handwriting when taking a test.

2. Start the test on time. If you have constructed a test that requires approximately 50 minutes to complete, make sure the students have 50 minutes.

3. Be sure the test is administered under normal conditions. Whether you consider the test easy or difficult, it is not fair to the students to have to take the test under abnormal conditions. Unfortunately, students in physical education classes often must complete written tests as they sit in gymnasium bleachers. This situation may influence the type of test items you choose to construct.

4. Read the directions to the students. In their haste to begin the test, many students will begin before reading the directions.

Item Analysis

After you have administered and scored the test, you are ready to determine the quality of the items through a statistical procedure called **item analysis.** Item analysis serves the following purposes:

• Indicates which items may be too easy or too difficult.

• Indicates which items may fail to discriminate clearly between the better and poorer students for reasons other than item difficulty.

• Indicates why an item has not functioned effectively and how it might be improved.

• Improves your skills in test construction.

The exact procedures used in item analysis depend on the type of items and test, the number of test takers, the computational facilities available, and the purpose of analysis. More confidence can be placed in item analysis when 100 or more tests are analyzed, but you can obtain an indication of the quality of the items through analysis of a smaller number of tests. Most item analyses are concerned with **item difficulty, discrimination power,** and **response quality.** The first three steps in item analysis are as follows:

1. Arrange the scored tests in order from high score to low score.

2. Determine the upper 27% of the test scores and place them in one group. Do the same for the bottom 27% of the test scores. These groups are referred to as upper group (UG) and lower group (LG). Although upper and lower groups of 27% are considered the best for maximizing the difference between the two groups, any percentage between 25% and 33% may be used.

3. Tally the number of times the correct response to each item was chosen on the tests of each group.

Item Difficulty. *Item difficulty* is defined as the proportion of test takers who answer an item correctly. If upper and lower groups are not formed, the **difficulty index** (p) may be found by dividing the number of test takers correctly answering each item by the total number taking the test.

$$p = \frac{\text{number answering correctly}}{\text{total number in group}}$$

If fifty students completed a test and thirty-one correctly answered an item, the item difficulty would be .62.

$$p = \frac{31}{50} = .62$$

Another acceptable method for determining the difficulty index requires the use of upper and lower groups.

$$p = \frac{\text{number correct in UG} + \text{number correct in LG}}{\text{number in UG} + \text{number in LG}}$$

If the number of test takers who answered correctly in the upper group is 16, the number who answered correctly in the lower group is 7, and the total number of test takers in each group is 20, the item difficulty is

$$p = \frac{16 + 7}{20 + 20} = \frac{23}{40} = .58$$

Since it is necessary to separate the test scores into upper and lower groups to determine the index of discrimination, you may prefer to use the second method to determine item difficulty. You should note that an easy item has a high index and a difficult item has a low index.

The typical norm-referenced test includes items with a range of difficulty, but the average test item difficulty should be around 50%. The difficulty for criterion-referenced tests is established at the minimum proficiency level, and, ideally, every student should pass every item at the end of the instructional unit. Because this is an unrealistic goal, however, items on criterion-referenced tests are usually constructed so that at least 80% to 85% of the students are expected to pass.

Interpretation of item difficulty is not always an easy task. The item may be easy either because its construction makes the answer obvious or because the students have learned the material in the item. On the other hand, it may be difficult either because it is constructed poorly or because the students have not learned the material. You should consider all of these things if the item difficulty indicates the item is unacceptable as it has been presented to the students. Table 6.3 shows the indexes that may be used to evaluate item difficulty.

Item Discrimination. Item discrimination determines how well the item differentiates between the good student and the poor student. If the item discriminates, more students with high scores will answer the item correctly than will students with low scores. The index of discrimination (D) is found by subtracting the number of correct responses of the lower group from the number of correct responses of the upper group and dividing the difference by the number of scores in each group. The formula is

$$D = \frac{\text{number correct in UG} - \text{number correct in LG}}{\text{number in each group}}$$

With the same values that were used previously to determine an item difficulty of .58, the index of discrimination is

$$D = \frac{16 - 7}{20} = \frac{9}{20} = .45$$

The index of discrimination can range from +1.00 to −1.00, but rarely do these extremes occur. A negative index indicates that more students in the lower group answered the item correctly than did students in the upper group. An item with a negative index has no place in a test. Generally, an index of .40 or above on a norm-referenced test indicates that the item discriminates well. Table 6.4 lists the rules for evaluating the index of discrimination for norm-referenced tests.

The usual item discrimination indexes will not work for criterion-referenced tests. One possible way to identify discriminating items for such tests is to administer the same

TABLE 6.3 Evaluation of Item Difficulty

Difficulty Index	Item Evaluation
.80 and higher	Reject item.
.71–.79	Accept if index of discrimination is acceptable, but revise if discrimination is marginal.
.30–.70	Accept item.
.20–.29	Accept if index of discrimination is acceptable, but revise if discrimination is marginal.
.19 and below	Reject item.

TABLE 6.4 Evaluation of Index of Discrimination

Index of Discrimination	Item Evaluation
.40 and above	Item discriminates; accept item.
.30–.39	Item provides reasonably good discrimination; may need improvement, particularly if item difficulty is marginal.
.20–.29	Item provides marginal discrimination; consider revision.
below .20	Item does not discriminate; reject item.

Source: Ebel, R. L., *Essentials of Educational Measurement,* 3d ed., Englewood Cliffs, N.J.: Prentice Hall, 1979

item before instruction (pre-test) and after instruction (post-test). Before instruction, few students should answer the item correctly, but after instruction most students should answer it correctly. If there is a large difference in the proportion of correct answers from pre-test to post-test, the item discriminates.

A test item with a difficulty index between .30 and .70 has a good chance of being a discriminating item, but you should not assume this always to be true. Before you judge the quality of an item, consider both the difficulty index and the index of discrimination.

Response Quality.   The choices of answers for each item in a multiple-choice test are called *responses*. The incorrect responses are referred to as *distractors* or *foils*.

Ideally, in a multiple-choice test, each response should be selected by some of the students. If a response is not selected by any student, it has contributed nothing to the test. As a rule of thumb, a response should be selected by at least 2% to 3% of the test takers.

Another consideration is the pattern of incorrect responses by the upper and lower groups. For example, if an incorrect response is selected by many students in the upper group but few in the lower group, the item might need revision. The item analysis of a multiple-choice test should include a record of the number of students who selected each response as well as the item difficulty and index of discrimination. Table 6.5 shows the analysis of five multiple-choice items.

TABLE 6.5   Example of Item Analysis for Multiple-Choice Test

60 students completed the test
Groups of 27% (16 test scores in each group); correct responses in bold print

Item		Responses				p	D
		A	**B**	C	D	.50	.63
1	Upper group	1	**13**	2	0		
	Lower group	4	**3**	5	4		
		A	B	**C**	D		
2	Upper group	0	1	**12**	3	.53	.44
	Lower group	3	4	**5**	4		
		A	**B**	C	D		
3	Upper group	0	**8**	0	8	.50	.00
	Lower group	1	**8**	0	7		
		A	B	C	D		
4	Upper group	**11**	3	2	0		
	Lower group	**4**	10	2	0	.47	.44
		A	B	C	**D**		
5	Upper group	2	4	3	**7**	.25	.38
	Lower group	7	4	4	**1**		

Item 1. All responses considered; difficulty and discrimination good. Retain item.

Item 2. All responses considered; difficulty and discrimination good. Retain item.

Item 3. Response C not considered and A considered only once; no discrimination. Reject item.

Item 4. Response D not considered; difficulty and discrimination acceptable. Retain item but replace D.

Item 5. All responses considered; difficulty and discrimination marginal. Revise item.

Item Revision

After completing the item analysis, you are ready to perform any necessary revision. Revision usually involves discarding or rewording some items, changing responses, and changing items to different types (for example, changing multiple-choice items to true-false items). If you perform the preceding steps the first time you administer a test, and analyze and revise the test after at least one additional administration of the test to a similar group, you will have a good test.

▬▬ ARE YOU ABLE TO DO THE FOLLOWING?

- Describe the five steps in constructing knowledge tests.

- Construct a table of test specifications and explain its use.

- Define *item analysis, item difficulty*, and *index of discrimination*, and conduct item analysis on test items.

Objective Test Items

With objective tests, choices of answers are provided for each test item. True-false, multiple-choice, and matching are objective test items. For each item, the test taker must select one of the choices provided. With true-false items, there are two choices; with multiple-choice, there usually are four or five choices; and with matching, there are many choices listed in a column. Many individuals claim that objective test items permit correct responses through simple recognition, rote memory, or association and do not measure the thought processes of comprehension, analysis, and application. These same individuals also believe that only essay tests can truly measure these thought processes. Objective items can measure different kinds of thought processes, but it takes time and effort to construct the items. Various tasks (verbs) usually are associated with

TABLE 6.6   Tasks to Measure Thought Processes

1. Knowledge: define, describe, identify, list, recall, recognize.
2. Comprehension: distinguish, estimate, explain, extrapolate, interpret, paraphrase, summarize.
3. Application: apply, classify, develop, modify, organize, produce, use.
4. Analysis: compare, contrast, deduce, determine, diagram, distinguish, examine, separate.
5. Synthesis: create, compose, contrast, devise, design, modify, plan.
6. Evaluation: appraise, critique, decide, defend, evaluate, judge, interpret.

each thought process. Table 6.6 includes examples of such tasks. [*In the discussion of all test items, examples of items are provided. The thought process measured by each of the items is indicated in brackets for illustrative purposes. You should not indicate these thought processes on tests that you construct.*]

True-False Items

The true-false item is a declarative statement, and the test taker must decide if the statement is correct or incorrect. The true-false item is widely used in teacher-made tests because items can be written rapidly and scored with ease.

Many teachers limit true-false items to factual content, but they can be used to test applications and principles. In addition, knowledge in the form of propositions can be measured. The following tennis items are examples of propositions:

If the score is 15–30, the server is ahead in points.

If the score is 15–30, the serve should be to the receiver's left service court.

Another excellent way to use the true-false item is to describe a situation and then to ask the students to respond to items about the situation. Game situations and strategies are very appropriate for this approach.

The following are advantages of true-false items:

1. A wide range of material may be covered in a single testing period. The response time required by a true-false item is less than that required by multiple-choice or completion items, so more items can be included on a test.

2. The scoring is easy.

3. In general, items are easy to construct. However, if true-false items are to measure thought processes other than simple knowledge, they will require some time to construct.

The following are disadvantages of true-false items:

1. Because there are only two possible answers, guessing could produce a score of 50% correct. Realizing this, many students do not study as they should.

2. Because the students have a 50% chance of guessing the correct answers, the reliability of the test items tends to be lower than that of other types of items.

3. The correct answer often depends on one word.

Guidelines for Constructing True-False Items. True-false items can be used effectively if you adhere to the following guidelines:

1. Avoid the use of absolute and relative modifiers. Words such as *all, always, never, no,* and *none* are clues that the item is probably false. Words such as *sometimes, usually,* and *typically* suggest that the item is probably true.

2. Include an equal number of true and false items, or include more false items than true ones. False items tend to discriminate more than true items.

3. Avoid the exact language of the textbook.

4. Avoid trick items. For example, using the wrong first name of an individual to make an item false is not a good practice.

5. Avoid negative and double negative terms. The inclusion of double negatives may confuse the students and

does not test their ability in terms of the subject matter. If you feel that negative statements should be used, *underline* the negative term or terms.

6. Avoid ambiguous statements. There should be no doubt the statement is completely true or completely false.

7. All items should be of the same approximate length. Some teachers have a tendency to make true statements longer than false statements.

8. Limit each item to a single concept. Items that include more than one concept are often confusing to the students.

One final comment about true-false items: An alternative format for the true-false items is to require the students to correct false statements. The major disadvantage of this technique is that often the item can be corrected in several ways. A better technique is to have the students identify only the false element in the item.

Examples of True-False Items. For each of the following statements, print a *T* in the blank in front of the statement if you believe it to be true and an *F* if you believe it to be false. Each item has a value of 3 points.

_____ 1. If the standard deviation of a group of scores increases, the variability increases. [*comprehension*]

_____ 2. A T-score of 60 is located one standard deviation above the mean. [*knowledge*]

_____ 3. A correlation coefficient of +.60 is twice as significant as a correlation coefficient of +.30. [*analysis*]

_____ 4. If the tail of a distribution curve is to the right, the skew is negative. [*comprehension*]

Read the described tennis situation and the statements that follow. If you believe the statement to be true, print a *T* in the blank in front of the statement. If you believe the statement to be false, print an *F.* Each item has a value of 3 points.

Player A makes a good serve and player B successfully returns it. Either player will now lose a point if

_____ 1. the ball bounces twice on his or her side of the court.

_____ 2. the player hits the ball and it touches the net before it lands in the opponent's court.

_____ **3.** after hitting the ball, the racket slips out of the player's hand.

_____ **4.** the player hits the ball before it crosses the net. [*application*]

Multiple-Choice Items

The multiple-choice item consists of two main components: the stem and three to five responses (one correct response and two to four incorrect responses, referred to as distractors or foils). The stem may be more than one sentence long, but it is usually a direct question or an incomplete statement. It should present the problem in enough detail so that there is no ambiguity about what is being asked. Multiple-choice items have several advantages:

1. They can measure almost any understanding or ability. However, as do other test items, they measure different abilities only if they are designed to do so. Too often multiple-choice items are constructed to measure only rote memory.

2. They can be used to test most types of material.

3. The chances of guessing the correct answer are much less than they are for true-false items.

4. They can be scored easily.

Multiple-choice items also have several disadvantages:

1. They are more difficult to construct than other objective tests. Considerable time is required to develop good items that each include at least four responses.

2. They sometimes encourage memorization of facts rather than understanding of concepts. As noted earlier, this deficiency can be corrected if the items are well planned.

3. Because fewer items can be asked than with true-false items (owing to the time element), less material can be covered.

Guidelines for Constructing Multiple-Choice Items. Multiple-choice items are not easy to construct, but the following guidelines will aid you in the task:

Stem Construction

1. The stem should be concise, be easy to read and understand, and contain the central issue of the item. It should not be necessary to repeat words in the responses. Avoid the use of irrelevant material in the stem. A properly constructed item has meaning by itself so that the good student knows the correct answer before reading all the responses. If the stem is an incomplete sentence or question, make the responses complete the stem.

2. Avoid absolute modifiers such as *always, never, all, none,* and so on.

3. Avoid negative wording; state the stem positively. If it is necessary to use negative words, capitalize each letter of the words or *underline* them.

4. Although not mandatory, it sometimes helps the student if the stem begins with a *w* word such as *which, why, where, what, when,* or *who.* This introduces the stem with the main point of the item.

5. Do not word the stem so that you are asking the student's opinion. If you use a stem that calls for an opinion, you may have difficulty defending one correct answer.

6. If the item is testing the definition, or meaning, of a word, the word to be defined should be in the stem and the responses should consist of alternative definitions or meanings.

Response Construction

1. All responses should be plausible, but there should be only one correct response. Ridiculous or obvious responses have no place in the test. The student who does not immediately know the correct response after reading the stem should have to consider all responses. If distractors are not chosen by some of the students, they should be eliminated from the test.

2. Use at least four responses for each item. If you can think of five good responses, use them. The use of five responses keeps the guessing factor at .20. However, if you can think of only three acceptable responses for an item, use just three.

3. All responses should be grammatically consistent, homogeneous in content, and approximately the same length. If some responses begin with a vowel but other responses in the same item do not, use "a(n)" in the stem to introduce the responses. Avoid the tendency to include more information in the correct response than in the incorrect responses (such as wording the stem so that the correct response needs to be qualified).

4. If the items are numbered, use *A, B, C, D,* and *E* to designate the responses. Also, unless limited by the number of pages, place the responses in vertical order rather than horizontal order for ease in reading.

5. Avoid patterns in the positions of the correct responses. Make it a point to place the correct response in each position approximately an equal number of times; that is, use *A, B, C, D,* and *E* equally.

6. Use the response "none of the above" or "all of the above" with care. If you use "none of the above," all options must be clearly wrong, or one must be clearly correct. If the student has only four responses to consider, the use of "all of the above" reduces the student's discrimination task to three responses. It would probably be best to include a plausible fourth response rather than use "all of the above."

7. When possible, list the responses in logical or sequential order. When variables or dates are arranged in sequence, the correct response occasionally should be first or last in the sequence. This arrangement helps the student to overcome the tendency to disregard the extremes of the sequence as probably not correct.

Examples of Multiple-Choice Items. Print the letter of the one correct answer on the blank line to the left of the item number. Each item has a value of 2 points.

_____ 1. For a knowledge test, a score of 55 has a percentile rank of 40. What do these values indicate?
A. 40 students answered 55% of the test correctly.
B. 40% of the students had a score of 55 or less.
C. 55% of the students had a score of 40 or less.
D. 40% of the students had a score of 55 or more. *[analysis]*

_____ 2. If the correlation coefficient between two variables is −.80,
A. the relationship is quite small.
B. the relationship does not always exist.
C. the two variables are significantly unrelated.
D. the value of one variable decreases as the value of the other variable decreases.
E. the value of one variable increases as the value of the other variable decreases. *[comprehension]*

_____ 3. Which muscle extends the lower leg and flexes the upper leg?
A. quadriceps femoris
B. biceps femoris
C. gluteus maximus
D. gastrocnemius *[knowledge]*

_____ 4. What is the approximate maximum heart rate (beats per minute) of a twenty-year-old individual?
A. 180
B. 190
C. 200
D. 210 *[application]*

Matching Items

The matching test usually consists of a column of items (stimulus words or phrases) on the left-hand side of a page and a column of options (alternatives) on the right. The student's task is to select the option that is correctly associated with the item. Matching items are similar to multiple-choice items in that the options serve as alternatives for all the items. They also are similar to short-answer items because they usually are limited to specific factual information (names, dates, and labels).

The following are advantages of matching items:

1. They are easy to construct and score.

2. They provide many scorable responses on each test page or for each unit of testing time.

3. They motivate students to integrate their knowledge and to consider relations among the items.

4. The odds of guessing the correct answer are low.

The following are disadvantages of matching items:

1. They are time-consuming for students to complete.

2. They usually test only factual information.

3. They are limited to association tasks.

Guidelines for Constructing Matching Items. To construct an effective and fair matching item test, use the following guidelines:

1. Include only homogeneous material in each matching exercise.

2. Make the basis for matching each item and option clear in the directions. The directions should inform the students if an option can be used more than once, if each item has only one correct answer, and how the marking is to be done.

3. Keep the sets of items relatively short (five or six in the lower grades and ten to fifteen in the upper grades). The shorter lists enable the students to respond more rapidly. If more matches are desired, arrange for several matching groups within a single test. Ideally, each group of matching items will involve a different topic.

4. Place all items and options for a matching exercise on one page. This arrangement enables the students to complete the exercise in less time and reduces the likelihood of errors caused by turning pages back and forth.

5. Use an appropriate format. Usually it is best to list the homogeneous items on the left and the options on the right. For ease of scoring, leave a blank space beside each numbered item for the letter of the matched option.

6. Arrange the responses in alphabetical or logical order. This arrangement reduces the time required for the student to find the correct answer.

7. Develop more options than items. Having two or three more options will reduce guessing.

Examples of Matching Items. Select the letter of one option from Column II that best associates with a term in Column I. Print your answer on the appropriate line. Each response has a value of 3 points. [*knowledge or association*]

Column I	Column II
_____ 1. Turnverein	A. Bloomer
_____ 2. Royal Central Institute of Gymnastics	B. Hitchcock
	C. Jahn
_____ 3. vertical jump	D. Ling
_____ 4. physical education costume for women	E. Naismith
	F. Sargent
_____ 5. basketball	G. Williams

Short-Answer and Completion Items

The differences between a short-answer item and a completion item are primarily the length and the format of the response. A short-answer item requires the student to respond to a question in a word, a phrase, or a sentence or two. In a completion item, the simplest short-answer form, one to several words are omitted from a sentence, and the student is asked to provide the missing information. Both items are suited to measure factual knowledge, comprehension of principles, and ability to identify and define concepts. Identification items also are a form of short-answer items.

The advantages of short-answer and completion items are the following:

1. They are affected much less by guessing than are true-false or multiple-choice items.

2. They come closer to assessing recall, as contrasted with recognition. Recall usually requires intensive study on the part of the student.

3. They are valuable when steps or procedures are to be learned.

4. They are easy to construct.

The disadvantages of these items are the following:

1. Scoring takes longer than for choice-type items, especially when only correct spelling is accepted.

2. Often, unless extreme care is taken in the construction of each item, a number of answers might be wholly or

partially correct. The scorer has to decide which responses are acceptable and how much credit to give for each variation. This feature usually means that only the test constructor is able to score the tests.

3. They encourage rote learning; however, there are occasions when recall and memorization are appropriate (first aid and cardiopulmonary resuscitation [CPR], for example).

Guidelines for Constructing Short-Answer and Completion Items. Though short-answer and completion items are easier to construct than objective test items, these guidelines should be observed when constructing the items:

1. Be sure that the item can be answered with a unique word, phrase, or number and that only one answer is correct.

2. Be sure the students know what type of response is required. Indicate also how precise the response should be. (Specifying the level of precision is especially important when computation of fractions or decimals is involved.)

3. Think of the answer first. Then try to write an item to which that answer is the only appropriate answer. By using this approach, you can avoid constructing items that have multiple correct answers.

4. With completion items, try to place the blank near the end of the sentence. This placement usually makes the intent of the item clearer and avoids the possibility of multiple answers.

5. Use no more than two blanks in an item. Too many blanks make the item confusing to the student.

6. Avoid lifting items directly from the textbook. One sentence taken out of context from a paragraph may fail to adequately present the concept of the entire paragraph.

7. Make the actual blanks for the responses the same length. Varying the length of the blank according to the length of the expected answer provides clues for the students. (For ease of scoring, provide short blank lines in the item and blank lines of appropriate length in a column to the right or left of the items for the student to write the responses.)

Examples of Short-Answer Items. Answer the following questions. They have a value of 3 points each.

1. What are the three measures of central tendency? [*knowledge*]

2. In a study of leg strength and hand grip, a correlation of $-.90$ was found. Interpret this correlation. [*comprehension*]

3. In a distribution of scores, the mean is 22 and the standard deviation is 2. What percent of the scores are between the scores of 16 and 28? [*application*]

Examples of Completion Items. Complete the items by writing the correct answer on the blank line to the left of each item. Each item has a value of 2 points.

_____ 1. The _____ is usually the most reliable measure of variability. [*knowledge*]

_____ 2. A T-score of 75 is found _____ standard deviations above the mean. [*application*]

_____ 3. In a T-scale, the mean is assigned to a T-score of _____. [*knowledge*]

Essay Test Items

The final test item to be discussed is the essay item, which is evaluated subjectively. Essay items are designed to measure the students' ability to use higher mental processes—identifying, interpreting, integrating, organizing, and synthesizing—and to express themselves by writing.

The following are advantages of essay items:

1. They are easily and quickly constructed.

2. They can measure complex concepts, thinking ability, and problem-solving skills.

3. They encourage students to learn how to effectively organize and express their own ideas.

4. They minimize guessing.

The following are disadvantages of essay items:

1. They usually are very time-consuming to score.

2. The scoring requires some decision making on the part of the scorer; thus, reliability may be decreased.

3. Because they take longer to answer, only a few items can be answered during one class period. This time constraint limits the field of knowledge that can be covered.

Guidelines for Constructing Essay Items. Though essay items seem the easiest test items to construct, the following guidelines should be observed when preparing them:

1. They should require the students to demonstrate a command of essential knowledge. Too often essay items call only for reproduction of materials presented in the textbook or class lectures.

2. Each item should be phrased so that only one answer is correct. When items have more than one correct answer, it is difficult to evaluate the student's level of achievement.

3. Indicate the scope and direction of the required answer. Vague phrasing leads to wide variation in responses and makes the task of evaluating the items even more difficult.

4. Require all students to answer the same items. If students answer different items, the basis for comparing the scores is limited. When students choose the items they can answer best, the range of test scores will probably be smaller, decreasing the reliability of the scores.

5. Indicate the approximate amount of time for the students to devote to each item and the point value of each item. Many students need guidelines in how to budget their working time. In addition, stating the amount of time that should be devoted to each item gives a clue as to the detail expected on a given item.

6. In general, it is better to use several short essay items rather than a few long ones. Short essay items are likely to be less ambiguous to the student and easier to score.

7. Write the ideal answer to the item. Writing the ideal answer gives you a clear idea of the item's reason and aids you in scoring the item.

Guidelines for Scoring Essay Items. Essay items can be difficult to evaluate. These guidelines may help.

1. Develop a method for scoring the tests. Some teachers identify essential points that should be included.

Other teachers rank each item according to the quality of response.

2. Evaluate the same item on all the students' papers before going on to the next item. It is also wise to occasionally check your consistency by reviewing how you evaluated an item on the first few papers you scored.

3. Try to conceal the name of the student whose test you are evaluating. Not knowing whose paper is being evaluated prevents the influence of any biases you may have toward students.

Examples of Essay Items. Read each item carefully and answer each one as completely as possible. The approximate amount of time that you should spend on each item and the point value of each item are indicated in parentheses.

1. Define *correlation,* and contrast the Spearman rank-difference correlation coefficient and the Pearson product-moment correlation. (10 minutes, 20 points) [*analysis, interpretation, organization, application*]

2. Define *standard scores,* and contrast T-scores, z-scores, and percentiles. (10 minutes, 20 points) [*analysis, interpretation, organization, application*]

3. A teacher is interested in determining whether his or her new teaching method is effective. Describe how he or she can determine its effectiveness. Include in your discussion
   a. what testing procedures he or she should use;
   b. when he or she should test; and
   c. what statistical analysis he or she should use.
   (15 minutes, 30 points) [*synthesis, integration, comprehension, analysis, application*]

■ ARE YOU ABLE TO DO THE FOLLOWING?

- Contrast the advantages and disadvantages of the test items described in the text.

- Construct true-false, multiple-choice, matching, short-answer and completion, and essay test items.

You have completed your study of knowledge test items. As you now know, much work is required for construction of a good test, and each type of test item has advantages and disadvantages. All test items, however, can serve to measure the cognitive achievement of the students if the items are well constructed.

Review Problems

1. Construct a knowledge test for a high school tennis class. The test should include a table of specifications, thirty multiple-choice items, and twenty true-false items. Ask a friend to take the test and provide comments about any items that might need to be rephrased or responses that are obviously incorrect or obviously correct.

2. A physical education teacher administered a fifty-item knowledge test to his or her 200 ninth-grade students. After scoring the tests, he or she determined the upper 27% and the lower 27% of the scores. He or she tabulated the following results for the first five items:

Item	Group	No. of Correct Answers
1.	Upper	44
	Lower	8
2.	Upper	45
	Lower	39
3.	Upper	35
	Lower	28
4.	Upper	14
	Lower	2
5.	Upper	37
	Lower	14

Calculate the item difficulty and index of discrimination for each item, and interpret your findings.

Chapter Review Questions

1. What is the purpose of a table of test specifications and what do you include in the table?

2. What do item difficulty and item discrimination indicate?

3. Describe the procedures for determining item difficulty and item discrimination.

4. What is the range of item difficulty indicating that a test item is acceptable?

5. What item discrimination value indicates that a test item is acceptable?

6. Is it possible for an item to have acceptable item difficulty and not have acceptable item discrimination? If so, how?

7 Assessment and Grading

After completing this chapter, you should be able to

1. Define *assessment*, *formative assessment*, and *summative assessment*.

2. List and describe the characteristics of authentic assessment.

3. Describe how you may use checklist, rating chart, analytical, and holistic rubrics in the assessment technique.

4. Describe portfolio assessment.

5. State purpose of and describe teacher self-assessment.

6. List and describe the use of grades.

7. List the three behavior areas and the factors commonly graded in these areas, and state why some factors should not be graded.

8. List and describe the criteria for grades.

9. Define *norm-referenced grading* and the grading methods of *natural breaks, standard deviation, percentage,* and *norms* (percentiles and T-scores); then describe the advantages and disadvantages of these methods.

10. Define *criterion-referenced grading* and the grading methods of *contract* and *percentage correct*; then describe the advantages and disadvantages of these methods.

11. Define *weighting of factors*, and describe a method for performing this technique.

12. Describe four methods for reporting term grades.

13. Describe your grading philosophy and develop a grading method that could be used in a teaching assignment.

Assessment and the assignment of grades are two important teaching responsibilities. These responsibilities are related, but they are also separate responsibilities. Occasionally, some individuals will use the words *assessment* and *evaluation* interchangeably. You should recall how these terms were defined in chapter 1. Evaluation is the interpretation of measurement; evaluation is an important part of assessment. Assessment is a process that includes measurement, evaluation, identification, and prescription.

Assessment should be performed continuously throughout the teaching of a skill. Through assessment the teacher can help the students perform at their maximum level and succeed in their class endeavors. Grading means that the teacher determines (through assessment) the achievement level of each student toward class objectives and assigns the appropriate grade at the conclusion of the teaching unit.

Many U.S. citizens do not believe teachers are fulfilling these responsibilities in an acceptable manner. Because of demands for school improvement and accountability for student learning, individuals and professional groups are seeking better ways to assess student performance. These individuals and professional groups believe that traditional methods (knowledge and skills tests) are too narrow in their measurement, do not integrate the essential performance skills of an activity, and are too artificial (not in the natural environment).

Now many school programs expect teachers to utilize alternative assessment methods in their professional responsibilities. The term *alternative assessment* simply means that students are assessed with nontraditional methods. The most popular form of alternative assessment is **authentic assessment.**

Authentic assessment provides ways for data or information to be gathered and organized so that accurate judgments can be made about each student. Once class goals have been stated, authentic assessment allows a teacher to do the following:

- Monitor the students' performance and determine where they are experiencing difficulties.

- Prescribe a correction for learning problems.

- Keep track of students' progress toward class goals and objectives.

- Fairly assign grades.

Characteristics of Authentic Assessment

Authentic assessment includes the characteristics described next. By including these characteristics, the teacher will experience greater success with authentic assessment.

Formal Record Keeping

Authentic assessment requires the maintenance of formal records. The completion of accurate records is time-consuming, and, although the teacher is responsible for the records, students may assist in this function. The need for records and the role of the students in completing these records will be described in the context of other authentic assessment characteristics.

Natural Surroundings

Authentic assessment is conducted while students are performing in a game or under gamelike conditions. Skills tests may be used for authentic assessment, but the students should be able to connect the expected skills to real-life (game) situations. For this reason, skill test components should be as gamelike as possible. In addition, rating charts of the skills that have been taught may be used to assess the students during game participation or skill practice. The form or technique of the students can be documented with the appropriate chart (described later in this chapter). Records also may be kept of the students' successful completion of skills during game play. The number of tennis serves returned during a match, the number of rebounds during a basketball game, and the number of successful passes during a soccer match are examples of the types of skills that can be recorded.

Formative and Summative Assessment

When conducted throughout the teaching unit, authentic assessment enables the teacher to provide students with regular feedback about progress toward the class goals and objectives. This assessment, called **formative assessment,** allows teachers to diagnose learning problems and prescribe any necessary changes in the teaching unit. Regular assessment does not imply daily assessment, but it does mean that it is done routinely and is not limited to designated testing times or days. Further, when done as part of the regular teaching process, authentic assessment can serve to motivate students to achieve the learning goals. Authentic assessment also should determine students' achievements of class goals and objectives at the conclusion of the teaching unit (called **summative assessment**). Typically, summative assessment is used in the assigning of grades, but both types of assessment should be used.

Technique (Form) and End Result

Assessments of each student's technique or form in performing the skills are conducted in authentic assessment. Although difficult, the assessment of technique should be as objective as possible. Through the use of **rubrics,** it is possible to be somewhat objective in technique assessment.

A rubric is a scoring guide, or a set of all key criteria, that is used to determine an individual's quality of performance. The guide usually consists of specific statements that describe various levels of skill performance. **Checklist, rating chart, analytical,** and **holistic rubrics** are often used in authentic assessment. Checklists and rating scales include the key components of a motor skill and provide students with the criteria for successful performance. Examples of a checklist for the topspin tennis serve and a rating scale for the tennis forehand/backhand are

TABLE 7.1 Checklist for Topspin Tennis Serve (Right-Handed Player)

Yes	No	Preparation
____	____	Continental grip (racket is held 1/8 of a turn from Eastern grip).
____	____	Body sideways to net.
____	____	Lower arm straight from elbow to fingers.
____	____	Feet spread about shoulder-width apart.
____	____	Court position correct in relation to center mark.
____	____	Ball held in thumb and first three fingers.
____	____	Hand with ball placed lightly against racket face.
____	____	Racket held at waist height and pointed toward service court.

Yes	No	Toss
____	____	Both hands drop simultaneously.
____	____	Racket hand moves across and in front of body.
____	____	Weight shifts to back foot as racket goes back.
____	____	Both hands are lifted into a Y shape.
____	____	Tossing arm extends completely before ball is released.
____	____	As ball leaves hand, racket is lowered into back-scratching position with palm of racket hand near ear.
____	____	Toss is slightly higher than server can reach.
____	____	If ball were allowed to drop, it would hit court in front of baseline and in front of heel.

Yes	No	Contact
____	____	Shoulders turn in throwing motion as ball rises.
____	____	Weight shifts to front foot as racket is "thrown" at ball.
____	____	Racket comes forward just as ball begins to drop; contact is made at the 1:00 position with slight outward roll of the forearm.

Yes	No	Follow-Through
____	____	Racket continues through ball toward target and finishes across body.
____	____	Palm of racket hand faces back leg.
____	____	Right leg falls across the baseline into playing court.

provided in tables 7.1 and 7.2, respectively. To use checklists and rating scales, it is especially important that you determine the specific skills that are to be assessed. If you choose to construct your own rating chart, you should follow the guidelines provided in table 7.3.

Analytical rubrics are used when the teacher wishes to assess a student's performance of each component of a skill. Analytical rubrics are detailed and require time to construct. However, they provide useful information about the student's strengths and weaknesses in separate skills. Table 7.4 provides an example of an analytical rubric for the tennis forehand/backhand. Only three scoring headings are included in table 7.4. If desired, additional scoring

headings may be included. For example, the five headings Excellent, Good, Satisfactory, Fair, and Poor may be used. Appropriate assessment statements should be provided for each heading.

Rather than assess each component of a skill, teachers may use a holistic rubric. With this rubric, no components of the skills are listed separately. Instead, broad statements that differentiate the levels of performance are grouped, and the teacher is expected to make a judgment about the student's performance. Holistic assessment is more efficient than analytical assessment and assesses the student while all components of a skill or game are performed. Table 7.5 is an example of holistic assessment of tennis play. As with an analytical

TABLE 7.2 Rating Scale for the Ability to Perform the Tennis Forehand/Backhand

5 Exceptional ability; ball consistently stroked with power; ball consistently lands close to baseline and bounces well beyond the baseline.

4 Above average ability; ball usually stroked with power; ball usually lands close to baseline and bounces beyond the baseline.

3 Average ability; occasional power; capable of hitting ball deep but inconsistent in doing so.

2 Below average ability; no power; ball consistently hit into opponent's forecourt.

1 Inferior ability; ball is rarely hit over net.

TABLE 7.3 Guidelines for Construction of a Rating Scale

1. Determine the specific skills to be assessed. The rating scale must reflect the objectives of the instructional program, and the objectives should be stated in terms of observable behavior.

2. Identify the traits that determine success. The expected traits for success at the beginner's level are different from those of an experienced player. The rating scale should include the skills that are necessary for the level of play being assessed.

3. Determine the levels of success or ability for each skill. A five-point rating scale usually provides enough spread to differentiate the ability levels.

4. Define each category or ability level by observable behavior. Descriptive phrases should accompany each numerical value, and there must be no doubt as to the ability level that is expected for each numerical value.

5. The form should permit the immediate recording of the rating of the observed skill.

Source: Adapted from Hensley, L. D., Morrow, J. R. and East, W. B., "Practical measurement to solve practical problems," *Journal of Physical Education, Recreation and Dance,* vol. 6, no. 3, 1990, 42–44; and Verducci, F. M., *Measurement Concepts in Physical Education.* St. Louis: C. V. Mosby, 1980.

rubric, additional scoring headings may be included in holistic assessment.

As indicated in these examples, analytical and holistic rubrics can be used to assess technique and end results of students' performances. Skills tests also may be used to assess the end result of performance.

TABLE 7.4 Analytical Rubric for Assessing the Tennis Forehand/Backhand

	Excellent	Satisfactory	Needs Improvement
Grip	Consistently maintains correct grip.	Uses correct grip most of time.	Rarely uses correct grip.
Balance and Footwork	Consistently maintains good balance and body position for shot.	Maintains good balance and body position for shot most of time.	Often fails to maintain good balance and body position for shot.
Swing Mechanics	Backswing and follow-through consistently correct.	Backswing and follow-through correct most of time.	Backswing and/or follow-through rarely correct.
Power	Ball consistently lands close to baseline.	Ball often lands close to baseline.	Ball rarely lands close to baseline.
Shot Placement	Able to vary shot placement when necessary.	Able to vary shot placement most of the time.	Rarely able to vary shot placement.
Court Position	Consistently returns to correct court position after shot.	Often returns to correct court position after shot.	Rarely returns to correct court position after shot.
Unforced Errors	Consistently avoids unforced errors.	Avoids excessive number of unforced errors.	Often commits unforced errors.
Comments			

TABLE 7.5   Holistic Assessment for Tennis Ability

Excellent	Consistently executes all strokes and serve with good form. Hits with power and varies shot placement. Anticipates the shots and movements of opponent. Limits the number of unforced errors and maintains good court position. Demonstrates knowledge of game rules and good sportsmanship at all times.
Satisfactory	Occasionally fails to execute strokes and/or serve with good form. Able to hit with power and vary shot placement. Usually anticipates shots and movements of opponent. Makes acceptable number of unforced errors and usually maintains good court position. Demonstrates knowledge of game rules and sportsmanship at all times.
Needs Improvement	Often fails to execute strokes and/or serve with good form. Rarely hits with power and unable to vary shot placement. Does not anticipate shots and movements of opponent. Commits unacceptable number of unforced errors and often fails to maintain good court position. Does not demonstrate knowledge of game rules. Does not demonstrate good sportsmanship at all times.

Comments

Student Self-Assessment and Peer Assessment

Authentic assessment should include student self-assessment and peer assessment. The teacher should explain and demonstrate assessment techniques, but the students can be taught how to assess their own skill. The students must understand how the assessments will be used and the necessity of accuracy and consistency.

End-result assessment usually is easy for the students to conduct. Just as the teacher does, the students count, time, or measure their own or their peers' performance. Daily accomplishments can be recorded as well as the number of times a skill is practiced. Directions as to how the end result is to be recorded should be provided.

Technique assessment is more difficult for the students. Charts or forms that include clearly stated performance criteria must be provided. The same charts or forms used by the teacher can be used by the students (see tables 7.1 and 7.2). Students may perform self-assessment if their performance can be videotaped; otherwise, peer assessment of technique probably is best. The teacher should spot-check the records and regularly review performance expectations. In addition to assisting in the assessment process, watching and analyzing the performance of their peers will help students learn more about a skill.

Portfolio Assessment

Portfolio assessment can be included in authentic assessment. With portfolio assessment, the students are responsible for collecting the portfolio contents. The portfolio may include written assignments (e.g., analysis of a skill and historical report of a sport), a preassessment of skill level, performance goals, a planned program for improvement, a self-assessment of performance through a videotape, a technique or form assessment by a peer, a record of practice sessions, written tests, class notes, and other items on which the teacher and students have agreed. The purpose of the portfolio is to document and exhibit the students' progress, achievements, and effort. In addition, the teacher may use the students' portfolios to determine if class objectives were fulfilled, to communicate with parents, and to evaluate the program.

◆ ◆ ◆   POINT OF EMPHASIS   ◆ ◆ ◆

- Authentic assessment is a time-consuming process, but it provides you with a consistent and accurate way to monitor students. As a teacher, you should invest the time needed for the benefit of students.

If portfolio assessment is used, the students must understand how the portfolio will be evaluated. In addition, guidelines and directions should be provided regarding organization and construction style. The following are a few important considerations: What is the date of completion? Is there a designated form for skill assessment? Are all items to be dated and placed in a notebook, or may some other method be used? When and where will the portfolios be collected? When and where will they be returned? Other considerations will become apparent as portfolio assessment is used. It is important to communicate these considerations to the students early in the process.

Society of Health and Physical Educators (SHAPE America)

The Society of Health and Physical Educators (SHAPE America) publishes *National Standards for K-12 Physical Education*. The standards describe what a student should know and be able to do after participation in a highly effective physical education program. The term *physical literacy* is used in the standards to emphasize the three domains of physical education—psychomotor, cognitive, and affective.

> **Standard 1.** The physically literate individual demonstrates competency in a variety of motor skills and movement patterns.
>
> **Standard 2.** The physically literate individual applies knowledge of concepts, principles, strategies, and tactics related to movement and performance.
>
> **Standard 3.** The physically literate individual demonstrates the knowledge and skills to achieve and maintain a health-enhancing level of physical activity and fitness.
>
> **Standard 4.** The physically literate individual exhibits responsible personal and social behavior that respects self and others.
>
> **Standard 5.** The physically literate individual recognizes the value of physical activity for health, enjoyment, challenge, self-expression, and/or social interaction.

With each standard and grade level, student expectations and performance outcomes are included. As a framework for the development of realistic and achievable expectations for student performance, this publication can serve as a valuable resource for the physical education teacher.

Teacher Self-Assessment

As a physical education teacher, you probably will be asked to perform self-assessment. Some states and professional organizations provide tools, or forms, that are used for teacher self-assessment. Regardless of the particular tool you use, to be an effective teacher (i.e., to experience success in your teaching and relationships with the administration), you should perform self-assessment. The following is an example of teacher self-assessment. Rate each practice with the provided scale, or if you prefer, answer yes or no.

1. Never 2. Rarely 3. Sometimes 4. Frequently 5. Always

Know Yourself

1. Do you like yourself?
   If you fail to like and care for yourself, you will also fail to care for your work, your students, and your fellow teachers.

2. Do you periodically determine your strengths and weaknesses? Do you recognize your shortcomings? Realizing that as a human being, you are never without faults, you recognize your shortcomings and seek to improve them. You are not satisfied with your current skills and abilities.

3. Do you seek to improve yourself through attendance at professional meetings and workshops, the reading of professional literature, and the advice of fellow teachers?
   Growth through professional meetings and literature will cost time, effort, and money, but you are willing to make these sacrifices.

4. Do you know what you want to accomplish in your profession? Do you have professional goals and objectives?
   Goals are not chosen out of ignorance or fear. Neither are they chosen because of what you believe to be expected by the administration. In determining goals, it is sometimes necessary to change or modify them with new students, new knowledge, or a change in financial support.

Be a Winner

1. **Do you live up to your self-expectations?**
   As a winning teacher, you know that responsibilities consist of doing, trying, succeeding, and making mistakes. You learn from your mistakes and attempt to correct those that can be corrected. You look for causes of any poor teaching, rather than just the results of such teaching.

2. **Do you feel guilty about being a winner?**
   You recognize that students, teachers, and administrators who do not fulfill their responsibilities or continually make mistakes lose the most. You are critical only of what can be corrected and you look for ways to assist others in better fulfilling their responsibilities.

Accept Difference of Opinions

1. **Do you state your opinion on various issues?**
   All teachers occasionally have difference of opinions with the administration, other teachers, and possibly students. However, many teachers fail to state their opinion on issues. You assert your opinion, but you respect and seek to understand the rights of others to assert their opinion.

2. **Do you recognize there are times when it is best not to fight the battle?**
   You use judgment and fight only the important battles. You battle only when relief or corrections can be obtained.

Emotions

1. **Do you recognize that students learn best when placed in pleasant surroundings?**
   You understand that sudden displays of anger may obtain immediate results, but these results are not usually long lasting.

2. **Do you recognize that anger that originates outside the teaching area should not be directed at the students?**
   Teachers, just as other individuals, are often guilty of misplacing anger and directing it at those who are not responsible for its origin.

As stated earlier, there are various forms, or tools, available for teacher self-assessment. Regardless of the instrument used, you should welcome the opportunity to assess your performance as a teacher.

Grading

As we begin the discussion of grading in physical education, think back to your middle grades and senior high school days. Do you remember the grades you received in your physical education classes? Do you remember the factors that were used to determine your grades? Did you and the other students feel you were graded fairly? Your instructors may have explained the factors that would be used to determine the grades and that all students would be evaluated objectively, but many instructors do not choose objective factors for grade determination. Instead, they base grades merely on attendance, participation, and effort. Students who miss some classes, fail to always take part in class activities, and appear to be giving less than their best effort do not receive high grades. In other words, the instructor subjectively categorizes the students. There is nothing wrong with rewarding students for effort, but grades earned in physical education classes should involve more than attendance, participation, and effort.

Proponents of grades based on participation argue that if objective grading is used, some students earn low grades and lose interest in physical education. It is possible that a few students who do not earn high grades will be upset, but they will not lose interest in a class because of grades. They lose interest when effective teaching does not take place. Effective teaching includes fair and objective grading.

Grades are recognized as symbols that denote progress and achievement toward established criterion-referenced or norm-referenced course objectives. As the teacher, you will decide whether the course objectives will be criterion-referenced or norm-referenced, but grades should always be related to the objectives. Different acceptable grading methods are available, and formative and summative assessment can be used with most, if not all, of them. The choice is yours. It is essential, however, that you be consistent and fair.

Use of Grades

If you enter the teaching profession, you will have the responsibility of reporting grades for every one of your students each term. Grades may be reported differently, but they have important uses for four groups: students, parents, teachers, and administrators. You should be prepared to discuss with the four groups your grading policies and how you determine the students' grades.

Students

Grades inform the students of their achievement levels. When students know the course objectives, the evaluation methods, and the grade standards, they usually are not surprised by the grades they earn. However, most students like to be informed of their achievement levels by the teacher, and certain students will be challenged by this feedback to work for higher marks. This motivation is more likely to occur if you provide feedback to the students throughout the term and if the students feel that you have a sincere interest in them. Unfortunately, for some students a good grade, rather than the attainment of course objectives, becomes the primary goal. Though it is difficult to prevent, you should attempt to counsel the students about this type of attitude.

Parents

Grades inform the parents of the progress and achievement of their children. Displeased when their children do not get the grades hoped for, some parents will ask you why their son or daughter did not receive a better grade in physical education. You will have a difficult time with many of these parents if you explain that their children did not have a good attitude, did not work hard enough in the class, and therefore did not deserve a better grade. On the other hand, if you explain the objectives of the instructional unit and how you evaluate the students, and provide the scores their children earned, your task will be less difficult. Not all parents will agree with your methods of evaluation, but at least they will understand and probably appreciate the seriousness with which you consider grades. You may avoid such disagreements by sending the parents information about the purposes and objectives of physical education, and your grading philosophy, at the beginning of the school year.

Teachers

Teachers are accountable for the students' achievement of course objectives, and as stated earlier, grades are used to recognize the level of such achievement. To determine the students' grades, you must do a comprehensive evaluation of all students. This evaluation will enable you to better know the strengths and weaknesses of the students. In addition, after evaluating the accomplishments of the students, you can evaluate the effectiveness of your teaching and the efficiency of the program. If many students are failing to complete the objectives of the program, you need to examine your teaching methodology and the expectations of the program. It may be necessary to make changes in both.

The students' grades from previous physical education classes may be beneficial to you at the beginning of each school year. If the grades indicate the students' level of skill, you can readily identify the higher-skilled students and, if necessary, group the students. However, since different factors often are used to determine grades in physical education, you should assume that the grades indicate the skill level of the students only if you are familiar with the grading philosophy of the previous teacher.

Administrators

School administrators use grades to make decisions related to promotion, graduation, academic honors, athletic eligibility, and guidance. They also use grades to determine if students have fulfilled educational objectives. Further, administrators place grades in every student's permanent record, which can have a positive or negative influence when the student applies for a job or an admission to college.

Factors Used in Grading

Physical educators use many factors to determine students' grades. All factors can be grouped into three behavior areas: affective, cognitive, and psychomotor.

Affective Factors

Participation in a physical education program should influence the affective behavior (attitudes and feelings) of students. Let's examine the factors that are usually considered to reflect affective behavior.

Sportsmanship. You always should insist that the students play fairly. They should exhibit good sportsmanship as winners or losers in a game or an event. Those who do not should be disciplined. But can you expect students who exhibit poor sportsmanship at the beginning of the term to change after participation in your class? Usually, poor sportsmanship is due to emotional problems other than those that arise during a game situation, and more than grades is required to improve these behaviors. When sportsmanship is used in determining the grade, students are likely to interpret their grade as a penalty for misbehavior rather than as something that is earned.

Perhaps the best method for dealing with sportsmanship problems is to insist upon sportsmanship during class participation and to individually counsel students about their behavior. This method requires that you keep written records of incidents of poor sportsmanship. Try this approach, and your students may realize that you have a sincere interest in their personal development.

Attendance, Participation, and Showering. Skill development takes place through proper instruction, participation, and practice of fundamentals. Students who fail to attend class regularly and who have poor skills usually do not improve or fulfill other course objectives. If grades are related to the extent that the students fulfill course objectives, students who do not regularly attend class and who have poor skills will not earn good grades. A teacher may not have an attendance policy, but these students will be penalized for their poor attendance.

On the other hand, there may be highly skilled students who are able to complete the course objectives at a satisfactory level, or better, without regular attendance. Should you lower the grades of these students? Since most school programs have attendance policies, problems related to attendance should be handled by the principal, not by the teacher. Base your grades on completion of course objectives, not on attendance.

Perhaps more of a problem occurs when students attend class but, for some reason, do not come dressed to participate. Again, it is best not to use the grade as a threat but to attempt to make the class enjoyable and challenging for the students. If you are successful in developing this type of class atmosphere, the students will want to participate.

Similar to these two factors is the practice of grading the students on showering. Though the students should be instructed in the importance of showering after physical activity, there may be reasons that some students do not want to shower. For example, the showers may not permit privacy for the students who desire it, or the instructor may not allow enough time to cool down before showering. Even if these are not the reasons students avoid showering, grading for showering is not a good practice. Advise and encourage, but do not reward students for showering or penalize them for failing to shower.

Effort. Effort is difficult to evaluate objectively. A poorly skilled individual may appear to be putting forth much effort, whereas a highly skilled individual appears to be putting forth little effort. Should the highly skilled student be penalized? If effort is graded, it is possible that the poorly skilled individual will receive the same grade as the highly skilled individual. Is it fair to give these two students the same grade? Some teachers argue that when effort is graded, the students are motivated to try harder. Perhaps this is true, but as a teacher you have the responsibility to promote inner motivation. Even though it sounds idealistic, the students' desire to excel should come from within, not from external rewards.

If you wish to include effort as a course requirement, seek to develop an objective method for evaluating it. The authentic assessment techniques described earlier can be used to document effort. You also should develop realistic grading standards so that anyone who puts forth the effort can at least meet the minimum standards for the class.

Cognitive Factors

General agreement exists that grading in physical education should include mental factors. Though many teachers limit the cognitive evaluation to knowledge of rules, history, and fundamentals, the student also should be required to demonstrate the ability to understand, apply, and analyze rules, strategy, and technique. As stated in chapter 6, it takes time to construct tests that properly measure these factors, but the teacher has the responsibility to do so.

Psychomotor Factors

Most physical educators grade the psychomotor skill of students. The degree of emphasis will vary, but teachers usually grade skill in terms of the activity, game performance, and fitness.

The Activity.   Two aspects of skill are generally used when grading the skill in an activity: achievement and improvement. Grading for achievement consists of measuring the skill of the students at the conclusion of an instructional unit and assigning the appropriate grades. As they will for any cognitive or psychomotor skill, the levels of ability will vary; unless the standards for skill are very low, only a portion of the students are likely to earn high grades.

Perhaps the most important consideration when grading skill achievement is to establish realistic norm-referenced or criterion-referenced objectives. If a school system has a coordinated physical education program, it is easier to plan realistic objectives because teachers are aware of the students' movement experiences. Knowing the physical education objectives for the previous years and the skills the students were expected to develop enables a teacher to plan the appropriate objectives.

When a class has some students with limited movement experiences and other students with good movement experiences, it is difficult to establish fair objectives. The skill objective may be too low for the students with good movement backgrounds and too difficult for the other students. (The availability of beginning and advanced classes helps prevent this problem, but such classes are not possible in many school programs.) When this dilemma does occur, the approach of some teachers is to homogeneously group the students in a class and use different grading standards for each group.

However, if this method is used, problems can occur: (1) some students with better than average skill may deliberately seek to be placed in the lower-skilled group in an attempt to ensure a good grade and (2) if the student's record does not indicate placement in a beginning or advanced class, what do the grades for the different groups mean? Does the grade of B earned by a student in the lower-skilled group mean the same as a B earned by a student in the higher-skilled group? For these reasons, many physical education teachers agree that the level of achievement should be evaluated in the same way for all students in a particular class.

Some physical educators believe that students should be graded on skill improvement. It is desirable that all students improve their skill through participation in a physical education instructional unit, but is it fair to all students to grade on improvement? In addition, can improvement be measured accurately? Usually, improvement is measured by administering one test at the beginning and another at the end of an instructional unit and subtracting the first score from the second score. The difference in the scores is interpreted as the improvement score. Several problems are associated with this technique:

1. When students know that improvement is a factor in grading, some may deliberately score low on the first test to show much improvement on the second.

2. Testing some skills before a minimum level of proficiency has been developed can be dangerous (in gymnastics and wrestling, for example). In addition, fitness testing of obese students probably is best done after a decrease in body fat is accomplished.

3. For some activities, the instructional term may not be long enough for students to practice and show improvement. Also, if the instructional term is too long, the improvement of some students may be due to physical maturity rather than ability.

4. If all students perform at their best on the test given at the beginning of the instructional unit, the low-skilled students may have an advantage in the earning of high grades because they have greater potential for improvement. The high-skilled students will probably improve very little. To correct for this inequity, the instructor must develop a scale for improvement for each skill level. Several hundred scores should be

collected and analyzed to develop such a scale. The students with high skill should not be expected to improve as much as the students with low skill.

5. Subject areas such as math, English, science, and history do not grade on improvement. If physical education is to be viewed in the same way as other subjects, grades should not be based on improvement.

You can see that the disadvantages of grading on improvement appear to far outweigh the advantages. If you feel that it is important to report improvement, do so with a form separate from the grade report.

Game Performance.   Grading game performance for individual activities may be done through tournament play. Tournaments should be double elimination or round-robin play, however. Game performance also may be graded through the authentic assessment procedures previously described in this chapter.

Fitness.   Though the educational objective of physical fitness is unique to physical education, many physical educators do not include it in the grading process of all activities. It may not be practical to provide class time in all instructional units for fitness activities, but after a fitness unit has been completed, the students should be expected to maintain a specified level of physical fitness throughout the school term. The specific level of fitness for each student may vary, however. In addition, it is probably best to avoid the use of fitness tests for grading purposes. If physical fitness is a factor in the grading process, perhaps it is best to permit the students to earn participation points in fitness activities. The reasons for measurement of physical fitness are discussed in chapter 15.

▰▰▰ ARE YOU ABLE TO DO THE FOLLOWING?

- List the three behavior areas and the factors commonly graded in these areas, and state the reasons why some of these factors should not be graded.

Criteria for Grades

As you now are aware, many factors can be considered in the grading of students. Some factors can be accurately and fairly graded, but other factors should be reported directly to the students and parents (rather than included in the reported grade). Barrow and McGee (1979) provide the following criteria for grades. If you observe these criteria, you will have a grading process that is educationally sound and fair to the students.

1. Grades should be *related to the educational objectives.* If a factor has not been included as an instructional objective, it should not be graded.

2. The grades should have *validity, reliability,* and *objectivity.* Grades should indicate achievement of the factors that they purportedly represent. The validity of a grading method is low when the grades are not related to the instructional objectives.
   A grading system should be consistent. It should yield the same grade for the same performance, regardless of the number of times the grade is calculated. In addition, unless modifications are made, it should yield the same results for the same performance from year to year.
   Though it may be necessary to grade some factors subjectively (e.g., gymnastics), a grading system should be as objective as possible. A grading system has high objectivity if several teachers can perform the same measurements on students and arrive at the same final grade. If some factors can be measured only subjectively, checklists or rating scales should be used. Grades that are determined subjectively are usually unreliable and difficult to defend if challenged.

3. The *weight* (the percentage or portion of the total grade) of each graded factor should be related to the emphasis placed on the factor during the instructional unit. It is possible, but unlikely, that all graded factors will have equal weight. (Assigning weights to factors will be discussed later in this chapter.)

4. The weights of the factors and the method with which the final grade is determined should be *understandable* to the students and parents. Each student should be able to determine the earned grade before it is provided by the teacher. The technique for determining grades should be neither a secret to the students and parents nor so complicated that they do not understand it.

5. Whether grades are norm-referenced or criterion-referenced, they should *discriminate* the good student from the poor student. Students who perform at a high level should receive better grades than students

who perform at a lower level. As in other subject areas, physical education grades should discriminate between levels of attainment.

6. The grades should have *administrative economy.* An educationally sound grading system should be used, but the system should be feasible in terms of time, cost, and personnel. Remember, clerical help for the teacher is limited, and grades must be prepared in a short time period. If the grading system requires so much time that other teaching responsibilities suffer, it is not practical. Teachers generally use computers to record and determine grades, giving them more time for class preparation.

■ ARE YOU ABLE TO DO THE FOLLOWING?

- List and describe grading criteria.

Methods of Grading

Physical education teachers use many grading methods. Regrettably, not all are good. Grading systems are classified as either norm-referenced or criterion-referenced, and both include acceptable methods of grading.

Norm-Referenced Grading

The norm-referenced system of grading is based on the normal probability curve that was described in chapter 2. Norm-referenced standards compare the performance of the students with each other. Levels of performance that discriminate among ability groups are developed. The levels of ability may range from high to low; the appropriate grade is used to indicate the attained ability. There are many methods of norm-referenced grading, not all of which are acceptable. Several methods follow.

Natural Breaks Method. In general, when test scores are ranked, gaps occur in the distribution. These breaks may be used as cutoff points for letter grades. Though quick and convenient for the teacher, this method is not recommended. A student's grade depends only on where the gaps occur, and there certainly is no consistency from one term to another. A numerical grade may be a B one term but an A another term. Table 7.6 shows how this method may be used.

TABLE 7.6 Grades Assigned by Natural Breaks Method

95	79
95	77
93	77
93	76
92	76
91	75
91 A	73
......	73
88	72
87	72 C
87	......
86	69
85	68
85	66
83	64
82 B	63 D
......	......
	57
	55 F
	......

Standard Deviation Method. This method assumes that the scores are normally distributed and that the standard deviation can be used to determine the grades. So, the first thing you must do is to calculate the mean and the standard deviation of a distribution of scores. You then have several choices for arranging the distribution into sections for grading purposes. Table 7.7 shows three arrangements. For illustration purposes, look at the following calculations for a sample knowledge test that has a mean of 74 and a standard deviation of 6. The arrangement in example 3 of table 7.7 is used.

The C range is determined first, since its range affects the B and D ranges. The C range is found as follows:

$$C = \bar{X} \pm 0.5s$$
$$= 74 \pm (.5)6$$
$$= 74 \pm 3$$
$$C = 71 \text{ to } 77$$

TABLE 7.7 Grades Assigned by Standard Deviation Method

Example 1

Grade	Standard Deviation Range	Percent
A	2.0s or more above mean	2
B	Between +1.0s and +2.0s	14
C	Between +1.0s and −1.0s	68
D	Between −1.0s and −2.0s	14
F	2.0s or more below mean	2

Example 2

Grade	Standard Deviation Range	Percent
A	1.75s or more above mean	4
B	Between +0.75s and +1.75s	19
C	Between +0.75s and −0.75s	54
D	Between −0.75s and −1.75s	19
F	1.75s or more below mean	4

Example 3

Grade	Standard Deviation Range	Percent
A	1.5s or more above mean	7
B	Between +0.5s and +1.5s	24
C	Between +0.5s and −0.5s	38
D	Between −0.5s and −1.5s	24
F	1.5s or more below mean	7

The upper limit of the B range is found as follows:

$$B = \bar{X} + 1.5s$$
$$= 74 + (1.5)6$$
$$B = 83$$

The lower limit of the D range is found as follows:

$$D = \bar{X} - 1.5s$$
$$= 74 - (1.5)6$$
$$D = 65$$

The ranges for the grades are as follows:

$$A = \text{above } 83$$
$$B = 78 \text{ to } 83$$
$$C = 71 \text{ to } 77$$
$$D = 65 \text{ to } 70$$
$$F = \text{below } 65$$

If this method is used with a small class, the percentage of scores for each grade is not likely to be exactly the same as presented in table 7.7. (A small number of scores does not usually result in a normal distribution.) The standard deviation method of grading is best when scores are collected for several classes and grouped into one distribution. It may be necessary to collect the scores over two or more years, but the larger set of scores will result in an approximately normal distribution. Once you have established a grade range based on a large distribution of test scores, you can convert subsequent scores for the test into letter grades. Used in this manner, the standard deviation method is an acceptable norm-referenced grading system.

Percentage Method. Using the percentage method, the teacher decides what percentage of the class is to receive each letter grade, lists the scores in order, and assigns the grades. For example, suppose a teacher has a class of thirty students. Table 7.8 shows how many students would receive each letter grade with three different groups of percentages.

Examples 1 and 3 of table 7.8 also show one of the problems encountered with this method. The selected percentage may require the rounding of numbers, which results in a different total number of students than the actual number of students. Example 1 has a total of 29 students, and example 3 has 31 students. When the total is different from the actual number of students, the teacher must decide which letter grade is to be received by more or fewer students than indicated by the percentage.

There is another problem with this method. Suppose that in example 2, when the scores are listed in order, the highest five are the following:

94   92   91   91   91

TABLE 7.8   Grades Assigned by Percentage Method (Class of 30 Students)

Grade	Example 1		Example 2		Example 3	
	% of Students	No. of Students*	% of Students	No. of Students	% of Students	No. of Students*
A	7	2	10	3	15	5
B	24	7	20	6	20	6
C	38	11	40	12	30	9
D	24	7	20	6	20	6
F	7	2	10	3	15	5

*Will not total 30 because of rounding of numbers.

Only the highest three scores should receive the grade of A, but scores 3, 4, and 5 are the same. The teacher must decide whether only the highest two scores will receive an A or the highest five. If only two scores receive the grade of A, more than six students will be given a B. If five scores are given the grade of A, fewer scores will be given a B. This problem could occur anywhere in the distribution and with any percentage group.

This method has other disadvantages. Average-ability students will receive higher grades in a class with low-ability students than in a class with high-ability students. Also, consider what occurs if the class is homogeneous in ability. Though all students are approximately equal in ability, some students will receive high grades and some will receive low grades. Finally, there is no consistency with this method. The grade assigned to a particular score may vary from term to term.

The disadvantages of the percentage method can be overcome if it is used in the same way as the standard deviation method. A large number of scores should be collected before the percentage groups are designated. Once the percentage groups (A, B, C, D, and F) have been determined with a large number of scores for a particular test, subsequent test scores can be assigned the appropriate letter grade. The problems of the percentage method still may occur but only during the initial determination of the letter grades. Once the letter grades have been assigned to the scores, these problems are eliminated. Used specifically in this manner, the percentage method is acceptable for norm-referenced grading.

Norms Method.   Norms are performance standards based on analysis of scores. They are developed by collecting scores for a large number of individuals of the same gender and similar age, experience, ability, and other such characteristics. Norms may be developed at the national, state, or local level. At any of these levels, several hundred scores should be collected and analyzed before the norms are accepted. Percentiles, T-scores, and z-scores are forms of norms.

The norms method is an excellent system for norm-referenced grading for several reasons. The norms may be used for several years before new norms need to be developed. Also, they are unaffected by the group being tested because all students in the group could excel in performance and earn a high grade. Finally, they have consistency in that the grade for a given performance will be the same for a group during any school term. Table 7.9 shows how percentiles and T-scores may be used for grading purposes. The percentiles and T-scores may be adjusted to reflect + and − grades. The procedures for calculation of percentiles and T-scores have been described in chapter 2, and table 2.5 includes the relationship of percentiles and T-scores to the normal curve.

Criterion-Referenced Grading

Criterion-referenced standards are clearly defined; the students know exactly what is expected of them. Standards may be developed for each grade that can be earned, or the standards may be pass/fail. When standards are developed for each grade, the students choose to work for a particular grade, and they are not in competition with each other. If

TABLE 7.9   Grades Assigned by Percentiles and T-scores

Grade	Percentile	T-score
A	90–100	Above 62
B	80–89	59–62
C	70–79	56–58
D	60–69	53–55
F	Below 60	Below 53

pass/fail, the standards represent the level of ability that most students should be able to achieve during the instructional unit.

Contract Method.   The contract grading method can be used with a class or with each student. With the class contract, the quality, amount, and type of work to be performed to earn the various grades are the same for all members of the class. For example, in a tenth-grade softball class, the A grade standards for each girl might be the following:

- Score 19 or above on the overhand throw for accuracy.

- Score 19 or above on the fielding test.

- Score 90 or above on the written test.

- Write a one-page report on the technique of bunting.

- Write a one-page report on the technique of fielding a ground ball in the outfield and throwing to home plate.

Other standards would be written for the remaining grades. The teacher may or may not permit the class to assist in developing the contract. With the individual contract, the teacher and student agree upon the type, amount, and quality of work the student must do to earn a particular grade. Each student could have a different contract, and every student could earn an A grade.

This method of grading allows for individual differences in ability and for successful performance, as defined by the student. Too often when this method is used, however, the emphasis is on the quantity of work rather than on the quality of work. If quality standards can be designed, this system is acceptable for criterion-referenced grading.

Percentage Correct Method.   Teachers often use the percentage correct method for grading. With this method, the student is advised what percentage of attempts must be correct to earn the various grades. Table 7.10 shows four examples of this method. The percentage correct method also can be used with physical performance scores, but there will be no maximum score for performances such as throwing and jumping events. In these events, the grade of A or A+ would be any score greater than a specified score. The standards for the grades should be based on previous test scores that have been analyzed, not on standards the teacher arbitrarily selects.

When the percentage correct method is used, it is sometimes difficult to compare different tests, because the level of difficulty for the tests will not always be the same. A grade of 85 on one knowledge test may be a better score than a grade of 85 on another test, depending on the test

TABLE 7.10   Grades Assigned by Percentage Correct Method

Grade	Percentage Correct Score	
	Example 1	**Example 2**
A	90 to 100	93 to 100
B	80 to 89	85 to 92
C	70 to 79	77 to 84
D	60 to 69	70 to 76
F	Below 60	Below 70
	Example 3	**Example 4**
A+	98 to 100	98 to 100
A	94 to 97	95 to 97
A−	90 to 93	93 to 94
B+	87 to 89	91 to 92
B	83 to 86	87 to 90
B−	80 to 82	85 to 86
C+	77 to 79	83 to 84
C	73 to 76	79 to 82
C−	70 to 72	77 to 78
D+	67 to 69	75 to 76
D	63 to 66	72 to 74
D−	60 to 62	70 to 71
F	Below 60	Below 70

difficulty. (This problem could occur with psychomotor tests also.) When one test is considered more difficult than another, different weights may be assigned to the tests.

The percentage correct method is an acceptable criterion-referenced grading system if the grade standards are determined as objectively as possible. It is a better system when the instructor assigns weights to factors or tests with different degrees of difficulty. There are no limits on the number of students who may earn high grades, and the students know exactly what they must do to earn a particular grade.

■ ARE YOU ABLE TO DO THE FOLLOWING?

- Define *norm-referenced grading* and the grading methods of *natural breaks, standard deviation, percentage,* and *norms* (percentiles and T-scores).

- Describe the advantages and disadvantages of each.

- Define *criterion-referenced* grading and the grading methods of *contract* and *percentage correct.*

- Describe the advantages and disadvantages of each.

Which Method of Grading Is Best?

Only a few of the grading methods used in physical education have been presented in this chapter. These, and many others, are not without faults. As teachers gain experience, they develop a method that suits them best. However, all teachers, beginning and experienced, should use a grading system that fulfills the grading criteria previously described and that they agree with philosophically. If you teach, a major decision will be whether to use criterion-referenced grading or norm-referenced grading. Both have a place in the grading process, so you should be prepared to use either, depending on which best serves your needs and the needs of your students.

Weighting of Factors

Usually a teacher emphasizes certain factors in a teaching unit; that is, the teacher gives these factors more value than other factors in determining the unit grade. The importance of these factors is reflected in the weight (percentage of the total grade) assigned to each. If evaluation scores for all factors are averaged without the assigning of weights, all scores will have equal value. As previously stated, the use of weights should be considered with knowledge and physical performance tests, as well as when one test is more difficult than another. Table 7.11 shows how weights might be used to determine grades in a tennis unit. Note that the psychomotor area has a weight three times greater than the cognitive area. Also note that game performance and tournament standing are important components in the psychomotor area. If you choose to include game performance, use authentic assessment procedures to determine the grade. In addition, technique rating may include self-assessment, peer assessment, teacher assessment, or some combination of the three. If letter grades are assigned for weighted factors, a numerical table for conversion of letter grades, as shown in table 7.12, should be available.

TABLE 7.11 Use of Weights in Determining Grades for Tennis

Area	Weighting of Area	Factor	Weighting of Factor	Grade	Points
Psychomotor	6	Skill test	1	C+	6
		Game performance	2	B+	18
		Tournament standing	2	A+	24
		Technique	1	A−	10
Cognitive	2	Knowledge test	2	A−	20
TOTALS	8		8		78
COMMENTS	Grade = 78/8 = 9.75 (A−)				

TABLE 7.12   Numerical Conversion Table for Letter Grades

A+ = 12	B− = 7	D+ = 3
A = 11	C+ = 6	D = 2
A− = 10	C = 5	D− = 1
B+ = 9	C− = 4	F = 0
B = 8		

ARE YOU ABLE TO DO THE FOLLOWING?

- Define *weighting of factors*, and describe a method for performing this technique.

Reporting of Final Grades

Teachers may choose a grading method, but they usually do not choose how the grades are to be reported. All teachers within a school, or school system, are required to report grades in the same way.

Letter   The letter grades A, B, C, D, and F are most commonly used. Some school systems use + and − with the grades: A+, A, and A−. Often the use of letter grades requires the teachers to convert numerical grades into letter grades. A system, such as the one shown in table 7.11, is needed in this case.

Numerical   The numerical average is reported rather than a letter grade. The grade may be the average of the actual scores or of the percentage correct. Though letter grades are not reported with this method, some schools equate the numerical ranges

with letter grades: A = 93 to 100, B = 85 to 92, and so forth.

Pass/fail   The grade indicates only whether the student has been successful or unsuccessful in completing the course objectives.

Descriptors   Words, terms, and phrases are used to describe the student's performance. Examples are "excellent," "above average," "average," "below average," "working at near capacity," "making moderate use of ability," "working substantially below ability," "outstanding progress," "appropriate progress," "progress below capabilities," and "little or no progress."

ARE YOU ABLE TO DO THE FOLLOWING?

- Describe four methods for reporting grades.

Review Problem

Imagine that you are to be interviewed for a high school teaching position. You are asked to assume that your first teaching assignment will be the teaching of tennis classes and to bring the following to the interview:

- Your grading philosophy.
- A description of how you would use authentic assessment.
- A description of a grading system that includes the use of weighted factors.

Prepare each request as if you were going for the interview.

1. What is the difference between assessment and grading?

2. What is a rubric?

3. How can rubrics be used in authentic assessment?

4. Contrast norm-referenced grading and criterion-referenced grading.

5. Contrast the standard deviation and the norm methods of grading.

6. Contrast the contract and percentage correct methods of grading.

7. Describe the use of percentiles and T-scores in a grading system.

8. What is meant by the weighting of factors in a grading system?

8

Construction and Administration of Psychomotor Tests

After completing this chapter, you should be able to

1. Describe the four components of the psychomotor domain.

2. Select psychomotor tests that have been constructed properly.

3. Describe the procedures for construction of a psychomotor test.

4. Describe the pre-test, testing, and post-test responsibilities for the administration of psychomotor tests.

5. Properly administer psychomotor tests.

6. Define *motor ability*, *motor capacity*, and *motor educability*.

Test Construction Guidelines

Jansma (1988) describes four fundamental components of the psychomotor domain: physical, motor, fitness, and play. The physical component deals with the individual's anatomical or structural status. The motor component deals with the quality of movement patterns, or how well the individual moves. The fitness component refers to the quantity of movement, or how much movement can be sustained. The play component represents the culmination of development within the psychomotor domain. To be a good player, the individual needs physical, motor, and fitness competence.

Many published tests are available to measure these psychomotor domain components. There may be occasions, however, when no published test meets the particular needs of the group you wish to test, or you feel that you are capable of devising a better test. The following guidelines will help you construct a good test. Because there is agreement on the techniques for estimating the validity and reliability of norm-referenced tests, it probably would be best if you first developed a norm-referenced test. The guidelines presented here, or ones similar to them, were followed in the development of most of the tests presented in the following chapters.

Know What Is Required of a Good Test

Before constructing a psychomotor test, you should be familiar with the criteria of a good test. Review the criteria in chapter 5.

Define the Performance to Be Measured

The new test might be designed to measure a sport skill, a game situation, fitness, strength, flexibility, or other related performances. You should define the exact performance you want to measure and state the objective of the new test. The test taker should be able to relate the test to real-life situations (e.g., the components of a skill test should be similar to gamelike conditions). Suppose you want to construct a new tennis serve test. Do you want to include measurement of power in the test or just measure the ability to serve the ball into the correct area? If it is to be a strength test, do you want to measure the strength of the leg, arm, or another body part? It may be wise to name the muscles to be tested. If it is to be a flexibility test, you should identify the joint or body part that will be involved in the measurement of flexibility. Also, include in your definition characteristics of the group that will take the test (e.g., gender and age).

After you have identified and defined the performance to be measured, ask yourself the following questions:

1. Has the performance been included in the unit of instruction?

2. Can the performance be objectively measured?

3. Is there an existing test that will meet my needs?

Once you are satisfied with your answers to these questions, you are ready to analyze the performance that will be measured.

Analyze the Performance

To construct a good test, *you must analyze the performance to be measured by identifying all the components needed for successful performance.* (For example, performance in softball involves hitting, catching, throwing, and running.) After you have identified the components, select the ones you want to measure. It is important that you give careful thought to this guideline. The components that you identify will determine the items you include in your test.

Suppose you want to construct a test to measure hitting ability. The skill of hitting may be broken down into four parts: grip, stance, swing, and follow-through. Successful performance of the test should require the student to perform the fundamentals of these four parts in a mechanically sound way. (Note that this example emphasizes form more than how hard or where the ball is hit. You must decide if you wish to emphasize form more than results in any sports skills analysis or seek a balance between the two.)

Review the Literature

You should review tests that measure the same performance or related performance and the research performed to develop the tests. This review will serve several purposes:

1. You will become familiar with developing physical performance tests. You may find useful ideas that will aid you in your project.

2. You may choose to include previously published test items in your test.

3. You may find a previously validated test to use in establishing the validity of your test.

4. You will become more familiar with the performance components.

Devise the Test Items

You now are ready to devise the item or items that will be included in your test. (You may also select published test items.) It is a good idea to develop more items than you actually plan to include in the test and to select the best ones after analyzing all the items. Keep the following principles in mind:

1. Make the items as realistic as possible. If a sport skill is being measured, the item should be similar to the game situation. This consideration (authentic assessment) has been described in chapter 7. The items also must be appropriate for the gender and age of the individuals being tested.

2. Make the items simple to perform. You do not want to include an item the students have difficulty remembering. If they hesitate or forget during test performance, the validity and reliability of the test will be affected.

3. Make the items practical. They should be inexpensive and require a minimum amount of time to administer.

4. Determine the test layout—dimensions and administrative order of items.

5. Make the scoring simple. Simplicity of scoring will aid objectivity, lessen the time required to train any assistants needed to administer the test, and better enable the students to understand the scoring.

Prepare the Directions

The directions must be clear and precise, or the reliability and objectivity of the test will be affected. In addition, clear directions will prevent confusion among the students. When writing the directions, try to imagine questions that might be asked after the directions have been given to a group. Review the directions of tests found in this book and other textbooks to aid you in the wording.

Have the Test Reviewed by Your Peers

This is not the time to be hesitant in asking for assistance in your project. Ask other qualified individuals to study your test and offer constructive criticism. What may be clear or obvious to you may not be to others. Asking for input now may prevent problems once you administer the test. Remember, when you ask for help, do not be oversensitive if people do not agree with everything you have written. You do not have to accept all their suggestions; however, open-mindedness is important in constructing successful tests.

Administer the Test to a Small Group of Students

At this point, it would be wise to administer the test to a small group of students to determine if there are any problems with the directions, administration, and scoring. Though not essential, having someone else administer the test to the group while you observe and make notes of any problems may be beneficial. Your group must be representative of the group for which the test is designed. After the sample group has completed the test, make any necessary changes. If you administered more items than you plan to include in the final version of the test, you can remove the items that appear to be troublesome.

Determine the Validity, Reliability, and Objectivity

Having completed the previous guidelines, you are ready to determine the validity, reliability, and objectivity coefficients of your test by administering it to a large number of students. As was the small group, this large group must be representative of the group for which the test is designed.

For norm-referenced tests, concurrent validity is usually desired. Concurrent validity can be estimated through ratings of experts, tournament play, and previously validated tests. These procedures were described in chapter 5.

Develop the Norms

If you have constructed a norm-referenced test, a table of norms is needed. Review the calculations of z-scores, T-scores, and percentiles described in chapter 2; remember,

TABLE 8.1 Guidelines for Construction of Psychomotor Tests

Review criteria of a good test:
  Consider validity, reliability, objectivity, and administrative feasibility.

Define the performance to be measured:
  Identify components for successful performance.

Review the literature:
  Research tests that measure the same performance or related performance.

Devise the test items:
  Make items realistic, simple, and practical; determine layout; make scoring simple.

Prepare directions:
  Be clear and precise.

Have test reviewed by peers:
  Be open-minded.

Administer test to small group:
  Make sure small group is representative of group for which test is designed.

Determine validity, reliability, and objectivity:
  Administer test to large group; make sure group is representative of group for which test is designed.

Develop norms:
  Base norms on large number of scores.

norms are usually reported by age and gender. Because a large number of scores are required to develop the norms, it will be necessary to test several classes. If this is not possible, you can accumulate test scores over a period of two or three years. You must administer the test the same way each time, however. Table 8.1 summarizes the guidelines for construction of physical performance tests.

Determine Intercorrelations

Determining intercorrelations (the relationship of two items that may mean that they measure the same thing) is necessary only if your test includes several items (referred to as a *test battery*). When a test includes more than one item, all items should have high correlation with the criterion and low correlation with each other. The correlation of the items with each other is determined through a multiple correlation procedure. This procedure has been used with other statistical procedures to develop many of the physical fitness, motor ability, and sports skills tests used in physical education programs. In the construction of a test battery, not all the items initially administered to the subjects are expected to be included in the final test battery. When two items are highly correlated with each other, the two items are considered to measure the same thing. The item that has the highest correlation with the criterion remains as part of the test; the other item is discarded. Since multiple correlation will not be discussed in this book, you should refer to a statistics book for the appropriate procedure.

Table 8.2 indicates how the developers of three tests followed test construction guidelines. The tests are described in chapter 18.

▓▓▓ ARE YOU ABLE TO DO THE FOLLOWING?

- Describe the four components of the psychomotor domain.
- Select psychomotor tests that have been constructed properly.
- Describe the procedures for construction of a psychomotor test.

TABLE 8.2 Steps in Construction of Three Sports Skills Tests

	Hewitt's Tennis Achievement Test	Indoor Golf Skill Test for Junior High Boys	Racquetball Skills Test
Define the performance.	Tennis skills	Golf skills	Racquetball skills
Analyze the performance.	Service, forehand, and backhand (fundamental skills in tennis)	Power and accuracy with 5 iron (selected because it is used extensively when teaching golf skills)	Speed and accuracy with wall volley (fundamental components of racquetball)
Review the literature.	Included	Included	Included
Devise the test items.	Fulfills principles on page 100	Fulfills principles on page 100, except use of plastic ball not gamelike	Fulfills principles on page 100
Prepare the directions.	Clear and precise	Clear and precise	Clear and precise
Have the test reviewed.	Test reviewed by peers prior to publication	Test reviewed by peers prior to publication	Test reviewed by peers prior to publication
Administer the test to small group.	Not reported in source	Not reported in source	Not reported in source
Determine the validity, reliability, and objectivity.	Three groups: 16 college tennis players, 36 male and female advanced tennis players, and 91 beginners Validity: round-robin tournament correlated with test Reliability: test-retest Objectivity: coefficient not reported, but scoring objective	63 junior high boys Validity: scores on par-3, nine-hole course correlated with test Reliability: intraclass correlation Objectivity: coefficient not reported, but scoring objective	113 college males and 99 college females Validity: instructor's ratings correlated with test Reliability: intraclass correlation Objectivity: coefficient not reported, but scoring objective
Develop the norms.	Norms provided for three groups	Norms not provided	Norms provided for beginning racquetball classes
Determine intercorrelations.	Not necessary	Not necessary	Not necessary

Source: Adapted from Hensley, L. D., East, W. B. and Stillwell, J. L., "A racquetball skills test," *Research Quarterly,* vol. 50, 1979, 114–118; Hewitt, J. E., "Hewitt's tennis achievement test," *Research Quarterly,* vol. 37, 1966, 231–237; and Schick, J. and Berg, N. G., "Indoor golf skills test for junior high school boys," *Research Quarterly for Exercise and Sport,* vol. 54, 1983, 75–78.

Test Administration Responsibilities

Do you remember taking psychomotor tests during your middle grades and senior high school physical education classes? When the students arrived for class, were the instructors prepared to administer the tests, or were they rushing to complete test preparations? Were they familiar with the test items, or did they appear to be unsure as to how the items should be administered? Did they require all students to perform the items correctly, or did they permit some students to perform the items incorrectly? Did they interpret the test results to the class, or were the students informed of the test results only through a grade? These questions illustrate the many responsibilities associated with the administration of psychomotor tests.

The administration of psychomotor tests involves pre-test, testing, and post-test responsibilities. If a test is to be effective and the purposes of testing are to be fulfilled, the responsibilities in all three areas must be completed. The following testing responsibilities are (1) appropriate for a school or nonschool environment and (2) described as if the test has more than one item. These responsibilities are basically the same, however, regardless of what type of group is tested or how many items are included in a test.

Pre-Test Responsibilities

Pre-test responsibilities include everything that is to be done before the actual testing of the students. These responsibilities must be fulfilled if all testing responsibilities are to be completed successfully. These responsibilities are as follows:

1. Develop a test schedule. Consider the days and minutes necessary for testing and the order in which the items will be administered.

2. If the entire class cannot be tested at the same time, plan an appropriate testing procedure. It may be necessary to have a class activity with which all students are familiar. While part of the group is tested, the other students can participate in the activity.

3. Provide opportunities for the students to practice the test items or activities similar to the items. Through practice, the students will know how to perform the items and know exactly what is expected during the testing. The purpose of the test also should be described.

4. Prepare the scorecards. The scorecards should be easy to follow and to use. If scorecards are not to be used, be prepared to score the results in another manner.

5. Train all test assistants, and make sure they are familiar with their responsibilities. They should know how to administer the test and be aware of all safety precautions. In addition, they should be prepared to deal with any unplanned developments that may occur during testing.

6. Know exactly how the test instructions are to be given to the group. Practice giving the instructions. If the instructions are rather involved, it may be wise to write them on paper.

7. If smaller groups are needed, plan how they are to be formed. If the absence of several students could affect your method for forming groups, plan more than one method.

8. Review all safety precautions. No one should be injured while performing the test as a result of your failure to take safety precautions.

9. Provide all necessary equipment and floor or court markings. Test the equipment for safety, and make sure that nothing on the field or court is unsafe.

Testing Responsibilities

When all pre-test responsibilities are completed, the testing responsibilities are easier to perform. The essential responsibilities are as follows:

1. Organize the group for instructions. The purpose of the test should have been discussed during a previous class meeting, but if it has not been, do so at this time.

2. Give test instructions. Always face the group and speak clearly. Do not attempt to give the instructions or demonstrate the items with your back to the group.

3. Demonstrate test items. If more appropriate, items may be demonstrated after smaller groups are formed. Whenever possible, have someone demonstrate the items while you describe them.

4. If test assistants are available, form smaller groups. The number of groups formed may depend on the number of items on the test.

5. Administer the test items. Insist that all individuals perform the items correctly. Remember that the validity and reliability of the test are affected if not all students are required to perform the items in the same way.

6. If time allows, gather the group for reaction to the test and discussion.

Post-Test Responsibilities

If the test is to have meaning to the students, the following post-test responsibilities should be completed:

1. Score all test items. Scoring the test may require the use of norms. If norms (standardized or local) are available, scoring is a simple task. If they are not available, develop your own. Whether the test is norm-referenced or criterion-referenced, you should calculate the mean, mode, median, deciles, and standard deviation of the test. These values will be useful in reporting the test results to the class and in comparing classes.

2. If you are testing for grading purposes, determine the grade for each student.

3. Interpret the test results to the students. This interpretation should be presented immediately after the test has been taken, and it should involve more than just reporting the students' grades. If some students did not perform well on the test, discuss the possible reasons with them. Discussion of a student's performance should not embarrass the student. If necessary, conduct the performance review in a private conference with the student. Also, if criterion-referenced standards are used, students will want to know how the class did as a group.

4. Prescribe the appropriate program for all students. A program for improvement should be planned for students who did not perform well on the test; students with satisfactory or better scores should be provided opportunities for improvement also.

5. Evaluate the test. Did the test fulfill your reasons for testing? Was it a learning experience for the students? Did the pre-test, testing, and post-test procedures go well? Make notes of any changes you should make in your next administration of the test.

ARE YOU ABLE TO DO THE FOLLOWING?

- Describe the proper procedures for administration of psychomotor tests.

Types of Psychomotor Tests

Historically, different types of psychomotor tests have been popular. At one time, there was much interest in measurement of an individual's **motor ability** (defined as the innate and acquired ability of an individual to perform motor skills of a general nature, exclusive of highly specialized sport or gymnastic skills). However, the measurement of motor ability is no longer popular, and its decline can be attributed to three reasons. First, many physical educators question the existence of a general motor ability; they believe that abilities are highly specific to the performance task. Second, the construct validity of motor ability test batteries has never been established. Last, a consensus does not exist on what the components of motor ability are.

During the time that motor ability testing was common, tests were designed to measure **motor capacity** (the individual's potential ability to perform motor skills) and **motor educability** (the individual's ability to learn new motor skills). These tests also are no longer popular. Rather, it appears that now many physical educators measure the physical performance components of agility, balance, cardiorespiratory endurance, flexibility, muscular strength,

---

◆ ◆ ◆ POINT OF EMPHASIS ◆ ◆ ◆

- You should fulfill these major responsibilities whenever you administer psychomotor tests. If you fail to do so, the validity, reliability, and objectivity of the tests may be affected. Never take your test administration responsibilities lightly.

and muscular endurance. Though there is no common agreement on the basic components that underlie physical performance, it cannot be disputed that individuals with poor abilities in these areas are not likely to succeed in sports and other physical activities. Tests often are used to identify these individuals so that appropriate activities may be prescribed to improve their weak abilities. In addition, physical educators employed in schools and fitness centers are measuring the components of health fitness (cardiorespiratory fitness, flexibility, muscular strength, muscular endurance, and body composition) because of the current emphasis on well-being and health fitness.

Since the early 1900s, **sports skills** measurement has been conducted in many physical education programs. Most, if not all, middle grade and high school physical education programs include the development of sports skills as a major objective. It is important that valid, reliable, and objective tests be used to measure these skills.

ARE YOU ABLE TO DO THE FOLLOWING?

- Define *motor ability, motor capacity*, and *motor educability*.

Review Problem

Select three psychomotor tests (at least one of them should have several items) described in this book and refer to the provided references for descriptions of their construction procedures. Note whether the procedures are similar to the ones described in this chapter. Also note how the validity and reliability of the tests were determined.

Chapter Review Questions

1. An athletic trainer developed a new type of equipment and test for shoulder flexibility. He or she used the equipment and test with his or her athletes, but now wishes to promote the test for use by others. What should he or she do to establish the validity and reliability of the equipment and test?

2. As a test administrator, what things should you consider to assure the validity and reliability of the test you are using?

3. As a physical education teacher, you plan to administer a health-related physical fitness test to your high school students. What are your pre-test, testing, and post-test responsibilities?

9 Agility

After completing this chapter, you should be able to

1. Define and measure *agility*.

2. State why agility should be measured.

3. Describe responsibilities after the measurement of agility and prescribe activities to improve agility.

Agility, sometimes referred to as the maneuverability of the body, is the ability to rapidly change the position and direction of the body or body parts. Heredity is a major factor in an individual's level of agility, but agility also depends on strength, speed, coordination, and dynamic balance. Many individuals are able to improve agility by increasing their ability in these areas. Agility also can be improved through direct instruction, training, and practice of agility drills.

Agility is important in all activities and sports. Individual and team sports involve quick starts and stops, rapid changes of direction, efficient footwork, and quick adjustments of the body or body parts. Individuals with good agility have a better chance of success in a physical activity than individuals with poor agility. Agility test items are usually of three types: (1) change in running direction, (2) change in body position, and (3) change in body part direction. Examples of the three types are the dodge or obstacle run (change in running direction), squat thrusts (change in body position), and a test that requires a change in the position of the hands or feet (change in body part direction). Agility tests that require only movement of the hands or feet are rarely used in physical education. Agility may be specific to an activity or a sport; you should not expect, therefore, each individual to do equally well on all agility tests.

◆◆◆ POINTS OF EMPHASIS ◆◆◆

- Most of the tests presented in chapters 9 through 17 include norms or standards. As the test administrator, you must decide if and how to use the norms and standards. In some environments, you may conclude that it is best not to use any norms or standards but to use the raw scores of test performers for comparison to future or past scores on the same test.

- Psychomotor tests that measure the same attribute (agility, balance, cardiorespiratory fitness, etc.) may vary in degree of difficulty. Which test you choose to administer will be influenced by the particular population (age and movement experience) you are measuring.

Most valid agility tests serve to identify individuals with poor agility.

Why Measure Agility?

Improvement in agility is a worthy objective in both the nonteaching and teaching environment. All physical educators should encourage children, youth, and adults to maintain an active lifestyle. Some individuals may wish to be active through recreational activities. Individuals with good agility are more likely to enjoy their recreational activities than those with poor agility. In the school environment, agility levels of students should not be used in determining grades. How much improvement in agility will occur in the amount of time spent on agility instruction in the school environment is questionable. But if agility is an important factor in the performance of sports, and if you grade sports skills, agility is graded. Agility tests are sometimes used to classify students for a particular activity or sport, but a test that measures the skill within the activity or sport should be used for classification purposes.

Agility tests are best used for diagnostic purposes, to determine which individuals have poor agility. In testing for diagnostic purposes, criterion-referenced measurement is more appropriate than norm-referenced measurement. A predetermined score should be used to place individuals into acceptable and unacceptable agility groups, and activities designed to improve agility should be prescribed for the individuals placed in the unacceptable group. It is the instructor's responsibility to determine the appropriate activities. Individuals with unacceptable agility may need strength, speed, coordination, and dynamic balance development exercises, or simple agility drills may serve the purpose, depending on the individual. After completion of the prescribed activities or drills, improvement in agility can be determined by the administration of the same agility test.

Responsibilities after Measurement

Remember the assessment responsibilities described in chapter 1. If you diagnose some students with poor agility, you should identify the problems associated with their performance and prescribe ways to improve their agility. If the agility of some students is unacceptable because they have inadequate muscular strength, prescribe the appropriate program to develop muscular strength. You also may consider ways to improve speed, coordination, and dynamic balance to aid the students. Activities for the development of agility are described at the conclusion of this chapter.

ARE YOU ABLE TO DO THE FOLLOWING?

- Define *agility* and state why it should be measured.
- Describe responsibilities after the measurement of agility.

Tests of Agility

The agility tests selected for review are practical, inexpensive to administer, and satisfactory for both sexes. Sport-specific agility tests are available through the National Strength and Conditioning Association (NSCA) and other web sites.

Objectivity coefficients and norms are not reported for all the tests. Norms can be developed to meet your specific needs. You may want to develop local norms for the tests for which norms are reported. Your primary purpose in developing norms should be to establish a criterion-referenced standard for the tests that you choose to use.

Obtaining consistency and comparability of results requires that the agility tests be performed on a nonslip surface, and all individuals should wear shoes that provide good traction. In addition, the individuals should practice

◆ ◆ ◆   POINTS OF EMPHASIS   ◆ ◆ ◆

- Other than for athletes, the development and maintenance of agility are often not emphasized in activity-fitness programs. If your professional responsibilities include the promotion of an active lifestyle, you should include activities that develop and maintain agility.

- All agility test participants must have good traction with the test surface, which is accomplished through appropriate shoes and surface.

performing the agility tests and should be familiar with the performance requirements.

■ Right-Boomerang Run
(Gates and Sheffield 1940)

Test Objective. To measure running agility.

Age Level. Ten through college age.

Equipment. Stopwatch, tape measure, a chair or similar object for center station, and four cone markers for outside points.

Validity. With the sum of T-scores for a fifteen-item agility battery as the test criterion, a validity coefficient of .72 has been reported for females. With a similar sixteen-item battery, coefficients ranging from .78 to .87 have been reported for junior high males.

Reliability. .93 for females and .92 for males.

Norms. Table 9.1 reports norms for boys in the seventh and eighth grades.

Administration and Directions. A chair is placed 17 feet from the starting line, and a cone marker is placed 15 feet on each side of the center point. On the signal "Go," the student runs to the center station, makes a quarter turn right, runs around the

TABLE 9.1 Norms in Seconds for Right-Boomerang Run for Seventh- and Eighth-Grade Males

Performance Level	Score
Above average	12.9 and below
Average (42% to 69%)	13.0 to 13.9
Below average	14.0 and above

Adapted from Johnson, B. L. and Nelson, J. K., *Practical measurements for evaluation in physical education*, 4th ed., Edina, Minn.: Burgess Publishing, 1986.

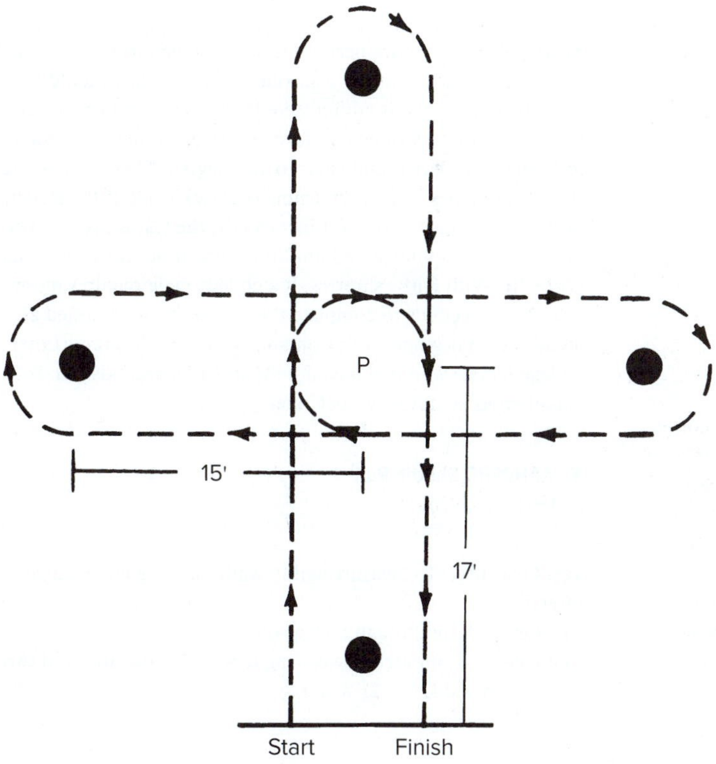

outside station and returns to the center, makes another quarter turn, and completes the course as shown in figure 9.1. The student should be instructed to run as fast as possible through the course and not to touch the chair or cones.

Scoring. The score is the time to the nearest one-tenth of a second to complete the course. A penalty of one-tenth second is deducted from the score for each time chairs or markers are touched.

FIGURE 9.1 Right-boomerang run.

■ Sidestepping
(North Carolina Motor Fitness Battery 1977)

Test Objective. To measure agility, endurance, and speed of lateral movement.

Age Level. Nine through seventeen.

Equipment. Stopwatch, measuring tape, and marking tape.

Validity. Face validity.

Reliability. Not reported.

Norms. Table 9.2 includes norms for males and females, ages nine through seventeen.

Administration and Directions. Two parallel lines are placed on the floor 12 feet apart as measured from the inside of the lines. The test performer assumes a starting position inside the lines, with one foot touching a line. On the signal "Start," the test performer (1) moves sideward with a sidestep, leading with the foot nearest the line to be approached; (2) repeats the sidestep until the foot has touched or gone beyond the line; and (3) moves to the other line in the same manner. The test performer must face the same direction at all times, must not cross his or her feet, and must not leap.

Scoring. One point is scored each time a foot touches or goes beyond a sideline. The final score is the number of times a line is touched in 30 seconds.

■ SEMO Agility Test
(Kirby 1971)

Test Objective. To measure agility while moving the body forward, backward, and sideward.

Age Level. High school and college.

Equipment. Four cone markers and a stopwatch.

Validity. .63 when correlated with the AAHPERD shuttle run test.

Reliability. .88 for high school and college males.

Objectivity. .97.

Norms. Kirby provided norms for college males.

Administration and Directions. Cones are placed in each corner of the free-throw lane of a basketball court or in the corners of a 12-by-19-foot rectangle that is on a good running surface (see figure 9.2). Beginning at point A facing the free-throw line, on the signal "Go," the test performer (1) sidesteps to outside of point B; (2) backpedals from B to D, passing inside D to be in a position facing A; (3) sprints to A, passing around the cone; (4) backpedals from A to C, passing inside C to be in a position facing B; (5) sprints to B, passing around the cone; and (6) sidesteps from B to the finish line at A.

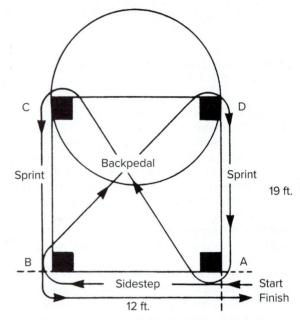

FIGURE 9.2 SEMO agility test.

Scoring. Two trials are permitted, with the better time recorded to the nearest one-tenth of a second. Practice trials should be given before the test is administered. Do not permit crossover steps when the sidestep is performed. Also, require the student to keep the back perpendicular to an imaginary line connecting the corner cones when performing the backpedal. If the student performs any part of the test incorrectly, the test is invalid. The test should be administered until the student performs one trial correctly. With Kirby's norms, if a college male requires more than 13.02 seconds to complete the course, he is classified as an advanced beginner. Johnson and Nelson (1986) report that a college female who requires more than 14.50 seconds also is classified as an advanced beginner.

■ AAHPERD Shuttle Run
(AAHPERD 1976a)

Test Objective. To measure agility while running and changing direction.

Age Level. Nine through college-age.

Equipment. Stopwatch, measuring tape, marking tape, and two blocks of wood (2″ × 2″ × 4″).

TABLE 9.2 Norms in Percentiles for Sidestep Test for Ages Nine through Seventeen

Percentile	Age								
	9	10	11	12	13	14	15	16	17
Males									
95	19	19	20	21	23	23	25	23	26
90	17	18	19	19	21	21	23	22	25
85	16	17	18		20		22	21	23
80	15		17	18	19	20	21		22
75		16					20	20	21
70			16	17	18	19			
65	14	15					19	19	20
60			15	16	17	18			
55	13	14						18	19
50				15			18		
45		14			16	17		17	18
40	12	13					17		
35			13	14	15	16			17
30	11	12					16	16	
25			12	13	14	15			16
20	10	11					15	15	15
15	9	10	11	12	13	14	14	14	14
10	8	9	10	11	11	13	13	13	12
5	7	8	8	9	10	11	11	10	10
Females									
95	18	19	21	20	20	21	21	21	21
90	16	17	18	18	19	19	20	19	20
85	15	16	17		18		19	18	
80			16	17		18	18		19
75		15			17			17	18
70	14		15	16		17	17		
65					16			16	
60		14				16			16
55	13		14	15			16		
50		13						15	
45					15				15
40	12		13	14		15	15		
35		12						14	
30	11		12	13	14				
25		11					14	14	13	14
20	10		11	12	13			12	13
15	9	10	10		12	13	13	11	
10	8	9	9	11	11	12	11	10	11
5	7	7	7	8	10	11	10	9	10

Source: Adapted from *North Carolina Motor Fitness Battery*, Raleigh, N.C.: North Carolina Department of Public Instruction, 1977.

Validity. Not reported by AAHPERD.

Reliability. Not reported by AAHPERD.

Norms. Table 9.3 provides quartile norms for ages nine through seventeen and up.

Administration and Directions. Lines are placed 30 feet apart with marking tape. The two blocks are placed adjacent to and outside of the line not being used as the starting line. On the signal "Go," the test performer (1) runs from the starting line to the blocks and picks one up, (2) returns to the starting line and places the block behind the line, (3) runs to pick up the second block, and (4) returns to the starting line and places the second block behind the line.

Scoring. Two trials are permitted. The better time to the nearest one-tenth second is accepted as the score. Rest should be allowed between trials. The student is not permitted to throw or drop the blocks. To eliminate this problem, test givers sometimes administer the test without the blocks; the student is instructed to touch behind the line.

■ **Barrow Zigzag Run**
(Barrow and McGee 1979)

Test Objective. To measure agility while running and changing direction.

Age Level. Grade seven through college. (Though this test was originally designed for males, it may be satisfactorily used with grade seven through college-age females.)

Equipment. Stopwatch and five standards that are used for high jump, volleyball, or badminton. Cones also may be used.

Validity. .74, with the total score for twenty-nine test items measuring eight factors.

Reliability. .80.

Objectivity. .99.

Norms. Table 9.4 reports norms for males in grades seven through eleven.

Administration and Directions. The course is designed as shown in figure 9.3. On the signal "Go," the test performer runs, as fast as possible, the prescribed course in a figure eight fashion for three complete laps. The standards should not be touched in any manner. If a foul is committed or the course is run improperly, the student is required to run the course again. (The validity and reliability of the test would probably be affected minimally if you required the students to run only two laps.)

Scoring. The score is the time to the nearest one-tenth second required to complete the course three times.

TABLE 9.3 Norms in Seconds for AAHPERD Shuttle Run for Ages Nine through Seventeen+

Percentile	Age							
	9–10	11	12	13	14	15	16	17+
Males								
95	10.0	9.7	9.6	9.3	8.9	8.9	8.6	8.6
75	10.6	10.4	10.2	10.0	9.6	9.4	9.3	9.2
50	11.2	10.9	10.7	10.4	10.1	9.9	9.9	9.8
25	12.0	11.5	11.4	11.0	10.7	10.4	10.5	10.4
0	17.0	20.0	22.0	16.0	18.6	14.7	15.0	15.7
Females								
95	10.2	10.0	9.9	9.9	9.7	9.9	10.0	9.6
75	11.1	10.8	10.8	10.5	10.3	10.4	10.6	10.4
50	11.8	11.5	11.4	11.2	11.0	11.0	11.2	11.1
25	12.5	12.1	12.0	12.0	12.0	11.8	12.0	12.0
0	18.0	20.0	15.3	16.5	19.2	18.5	24.9	17.0

Source: Adapted from AAHPERD, *AAHPERD youth fitness test manual*, Reston, Va.: American Alliance for Health, Physical Education, Recreation and Dance, 1976.

TABLE 9.4 Norms in Seconds for Barrow's Zigzag Run for Seventh- through Eleventh-Grade Males

	Grade				
Performance Level	7	8	9	10	11
Above average	25.2 and below	24.5 and below	24.6 and below	25.8 and below	25.8 and below
Average (T-score 45 to 55)	29.0 to 25.3	29.5 to 24.6	27.9 to 24.7	28.9 to 25.9	28.9 to 25.9
Below average	29.1 and above	29.6 and above	28.0 and above	29.0 and above	29.0 and above

Source: Adapted from Barrow, H. M. and McGee, R., *A practical approach to measurement in physical education*, 3d ed., Philadelphia: Lea & Febiger, 1979.

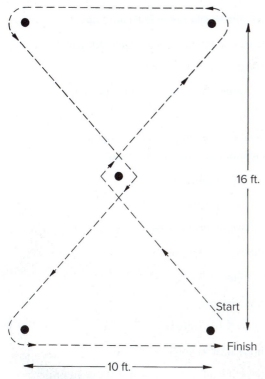

FIGURE 9.3 Barrow zigzag run.

Validity. Face validity is accepted.

Reliability. .94 (test-retest).

Norms. Baechle and Earle (2000) reported 50th percentile values for college athletes and sedentary college students. The values, however, were developed from various sample sizes and should be interpreted as descriptive, not normative.

Administration and Directions. Using adhesive tape, the hexagon is marked on the floor as shown in figure 9.4. The test performer stands in the middle of the hexagon, with the feet together, facing the front line. On the signal "Go," the test performer double-leg hops from the center of the hexagon over each side and back to the center in a continuous clockwise sequence. The hopping is continued until all six sides are jumped three times (three revolutions around the hexagon). The performer faces in the same direction throughout the test.

Scoring. The score is the time to the nearest one-tenth of the second to complete three revolutions (18 total jumps). The stopwatch is stopped when the performer lands in the center of the hexagon after the last jump. The best time of three trials is recorded as the final score. If the performer lands on the tape, loses balance and takes an extra step, or changes the original body direction, the trial is stopped and restarted. Comparison of clockwise and counterclockwise directions may be used to indicate if left and right movement abilities are imbalanced.

■ **Hexagon Test**
(Baechle and Earle 2000)

Test Objective. To measure agility while double-leg hopping in a circular manner.

Age Level. High school through adulthood.

Equipment. Stopwatch, adhesive tape, and tape measure.

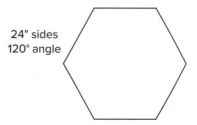

24" sides
120° angle

FIGURE 9.4 Hexagon test.

■ **T-Test**
(Semenick 1990)

Test Objective. To measure four-directional agility and body control.

Age Level. High school through adulthood.

Equipment. Stopwatch and four cones.

Validity. .42 (with hexagon test with college-aged males); .48 (with hexagon test with college-aged females).

Reliability. .98 (intraclass reliability).

Norms. Baechle and Earle (2000) report 50th percentile values for college athletes and sedentary college students. The values, however, were developed from various sample sizes and should be interpreted as descriptive, not normative.

Administration and Directions. The four cones are arranged as shown in figure 9.5. Facing forward, the test performer starts at point A. On the signal "Go," the performer, while facing forward at all times, (1) sprints to point B and touches the base of the cone with the right hand, (2) shuffles to the left 5 yards and touches the base of the cone at point C with the left hand, (3) shuffles to the right 10 yards and touches the base of the cone at point D with the right hand, (4) shuffles to the left 5 yards and touches the base of the cone at point B with the left hand, and (5) backpedals past point A. The time is recorded to the nearest one-tenth of a second when the performer passes point A.

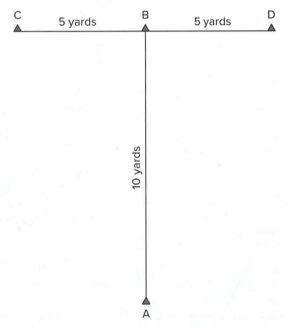

FIGURE 9.5 T-test.

Scoring. The best time of two trials is recorded as the final score. If the test performer fails to touch the base of any cone, crosses the feet when shuffling, or fails to face the front at all times, the trial is discontinued.

Activities to Develop Agility

McClenaghan and Gallahue (1978) suggest the following activities for the development of agility in young children. These activities, or modifications of them, also may be used for junior and senior high students with poor agility.

Changes in the Height of the Body in Jumps

1. Alternate jumping maximum and minimum heights.
2. Alternate fast and slow jumping.
3. Jump while tossing an object to yourself.
4. Hop on one foot.
5. Hop two to four times on one foot, then the same number of times on the other foot.
6. Jump over a stationary rope.
7. Jump over a swinging rope.
8. Jump over a turning rope.
9. Jump over a rope you are turning.
10. Jump rope with a partner.

Changes in Distance

1. Jump as far as you can.
2. Jump as near as you can.
3. Jump and land with your feet in different positions.
4. Jump backward.
5. Walk backward.
6. Run backward or sideward.
7. Leap over objects.
8. Jump different heights.
9. Jump and land lightly.
10. Jump and land on different surfaces.

Changes in Direction

1. Jump and turn (quarter, half, three-quarter, and full turn).

2. Jump forward, then sideward, then backward.

3. Jump in a circle, square, triangle, and so forth.

4. Run between chairs.

5. Run forward and change direction quickly, on command.

6. Slide sideways and change direction quickly, on command.

7. Jump over a turning rope and change your body position.

8. Move forward, sideward, or backward while jumping over a rope you are turning.

9. Run through a series of tires (laid flat on the ground).

10. Do tumbling tricks requiring your body to roll in various ways (log rolls, forward rolls, backward rolls, and so on).

Other Agility Activities

Side-Straddle Hop (Jumping Jacks). Stand erect with arms at sides and feet together; jump, spreading the legs to the side and at the same time bring the arms overhead; jump and return to starting position; attempt to perform in a smooth and continuous action. One side-straddle hop is counted each time you return to the starting position.

Heel Touch. Stand erect with hands at the sides; jump and touch both heels with the fingers. Each jump is counted as one.

Treadmill. Assume push-up position with right leg forward; keep hands in place while alternately bringing one leg forward and extending the other leg in a running position. One treadmill is counted each time the right leg is forward.

Zigzag Run. Arrange chairs in a position to provide a zigzag course; run as fast as possible in a zigzag course around the chairs.

Review Problems

1. Review additional agility tests found in other textbooks. Note the groups for whom the tests are intended and the validity, reliability, and objectivity coefficients.

2. Administer one of the tests described in this chapter to several of your fellow students. Ask them to provide constructive criticism of your test administration.

3. An elementary physical education teacher administered the ten-second squat thrust and the AAHPERD shuttle run tests to 15 ten-year-old boys. Determine the relationship of the two groups of scores. Interpret the correlation coefficient.

Student	10-Second Squat Thrust (Number)	AAHPERD Shuttle Run (Seconds)
A	7.00	9.8
B	6.50	10.8
C	5.50	11.4
D	7.50	9.6
E	5.25	12.0
F	6.50	10.4
G	6.75	10.5
H	6.00	11.0
I	5.75	11.4
J	5.00	12.5
K	6.00	11.3
L	6.75	10.3
M	5.75	11.2
N	6.50	10.7
O	5.75	11.5

Chapter Review Questions

1. What is the definition of agility? Is agility considered a health-related physical fitness component?

2. Why is it important to measure agility?

3. What are your responsibilities after you measure agility? In addition to agility drills, what other variables might individuals seek to improve to increase their agility?

10 | Balance

After completing this chapter, you should be able to

1. Define *balance, static balance,* and *dynamic balance,* and measure static and dynamic balance.

2. State why balance should be measured.

3. Describe responsibilities after the measurement of balance and prescribe activities to improve balance.

Balance is the ability to maintain equilibrium against the force of gravity. The balance center (semicircular canal) in the inner ear, the kinesthetic sense in the muscles and joints ("feel" of an activity), and visual perception contribute to balance. In certain positions, balance also is affected by strength. If the supporting muscles cannot hold the body weight, body parts, or an external weight firmly in position, balance is limited. For some individuals, increased strength results in improved balance.

Basically, there are two types of balance: **static** and **dynamic.** The recovery of balance, after the body's balance has been disturbed, may also be considered a type of balance. Static balance, the ability to maintain equilibrium while stationary, is often thought of as steadiness. Maintaining static balance requires that the person's center of gravity be over the base of support. Assuming a position to shoot a rifle, looking through a microscope, and posing for a photographer are examples of static balance.

Dynamic balance is the ability to maintain equilibrium while in motion or to move the body or parts of the body from one point to another and maintain equilibrium. Dancing, walking, driving a golf ball, and bowling are examples of dynamic balance. Static and dynamic balance are necessary for successful performance in physical activity, but the ability to recover balance is also essential in many activities. Running, kicking, hopping, dismounting from gymnastics apparatus, performing gymnastic floor exercises, and wrestling are examples of such activities. In fact, all human motion occurs as a result of the disturbance of the body's balance.

Why Measure Balance?

Balance is necessary in our usual, everyday activities. Individuals with poor balance are at a disadvantage in efficiently performing most physical activities. Also, these individuals are at a greater risk to fall and injure themselves during physical activity. Additionally, performance of any physical skill requires some degree of balance. Since balance can be improved, balance tests can be used to identify those individuals with poor balance. Activities then should be prescribed to improve their balance. However, as balance is specific to a body part or parts and may be specific to a sport or physical activity, different types of balance tests should be used for diagnostic purposes. Also, different types of activities designed to improve balance should be prescribed.

As was recommended for agility if teaching physical education, specific improvement in balance should not be used to determine grades. If balance is an important component of a physical activity, the student's performance in that activity will be affected by the degree of balance. Through the assigning of grades for performance in an activity, balance has been graded.

Responsibilities after Measurement

As with agility measurement, you may identify individuals who appear to not have the necessary strength to maintain good balance. Increasing the strength of these individuals may improve their balance. Balance also can be improved through intensive practice of activities that place individuals (1) in balanced positions that they attempt to maintain and (2) in balanced positions that help them develop a "feel" (kinesthetic sense) for such positions. Additionally, balance can be improved through activities that place individuals in a state of imbalance, forcing them to recover balance. A program that involves both strength development and a variety of balance activities may be best. You should seek to develop the program that achieves the desired results. Activities to develop balance are described at the conclusion of this chapter.

▨▨▨ **ARE YOU ABLE TO DO THE FOLLOWING?**

- Define *balance, static balance,* and *dynamic balance,* and state why static and dynamic balance should be measured?

- Describe responsibilities after the measurement of balance?

Tests of Balance

Balance tests are classified as static or dynamic. The tests reviewed are practical, inexpensive to administer, and satisfactory for both sexes. Reliability and objectivity coefficients are not available for all the tests, and, regrettably, the published norms are primarily for college-age individuals. It will be necessary to develop norms for the population with which you are working. It is recommended that balance test norms be used in the same manner as agility norms to develop criterion-referenced standards. Though not a factor in all balance tests, fatigue may influence the performance of some individuals. For this reason, it is best not to administer balance tests after any strenuous activity. So that the test performers will be familiar with the test, permit them to practice the test. Practice enables many individuals to score better.

Static Balance Tests

■ **Stork Stand**
(Johnson and Nelson 1986)

Test Objective. To measure stationary balance while the body weight is supported on the ball of the foot of the dominant leg.
Age Level. Ten through college-age.
Equipment. Stopwatch.

©David K. Miller

FIGURE 10.1   Stork stand.

Validity. Face validity.

Reliability. Coefficients of .85 and .87 have been reported using the test-retest method.

Objectivity. Johnson and Nelson (1986) report a study that found an objective coefficient of .99.

Norms. Table 10.1 reports norms for college students.

Administration and Directions. Individuals may be tested in pairs. The test performer stands on the foot of the dominant leg, places the other foot against the inside of the supporting knee, and places the hands on the hips as shown in figure 10.1. On the signal "Go," the performer raises the heel of the dominant foot from the floor and attempts to maintain balance as long as possible. The test administrator counts aloud the seconds. The partner of the test performer records the number of seconds the performer is able to maintain balance. The trial is ended when the hands are moved from the hips, when the ball of the dominant foot moves from its original position, or when the heel touches the floor. Three trials are administered.

Scoring. The best time, in seconds, of the three trials is the score. Since there is no time limit, and some individuals may be able to maintain their balance for some time, you may choose to halt the performance of those individuals who exceed the norm for above average.

Note: Modifications in the administration of this test can decrease or increase its difficulty. The participant may perform the test with the heel and ball of the foot in contact with the floor. To increase the difficulty, you may ask the participant to close the eyes, tilt the head, touch the index finger to the nose, or perform a quarter or half-squat (squats performed while weight is supported by heel and ball of foot).

FIGURE 10.2 Bass lengthwise stick test.

©David K. Miller

■ Bass Stick Test (Lengthwise)
(Bass 1939)

Test Objective. To measure stationary balance while the weight of the body is supported on a small base of support on the ball of the foot.

Age Level. Ten through college-age.

Equipment. Sticks 1″ × 1″ × 12″ (you may test one-half of the class at the same time if you have enough sticks), stopwatch, and adhesive tape.

Validity. Face validity is accepted.

Reliability. .90.

Norms. Table 10.1 reports norms for college students.

Administration and Directions. All sticks should be taped to the floor. Individuals may be tested in pairs. The test performer places a foot lengthwise on the stick (ball of the foot and heel should be in contact with the stick). On the signal "Go," the performer lifts the opposite foot from the floor, raises the heel of the dominant foot from the stick, and attempts to hold this position for a maximum of 60 seconds (see figure 10.2). The test administrator counts aloud the

TABLE 10.1 Norms in Seconds for Stork Stand, Bass Stick Test (Lengthwise), and Bass Stick Test (Crosswise) for College Students

Performance Level	Stork Stand	Bass Stick (LW)	Bass Stick (CW)
Males			
Above average	37 and above	306 and above	165 and above
Average	15 to 36	221 to 305	65 to 164
Below average	14 and below	220 and below	64 and below
Females			
Above average	23 and above	301 and above	140 and above
Average	8 to 22	206 to 300	60 to 139
Below average	7 and below	205 and below	59 and below

Source: Adapted from Johnson, B. L. and Nelson, J. K., *Practical measurements for evaluation in physical education*, 4th ed., Edina, Minn.: Burgess Publishing, 1986.

seconds while the partner of the performer records the number of seconds the performer is able to maintain balance. The trial is ended when any part of either foot touches the floor. Three trials are taken on each foot. If any performers lose their balance within the first 3 seconds of a trial, the trial is not considered an attempt.

Scoring. The score is the total time in seconds for all six trials, three on each foot.

■ Bass Stick Test (Crosswise)
(Bass 1939)

The crosswise stick test is the same as the lengthwise test except that the ball of the foot is placed crosswise on the stick. Table 10.1 includes norms for college students.

You will find additional static balance tests directly related to gymnastics performance in other measurement textbooks. Head balance, head and forearm balance, and handstands are examples of such tests.

Dynamic Balance Tests

■ Johnson Modification of the Bass Test of Dynamic Balance
(Johnson and Nelson 1986)

Test Objective. To measure the ability to maintain balance during movement and upon landing from a leap.

Age Level. High school through college.

Equipment. Stopwatch, tape measure, and floor tape.

Validity. Face validity; .46 when correlated with Bass test of dynamic balance.

Reliability. .75 using test-retest.

Objectivity. .97.

Norms. Johnson and Nelson (1986) provide norms for college women.

Administration and Directions. Eleven pieces of tape (1″ × 3/4″) are placed in the pattern shown in figure 10.3. The test performer (1) stands with the right foot placed on the starting mark; (2) leaps to the first tape mark, lands on the ball of the left foot, and attempts to hold for 5 seconds; (3) leaps to the second tape mark, lands on the ball of the right foot, and attempts to hold for 5 seconds; and (4) continues to the other tape marks, alternating feet and attempting to hold a steady position for 5 seconds. The ball of the foot must completely cover the tape. The test administrator should count aloud the seconds of each balance.

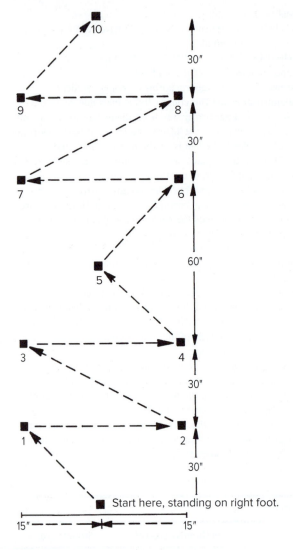

FIGURE 10.3 Floor pattern for modified Bass dynamic balance test.

Scoring. The test scoring is as follows:

1. 5 points for landing successfully on the tape mark (tape completely covered).
2. 1 point (up to 5 seconds) for each second the steady position is held on the tape marks.

A maximum of 10 points per tape mark and 100 points for the test may be earned. The test performer is penalized 5 points for any of the following landing errors:

- Failing to stop upon landing.

- Touching the floor with any part of the body other than the ball of the landing foot.
- Failing to completely cover the tape mark with the ball of the foot.

If the test performer makes a landing error, the correct balance position may be assumed and held for a maximum of 5 seconds.

If the test performer lands successfully on the tape mark but commits any of the following errors before completing the 5-second count, a penalty of 1 point is taken away:

- Touching the floor with any part of the body other than the ball of the landing foot.
- Failing to hold the landing foot steady while in the steady position.

If balance is lost, the test performer must return to the proper mark and leap to the next mark.

■ Balance Beam Walk
(Jensen and Hirst 1980)

Test Objective. To measure balance while walking on a balance beam.
Age Level. Nine through college-age.
Equipment. Regulation balance beam and stopwatch.
Validity. Face validity.

Norms. No norms reported.
Administration and Directions. Standing on one end of the beam, the test performer slowly walks the full length of the beam, pauses for 5 seconds, turns around, and walks back to the starting point. Three trials are allowed.
Scoring. Pass/fail. There is no time limit for this beam walk (the test performer walks until he or she falls), so the test could require much class time to administer. You may want to shorten the time for test administration or to increase the difficulty of the test by limiting the amount of time permitted to complete the test. The test difficulty may also be increased through the use of a 2-inch balance beam.

■ Modified Sideward Leap
(Scott and French 1959; Safrit 1986)

Test Objective. To measure the ability to maintain balance during movement and upon landing from a leap.
Age Level. Junior high through college.
Equipment. Stopwatch, tape measure, and floor tape.
Validity. Face validity.
Reliability. .66 to .88 at differing age levels.
Norms. No norms reported.
Administration and Directions. Place three 1-inch square spots in a straight line, 18 inches apart, as shown in figure 10.4.

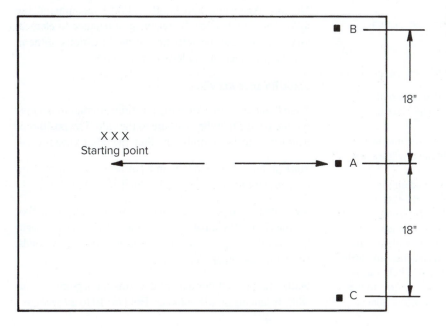

FIGURE 10.4 Floor marking for the modified sideward leap test.

Place additional spots at right angles to the line. These spots should be 3 inches apart and range in distance from spot A (24 to 40 inches) according to the height of the test performers. Three or four spots properly placed will usually cover the range in height. Place a small cork (may be the bottom of an old badminton bird) or other light object on spot B.

The test performer (1) places the left foot on mark X with the right side toward spot A (the correct spot for each individual may be determined through practice); (2) leaps sideward and lands on the ball of the right foot on spot A (the leap should require both feet to be off the floor at the same time, but it should not require extensive effort); (3) immediately leans forward and, using only one hand, pushes the cork off spot B (the floor should not be touched with either hand); and (4) holds a balanced position for 5 seconds (the position may be either forward or erect). Four trials are administered: two as in the previous text and two with the student placing the right foot on mark X, landing on the ball of the left foot, and leaning forward to spot C.

Scoring. The maximum number of points for each trial is 15:

1. 5 points for landing correctly on spot A.
2. 5 points for leaning and pushing the object off spot B or C.
3. 1 point for each second that balance is held on spot A, up to 5 seconds.

■ **Star Excursion Balance Test**
(Gribble and Hertel 2003)

Test Objective. To measure dynamic balance and postural control with a single-leg stance.
Age Level. High school through adulthood.
Equipment. Tape measure and marking tape.
Validity. Face validity.
Reliability. Hertel, Miller, and Denegar (2000) reported intratester reliability coefficients of .78 to .96 and intertester reliability coefficients of .81 to .93.
Norms. Although no norms are reported, the test may be used to determine if major differences exist in lift and right leg performances, particularly after an injury.
Administration and Directions. A grid is formed on the floor with 8 lines of tape extending out 45° from each other as shown in figure 10.5. A line length of 15" to 20" from the center should be sufficient. Placing 1/2" marks on the tape will facilitate scoring. Standing in the middle of the grid on both feet, facing anteriorly, the test performer (1) reaches anteriorly with the right foot as far as possible and makes a light touch on the line with the ball of the foot or toes; (2) returns to the double leg stance without allowing contact to affect balance;

FIGURE 10.5 Star Excursion balance test.

©David K. Miller

(3) progressing clockwise, repeats this action on each of the 8 lines. Three trials with each leg are administered. It is recommended that 5 to 6 practice trials in each direction be permitted prior to administration of the test.
Scoring. The score is the distance from the center of the grid to the point of touch with the reaching foot. The test is repeated if the performer loses balance or removes a foot from the center of the grid.

Activities to Develop Balance

Nichols, Arsenault, and Giuffre (1980) recommend the following activities for the teaching of balance to elementary students, but the activities, or modifications of them, may be practiced at any level of instruction.

Static Balance Activities

Knee Balance. In a kneeling position, attempt to balance on one knee while the arms are to the side. The position is held for 10 to 15 seconds, and then the other knee is used.

Stork Stand. While in the same position as the stork stand test, attempt to hold the position for 10 to 20 seconds.

Swan Stand. Lean forward at the hips and lift the right foot off the floor. While balancing on the left foot, lift the right leg behind as high as possible. Hold for 10 to 15 seconds. Repeat on the other foot.

V-Sit. Sit on the floor and lift the arms and legs into the air while balancing on the buttocks. Hold for 10 to 20 seconds.

Dynamic Balance Activities

Tape Line.   Tape a line on the floor, and then (1) walk forward, backward, and sideways; (2) walk while balancing a book or a beanbag on the head; and (3) run, hop, or skip in different directions.

Hopping.   Try to (1) hop over objects using the left foot and then the right, (2) hop with the eyes closed, (3) hop while holding onto different objects, or (4) hop in and out of tires.

Rug Twister.   Place a rug sample so that the rubber backing faces upward. Stand on the rug and twist back and forth to move around the floor.

Hop Leap.   Place tape marks on the floor approximately 1 yard apart. Leap from mark to mark, alternating the landing foot. Maintain a one-foot static balance on each mark for 5 seconds.

Recapturing Balance Activities

1. Jump off a low bench, landing with both feet inside a hoop.

2. Jump forward off a chair and clap the hands above the head while in midair.

3. Jump forward off a chair with one foot going forward and the other backward, and land with the legs back together.

4. Jump forward off a low bench, make a half turn in midair, and land facing the bench.

5. Jump sideways off a low bench. Jump backward.

6. Jump forward off a chair and catch a ball in midair.

The balance beam and walking boards can be used for many types of balance activities. The boards should be of different widths, heights, and inclines to provide challenges that increase in difficulty. When the students are first using the balance beam, it may be best to have it at a low height. As the students gain confidence, the height can be increased.

Review Problems

1. Review additional balance tests found in other textbooks. Note the groups for whom the tests are intended and the validity, reliability, and objectivity coefficients.

2. Administer one static balance test and one dynamic balance test described in this chapter to several of your classmates. Ask them to provide constructive criticism of your test administration.

Chapter Review Questions

1. What is the definition of balance?

2. What is the difference between static balance and dynamic balance?

3. What variable plays an important role in the ability to maintain balance?

4. Why is it important to measure balance, and what are your responsibilities after the measurement of balance?

11 | Cardiorespiratory Fitness

After completing this chapter, you should be able to

1. Define and measure cardiorespiratory fitness.

2. State why cardiorespiratory fitness should be measured.

3. Describe the purpose of pre-test/pre-activity screening, and state who should undergo medical clearance before they participate in cardiorespiratory fitness testing.

4. Describe responsibilities after the measurement of cardiorespiratory fitness, and prescribe activities and exercises to develop cardiorespiratory fitness.

Cardiorespiratory fitness is the ability to perform large muscle, whole body physical activity of moderate to high intensity for relatively long periods of time. It is the ability of the circulatory and respiratory systems to adjust to vigorous exercise and to recover from the effect of such exercise. It involves the functioning of the heart and lungs, the blood and its capacity to carry oxygen, the blood vessels and capillaries supplying blood to all parts of the body, and the muscle cells, which use the oxygen to provide the energy necessary for endurance exercise. Activities such as aerobic dance, distance running, brisk walking, swimming, bicycling, and cross-country skiing are associated with cardiorespiratory fitness. Terms such as aerobic power, aerobic fitness, cardiovascular endurance, and cardiorespiratory endurance essentially mean cardiorespiratory fitness.

Cardiorespiratory fitness indicates a high state of efficiency of the circulatory and respiratory systems in supplying oxygen to the working muscles. The more oxygen you are able to take in and utilize, the longer you are able to work (exercise) before fatigue or exhaustion occurs. Generally, the more intense the work or performance of an activity, the greater the amount of oxygen processed by the body (oxygen uptake). The greatest rate at which oxygen can be taken in and utilized during exercise is referred to as *maximal oxygen consumption* ($\dot{V}O_2max$). $\dot{V}O_2max$ is also termed maximal oxygen intake, maximal oxygen uptake, or aerobic capacity. Because oxygen consumption is related to body weight, $\dot{V}O_2max$ is usually reported as the volume of oxygen consumed per kilogram of body weight per minute of work ($mL \cdot kg^{-1} \cdot min^{-1}$). The $\dot{V}O_2max$ an individual can attain measures the effectiveness of the heart, lungs, and vascular system in delivering oxygen during heavy work and the ability of the working cells to extract it. The higher the $\dot{V}O_2max$ attained, the more effective the circulatory and respiratory systems. $\dot{V}O_2max$ in untrained college males generally ranges from 42 to 45 $mL \cdot kg^{-1} \cdot min^{-1}$ of work, whereas values for females are 3 to 4 milliliters lower at the same level of fitness. Many endurance athletes have been able to achieve values as high as 65 to 80 $mL \cdot kg^{-1} \cdot min^{-1}$.

Why Measure Cardiorespiratory Fitness?

Because flexibility, muscular strength, and muscular endurance exercises may reduce the frequency of musculoskeletal problems and other health problems, they should be included in an exercise program. However, the most important aspect of an exercise program is cardiorespiratory conditioning. Performed with the correct intensity, duration, and frequency, cardiorespiratory conditioning activities serve the following purposes:

1. Increase physical working capacity at all ages.

2. Decrease the risk of developing obesity and problems associated with obesity.

3. Decrease the risk of coronary artery disease and stroke.

4. Decrease the risk of diabetes (enhance the body's ability to use insulin).

5. Help maintain bone density (weight-bearing activity).

6. Reduce the risk of certain cancers (especially colon and breast).

7. Help reduce the symptoms of arthritis.

8. Aid in the management of both stress and depression.

9. Enable most people to feel better, physically and mentally.

These health benefits are very important. In your professional responsibilities, you should be prepared to help individuals attain them. Through measurement you can identify individuals who have poor cardiorespiratory fitness and then prescribe the appropriate activities for them. Some individuals are motivated when taking the test to adopt or to continue an active and healthful lifestyle. In addition, cardiorespiratory tests may be used to screen individuals for other activities. However, the screening test should not take the place of a medical examination, and maximal effort should not be required unless the test is conducted under proper conditions (emergency care equipment available along with personnel qualified to use it).

Cardiorespiratory fitness testing is often performed before and after participation in physical conditioning activities to measure changes in fitness. Sometimes, in the school environment, the cardiorespiratory test results may be included in the determination of a unit grade. Unless prohibited because of medical problems, all individuals can experience change in cardiorespiratory fitness through proper conditioning activities. However, if a score on a cardiorespiratory fitness test is to be used in the grading process, reasonable objectives should be stated at the beginning of the unit and an appropriate amount of time

(weeks) should be provided for the attainment of the objectives. Additionally, the grading process may be based upon fitness goals for each individual. After the administration of a pre-test, appropriate goals can be planned for each student. Students who demonstrate a high level of fitness on the pre-test should not be expected to demonstrate significant changes in their fitness scores. Students also may be asked to maintain daily records of their physical activities. Whatever grading methods are used, all students should have the opportunity for success.

The *ACSM's Health-Related Physical Fitness Assessment Manual* (American College of Sports Medicine 2018) provides further information about the benefits of cardiorespiratory fitness. Additionally, the ACSM manual is an excellent reference for measurement of all health-related physical fitness components (described in chapter 15).

Pre-Test/Pre-Activity Screening

When testing adults, it is critical that pre-testing/pre-activity screening be conducted to identify at-risk individuals. The screening may include medical clearance by a physician. The American College of Sports Medicine recommends identification of the risk factors and risk classifications for adults prior to cardiorespiratory fitness testing that are described in table 11.1.

At the very least, a screening questionnaire should be required of all adults before the administration of a cardiorespiratory fitness test. The Physical Activity Readiness Questionnaire (PAR-Q+) in figure 11.1 is widely used for this purpose. The *ACSM's Health-Related Physical Fitness Assessment Manual* (2018) and *CSEP-Physical Activity Training for Health* (CSEP-PATH) (2013) also include screening resources. Screening questionnaires serve to prevent individuals from participating in physical tests and activities that may be too strenuous for them and may indicate the need of physician supervision for any type of cardiorespiratory fitness testing. Certainly, all individuals with symptoms of cardiopulmonary disease or known cardiopulmonary disease should be tested only with physician supervision. As a test administrator, you should recognize that good judgment may mean the postponement of cardiorespiratory fitness testing when the influence of any of the test variables could jeopardize the health of the test performer.

TABLE 11.1 Risk Factors and Classification for Cardiovascular Disease (CVD)

Positive Risk Factor	Defining Criteria
Age	Male ≥45 yr; Female ≥55 yr
Family history	Father or brother with CVD before 55 yr of age; mother or sister with CVD before 65 yr of age
Cigarette smoking	Current smoker or quit within previous 6 months
Sedentary lifestyle	Not exercised for at least 30 minutes at moderate intensity on at least 3 days/week for previous 3 months
Obesity	BMI ≥30 (Male and female) or male waist girth >40 in.; female waist girth >35 in.
Hypertension	Systolic blood pressure ≥140 mm Hg and/or diastolic blood pressure ≥90 mm Hg
Dyslipidemia	LDL ≥130 mg/dl or HDL <40 mg/dl or total cholesterol ≥200 mg/dl
Prediabetes	Fasting plasma glucose ≥100 mg/dl
Risk Classification	
Low risk	No CVD symptoms (asymptomatic) and no more than one risk factor confirmed
Moderate risk	Asymptomatic and two or more risk factors confirmed
High risk	Symptomatic and known cardiovascular, pulmonary, or metabolic disease

Source: Adapted from ACSM, *ACSM's health-related physical fitness assessment manual,* Philadelphia: Wolters Kluwer Health, 2010.

Responsibilities after Measurement

After completion of the measurement process, the appropriate cardiorespiratory fitness program should be prescribed for all individuals. The selection of a cardiorespiratory fitness program for a group often is determined by the facilities and equipment available. In the school environment, students usually must participate in the same program. When possible, however, every effort should be made to individualize the students' programs. The intensity level usually will not be the same for every student tested, and students with a high level of fitness probably will need less monitoring or guidance than students with low fitness. As a teacher, you also may consider the use of activity journals in which the students record their daily physical activities. Upon review of the students' journals, appropriate recommendations regarding their physical activities can be made. Guidelines for the development of cardiorespiratory fitness are described at the conclusion of this chapter.

▬▬ ARE YOU ABLE TO DO THE FOLLOWING?

- Define *cardiorespiratory fitness* and state why it should be measured.

- Describe the purpose of pre-test/pre-activity screening, and state who should undergo medical clearance before they participate in cardiorespiratory fitness testing.

- Describe responsibilities after the measurement of cardiorespiratory fitness.

◆ ◆ ◆   **POINT OF EMPHASIS**   ◆ ◆ ◆

- In choosing which cardiorespiratory test to administer to a group, you should always consider the criteria of a good test described in chapter 5. You also must consider other factors. For example, some individuals may truly dislike running or be prohibited from weight-bearing activities because of joint problems. Also, some individuals may be such inefficient swimmers that they perform poorly on swimming tests. It is not practical to administer several different tests to members of a group, but you should seek to use a test that best meets the abilities and interests of all the members of the group.

2018 PAR-Q+

The Physical Activity Readiness Questionnaire for Everyone

The health benefits of regular physical activity are clear; more people should engage in physical activity every day of the week. Participating in physical activity is very safe for MOST people. This questionnaire will tell you whether it is necessary for you to seek further advice from your doctor OR a qualified exercise professional before becoming more physically active.

GENERAL HEALTH QUESTIONS

Please read the 7 questions below carefully and answer each one honestly: check YES or NO.	YES	NO
1) Has your doctor ever said that you have a heart condition ☐ OR high blood pressure ☐ ?	☐	☐
2) Do you feel pain in your chest at rest, during your daily activities of living, **OR** when you do physical activity?	☐	☐
3) Do you lose balance because of dizziness **OR** have you lost consciousness in the last 12 months? Please answer **NO** if your dizziness was associated with over-breathing (including during vigorous exercise).	☐	☐
4) Have you ever been diagnosed with another chronic medical condition (other than heart disease or high blood pressure)? **PLEASE LIST CONDITION(S) HERE:** _____	☐	☐
5) Are you currently taking prescribed medications for a chronic medical condition? **PLEASE LIST CONDITION(S) AND MEDICATIONS HERE:** _____	☐	☐
6) Do you currently have (or have had within the past 12 months) a bone, joint, or soft tissue (muscle, ligament, or tendon) problem that could be made worse by becoming more physically active? Please answer **NO** if you had a problem in the past, but it *does not limit your current ability* to be physically active. **PLEASE LIST CONDITION(S) HERE:** _____	☐	☐
7) Has your doctor ever said that you should only do medically supervised physical activity?	☐	☐

☑ **If you answered NO to all of the questions above, you are cleared for physical activity.**
Please sign the PARTICIPANT DECLARATION. You do not need to complete Pages 2 and 3.

- ▶ Start becoming much more physically active – start slowly and build up gradually.
- ▶ Follow International Physical Activity Guidelines for your age (www.who.int/dietphysicalactivity/en/).
- ▶ You may take part in a health and fitness appraisal.
- ▶ If you are over the age of 45 yr and NOT accustomed to regular vigorous to maximal effort exercise, consult a qualified exercise professional before engaging in this intensity of exercise.
- ▶ If you have any further questions, contact a qualified exercise professional.

PARTICIPANT DECLARATION
If you are less than the legal age required for consent or require the assent of a care provider, your parent, guardian or care provider must also sign this form.

I, the undersigned, have read, understood to my full satisfaction and completed this questionnaire. I acknowledge that this physical activity clearance is valid for a maximum of 12 months from the date it is completed and becomes invalid if my condition changes. I also acknowledge that the community/fitness centre may retain a copy of this form for records. In these instances, it will maintain the confidentiality of the same, complying with applicable law.

NAME _____ DATE _____

SIGNATURE _____ WITNESS _____

SIGNATURE OF PARENT/GUARDIAN/CARE PROVIDER _____

⬤ **If you answered YES to one or more of the questions above, COMPLETE PAGES 2 AND 3.**

⚠ **Delay becoming more active if:**

- ✓ You have a temporary illness such as a cold or fever; it is best to wait until you feel better.
- ✓ You are pregnant - talk to your health care practitioner, your physician, a qualified exercise professional, and/or complete the ePARmed-X+ at **www.eparmedx.com** before becoming more physically active.
- ✓ Your health changes - answer the questions on Pages 2 and 3 of this document and/or talk to your doctor or a qualified exercise professional before continuing with any physical activity program.

FIGURE 11.1 The Physical Activity Readiness Questionnaire (PAR-Q+).
(Courtesy of the Canadian Society for Exercise Physiology.)

Warburton DER, Jamnik VK, Bredin SSD, and Gledhill N on behalf of the PAR-Q+ Collaboration. The Physical Activity Readiness Questionnaire for Everyone (PAR-Q+) and Electronic Physical Activity Readiness Medical Examination (ePARmed-X+). *Health & Fitness Journal of Canada* 4(2):3–23, 2011. ©2018 PAR-Q+ Collaboration. Used with permission

2018 PAR-Q+

FOLLOW-UP QUESTIONS ABOUT YOUR MEDICAL CONDITION(S)

1.   Do you have Arthritis, Osteoporosis, or Back Problems?

If the above condition(s) is/are present, answer questions 1a-1c   If **NO** ☐ go to question 2

1a.	Do you have difficulty controlling your condition with medications or other physician-prescribed therapies? (Answer **NO** if you are not currently taking medications or other treatments)	YES ☐ NO ☐
1b.	Do you have joint problems causing pain, a recent fracture or fracture caused by osteoporosis or cancer, displaced vertebra (e.g., spondylolisthesis), and/or spondylolysis/pars defect (a crack in the bony ring on the back of the spinal column)?	YES ☐ NO ☐
1c.	Have you had steroid injections or taken steroid tablets regularly for more than 3 months?	YES ☐ NO ☐

2.   Do you currently have Cancer of any kind?

If the above condition(s) is/are present, answer questions 2a-2b   If **NO** ☐ go to question 3

2a.	Does your cancer diagnosis include any of the following types: lung/bronchogenic, multiple myeloma (cancer of plasma cells), head, and/or neck?	YES ☐ NO ☐
2b.	Are you currently receiving cancer therapy (such as chemotheraphy or radiotherapy)?	YES ☐ NO ☐

3.   Do you have a Heart or Cardiovascular Condition? *This includes Coronary Artery Disease, Heart Failure, Diagnosed Abnormality of Heart Rhythm*

If the above condition(s) is/are present, answer questions 3a-3d   If **NO** ☐ go to question 4

3a.	Do you have difficulty controlling your condition with medications or other physician-prescribed therapies? (Answer **NO** if you are not currently taking medications or other treatments)	YES ☐ NO ☐
3b.	Do you have an irregular heart beat that requires medical management? (e.g., atrial fibrillation, premature ventricular contraction)	YES ☐ NO ☐
3c.	Do you have chronic heart failure?	YES ☐ NO ☐
3d.	Do you have diagnosed coronary artery (cardiovascular) disease and have not participated in regular physical activity in the last 2 months?	YES ☐ NO ☐

4.   Do you have High Blood Pressure?

If the above condition(s) is/are present, answer questions 4a-4b   If **NO** ☐ go to question 5

4a.	Do you have difficulty controlling your condition with medications or other physician-prescribed therapies? (Answer **NO** if you are not currently taking medications or other treatments)	YES ☐ NO ☐
4b.	Do you have a resting blood pressure equal to or greater than 160/90 mmHg with or without medication? (Answer **YES** if you do not know your resting blood pressure)	YES ☐ NO ☐

5.   Do you have any Metabolic Conditions? *This includes Type 1 Diabetes, Type 2 Diabetes, Pre-Diabetes*

If the above condition(s) is/are present, answer questions 5a-5e   If **NO** ☐ go to question 6

5a.	Do you often have difficulty controlling your blood sugar levels with foods, medications, or other physician-prescribed therapies?	YES ☐ NO ☐
5b.	Do you often suffer from signs and symptoms of low blood sugar (hypoglycemia) following exercise and/or during activities of daily living? Signs of hypoglycemia may include shakiness, nervousness, unusual irritability, abnormal sweating, dizziness or light-headedness, mental confusion, difficulty speaking, weakness, or sleepiness.	YES ☐ NO ☐
5c.	Do you have any signs or symptoms of diabetes complications such as heart or vascular disease and/or complications affecting your eyes, kidneys, **OR** the sensation in your toes and feet?	YES ☐ NO ☐
5d.	Do you have other metabolic conditions (such as current pregnancy-related diabetes, chronic kidney disease, or liver problems)?	YES ☐ NO ☐
5e.	Are you planning to engage in what for you is unusually high (or vigorous) intensity exercise in the near future?	YES ☐ NO ☐

FIGURE 11.1   The Physical Activity Readiness Questionnaire (PAR-Q+). (*continued*)

2018 PAR-Q+

6. **Do you have any Mental Health Problems or Learning Difficulties?** *This includes Alzheimer's, Dementia, Depression, Anxiety Disorder, Eating Disorder, Psychotic Disorder, Intellectual Disability, Down Syndrome*

If the above condition(s) is/are present, answer questions 6a-6b   If **NO** ☐ go to question 7

6a.	Do you have difficulty controlling your condition with medications or other physician-prescribed therapies? (Answer **NO** if you are not currently taking medications or other treatments)	YES ☐ NO ☐
6b.	Do you have Down Syndrome **AND** back problems affecting nerves or muscles?	YES ☐ NO ☐

7. **Do you have a Respiratory Disease?** *This includes Chronic Obstructive Pulmonary Disease, Asthma, Pulmonary High Blood Pressure*

If the above condition(s) is/are present, answer questions 7a-7d   If **NO** ☐ go to question 8

7a.	Do you have difficulty controlling your condition with medications or other physician-prescribed therapies? (Answer **NO** if you are not currently taking medications or other treatments)	YES ☐ NO ☐
7b.	Has your doctor ever said your blood oxygen level is low at rest or during exercise and/or that you require supplemental oxygen therapy?	YES ☐ NO ☐
7c.	If asthmatic, do you currently have symptoms of chest tightness, wheezing, laboured breathing, consistent cough (more than 2 days/week), or have you used your rescue medication more than twice in the last week?	YES ☐ NO ☐
7d.	Has your doctor ever said you have high blood pressure in the blood vessels of your lungs?	YES ☐ NO ☐

8. **Do you have a Spinal Cord Injury?** *This includes Tetraplegia and Paraplegia*

If the above condition(s) is/are present, answer questions 8a-8c   If **NO** ☐ go to question 9

8a.	Do you have difficulty controlling your condition with medications or other physician-prescribed therapies? (Answer **NO** if you are not currently taking medications or other treatments)	YES ☐ NO ☐
8b.	Do you commonly exhibit low resting blood pressure significant enough to cause dizziness, light-headedness, and/or fainting?	YES ☐ NO ☐
8c.	Has your physician indicated that you exhibit sudden bouts of high blood pressure (known as Autonomic Dysrefiexia)?	YES ☐ NO ☐

9. **Have you had a Stroke?** *This includes Transient Ischemic Attack (TIA) or Cerebrovascular Event*

If the above condition(s) is/are present, answer questions 9a-9c   If **NO** ☐ go to question 10

9a.	Do you have difficulty controlling your condition with medications or other physician-prescribed therapies? (Answer **NO** if you are not currently taking medications or other treatments)	YES ☐ NO ☐
9b.	Do you have any impairment in walking or mobility?	YES ☐ NO ☐
9c.	Have you experienced a stroke or impairment in nerves or muscles in the past 6 months?	YES ☐ NO ☐

10. **Do you have any other medical condition not listed above or do you have two or more medical conditions?**

If you have other medical conditions, answer questions 10a-10c   If **NO** ☐ read the Page 4 recommendations

10a.	Have you experienced a blackout, fainted, or lost consciousness as a result of a head injury within the last 12 months **OR** have you had a diagnosed concussion within the last 12 months?	YES ☐ NO ☐
10b.	Do you have a medical condition that is not listed (such as epilepsy, neurological conditions, kidney problems)?	YES ☐ NO ☐
10c.	Do you currently live with two or more medical conditions?	YES ☐ NO ☐

PLEASE LIST YOUR MEDICAL CONDITION(S) AND ANY RELATED MEDICATIONS HERE: _____

_____

GO to Page 4 for recommendations about your current medical condition(s) and sign the PARTICIPANT DECLARATION.

FIGURE 11.1 The Physical Activity Readiness Questionnaire (PAR-Q+). *(continued)*

2018 PAR-Q+

☑ **If you answered NO to all of the FOLLOW-UP questions (pgs. 2-3) about your medical condition, you are ready to become more physically active - sign the PARTICIPANT DECLARATION below:**

▶ It is advised that you consult a qualified exercise professional to help you develop a safe and effective physical activity plan to meet your health needs.

▶ You are encouraged to start slowly and build up gradually - 20 to 60 minutes of low to moderate intensity exercise, 3-5 days per week including aerobic and muscle strengthening exercises.

▶ As you progress, you should aim to accumulate 150 minutes or more of moderate intensity physical activity per week.

▶ If you are over the age of 45 yr and **NOT** accustomed to regular vigorous to maximal effort exercise, consult a qualified exercise professional before engaging in this intensity of exercise.

◯ **If you answered YES to one or more of the follow-up questions about your medical condition:**

You should seek further information before becoming more physically active or engaging in a fitness appraisal. You should complete the specially designed online screening and exercise recommendations program - the **ePARmed-X+ at www.eparmedx.com** and/or visit a qualified exercise professional to work through the ePARmed-X+ and for further information.

⚠ **Delay becoming more active if:**

✓ You have a temporary illness such as a cold or fever; it is best to wait until you feel better.

✓ You are pregnant - talk to your health care practitioner, your physician, a qualified exercise professional, and/or complete the ePARmed-X+**at www.eparmedx.com** before becoming more physically active.

✓ Your health changes - talk to your doctor or qualified exercise professional before continuing with any physical activity program.

● You are encouraged to photocopy the PAR-Q+. You must use the entire questionnaire and NO changes are permitted.
● The authors, the PAR-Q+ Collaboration, partner organizations, and their agents assume no liability for persons who undertake physical activity and/or make use of the PAR-Q+ or ePARmed-X+. If in doubt after completing the questionnaire, consult your doctor prior to physical activity.

PARTICIPANT DECLARATION

● All persons who have completed the PAR-Q+ please read and sign the declaration below.

● If you are less than the legal age required for consent or require the assent of a care provider, your parent, guardian or care provider must also sign this form.

I, the undersigned, have read, understood to my full satisfaction and completed this questionnaire. I acknowledge that this physical activity clearance is valid for a maximum of 12 months from the date it is completed and becomes invalid if my condition changes. I also acknowledge that the community/fitness center may retain a copy of this form for records. In these instances, it will maintain the confidentiality of the same, complying with applicable law.

NAME _____   DATE _____

SIGNATURE _____   WITNESS _____

SIGNATURE OF PARENT/GUARDIAN/CARE PROVIDER _____

─── For more information, please contact ───
www.eparmedx.com
Email: eparmedx@gmail.com

Citation for PAR-Q+
Warburton DER, Jamnik VK, Bredin SSD, and Gledhill N on behalf of the PAR-Q+ Collaboration. The Physical Activity Readiness Questionnaire for Everyone (PAR-Q+) and Electronic Physical Activity Readiness Medical Examination (ePARmed-X+). Health & Fitness Journal of Canada 4(2):3-23, 2011.

Key References
1. Jamnik VK, Warburton DER, Makarski J, McKenzie DC, Shephard RJ, Stone J, and Gledhill N. Enhancing the effectiveness of clearance for physical activity participation; background and overall process. APNM 36(S1):S3-S13, 2011.
2. Warburton DER, Gledhill N, Jamnik VK, Bredin SSD, McKenzie DC, Stone J, Charlesworth S, and Shephard RJ. Evidence-based risk assessment and recommendations for physical activity clearance; Consensus Document. APNM 36(S1):S266-s298, 2011.
3. Chisholm DM, Collis ML, Kulak LL, Davenport W, and Gruber N. Physical activity readiness. British Columbia Medical Journal. 1975;17:375-378.
4. Thomas S, Reading J, and Shephard RJ. Revision of the Physical Activity Readiness Questionnaire (PAR-Q). Canadian Journal of Sport Science 1992;17:4 338-345.

The PAR-Q+ was created using the evidence-based AGREE process (1) by the PAR-Q+ Collaboration chaired by Dr. Darren E. R. Warburton with Dr. Norman Gledhill, Dr. Veronica Jamnik, and Dr. Donald C. McKenzie (2). Production of this document has been made possible through financial contributions from the Public Health Agency of Canada and the BC Ministry of Health Services. The views expressed herein do not necessarily represent the views of the Public Health Agency of Canada or the BC Ministry of Health Services.

Copyright © 2018 PAR-Q+ Collaboration 4 / 4
01-11-2017

FIGURE 11.1   The Physical Activity Readiness Questionnaire (PAR-Q+). (*continued*)

Tests of Cardiorespiratory Fitness

The best single measure of cardiorespiratory fitness is $\dot{V}O_2max$, but performing this measurement requires expensive equipment (a treadmill or bicycle ergometer and expired gas analysis equipment) and trained personnel. Because of these requirements, $\dot{V}O_2max$ tests are rarely performed in physical education classes and in other environments only by certified individuals. Exercise physiology classes provide more detailed instructions about laboratory methods used to determine $\dot{V}O_2max$. Cardiorespiratory fitness tests that require inexpensive equipment and that can be administered to large groups are presented here. However, validity, reliability, and objectivity coefficients are not available for all the tests presented.

Because oxygen consumption has a direct linear relationship to heart rate, cardiorespiratory fitness can be estimated by measurement of the heart rate during and after testing. Though electronic measurement of the heart rate is preferred for accuracy, it is not practical or feasible in the testing of groups. In group testing, the heart rate is usually measured by counting the pulse rate at the radial artery in the wrist or at the carotid artery in the neck (lightly place the first two fingers at these sites). Because counting errors affect the validity of the test, it is essential that those individuals who are responsible for counting the pulse rate practice the procedure several times before the test is administered. Running tests (the timing of running a specified distance or the distance an individual can run in a stated time) are also highly correlated with maximum oxygen consumption. Scoring accuracy is greater with running tests, since it is necessary only to count the number of laps around a particular course or to record the time for running a specified distance.

Regardless of the type of cardiorespiratory test administered, many variables can influence cardiorespiratory functions. It has been found that exercise, age, gender, environmental temperature, humidity, altitude, digestion, loss of sleep, changes in body position, emotional and nervous conditions, body fat level, running efficiency, and motivation can influence cardiorespiratory fitness testing. It is not possible to control all of these variables, but you should be aware of them and recognize their influence on the tests.

In addition to the tests presented in this chapter, other cardiorespiratory fitness tests and norms are included as components of health-related physical fitness and skill-related physical fitness tests in chapter 15. If you choose to do so, you may administer any of these cardiorespiratory tests independent of the other test items.

■ 12-Minute and 9-Minute Runs
(AAHPERD 1980a)

Test Objective. To measure cardiorespiratory fitness.
Age Level. Grade 7 through adult for 12-minute run and ages five to college-age for 9-minute run.
Equipment. A stopwatch, a whistle, and any flat, measured area. Sharp turns usually slow the runner, so it is best if the running course does not have them. If sharp turns are unavoidable, however, do not compare the running times for the curvy course with running times for a course that has no sharp turns. Different norms should be prepared for the course with sharp turns.
Validity. A validity coefficient of .90 has been reported when maximum oxygen consumption was used as the criterion.
Reliability. When the test-retest method was used, a coefficient of .94 was reported.
Norms. Tables 11.2 and 11.3 report norms for the 12-minute run and table 11.4 reports norms for the 9-minute run.
Administration and Directions. All test performers should practice distance running and understand the advantage of maintaining a constant pace before attempting the test. The runners should be motivated to give their best effort, or the validity of the test will be affected. The running course should be marked so that the test administrator can determine with ease and promptness the exact distance in yards covered by the runner. Placing markers every 10 to 25 yards facilitates the scoring process. In addition, assigning a spotter to each runner makes the scoring process more efficient. After the test performers have warmed up, they gather behind a line, and on the starting signal, they run (walking is permitted) as many laps as possible around the course. The spotters count the number of laps for the runners, and when the signal (whistle) to stop is given, they run to the spots of the runners. The runners should be instructed to keep moving until they have cooled down.
Scoring. Both runs are scored to the nearest 10 yards. The importance of accurate counting of laps should be emphasized to the spotters.

TABLE 11.2   Norms for 12-Minute Run (Yards) and 1.5-Mile Run (Minutes and Seconds) for Ages Thirteen through Eighteen

Percentile	Males		Females	
	12-Minute Run (Yards)	1.5-Mile Run (Time)	12-Minute Run (Yards)	1.5-Mile Run (Time)
95	3,297	8:37	2,448	12:17
75	2,879	10:19	2,100	15:03
50	2,592	11:29	1,861	16:57
25	2,305	12:39	1,622	18:50
5	1,888	14:20	1,274	21:36

Source: Adapted from AAHPERD, *AAHPERD youth fitness test manual,* Reston, Va.: American Alliance for Health, Physical Education, Recreation and Dance, 1976.

■ **1-Mile and 1.5-Mile Runs**
(AAHPERD 1976a, 1980a)

Test Objective. To measure cardiorespiratory fitness.
Age Level. Five through adult for 1-mile run and thirteen through adult for 1.5-mile run.
Equipment. A stopwatch and a flat, measured area.
Validity and Reliability. Both runs are valid tests because they are related to maximum oxygen consumption. As do other similar tests, these runs have acceptable reliability when administered to properly prepared performers.
Norms. Table 11.5 reports norms for the 1-mile run, and tables 11.2 and 11.3 report norms for the 1.5-mile run.
Administration and Directions. Again, all performers should practice distance running and understand the advantage of maintaining a constant pace before attempting the test. Assigning a partner, or spotter, to each runner aids in the recording of the scores. After the runners have warmed up, they gather behind a starting line, and on the signal to start, they run (walking is permitted) the distance as fast as possible. The partner of each runner is at the finish line and records the test time of the runner. The test administrator calls out the times as the runners cross the finish line.
Scoring. The score is the time in minutes and seconds to complete the run.

■ **Steady-State Jog or Continuous Movement**
(American Health and Fitness Foundation 1986)

Test Objective. To measure cardiorespiratory fitness.
Age Level. Grades K through 12.
Equipment. Flat running surface and stopwatch.

Validity. Face validity.
Reliability. Not reported.
Norms. Table 11.6 reports criterion-reference standards.
Administration and Directions. Students in grades K–1 and grades 2–3 are instructed to jog or move continuously for 12 minutes and 15 minutes, respectively. Students in grades 4–12 are instructed to jog at a steady pace for 20 minutes. The goal is to meet the criterion-reference standard if possible. If students in grades 4–12 can attain the criterion-reference standard by walking rapidly, or by a combination of walking and running, it is acceptable.
Scoring. The distance covered is recorded to the nearest 1/10 mile.

■ **1-Mile Walk**
(Kline et al. 1987; Rippe 1991)

Test Objective. To measure cardiorespiratory fitness through walking.
Age Level. Twenty through sixty-plus.
Validity. Coefficients of .79 for ages 20–29 and .92 for ages 30–69 have been reported.
Reliability. A coefficient of .98 was found for ages 30–69 years.
Equipment. A flat, measured surface and a stopwatch.
Norms. Fitness level charts for gender and age groups are provided in figure 11.2. The charts are based on weights of 170 pounds for men and 125 pounds for women. If the test taker weighs substantially less, his or her relative cardiorespiratory fitness level will be slightly underestimated. If the test taker weighs substantially more, his or her cardiorespiratory fitness will be slightly overestimated.
Administration and Directions. All test performers should practice counting their pulse at the radial or carotid artery before

TABLE 11.3 Norms for 12-Minute Run (Yards) and 1.5-Mile Run (Minutes and Seconds) for Ages Twenty through Seventy-Nine

Males

Age

Percentile	20–29		30–39		40–49	
	12-Minute Run (Yards)	1.5 Mile Run (Time)	12-Minute Run (Yards)	1.5Mile Run (Time)	12-Minute Run (Yards)	1.5 Mile Run (Time)
95	3,274	9:17	3,203	9:33	3,115	9:51
75	2,922	10:43	2,851	11:06	2,746	11:40
50	2,693	11:58	2,622	12:24	2,517	13:12
25	2,482	13:36	2,394	14:05	2,306	14:43
5	2,112	17:04	2,077	17:25	1,989	18:48

Age

Percentile	50–59		60–69		70–79	
	12-Minute Run (Yards)	1.5 Mile Run (Time)	12-Minute Run (Yards)	1.5 Mile Run (Time)	12-Minute Run (Yards)	1.5 Mile Run (Time)
95	2,957	10:37	2,798	11:26	2,693	11:58
75	2,605	12:36	2,429	13:52	2,270	15:14
50	2,358	14:23	2,200	15:56	2,059	17:38
25	2,165	16:28	1,989	18:33	1,866	20:36
5	1,866	20:38	1,707	24:03	1,566	27:58

Females

Age

Percentile	20–29		30–39		40–49	
	12-Minute Run (Yards)	1.5 Mile Run (Time)	12-Minute Run (Yards)	1.5 Mile Run (Time)	12-Minute Run (Yards)	1.5 Mile Run (Time)
95	2,974	10:28	2,869	11:00	2,763	11:33
75	2,622	12:24	2,552	12:53	2,446	13:45
50	2,411	14:04	2,341	14:34	2,235	15:34
25	2,165	16:21	2,112	16:56	2,024	18:05
5	1,901	20:03	1,813	21:34	1,778	22:22

Age

Percentile	50–59		60–69		70–79	
	12-Minute Run (Yards)	1.5 Mile Run (Time)	12-Minute Run (Yards)	1.5 Mile Run (Time)	12-Minute Run (Yards)	1.5 Mile Run (Time)
95	2,552	12:53	2,394	14:05	2,376	14:21
75	2,270	15:13	2,130	16:46	2,006	18:21
50	2,094	15:34	1,971	19:04	1,901	20:02
25	1,918	18:05	1,883	22:21	1,742	23:20
5	1,672	22:22	1,619	26:19	1,514	30:00

Source: Adapted from American College of Sports Medicine, *ACSM's health-related physical fitness assessment manual,* 5th ed., Philadelphia: Wolters Kluwer, 2018.

TABLE 11.4 Norms in Yards for 9-Minute Run for Ages Five through College-Age

Percentile	Age													College
	5	6	7	8	9	10	11	12	13	14	15	16	17+	
Males														
95	1,760	1,750	2,020	2,200	2,175	2,250	2,250	2,400	2,402	2,473	2,544	2,615	2,615	2,640
75	1,320	1,469	1,683	1,810	1,835	1,910	1,925	1,975	2,096	2,167	2,238	2,309	2,380	2,349
50	1,170	1,280	1,440	1,595	1,660	1,690	1,725	1,760	1,885	1,956	2,027	2,098	2,169	2,200
25	990	1,090	1,243	1,380	1,440	1,487	1,540	1,500	1,674	1,745	1,816	1,887	1,958	1,945
5	600	816	990	1,053	1,104	1,110	1,170	1,000	1,368	1,439	1,510	1,581	1,652	1,652
Females														
95	1,540	1,700	1,900	1,860	2,050	2,067	2,000	2,175	2,085	2,123	2,161	2,199	2,237	2,230
75	1,300	1,440	1,540	1,540	1,650	1,650	1,723	1,760	1,785	1,823	1,861	1,899	1,937	1,870
50	1,140	1,208	1,344	1,358	1,425	1,460	1,480	1,590	1,577	1,615	1,653	1,691	1,729	1,755
25	950	1,017	1,150	1,225	1,243	1,250	1,345	1,356	1,369	1,407	1,445	1,483	1,521	1,460
5	700	750	860	970	960	940	904	1,000	1,069	1,107	1,145	1,183	1,221	1,101

Source: Adapted from *AAHPERD health related physical fitness test manual*, Reston, Va.: American Alliance for Health, Physical Education, Recreation and Dance, 1980; and R. R. Pate, Norms for college students: Health related physical fitness test, Reston, Va.: AAHPERD, 1985.

TABLE 11.5 Norms in Minutes and Seconds for 1-Mile Run for Ages Five through College-Age

Percentile	5	6	7	8	9	10	11	12	13	14	15	16	17+	College
						Males								
95	9:02	9:06	8:06	7:58	7:17	6:56	6:50	6:27	6:11	5:51	6:01	5:48	6:01	5:30
75	11:32	10:55	9:37	9:14	8:36	8:10	8:00	7:24	6:52	6:36	6:35	6:28	6:36	6:12
50	13:46	12:29	11:25	11:00	9:56	9:19	9:06	8:20	7:27	7:10	7:14	7:11	7:25	6:49
25	16:05	15:10	14:02	13:29	12:00	11:05	11:31	10:00	8:35	8:02	8:04	8:07	8:26	7:32
5	18:25	17:38	17:17	16:19	15:44	14:28	15:25	13:41	10:23	10:32	10:37	10:40	10:56	9:47
						Females								
95	9:45	9:18	8:48	8:45	8:24	7:59	7:46	7:26	7:10	7:18	7:39	7:07	7:26	7:02
75	13:09	11:24	10:55	10:35	9:58	9:30	9:12	8:36	8:18	8:13	8:42	9:00	9:03	8:15
50	15:08	13:48	12:30	12:00	11:12	11:06	10:27	9:47	9:27	9:35	10:05	10:45	9:47	9:22
25	17:59	15:27	14:30	14:16	13:18	12:54	12:10	11:35	10:56	11:43	12:21	13:00	11:28	10:41
5	19:00	18:50	17:44	16:58	16:42	17:00	16:56	14:46	14:55	16:59	16:22	15:30	15:24	12:43

Source: Adapted from *AAHPERD health related physical fitness test manual*, Reston, Va.: American Alliance for Health, Physical Education, Recreation and Dance, 1980; and R. R. Pate, Norms for college students: Health related physical fitness test, Reston, Va.: AAHPERD, 1985.

TABLE 11.6 Steady-State Jog or Continuous Movement

Grade	Criterion-Reference Standard
K–1	12-minute jog or 12-minute continuous activity
2–3	15-minute jog or 15-minute continuous activity
4	1.8 miles
5	2.0 miles
6	2.2 miles
7–12	2.4 miles

Source: Adapted from *FYT program manual,* Austin, Tex.: American Health and Fitness Foundation, 1986.

taking the test. After stretching for 5–10 minutes, the participants gather behind the starting line. On the signal to start, they walk 1 mile as fast as possible. Immediately at the end of the 1-mile walk, the test performers count their pulse for 15 seconds.
Scoring. The heart rate is multiplied by four, recorded, and located on the appropriate fitness test chart in figure 11.2. The point where the 1-mile time (horizontal axis) and the recorded heart rate (vertical axis) cross is the fitness score.

■ **3-Mile Walk (No Running)**
(Cooper 1982)

Test Objective. To measure cardiorespiratory fitness through walking.

Age Level. Thirteen through sixty-plus.
Validity. Accepted because of linear relationship between workload, heart rate, and $\dot{V}O_2$max.
Reliability. Not reported.
Equipment. A flat, measured surface and a stopwatch.
Norms. Cooper (1982) provides fitness standards for male and female age groups, age thirteen through sixty-plus. Table 11.7 reports the "good" classification standards for the 3-mile walking test. Lower times place test performers in the excellent classification and higher times place them in the fair to very poor classifications.
Administration and Directions. All test performers should practice walking for speed and endurance before attempting the test. After warming up, the test performers gather behind the starting line. On the signal to start, they attempt to cover 3 miles in the fastest time possible, without running. A partner for each walker is at the finish line to record the finishing time as the test administrator calls it out.
Scoring. The time in minutes and seconds to walk the 3 miles is the score.

■ **12-Minute Swim**
(Cooper 1982)

Test Objective. To measure cardiorespiratory fitness through swimming.
Age Level. Thirteen through sixty-plus.
Equipment. Swimming pool, stopwatch, and whistle.
Validity. Accepted because of linear relationship between workload, heart rate, and $\dot{V}O_2$max.
Reliability. Not reported.

20–29

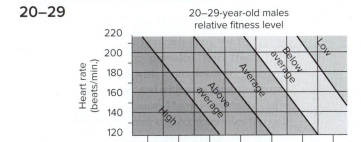

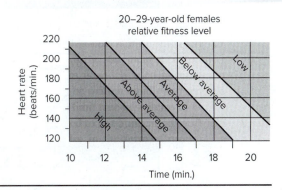

FIGURE 11.2 1-mile walking fitness chart. *(continued)*
(All charts and tables taken from the *One Mile Walk Test* by Dr. James Rippe and colleagues. Reprinted with author's permission.)

Source: All charts and tables taken from the *One Mile Walk Test* by Dr. James Rippe and colleagues. Reprinted with author's permission.

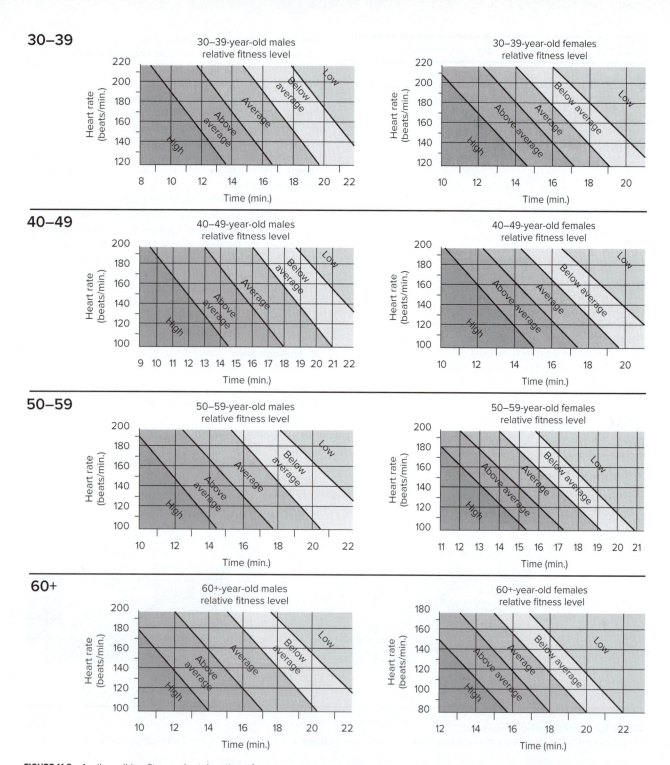

FIGURE 11.2 1-mile walking fitness chart. (*continued*)

Norms. Cooper (1982) provides fitness standards for male and female age groups, age thirteen through sixty-plus. Table 11.7 reports the "good" classification standards. Greater distances place the test performers in the excellent classification, and lesser distances place them in the fair to very poor classification.

Administration and Directions. All test performers should practice swimming for distance and pacing before attempting the test. The swimming course performers gather at one end of the pool. Each performer is instructed to swim in an individual lane. On the signal to start, they push off from the side and swim as far as possible in 12 minutes, using any stroke and resting when necessary. A test partner counts the laps and observes where the swimmer is when the signal to stop is given. The swimmer continues to swim to cool down.

Scoring. The distance in yards swum is the score.

■ 12-Minute Cycling
(Cooper 1982)

Test Objective. To measure cardiorespiratory fitness through cycling.

Age Level. Thirteen through sixty-plus.

Equipment. A bicycle with no more than three gears and a flat, measured distance.

Validity. Accepted because of linear relationship between workload, heart rate, and $\dot{V}O_2$max.

Reliability. Not reported.

Norms. Cooper (1982) provides fitness standards for male and female age groups, age thirteen through sixty-plus. Table 11.7 reports the "good" classification standards. Greater distances place the test performers in the excellent classification, and lesser distances place them in the fair to very poor classifications.

Administration and Directions. All test performers should practice cycling for distance and pacing before attempting the test. The cycling course should be on a hard, flat surface in an area where traffic is not a problem. Every quarter-mile should be marked. On the day of the test, the wind should be less than 10 mph. After warming up, the test performers gather at the starting line, and on the signal to start, they attempt to cycle as far as possible in 12 minutes. A test partner spots the position of the cyclist when the signal to stop is given. All cyclists should continue to move until they have cooled down.

Scoring. The score is the distance in miles cycled.

TABLE 11.7 Standards for Classification of Good Fitness for 3-Mile Walk, 12-Minute Swim, and 12-Minute Cycling Tests for Ages Thirteen through Sixty+

Test	Age					
	13–19	20–29	30–39	40–49	50–59	60+
Males						
3-mile walk (minutes:seconds)	33:00 to 37:30	34:00 to 38:30	35:00 to 40:00	36:30 to 42:00	39:00 to 45:00	41:00 to 48:00
12-minute swim (yards)	700 to 799	600 to 699	550 to 649	500 to 599	450 to 549	400 to 499
12-minute cycling (miles)	4.75 to 5.74	4.50 to 5.49	4.25 to 5.24	4.00 to 4.99	3.50 to 4.49	3.00 to 3.99
Females						
3-mile walk (minutes:seconds)	35:00 to 39:30	36:00 to 40:30	37:30 to 42:00	39:00 to 44:00	42:00 to 47:00	45:00 to 51:00
12-minute swim (yards)	600 to 699	500 to 599	450 to 549	400 to 499	350 to 449	300 to 399
12-minute cycling (miles)	3.75 to 4.74	3.50 to 4.49	3.25 to 4.24	3.00 to 3.99	2.50 to 3.49	2.00 to 2.99

Source: Adapted from Cooper, K. H., The aerobics program for total well-being, New York: M. Evans & Company, 1982.

Note: Lower times or greater distances place the individual in the excellent fitness category, and higher times or lesser distances place the individual in the fair to very poor fitness categories.

■ **Queens College Step Test**
(Katch and McArdle 1977; McArdle et al. 1972)

Test Objective. To measure cardiorespiratory fitness with a submaximal step test.

Age Level. College.

Equipment. Gymnasium bleachers and a metronome. To facilitate testing, record the instructions and commands (cadence) on tape. It is helpful to the test performers if the cadence is maintained through the commands "up, up, down, down," rather than through the metronome. Recording the instructions and commands standardizes the administration of the test and permits you to circulate among the performers during the test.

Validity. When $\dot{V}O_2$max was used as the criterion, correlation coefficients of −.75 and −.72 were found for college-age women and men, respectively.

Reliability. Coefficients of .92 and .89 were found for college-age women and men, respectively.

Norms. Table 11.8 reports norms.

Administration and Directions. Before administration of the test, provide all participants ample time to practice measuring the pulse rate by palpating the carotid artery for 15-second intervals. Test performers should have a partner to count the pulse rate. Since the test cadence is different for males and females, pair a male with a female; then you can test the males as a group and the females as a group.

TABLE 11.8 Norms for the Queens College Step Test for College Students

	Males		Females	
Percentile	Heart Rate	$\dot{V}O_2$	Heart Rate	$\dot{V}O_2$
95	124	59.3	140	40.0
75	144	50.9	158	36.6
50	156	45.8	166	35.1
25	168	40.8	176	33.3
5	184	34.1	196	29.6

Equations for predicting $\dot{V}O_2$max

Males: $\dot{V}O_2$max (mL·kg^{-1}·min^{-1}) = 111.33 − 0.42
(pulse rate; beats/min)

Females: $\dot{V}O_2$max (mL·kg^{-1}·min^{-1}) = 65.81 − 0.1847
(pulse rate; beats/min)

Source: Adapted from Katch, F. I. and McArdle, W. D., *Nutrition, weight control, and exercise*, Boston: Houghton Mifflin, 1977.

Demonstrate the test and allow the test performers a brief practice period (15 to 20 seconds) to learn the cadence. After the practice period, permit the participants to rest. To perform the test, all participants step up and down on the bleacher for 3 minutes. The cadence for males is 24 steps/minute (metronome set at 96 beats/minute), and the cadence for females is 22 steps/minute (metronome set at 88 beats/minute). At the end of 3 minutes, the test performers remain standing while the partners count their pulse rate for 15 seconds, beginning 5 seconds after completion of the test. (Pulse count should be completed 20 seconds after test performer has completed test.)

Scoring. Multiply the 15-second pulse rate by four to obtain the performer's score in beats per minute. Katch and McArdle (1977) also developed regression equations to predict $\dot{V}O_2$max from heart rate (beats per minute). They are included in table 11.5.

■ **Harvard Step Test**
(Brouha 1943)

Note: This is a strenuous test and should not be used on older individuals.

Test Objective. To estimate the capacity of the body to adjust to and recover from hard muscular work.

Age Level. College males.

Equipment. A bench or platform 20 inches high, a stopwatch, and a metronome. Recording the commands "up, up, down, down" helps the performers maintain the cadence and permits you to circulate among them.

Validity. Studies on Harvard undergraduates showed that athletes scored higher than nonathletes, and the scores of the athletes increased with more training and decreased after they stopped training.

Norms. Classification standards are given in the discussion of scoring.

Administration and Directions. Permit the test performers to practice counting their pulse at the radial or carotid artery. Pair up the test performers. Test performers step up and down on a bench 30 times/minute for 5 minutes, unless they must stop earlier because of fatigue. The body should be erect each time the performer steps onto the bench and the lead foot may be changed during the test. As soon as performers stop the test, they sit down and remain sitting throughout the pulse count. There are two forms of the test. In the long form, the pulse is counted for 30 seconds on three occasions: 1 minute after exercise (1 to 1 1/2 minutes), 2 minutes after exercise (2 to 2 1/2 minutes), and 3 minutes after exercise (3 to 3 1/2 minutes). In the short form, the pulse is counted for only 30 seconds, 1 minute after exercise (1 to 1 1/2 minutes).

Scoring. In the long form, a physical efficiency index (PEI) is computed with the formula

$$PEI = \frac{\text{duration of exercise in seconds} \times 100}{2 \times \text{sum of pulse counts in recovery}}$$

The PEI standards for the long form are as follows:

below 55	— poor
55 to 64	— low average
65 to 79	— high average
80 to 89	— good
above 89	— excellent

For individuals who do not complete the 5-minute test, the following scoring standards may be used:

less than 2 minutes	25
from 2 to 3 minutes	38
from 3 to 3½ minutes	48
from 3½ to 4 minutes	52
from 4 to 4½ minutes	55
from 4½ to 5 minutes	59

In the short form, the scoring formula is

$$PEI = \frac{\text{duration of exercise in seconds} \times 100}{5.5 \times \text{pulse count for 1 to 1½ minutes after exercise}}$$

The PEI standards for the short form are as follows:

below 50	— poor
50 to 80	— average
above 80	— good

Modifications of the Harvard Step Test have been made so that it may be used on both sexes in elementary grades through college. The modifications group the norms into elementary, junior high, and high school. The grades and ages of these groups are elementary grades 1–6 (ages 6–12), junior high grades 7–9 (ages 12–15), and high school grades 10–12 (ages 15–18).

■ Harvard Step Test for Junior and Senior High Males
(Gallagher and Brouha 1943)

Males twelve through eighteen years of age with a body surface area (based on height and weight) less than 1.85 square meters use an 18-inch bench, whereas males of the same age with a surface area of 1.85 square meters or more use a 20-inch bench. A nomogram for estimating body surface is provided in the reference. Both groups perform 30 steps/minute for 4 minutes. The sequence of pulse counts and the formula for scoring are the same as those used for college males. The classification standards for this test are as follows:

50 or less	— very poor
51 to 60	— poor
61 to 70	— fair
71 to 80	— good
81 to 90	— excellent
92 or more	— superior

■ Harvard Step Test for Junior High, Senior High, and College Females
(Skubic and Hodgkins 1963)

For this test, the bench is 18 inches high, the sequence is 24 steps/minute, the duration of exercise is 3 minutes, and only one 30-second pulse count is taken 1 minute after exercise (1 to 1½ minutes). The cardiovascular efficiency score (CES) is determined by the formula

$$CES = \frac{\text{no. of seconds completed} \times 100}{\text{recovery pulse} \times 5.6}$$

Norms for the three female groups are reported in table 11.9.

■ Harvard Step Test for Elementary School Males and Females
(Brouha and Ball 1952)

For this test, the bench is 14 inches high and the cadence is 30 steps/minute. The duration of the exercise is adjusted by ages: 3 minutes for ages eight through twelve and 2 minutes for age seven. The pulse count, scoring formula, and classification standards are the same as those used for the original Harvard Step Test.

■ YMCA 3-Minute Step Test
(Golding 2000)

Test Objective. To measure cardiorespiratory fitness with a submaximal step test.
Age Level. Eighteen through sixty-five-plus.

TABLE 11.9 Norms for Cardiovascular Efficiency Test (Step Test) for Junior High, Senior High, and College Females

	Junior High*		Senior High*		College**	
Rating	**Cardiovascular Efficiency Score**	**30-Second Recovery Rate**	**Cardiovascular Efficiency Score**	**30-Second Recovery Rate**	**Cardiovascular Efficiency Score**	**30-Second Recovery Rate**
Excellent	72–100	44 or less	71–100	45 or less	71–100	45 or less
Very good	62–71	45–52	60–70	46–54	60–70	46–54
Good	51–61	53–63	49–59	55–66	49–59	55–66
Fair	41–50	64–79	40–48	67–80	39–48	67–83
Poor	31–40	80–92	31–39	81–96	28–38	84–116
Very poor	0–30	93 & above	0–30	97 & above	0–27	117–120

*Source: Skubic, V. and Hodgkins, J., "Cardiovascular efficiency test scores for junior and senior high school girls in the United States," *Research Quarterly*, vol. 35, 1964, 184–192.
**Hodgkins, J. and Skubic, V., "Cardiovascular efficiency test scores for college women in the United States," *Research Quarterly*, vol. 34, 1963, 454–461, 1963.

Equipment. A bench 12 inches high, a stopwatch, and a metronome.
Validity. Accepted because of linear relationships between workload, heart rate, and $\dot{V}O_2$max.
Reliability. Not reported.
Norms. Table 11.10 reports below average to good norms. Scores below and above these norms are poor and excellent scores, respectively.
Administration and Directions. All test performers should have a partner to count the carotid pulse (allow time to practice counting a partner's carotid pulse). On the signal to begin, the test performer steps up with one foot, then the other, steps down with the first foot, and then the other foot. The knees must straighten with the step on the bench. The complete step represents 4 counts (up, up, down, down). The step is done at a cadence of 96 counts/minute or 24 complete step executions/minute (one 4-count step every 2.5 seconds). At the conclusion of 3 minutes, the test performer quickly sits down, and the partner counts the pulse for 1 minute.
Scoring. The score is the total 1-minute post-test pulse count.

Development of Cardiorespiratory Fitness

Many individuals can begin an exercise program of low to moderate intensity without medical clearance. The pre-test/pre-activity screening procedures described earlier in this chapter should be followed before adults start an exercise program, however.

Cardiorespiratory fitness is developed through aerobic activities, such as running, walking, swimming, cross-country skiing, or bicycling for a relatively long distance or jumping rope for an extended period at an appropriate intensity. Individuals should select an aerobic activity or activities they enjoy and to which they can make a commitment to continue. Running is the most convenient aerobic activity for development and maintenance of cardiorespiratory fitness, though some people find it tedious. In addition, individuals with joint problems (in the back, knees, and ankles) and foot disorders are unable to run for an extended period. Though some sports activities and forms of training require intense effort for short periods of time, they are inappropriate for development of cardiorespiratory fitness because they are not aerobic. These activities can, however, provide other exercise benefits and are highly recommended for those benefits.

Current exercise guidelines for adults recommend at least 150 minutes per week of moderate physical activity or 75 minutes per week of vigorous physical activity. Combinations of moderate and vigorous intensity also can be performed. Many individuals exercise more than five days a week but modify the intensity or the duration on alternate days. The avoidance of two consecutive days of intense or long exercise sessions prevents chronic fatigue for most individuals.

Highly organized exercise programs usually are not preferable for children and teens. They should, however,

TABLE 11.10 Pulse Count Norms for YMCA 3-Minute Step Test for Ages Eighteen through Sixty-Five+

Ratings*	Age					
	18–25	26–35	36–45	46–55	56–65	65+
Males						
Good (75–85%)	84–79	85–79	88–80	93–87	94–86	92–87
Above Average (60–70%)	93–88	94–88	98–92	101–95	100–97	102–94
Average (45–55%)	100–95	102–96	105–100	111–103	109–103	110–104
Below Average (30–40%)	107–102	110–104	113–108	119–113	117–111	118–114
Females						
Good (75–85%)	93–85	92–85	96–89	101–95	103–97	101–96
Above Average (60–70%)	102–96	101–95	104–100	110–104	111–106	111–104
Average (45–55%)	110–104	110–104	112–107	118–113	118–113	121–116
Below Average (30–40%)	120–113	119–113	120–115	124–120	127–119	126–123

Source: Adapted from Golding, L. A. ed., *YMCA fitness testing and assessment manual,* 4th ed., Champaign, Ill.: Human Kinetics, 2000.

Note: Higher pulse count places individual at lower percentile.

have at least 60 minutes of daily physical activity that develops and maintains cardiorespiratory fitness.

Determining the intensity at which one should exercise is critical; however, if training effects are to occur, the principle of overload must be observed. Overload is a gradual increase in the intensity of the physical activity. For the cardiovascular and respiratory systems (or any other physiological components of fitness) to improve, they must work harder than they are used to working. Stress must be imposed upon them so that over a period of time they will be able to accommodate the additional stress. Sedentary persons who initiate an exercise program should begin at a relatively low intensity and gradually increase the level of exertion. With great expectations of physical development, many individuals undertake a program but mistakenly begin their activity at an intensity that is too high for them. Their efforts result in soreness and discomfort, which hinder continuation of the program. Also, upon recovery from the soreness, these individuals have no desire to resume the exercise program.

For adults, physical activity that noticeably increases the heart rate may be considered moderate effort. Activity that substantially increases the heart rate and causes rapid breathing may be considered vigorous effort. Monitoring the heart rate is the easiest method of determining the intensity of exercise. Unless advised differently by a qualified physician, most individuals should exercise at 60% to 75% of their maximal heart rate range. This range may be found by completing the following steps:

1. Estimate the maximal heart rate (220 minus age). Note that it is only an estimate of maximal heart rate. There are several different equations that may be used to predict the maximal heart rate, but most have a standard error of estimate of $\pm$ 10 to 15 beats per minute (bpm). Do not expect all individuals to have the maximal heart predicted with any equation.

2. Subtract the resting heart rate from the value found in step 1.

3. Multiply the value found in step 2 by .60.

4. Add the value found in step 3 to the resting heart rate (this value is the minimal target heart rate).

5. Multiply the value found in step 2 by .75 and add to the resting heart rate (this value is the maximal target heart rate).

Sedentary individuals should begin an exercise program at 50% to 60% of their maximal heart rate range and increase the percentage as cardiorespiratory fitness improves.

In addition to heart rate as an indicator of exercise intensity, Borg's Rating of Perceived Exertion (RPE) can be used (Borg 1973, 1982). During an exercise session or a stress test, individuals are asked to rate on a numerical scale how they feel in relation to their level of exertion. Perceived exertion is defined as the total amount of exertion and physical fatigue. Factors such as breathing difficulties or aches and pain should not be considered. With the proper instruction, it is possible for individuals to exercise at a particular RPE based on their feeling of exertion, which relates to measures such as heart rate and oxygen consumption. In other words, individuals listen to their bodies.

Table 11.11 shows the original and revised scales for ratings of perceived exertion. The original scale used the rankings of 6 to 20 to approximate the heart values from rest to maximum (60–200). The revised scale represents an attempt to provide a ratio scale of RPE values. According to Borg, the old scale provides the simplest estimate of perceived exertion. The revised category scale may be especially suitable for determining other subjective symptoms, such as breathing difficulties, aches, and pains.

The exercise period should include 5 to 10 minutes of flexibility exercises and a minimum of 20 minutes of aerobic activity. As the level of fitness improves, the duration of the exercise period can be increased.

All of the above guidelines apply to organized cardiorespiratory fitness programs and, if followed, will lead to better cardiorespiratory fitness. For highly sedentary individuals, however, improvement in cardiorespiratory fitness can occur with very small increases in daily activity. Ten- to fifteen-minute increments of walking or other types of mild physical activity, performed several times during the day, can lead to improvements in cardiorespiratory fitness.

TABLE 11.11 Rating of Perceived Exertion Scales

Original Rating Scale	Revised Rating Scale
6	0 Nothing at all
7 Very, very light	0.5 Very, very weak (just noticeable)
8	1 Very weak
9 Very light	2 Weak (light)
10	3 Moderate
11 Fairly light	4 Somewhat strong
12	5 Strong (heavy)
13 Somewhat hard	6
14	7 Very strong
15 Hard	8
16	9
17 Very hard	10 Very, very strong (almost max)
18	
19 Very, very hard	
20	

Source: Borg, G. A. V., "Psychophysical bases of perceived exertion," *Medicine and Science in Sports and Exercise,* vol. 14, no. 5, 1982, 377–381.

Review Problems

1. Review additional step tests found in other textbooks. Note the groups for whom the tests are intended and the validity and reliability coefficients.

2. Administer one step test and one running test described in this chapter to several of your classmates. Ask them to provide constructive criticism of your test administration.

3. Imagine that you are responsible for testing the cardiorespiratory fitness of a group of 50- to 60-year-old adults. Describe the procedure you would follow to determine who would be tested. Also explain which tests you would choose and the reasons for your choice of tests.

4. If possible, observe the administration of cardiorespiratory fitness tests at health and fitness clubs in your community. Observe how the instructions are given, how the results are interpreted to the group, and what safety precautions are followed.

Chapter Review Questions

1. What is cardiorespiratory fitness?

2. What is the definition of maximal oxygen consumption?

3. Why is it important to measure cardiorespiratory fitness?

4. What is the purpose of prescreening before the conduction of cardiovascular fitness testing?

5. What are your responsibilities after the measurement of cardiorespiratory fitness?

12 Flexibility

After completing this chapter, you should be able to

1. Define and measure *flexibility*.

2. State why flexibility should be measured.

3. Describe the difference between relative and absolute flexibility tests.

4. State the guidelines that should be followed in the administration of flexibility tests.

5. Describe responsibilities after the measurement of flexibility and prescribe activities to improve flexibility.

Flexibility is the ability to move the body joints through a maximum range of motion without undue strain. When describing or measuring flexibility, the terms *flexion* (joint angle is decreased) and *extension* (joint angle is increased) are used. Flexibility is not a general factor, but it is specific to given joints and to particular sports or physical activities. An individual with good flexibility in the shoulders may not have good flexibility in the lower back or posterior upper legs. Flexibility depends more on the soft tissues (ligaments, tendons, and muscles) of a joint than on the bony structure of the joint itself. However, the bony structures of certain joints do place limitations on flexibility, as illustrated by extension of the elbow or knee and hyperextension and abduction of the spinal column.

Flexibility is related to body size, gender, age, and physical activity. Any increase in body fat usually decreases flexibility. In general, females are more flexible than males. Anatomical distinctions or differences in regular physical activity may account for these flexibility differences. During the early school years flexibility increases, but a leveling off or decrease begins in early adolescence. The dramatic loss of flexibility during the aging process is probably due to failure to maintain an active program of movement.

In general, active individuals are more flexible than inactive individuals. The soft tissues and joints tend to shrink, losing extensibility when the muscles are maintained in a shortened position. Habitual postures and chronic heavy work through restricted ranges of motion also can lead to adaptive shortening of muscles. Physical activity with wide ranges of movement helps prevent this loss of extensibility. In general, then, flexibility is more related to habitual movement patterns for each individual and for each joint than to age or to gender.

Why Measure Flexibility?

Flexibility is an important component of health-related fitness, and the lack of it can create functional problems or disorders for many individuals. Medical records indicate that low-back pain is one of the most prevalent health complaints in the United States, and many low-back disorders are caused by poor muscle tone, poor flexibility of the lower back, and inadequate abdominal muscle tone. In addition, anyone with a stiff spinal column is at a disadvantage in many physical activities and also fails to get full value from the shock-absorbing arrangement of the spine when walking, running, or jumping. Lack of flexibility in the back can be responsible for bad posture, compression of peripheral nerves, painful menstruation, and other ailments. Furthermore, short muscles limit work efficiency. They become sore when they perform physical exertion, and without a good range of movement, the individual is more likely to incur torn ligaments and muscles during physical activities.

Because individuals with good flexibility have greater ease of movement, less stiffness of muscles, enhancement of skill, and less chance of injury during movement, the measurement of flexibility should be included in all physical education and wellness programs. Individuals with poor flexibility should be identified, and the appropriate exercises and activities prescribed for them. Flexibility tests are usually administered to identify individuals with too little range of joint movement, but they also can be administered to determine if individuals have too much flexibility in certain joints. Too much range of movement can result in joint instability and can increase the possibility of injury.

Though flexibility is usually measured for diagnostic purposes, many physical education teachers believe it is acceptable to grade flexibility performance. However, since the degree of flexibility most desirable for health purposes has not been determined, the grading of flexibility is questionable. If flexibility performance is graded, the standards should be reasonable, and the students should be informed of the standards at the beginning of the unit.

Responsibilities after Measurement

As previously stated, individuals with poor flexibility are susceptible to musculoskeletal problems as well as other ailments. Once these individuals have been identified, the appropriate flexibility exercises should be prescribed for them.

Three stretching techniques can be used to improve flexibility: static stretching, ballistic stretching, and proprioceptive neuromuscular facilitation (PNF). **Static stretching** involves slowly moving to a position to stretch the designated muscles and holding the position for a specified length of time. The recommended length of time for holding the stretch varies from 20 to 30 seconds, and the stretch for each muscle is repeated two or three times in each stretching session.

Ballistic stretching makes use of repetitive bouncing motions. Though ballistic stretching can improve flexibility, it is not often recommended as a stretching technique. If the force produced by the effort to stretch is greater than

the extensibility the muscle tissues can tolerate, the muscle may be injured. In addition, the use of a fast, forceful, bobbing type of stretching induces the stretch reflex (the reflex contraction of a muscle in response to being suddenly stretched beyond its normal length). The purpose of this reflex action is to prevent injury caused by overstretching. The amount and rate of the stretch reflex contraction vary directly in proportion to the amount and rate of the movement causing the stretch. The faster and more forceful the stretch, the faster and more forceful the reflex contraction of the stretched muscle. As the individual is attempting to stretch the muscle through a bouncing action, the stretch reflex responds to prevent the muscle from being stretched. This combination may result in muscle injury.

There are a number of **PNF** techniques used for stretching, but all involve a combination of alternating contraction and relaxation of both agonist and antagonist muscles. The disadvantage of the PNF techniques is that they require the assistance of a partner.

Both static stretching and PNF techniques will improve flexibility, but there is lack of agreement regarding which technique is superior. It is difficult to compare flexibility studies, because different designs for training programs, length of stretch time, and number of PNF repetitions influence the results of the studies. Since it is accepted that static stretching improves flexibility and no partner is required to perform the exercises, only descriptions of static stretching exercises are provided at the conclusion of this chapter.

Note: If your responsibilities are with athletes, you may choose not to use static stretching in certain situations. Some studies have concluded that athletes who perform a static stretch routine prior to participation in power or explosive type events experience a decrease in performance success. It may be best that athletes in such events conduct a general warm-up session and sports-specific, dynamic stretches prior to their performance. Static stretching sessions may then be conducted after performance and on training days when the athletes are not participating in an athletic event.

ARE YOU ABLE TO DO THE FOLLOWING?

- Define *flexibility* and state why it should be measured.
- Describe responsibilities after the measurement of flexibility.

Tests of Flexibility

For clinical assessment of flexibility, devices such as the Leighton Flexometer, the electrogoniometer, and the goniometer are used. These devices provide a rotary measure, in which degrees of rotation around a 360° arc are determined. There also are many valid, practical tests that may be used in physical education and wellness programs and that may be administered to both sexes. These tests provide a linear measure and utilize tape measures, rulers, and yardsticks. Such tests will be covered in this chapter. None of the tests that will be described poses risk of injury to the performer.

There are two types of linear flexibility tests. **Relative flexibility tests** are designed to be relative to the length or width of a specific body part. In these tests, the movement and the length, or width, of an influencing body part are measured. **Absolute flexibility tests** are designed to measure only the movement in relation to an absolute performance goal. Both types of test are presented.

Before administering any flexibility tests, you should instruct all test performers to do the following:

1. Perform 5 to 10 minutes of light aerobic exercise to warm up their muscles (warm muscles stretch better than cold ones).

2. Perform slow, sustained static stretching of all joints to be tested.

3. Declare if they have any back problems.

If any test performers have back problems, permit them to practice the test items. If they experience any discomfort, discontinue the test.

■ Sit and Reach Test
(AAHPERD 1980a)

Note: Other similar tests for measurement of lower back and posterior thigh flexibility may be used. The V-sit reach test, the sit and reach test included in the YMCA Fitness Test, and the back-saver sit and reach included in the FitnessGram are appropriate tests. If norms are used, you should always use the norms of the test that you administer. These tests are described in chapter 15. Additionally, although sit and reach tests claim to measure lower back flexibility, they better measure hamstring flexibility. An acceptable performance on sit and reach tests does not necessarily mean the individual will be free of back pain. Prevention of low-back pain involves other factors such as weight and trunk muscular strength and endurance.

Test Objective. To measure the flexibility of the lower back and posterior thighs.

Age Level. Five through adulthood.

Equipment. Figure 12.1 includes the specifications of the box used for this test. It is crucial that the 9-inch mark be exactly in line with the vertical panel against which the test performer's feet will be placed. This flexibility test and box are included in many fitness tests. Some tests, however, report the score in centimeters. If centimeters are used, the 23-centimeter line should be exactly in line with the vertical panel against which the test performer's feet will be placed. If the AAHPERD norms are used, the specially constructed box, or benches that are only 12 inches high, should be used when administering this test. If local norms are established, benches turned on their sides, or the bottom row of bleachers that are a few inches higher than 12 inches, may be used. Yardsticks may be taped to the benches or bleachers so that several students can be measured at the same time.

Validity. Logical validity has been claimed. The AAHPERD sit and reach test has been validated against several other tests, and coefficients ranging between .80 and .90 have been found.

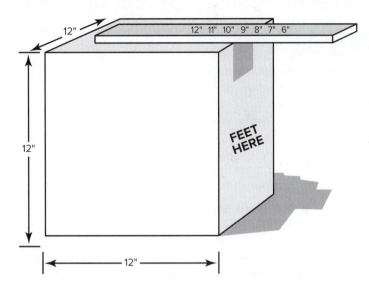

FIGURE 12.1 Sit and reach box.

Reliability. .70 or higher.

Objectivity. Not reported.

Norms. Table 12.1 includes norms for ages five through college-age.

Administration and Directions. The test apparatus should be prevented from slipping (may be placed against a wall), and the test performer should not be wearing shoes. The performer (1) sits at the test apparatus with the knees fully extended and the feet shoulder-width apart, flat against the end of the board; (2) with the palms down and hands placed on top of each other, extends the arms forward; and (3) reaches directly forward four times and holds the position of the maximum reach

TABLE 12.1 Norms in Inches for Sit and Reach Test for Ages Five through College

Percentile	Age													
	5	6	7	8	9	10	11	12	13	14	15	16	17+	College
							Males							
95	12.50	13.50	13.00	13.50	13.50	13.00	13.50	13.75	14.25	15.50	16.25	16.50	17.75	17.75
75	11.50	11.50	11.00	11.50	11.50	11.00	11.50	11.50	12.00	13.00	13.50	14.25	15.75	15.50
50	10.00	10.25	10.00	10.00	10.00	10.00	10.00	10.25	10.25	11.00	12.00	12.00	13.50	13.50
25	8.75	8.75	8.75	8.75	8.75	8.00	8.25	8.25	8.00	9.00	9.50	10.00	11.00	11.50
5	6.75	6.25	6.25	6.25	4.75	4.75	5.25	4.75	4.75	6.00	5.25	4.50	6.00	7.50
							Females							
95	13.50	13.50	13.50	14.25	13.75	13.75	14.50	15.75	17.00	17.50	18.25	18.25	17.50	18.50
75	12.00	12.00	12.25	12.25	12.25	12.25	12.50	13.50	14.25	15.00	16.25	15.50	15.75	16.25
50	10.75	10.75	10.75	11.00	11.00	11.00	11.50	12.00	12.25	13.00	14.25	13.50	13.75	14.50
25	9.00	9.00	9.50	9.00	9.00	9.50	9.50	10.00	9.50	11.00	12.25	12.00	12.25	12.50
5	7.00	7.00	6.25	6.75	6.75	6.25	6.25	6.00	6.75	7.00	7.50	5.50	8.75	9.50

Source: Adapted from *AAHPERD, Health related physical fitness test manual,* Reston, Va.: AAHPERD, 1980; and Pate, R. R., *Norms for college students: Health related physical fitness test,* Reston, Va.: American Alliance for Health, Physical Education, Recreation and Dance, 1985.

FIGURE 12.2 Sit and reach test.

©David K. Miller

on the fourth trial for one second (see figure 12.2). The test administrator may place a hand on the knees of the performer to discourage knee flexion, but the knees should not be hyperextended.

Scoring. The score is the most distant point reached on the fourth trial, measured to the nearest 1/4 inch or the nearest centimeter. The test administrator should be in a position to note the most distant line touched by the fingertips of both hands. If the hands reach unevenly, the position is not held for 1 second, or the knees bend, the test should be readministered. You should be aware that it is normal for many boys and girls not to reach the 9-inch level during the preadolescent and adolescent growth spurt (ages ten through fourteen). It is not unusual for the legs to become proportionately longer in relation to the trunk during this period. Flexibility exercises should be prescribed for individuals who score below P_{50}, as any score below this percentile represents poor flexibility in the posterior thigh, lower back, or posterior hip. Individuals who score below P_{25} have a critical lack of flexibility.

■ Modified Sit and Reach Test
(Hoeger and Hoeger 2005)

Individuals with short legs relative to the trunk and arms may have an advantage when performing the sit and reach test previously described. To account for this potential bias, the modified sit and reach test was developed.

Test Objective. To measure the flexibility of the lower back and posterior thighs.

Age Level. Under eighteen through fifty-plus.

Equipment. 12-inch sit and reach box (dimensions described in previous test) and yardstick (used with box).

Validity. Logical validity.

Reliability and Objectivity. Not reported.

Norms. Table 12.2 includes norms for ages under eighteen through fifty-plus.

Administration and Directions. With the shoes removed, the test performer does the following:

1. Sits on the floor with hips, back, and head against the wall; extends legs fully; and places the feet against the sit and reach box.
2. Places the hands one on top of the other and reaches forward as far as possible without letting the head and back come off the wall (the shoulders may be rounded but back remains in contact with wall).

   A yardstick is placed on the box with the zero end pointed toward the test performer and touching his/her extended hands. The yardstick is held in this position by the test administrator. This procedure establishes the relative zero point for each test performer.
3. Gradually reaches forward three times, as the yardstick is held firmly in place, and holds the third stretch as far as possible for two seconds.

Scoring. Two trials are administered. The score is the number of inches reached to the nearest one-half inch.

TABLE 12.2 Norms for the Modified Sit and Reach Test for Ages under Eighteen through Fifty-Plus

	Age			
	≤18	19–35	36–49	≥50
Percentile	**Males**			
95	19.6	18.9	18.2	15.8
80	17.8	17.0	14.6	13.3
60*	15.2	15.0	13.4	11.5
40	14.0	13.5	11.6	9.7
20	11.8	11.6	9.9	8.8
	Females			
95	19.5	19.3	19.2	15.7
80	17.8	16.7	16.2	14.2
60*	16.0	15.8	14.5	12.3
40	14.5	14.5	12.8	10.1
20	12.6	12.6	11.0	8.3

*Health-related physical fitness standard.

Source: Adapted from Hoeger, W. W. and Hoeger, S. A., *Lifetime physical fitness and wellness: A personalized program,* 8th ed., Belmont, Cal.: Wadsworth, 2005.

■ V-Sit Reach Test
(President's Council on Physical Fitness and Sports 2012)

Test Objective. To measure the flexibility of the lower back and hamstrings.

Age Level. Six through seventeen.
Equipment. Yardstick or measuring tape.
Validity. Face validity.
Reliability and Objectivity. Not reported.
Norms. Table 12.3 includes the 50th and 85th percentile norms for ages six through seventeen.
Administration and Directions. A straight line 2 feet long is marked on the floor as the baseline. A measuring line is drawn perpendicular to the midpoint of the baseline extending 2 feet on each side and is marked off in inches. The point where the baseline and the measuring line intersect is the zero (0) point. The test participant sits on the floor, without shoes, with the measuring line between the legs and the soles of the feet immediately behind the baseline. The heels should be 8 to 12 inches apart. With palms down and thumbs clasped so that the hands are together, the participant places the hands on the measuring line. With the legs held flat by a partner, the test participant slowly reaches forward as far as possible. After three practice trials, the fourth reach is held for 3 seconds while the distance is recorded.
Scoring. The distance held beyond the baseline for three seconds is recorded as a positive score.

■ Sit and Reach Wall Test
(Robbins, Powers, and Burgess 1991)

The sit and reach wall test may be used to provide a quick estimate of lower back and posterior thigh flexibility. It requires only a wall and can be performed quickly by a large number of people.
Test Objective. To measure the flexibility of the lower back and posterior thighs.

TABLE 12.3 Percentile Norms for the V-Sit Reach Test for Ages Six through Seventeen

	Age											
	6	7	8	9	10	11	12	13	14	15	16	17
Percentile	**Males**											
50	+1.0	+1.0	+0.5	+1.0	+1.0	+1.0	+1.0	+0.5	+1.0	+2.0	+3.0	+3.0
85	+3.5	+3.5	+3.0	+3.0	+4.0	+4.0	+4.0	+3.5	+4.5	+5.0	+6.0	+7.0
	Females											
50	+2.5	+2.0	+2.0	+2.0	+3.0	+3.0	+3.5	+3.5	+4.5	+5.0	+5.5	+4.5
85	+5.5	+5.0	+4.5	+5.5	+6.0	+6.5	+7.0	+7.0	+8.0	+8.0	+9.0	+8.0

Source: Adapted from the President's Council on Physical Fitness and Sports, *President's challenge physical fitness program,* Washington, D.C.: President's Council on Physical Fitness and Sports, 2012.

TABLE 12.4 Norms for Sit and Reach Wall Test for High School and College Students

Performance Level	Score
Excellent	Palms touch wall
Good	Knuckles touch wall
Average	Fingertips touch wall
Poor	Cannot touch wall

Source: Robbins, Powers, and Burgess 1991.

Age Level. Junior high through college-age.
Equipment. A wall.
Validity. Logical validity.
Reliability and Objectivity. Not reported.
Norms. Table 12.4 provides norms for high school and college students.
Administration and Directions. Individuals should be permitted to warm up before stretching. With shoes removed, the performer (1) sits facing a wall, with the knees straight and feet flat against the wall; (2) reaches as far as possible to touch fingertips, knuckles, or palms to the wall; and (3) holds position for 3 seconds.
Scoring. See table 12.4.

■ **Trunk and Neck Extension Test**
(Johnson and Nelson 1986)

Test Objective. To measure the ability to extend the trunk (relative flexibility).
Age Level. Six through college-age.
Equipment. Mat and yardstick or tape measure.
Validity. Face validity.
Reliability. .90 through test-retest.
Objectivity. .99.
Norms. Table 12.5 reports norms for college students.
Administration and Directions. The test performer should sit in a hard chair, and the test administrator should measure to the nearest 1/4 inch the distance from the tip of the performer's nose to the seat of the chair in which the performer is sitting. (The chin must be level when the distance is measured.) The test performer then assumes a prone position on a mat, placing both hands on the lower back. With a partner holding the hips against the mat, the performer raises the trunk in a slow and controlled manner as high as possible from the mat. The

TABLE 12.5 Norms in Inches for Trunk and Neck Extension and Trunk Extension Tests for College Students

Performance Level	Trunk and Neck Extension	Trunk Extension
Males		
Above average	6 to 0	19 and above
Average	8 to 6¼	16 to 18
Below average	8¼ and above	15 and less
Females		
Above average	5¾ to 0	21 and above
Average	7¾ to 6	18 to 20
Below average	8 and above	17 and less

Source: Adapted from Johnson, B. L. and Nelson, J. K., *Practical measurements for evaluation in physical education*, 4th ed., Edina, Minn.: Burgess Publishing, 1986; and Miller, D. K. and Allen, T. E., *Fitness: A lifetime commitment*, 4th ed., New York: Macmillan Publishing, 1990.

distance from the tip of the nose to the mat is measured (see figure 12.3). If any back discomfort occurs, the test should be stopped immediately.
Scoring. The best of three lifts is subtracted from the trunk and neck length measurement. The closer the trunk lift is to the trunk and neck length, the better the score.

■ **Trunk Extension Test**
(Miller and Allen 1990)

The trunk extension test is very similar to the trunk and neck extension previously described. The difference is that this test measures absolute flexibility and does not require measurement of any body parts.
Age Level. Six through college-age.
Equipment. Mat and yardstick or tape measure.
Validity. Face validity.
Reliability and Objectivity. Not reported.
Norms. Table 12.5 reports norms for college students.
Administration and Directions. The test performer lies prone on a mat with a partner holding the hips against the mat. The fingers are interlocked behind the neck, and the chest and head are raised in a slow and controlled manner off the mat as far as possible. The distance in inches is measured from the mat to

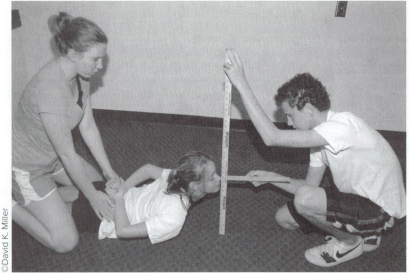

FIGURE 12.3   Trunk and neck extension test.

FIGURE 12.4   Trunk extension test.

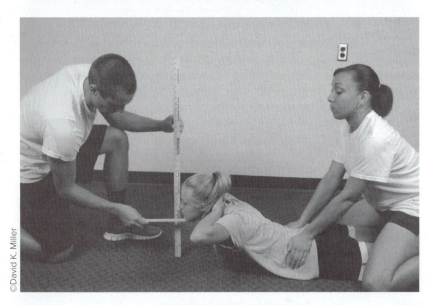

the chin (see figure 12.4). If any back discomfort occurs, the test should be stopped immediately.

Scoring. The best of three lifts is the score.

■ Trunk Rotation Test

Test Objective. To measure trunk and shoulder flexibility.

Age Level. Six through adulthood.

Equipment. Tape and a ruler.

Validity. Face validity.

Reliability and Objectivity. Not reported.

Norms. No norms reported.

Administration and Directions. Mark a vertical line on a wall with tape. The test performer should (1) stand about the length of the arms from the wall with the back toward the wall and directly in front of the tape; (2) place the feet shoulder width apart and extend the arms in front of the body, parallel to the floor; (3) slowly rotate the trunk to the right as far as possible and touch the wall with the fingertips. The wall touch must be briefly maintained. The shoulders, hips, and knees may turn, but the feet are not permitted to move. The test should be repeated for the left side to compare right and left rotations.

Scoring. A touch before the line is a negative score and a touch after the line a positive score. The greater the score is above "0", the better the score.

■ **Shoulder and Wrist Elevation Test**
(Johnson and Nelson 1986)

Test Objective. To measure shoulder and wrist flexibility (relative flexibility).
Age Level. Six through college-age.
Equipment. Mat and two yardsticks, or one yardstick and a tape measure.
Validity. Face validity.
Reliability. .93 through test-retest.
Objectivity. .99.
Norms. Norms for college students are reported in table 12.6.
Administration and Directions. The arm length of the test performer should be measured from the acromion process (shoulder tip) to the middle fingertip, as the arms hang down. The test performer then assumes a prone position with the arms extended directly in front of the shoulders and holds a yardstick, with the hands about shoulder-width apart. The

yardstick is raised upward as far as possible while keeping the chin on the floor. Because it is difficult to elevate the shoulders without extending the wrists, the movements of the two joints are combined for the test score. When the highest point is reached, the distance is measured to the nearest 1/4 inch. Though some individuals are extremely flexible and can move the yardstick beyond the highest vertical point, the measurement is still taken at the highest vertical point.
Scoring. The score is the best of three trials subtracted from the arm length. The closer the lift is to the arm measurement, the better the score.

■ **Shoulder Lift**
(Miller and Allen 1990)

The shoulder lift test is very similar to the shoulder and wrist elevation test, but it measures shoulder flexibility only. It measures absolute flexibility rather than relative flexibility.
Age Level. Six through college-age.
Equipment. Mat and two yardsticks, or one yardstick and a tape measure.
Validity. Face validity.
Reliability and Objectivity. Not reported.
Norms. Table 12.6 reports norms for college students.
Administration and Directions. The test performer lies prone on the mat with the chin to the mat and the arms extended forward directly in front of the shoulders. A yardstick is held with the hands about shoulder-width apart. The wrists and elbows are kept straight as the yardstick is raised upward as far as possible, with the chin touching the mat. The distance in inches is measured from the bottom of the yardstick to the mat (see figure 12.5).
Scoring. The score is the best of three trials. Figures 12.6 through 12.13 (Jensen and Hirst 1980; Robbins, Powers, and Burgess 1991) illustrate observation measures of flexibility. No score is recorded, but the measures may be used to identify individuals with inadequate flexibility.

Exercises to Develop Flexibility

These static exercises are appropriate for the general population. They are designed to improve flexibility throughout the body, but the most important areas to consider are neck and shoulder flexion, back extension, trunk and hip flexion (including lower back and posterior upper-leg muscles), and posterior lower-leg extension (ankle flexion). Unless stated otherwise, the following

TABLE 12.6 Norms in Inches for Shoulder and Wrist Elevation and Shoulder Lift for College Students

Performance Level	Shoulder and Wrist Elevation	Shoulder Lift
Males		
Above average	8¼ to 0	22 and above
Average	11½ to 8½	17 to 21
Below average	11¾ and above	16 and less
Females		
Above average	7½ to 0	23 and above
Average	10¾ to 7¾	19 to 22
Below average	11 and above	18 and less

Source: Adapted from Johnson, B. L. and Nelson, J. K., *Practical measurements for evaluation in physical education,* 4th ed., Edina, Minn.: Burgess Publishing, 1986; and Miller, D. K. and Allen, T. E., *Fitness: A lifetime commitment,* 4th ed., New York: Macmillan Publishing, 1990.

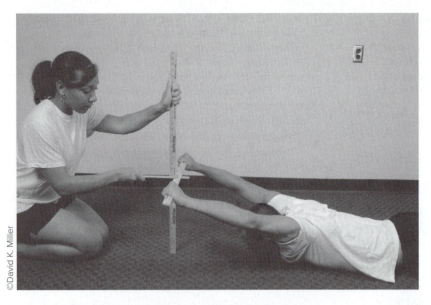

©David K. Miller

FIGURE 12.5   Shoulder lift test.

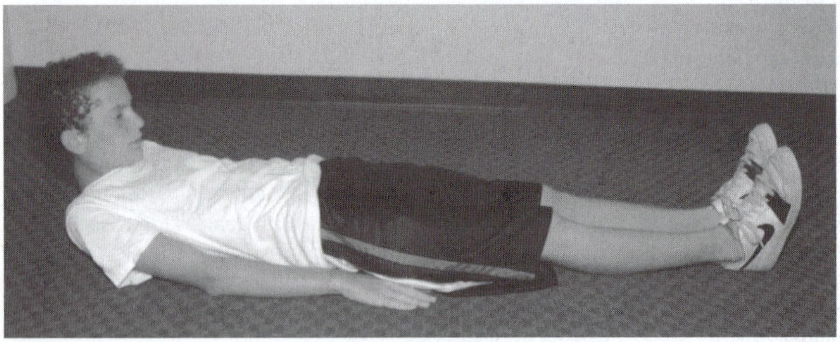

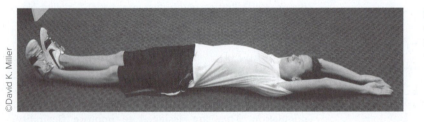

©David K. Miller

FIGURE 12.6   Normal flexibility for the neck allows the chin to move closer to the upper chest.

©David K. Miller

FIGURE 12.7   Normal flexibility of chest muscles allows arms to be flexed to 180° of shoulders.

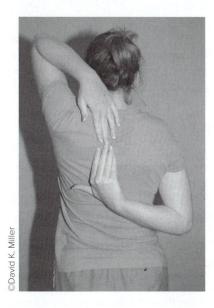

FIGURE 12.8　Normal flexibility of shoulder girdle allows fingertips to touch.

FIGURE 12.11　Normal flexibility of lower back allows thighs to touch chest.

FIGURE 12.9　Normal flexibility in the hips and lower back allows for flexion to about 135°.

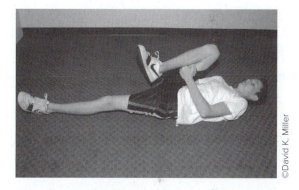

FIGURE 12.12　Normal flexibility of iliopsoas muscle (hip flexor) allows thigh to touch chest. Extended leg should remain on floor and straight.

FIGURE 12.10　Normal flexibility of the hamstring muscles allows straight-leg lifting to 90° from supine position.

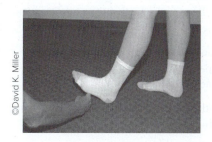

FIGURE 12.13　Normal flexibility of the gastrocnemius muscle (calf) allows the ball of the foot to clear the floor by a height equal to the width of two fingers.

guidelines should be observed for best results when performing the exercises:

- Spend 20 to 30 seconds in a gentle, static stretch with each exercise, and perform each exercise two or three times.

- Increase the extent of the stretch gradually and progressively, with full extension, flexion, or both being placed on the joint.

- Breathe slowly, rhythmically, and with control.

- Stretch beyond the normal length of the muscle but only to the point that a slight stretch pain is felt.

- Practice regularly; perform the exercises several times each day.

Flexibility is highly specific to each joint and activity; therefore, flexibility exercises should be performed for each joint in which increased flexibility is desired.

Neck

1. Place the hands behind the head and gradually press down; hold. The posterior neck muscles should feel stretched.

2. Bend the neck from side to side and then from front to back. Do not rotate the head.

Shoulder and Upper Chest

1. Stand in a doorway and grasp the door jamb above the head. Lean forward through the doorway until the stretch is felt.

2. Stand with the feet shoulder-width apart and lock the hands behind the waist. Straighten the arms, raise, and hold. Bending forward at the waist is a good variation.

3. Extend the arms overhead and interlace the fingers with the palms facing upward. Push upward and slightly backward.

4. Interlace the fingers in front of the chin with the palms turned out. Extend the arms forward.

5. Bring the right hand over the right shoulder to the upper back and reach down as far as possible. Bring

the left hand under the left shoulder to the upper back. Grab the fingers and hold. If you are unable to grasp the fingers together, hold a towel between them. Gradually move the left hand up the towel. Reverse the hand positions and repeat.

Upper Back

1. Lie on the back with the knees bent and the feet flat on the floor. Interlace the fingers behind the head and gently pull forward until you feel a comfortable stretch. This stretch also may be performed while in the standing position.

Lower Back

1. Lie on the back with the knees bent and the feet flat on the floor. Place the hands under the knees and pull both thighs to the chest with your hands while simultaneously raising the head.

2. Sit on the floor with the legs crossed and the arms at the sides. Tuck the chin and curl forward. Slide the hands forward on the floor, allowing the back to be rounded.

Trunk

1. Stand with the feet shoulder-width apart and the toes pointed straight ahead. Extend both arms overhead; grasp the left hand with the right hand and bend slowly to the right. Pull the left arm over the head and down toward the ground with the right hand. Bend to the left, reversing the hand positions.

2. Stand and hold a towel overhead with the hands about 12 inches apart, the elbows straight, and the feet 18 to 24 inches apart. Bend to one side as far as possible, keeping the elbows straight. Repeat on the other side.

3. Sit on the floor with the right leg extended; cross the left foot over the right knee and place the foot flat on the floor. Place the left hand on the floor behind the hips and use the right hand to slowly twist the spine to the left. Look over the left shoulder. Repeat to the other side.

Posterior Hip, Upper Leg, and Lower Back

1. Sit on the floor with the legs straight and the feet together. Bend forward at the waist (do not dip the head or round the back) and slide the hands down the lateral sides of the legs. Try to place the chest on the thighs and grasp the outer borders of the feet. Keep the toes pointed back to stretch the posterior lower-leg muscles.

2. Sit on the floor. Extend one leg and place the sole of the other foot against the knee of the extended leg. Lean forward at the waist and attempt to pull the toes of the extended leg back to exert a stretch in the calf and hamstrings. Repeat with the other leg.

3. Lie flat on the back. Raise one leg straight up with the knee extended and ankle flexed at 90°. Grasp the leg around the calf and pull toward the head. Repeat with the opposite leg.

Anterior Hip and Thigh

1. In a standing position, draw one knee (hands under knee) up to the chest and pull it tightly to the chest with the hands. Repeat with the other knee.

2. Support yourself by leaning against a wall with the right hand; stand on the right leg and bend the left knee. Grasp the ankle behind you with the left hand and gently pull backward; keep the knee pointed down. Repeat with the other leg.

3. Squat with the bent knee of one leg forward and the other leg extended behind you. Push forward until the knee of the front leg is directly over the ankle. The knee of the backward extended leg should be resting on the floor. Without changing the position of the legs and feet, lower the front of your hips downward to create an easy stretch. Reverse the position of the legs and repeat.

Groin Area

1. Sit on the floor. Put the soles of the feet together and grasp the toes. Gently pull yourself forward, bending at the hips.

2. Sit on the floor with the back pressed against a wall or anything that will give support. With the back straight and the soles of the feet together, gently push down on the inside of the thighs with the hands.

Posterior Lower Leg

1. Face a wall, standing approximately 3 to 4 feet away. Lean forward and place the palms against the wall, with the arms straight and at shoulder height. Keep the feet flat and the body in a straight line. Allow the elbows to bend while leaning forward more. Do not allow the heels to rise off the floor.

2. Assume the same position as described in the previous exercise. Perform the same routine but also bend at the knees. Do not allow the heels to rise off the floor. You should feel the stretch in the area closer to the Achilles tendon.

Foot and Ankle

1. Sit on the floor with the left leg extended. Bend the right leg and provide support under the lower calf with the right hand. Grasp the right foot with the left hand and gently rotate the foot clockwise and counterclockwise through a complete range of motion. Repeat with the other foot.

2. Stand with the feet apart. Reach back with one foot and touch the floor with the upper side of the toes. Press down until a stretch is felt. Repeat with the other foot.

Review Problems

1. Review additional flexibility tests found in other textbooks. Note the groups for whom the tests are intended and the validity, reliability, and objectivity coefficients.

2. Administer one of the tests described in this chapter to several of your classmates. Ask them to provide constructive criticism of your test administration.

3. A physical education teacher administered the sit and reach test to 20 fifteen-year-old students. After the students followed a 10-week flexibility program for the lower back and posterior thighs, the

teacher again administered the test. Determine if the students significantly improved their flexibility scores.

Student	Pre-Test Score	Post-Test Score
A	17.50	18.25
B	16.75	17.50
C	17.00	17.75
D	15.50	16.25
E	15.00	15.75
F	18.50	18.50
G	18.00	18.50
H	14.25	16.25
I	17.00	17.25
J	16.50	17.25
K	15.75	15.75
L	17.50	18.00
M	16.75	17.75
N	15.75	16.50
O	15.50	16.25
P	16.25	16.25
Q	15.75	16.00
R	15.25	15.25
S	16.00	16.50
T	17.00	17.75

Chapter Review Questions

1. What is flexibility?

2. How do body size, gender, age, and physical activity relate to flexibility?

3. Why is it important to measure flexibility?

4. What is the difference between relative flexibility tests and absolute flexibility tests?

5. What guidelines should be followed in the administration of flexibility tests?

6. What are your responsibilities after the measurement of flexibility? What type of stretching program would you recommend and why?

13

Muscular Strength, Endurance, and Power

After completing this chapter, you should be able to

1. Define *muscular strength, dynamic strength, static strength, dynamic and static muscular endurance,* and *power.*

2. State why muscular strength, endurance, and power should be measured.

3. Measure muscular strength, endurance, and power.

4. Describe responsibilities after the measurement of muscular strength, endurance, and power and prescribe activities to improve muscular strength and endurance.

Muscular strength is the ability of a muscle or muscle group to exert maximum force. **Dynamic strength** is force exerted by a muscle group as a body part moves. Dynamic strength also may be referred to as isotonic strength. **Static strength** is the force exerted against an immovable object; that is, movement does not take place. This type of strength is also referred to as isometric strength. Both types of strengths are best measured by tests that require one maximum effort.

Muscular endurance is the ability of a muscle or muscle group to resist fatigue and to make repeated contractions against a defined submaximal resistance **(dynamic endurance).** It also may be the ability to maintain a certain degree of force over time **(static endurance).** Muscular strength and endurance are closely related, though weight-training methods for them are typically different. In general, strength is best developed through a high-resistance, low-repetition program, whereas endurance is improved through a low-resistance, high-repetition program. Strength and endurance can be improved through either program, however. Also, it is necessary to have some strength to develop endurance. For example, to develop abdominal muscular endurance through sit-ups, you must have the strength to perform at least one sit-up. The inability to perform one sit-up is due to lack of strength, not to lack of endurance.

Muscular power is the ability to generate maximum force in the fastest possible time. It also may be defined as the ability to release maximum muscular force in an explosive manner. Power is equal to the product of force times velocity. Force is generated by muscle strength (strength is a component of power), and velocity is the speed at which the force is used. Although power is not considered an essential component of physical fitness or good health, it is often the characteristic of a good athlete. Power usually is measured by some type of jump, throw, or charge (the vertical jump, shot put, or a charge at a blocking sled).

Why Measure Muscular Strength, Endurance, and Power?

In modern American society, most individuals do not need upper body muscular strength and endurance to perform work and routine daily activities. Additionally, many children and adolescents fail to participate in activities that require muscular strength and endurance. Consequently, a lack of adequate strength and endurance causes many of us to experience health problems.

Strong muscles help protect the joints, making them less susceptible to sprains, strains, and other injuries. Strength is necessary for good posture. Such postural problems as sagging abdominal muscles, round shoulders, and low-back pain may be prevented if adequate strength is maintained. In addition, strength will enable you to perform routine tasks more efficiently and to experience more satisfaction from leisure sport participation.

The need for muscular endurance is demonstrated in many of our daily activities. Have you ever experienced occasions when it was necessary to "keep going," though your arms, legs, or entire body felt too tired to do so? Perhaps your arms felt this way when carrying the groceries from the car into the house. You had the strength to pick up the groceries, but they felt heavier and heavier the farther you carried them. This phenomenon can occur when a person is pushing a stalled car, carrying a heavy suitcase, or performing any task that involves sustained muscular contraction. Even if you do not lift and carry heavy loads, you probably lift light loads repeatedly or lift and move your body throughout the day. To avoid end-of-day fatigue, you need muscular endurance. Also, possessing adequate muscular endurance enables you to maintain good posture, thereby decreasing the likelihood that you will experience backaches and muscular injury while performing routine tasks.

Children and adolescents also may experience some of these same problems if they do not have the necessary strength and endurance. They certainly are more susceptible to poor posture (which can lead to future health problems) and quicker fatigue in their play and daily activities. Additionally, they are less likely to experience success in games and activities that require a level of strength and endurance.

As previously stated, muscular power is often a characteristic of a good athlete, but it is rarely necessary to have power when performing daily tasks. Because it is not considered to be an essential component of health and physical fitness, it is not usually emphasized in physical education and wellness programs. Occasionally, leisure sports participants feel that increasing their power will improve their sport performance.

Responsibilities after Measurement

After measurement of muscular strength and endurance, you should seek to help the individuals who need to improve in these components. Improvement will take place within a few weeks if the correct program or exercises are done on a regular basis. For children, a highly organized program often is not necessary. They usually can improve their strength through activities that require them to move and lift their own body. For others, weight-training programs typically involve the use of free weights, Nautilus equipment, or other similar equipment. In such programs, the major muscle groups should be used, the exercises should be performed a minimum of two days each week, and 8 to 12 repetitions of each exercise should be completed. Muscular strength and endurance can be improved without the use of expensive equipment or a special room, however. Exercises and guidelines for the development of muscular strength and endurance are provided at the conclusion of this chapter.

ARE YOU ABLE TO DO THE FOLLOWING?

- Define *muscular strength, dynamic and static muscular strength, dynamic and static muscular endurance,* and *power.*

- State why muscular strength, muscular endurance, and muscular power should be measured.

- Describe responsibilities after the measurement of muscular strength and endurance.

Tests of Muscular Strength and Endurance

In the laboratory and rehabilitation setting, dynamometers, cable tensiometers, and electromechanical instruments are used to measure muscular strength and endurance. This equipment is expensive and is typically used in research

◆ ◆ ◆ POINT OF EMPHASIS ◆ ◆ ◆

- For the older population, the decline in muscle strength affects other functions such as agility, balance, and coordination. Improvement in muscular strength and endurance in these individuals can improve these abilities.

studies when accuracy of measurement is essential. Two types of dynamometers are used to measure static strength, one for handgrip and one for back and leg strength. Cable tensiometers may be used to measure static strength of many different muscle groups. Electromechanical instruments measure static and dynamic strength, endurance, and power. Through measurement of the intensity and frequency (in terms of electrical activity) of muscle contractions, these instruments are capable of determining the maximum contraction of a muscle group at a constant speed throughout the entire range of the movement. Many public schools and fitness centers have weight-training machines and free weights, but few have dynamometers, cable tensiometers, and electromechanical instruments.

Tests with Weight-Training Equipment

If weight-training equipment is available, the measurement of dynamic muscular strength and endurance is a simple procedure. It is important, however, that handgrip, knee flexion, foot placement, and all other considerations that may influence test performance be standardized and enforced. In addition, since motivational factors can influence the test results, the test administration must be standardized for motivational considerations. Test participants should warm up but avoid overworking, and safety precautions should be observed, especially if free weights are used.

Before testing, the American College of Sports Medicine (2010b) recommends that the following be considered:

- Participants should be familiarized with the equipment and test procedures.

- Participants should be provided an adequate warm-up period.

- Standardization of performance position should be followed for all tests.

- Adequate rest should be provided between tests.

Dynamic strength is measured with one repetition maximum (1-RM). Because a direct relationship exists between body weight and weight lifted (heavier individuals generally can lift more), the maximum weight that can be lifted should be interpreted in relation to the individual's weight.

Although 1-RMs may be administered to measure most muscle groups, the body's major muscle groups may be tested with the bench press, standing press, arm curls, and leg press. The bench press and leg press are described in this chapter.

Muscular endurance tests may be relative or absolute. In a relative endurance test, the performer works with a weight that is proportionate to the maximum strength of a particular muscle group or to body weight. In an absolute endurance test, all performers work with the same amount of weight (the weight has no relationship to maximum strength or body weight of the test performer). In a test for muscular endurance, the weight should be lifted and returned without jerky movements. A 3-second cadence may be used for each lift to encourage continuous, smooth movement. The score is the number of repetitions completed, and the test is completed when a lift can no longer be properly executed or performed with the cadence. Pollock, Wilmore, and Fox (1978) suggest that a fixed percentage of 70% of the maximum strength be used to test muscle endurance. This percentage would be the same for all muscle groups tested. No norms have been developed for this procedure, but on the basis of limited test data, the individual seeking health fitness should be able to perform 12 to 15 repetitions, and the competitive athlete should be able to perform 20 to 25 repetitions of each of the lifts tested.

■ 1-Repetition Maximum (RM) Bench Press
(ACSM 2010b)

Test Objective. To measure strength of the arm extension muscles.

Age Level. Twenty through sixty-plus.

Equipment. Free weights and weight bench; Nautilus or similar equipment may be used.

Validity. Research shows that the best weight-lifting test for predicting total dynamic strength is the 1-RM bench press.

Norms. Table 13.1 provides norms.

Administration and Directions. Free weight equipment is preferred over equipment like Nautilus, and a spotter must be present at all times. For the test, (1) the test performer keeps the back on the bench, both feet on the floor, and the hands shoulder-width apart with palms up on the bar; (2) a spotter hands the bar to the test performer, and the lift is started with the arms fully extended; and (3) the bar is lowered to the chest and pushed back up until the arms are locked. The test performer first should practice the bench press with a light warm-up of 5 to 10 repetitions at 40 to 60% of perceived

TABLE 13.1 Norms for 1-Repetition Maximum (RM) Bench Press Test

Performance Level	Age				
	20–29	30–39	40–49	50–59	60+
Males					
Above average (70–80%)	1.22–1.32	1.04–1.12	.93–1.00	.84–.90	.77–.82
Average (50–60%)	1.06–1.14	.93–.98	.84–.88	.75–.79	.68–.72
Below average (30–40%)	.93–.99	.83–.88	.76–.80	.68–.71	.63–.66
Females					
Above average (70–80%)	.74–.80	.63–.70	.57–.62	.52–.55	.51–.54
Average (50–60%)	.65–.70	.57–.60	.52–.54	.46–.48	.45–.47
Below average (30–40%)	.56–.59	.51–.53	.47–.50	.42–.44	.40–.43

Source: Adapted from *ACSM's health-related physical fitness assessment manual*, 5th ed., Philadelphia: Wolters Kluwer Health Ltd, 2018. Original source: Cooper Institute, *Physical fitness assessments and norms for adults and law enforcement*, Dallas: Cooper Institute, 2009.

maximum. After a 1-minute rest, the test performer does 3 to 5 repetitions at 60 to 80% of perceived maximum. The performer should be close to the perceived maximum; a small amount of weight is added and 1-RM is attempted. If the lift is successful, a 3- to 5-minute rest period is provided, and the test is continued until a failed lift occurs. The 1-RM should be found in 3 to 5 efforts.

Scoring. A ratio is determined by dividing the maximum weight lifted by the test performer's weight in pounds.

■ **1-Repetition Maximum (RM) Leg Press**
(ACSM 2010b)

Test Objective. To test strength of the lower leg extension muscles.
Age Level. Twenty through sixty-plus.
Equipment. Leg press equipment.
Validity. Face validity.
Norms. Table 13.2 provides norms.

TABLE 13.2 Norms for 1-Repetition Maximum (RM) Leg Press Test

Performance Level	Age				
	20–29	30–39	40–49	50–59	60+
Males					
Above average (70–80%)	2.05–2.13	1.85–1.93	1.74–1.82	1.64–1.71	1.56–1.62
Average (50–60%)	1.91–1.97	1.71–1.77	1.62–1.68	1.52–1.58	1.43–1.49
Below average (30–40%)	1.74–1.83	1.59–1.65	1.51–1.57	1.39–1.46	1.30–1.38
Females					
Above average (70–80%)	1.58–1.68	1.39–1.47	1.29–1.37	1.17–1.25	1.13–1.18
Average (50–60%)	1.44–1.50	1.27–1.33	1.18–1.23	1.05–1.10	.99–1.04
Below average (30–40%)	1.27–1.37	1.15–1.21	1.08–1.13	.95–.99	.88–.93

Source: Adapted from *ACSM's health-related physical fitness assessment manual*, 5th ed., Philadelphia: Wolters Kluwer Health Ltd, 2018. Original source: Cooper Institute, *Physical fitness assessments and norms for adults and law enforcement*, Dallas: Cooper Institute, 2009.

Administration and Directions. The administration and directions followed for the 1-Repetition Maximum (RM) Bench Press can be used for the leg press test.
Scoring. A ratio is determined by dividing the maximum weight pressed by the test performer's weight in pounds.

■ **YMCA Bench Press Test**
(Golding 2000)

Test Objective. To test dynamic muscle endurance of the upper arm and shoulder girdle muscles.
Age Level. Eighteen through sixty-five-plus.
Equipment. A metronome, 35-pound barbell, 80-pound barbell, and weight bench.
Norms. Table 13.3 provides norms.
Administration and Directions. Use a 35-pound barbell with females and an 80-pound barbell with males. Set the metronome to 60 beats per minute. For the test, the test performer (1) lies supine on the bench with the feet flat on the floor, (2) receives the barbell from a spotter with the arms flexed (weight rests on the chest) and the hands shoulder-width apart, (3) presses the weight up and lowers the weight at a cadence of 30 repetitions per minute, and (4) continues until the arms cannot fully extend or the cadence cannot be maintained. The arms must be fully extended and returned to the chest with each lift.

Tests Requiring Limited Equipment

The following tests for muscular strength, endurance, and power are simple and practical, and they require little equipment for administration. However, reliability and objectivity coefficients are not reported for all the tests, and many of them are not appropriate for both sexes. If a test is designed primarily for one sex, that sex is indicated. Participants should be permitted to practice the tests and rest. Rest should be permitted when two or more test trials are administered.

■ **Sit-Ups (Strength)**
(Johnson and Nelson 1986)

Test Objective. To measure strength of abdominal and trunk flexion muscles.
Age Level. Twelve through college-age.
Equipment. A mat, weight bar, dumbbell bar, weight plates, and a 12-inch ruler.
Validity. Face validity.
Reliability. .91.
Objectivity. .98.
Norms. Johnson and Nelson (1986) provide norms (weight lifted divided by body weight) for college students.
Administration and Directions. The sit-up is performed with a weight plate, a dumbbell, or a barbell behind the neck. If a dumbbell or barbell is used, the attached weight plates must not have a greater circumference than standard 5-pound plates. The

TABLE 13.3 Norms for YMCA Bench Press Test

Performance Level	Age					
	18–25	26–35	36–45	46–55	56–65	>65
Males						
Above average (60–70%)	29–33	26–29	22–25	16–20	12–14	10
Average (45–55%)	24–28	21–24	18–21	12–14	9–11	7–8
Below average (30–40%)	20–22	17–20	14–17	9–11	5–8	4–6
Females						
Above average (60–70%)	25–28	24–28	21–24	14–18	12–14	8–10
Average (45–55%)	20–22	18–22	16–20	10–13	8–10	5–7
Below average (30–40%)	16–18	14–17	12–14	7–9	5–6	3–4

Source: Golding, L. A. (ed.), *YMCA fitness testing and assessment manual*, 4th ed., Champaign, Ill.: Human Kinetics, 2000.

test performer (1) selects the amount of weight that is to be held during the sit-up; (2) assumes a supine position on a mat so the selected weight is behind the neck, flexes the knees, and places the feet flat on the mat; (3) with a test partner holding a ruler under the knees, slides the feet toward the buttocks until the ruler can be held in place by the flexion of the lower legs; (4) slowly slides the feet forward until the ruler falls—at that point the test administrator marks the heel line and the buttocks line, indicating the distance that should remain between the heels and the buttocks during the test; and (5) as the partner holds the performer's feet firmly to floor, attempts to sit up while holding the weight behind the neck (see figure 13.1). The test administrator should be prepared to remove the weight at the completion of the sit-up.

Scoring. Two sit-ups are permitted, and the greatest amount of weight lifted is recorded. The test score may be (1) the amount of weight lifted or (2) the amount of weight lifted divided by body weight.

■ **Sit-Ups (Endurance)**
(AAHPERD 1980a; Pollock, Wilmore, and Fox 1978)

Test Objective. To measure abdominal strength and endurance.
Age Level. Five through adulthood.

FIGURE 13.1 Sit-ups test for strength.

Equipment. Mats and a stopwatch.
Validity. Logical validity.
Reliability. .68 to .94 for modified sit-ups test.
Norms. Tables 13.4 through 13.7 provide norms.
Administration and Directions. Three types of sit-ups tests may be administered; all three are performed for 60 seconds. With the modified sit-ups test, the test performer assumes a supine position on the mat with the knees flexed, feet flat on the mat,

TABLE 13.4 Norms for Sit-Ups Test with Hands Crossed on Chest (Muscular Endurance) for Ages Five through College-Age

| | Age | | | | | | | | | | | | | |
Percentile	5	6	7	8	9	10	11	12	13	14	15	16	17+	College
						Males								
95	30	36	42	48	47	50	51	56	58	59	59	61	62	60
75	23	26	33	37	38	40	42	46	48	49	49	51	52	50
50	18	20	26	30	32	34	37	39	41	42	44	45	46	44
25	11	15	19	25	25	27	30	31	35	36	38	38	38	38
5	2	6	10	15	15	15	17	19	25	27	28	28	25	30
						Females								
95	28	35	40	44	44	47	50	52	51	51	56	54	54	53
75	24	28	31	35	35	39	40	41	41	42	43	42	44	42
50	19	22	25	29	29	32	34	36	35	35	37	33	37	35
25	12	14	20	22	23	25	28	30	29	30	30	29	31	30
5	2	6	10	12	14	15	19	19	18	20	20	20	19	21

Source: Adapted from *AAHPERD health related physical fitness test manual*, Reston, Va.: American Alliance for Health, Physical Education, Recreation and Dance, 1980; and Pate, R. R., *Norms for college students: Health related physical fitness test*, Reston, Va.: AAHPERD, 1985.

TABLE 13.5 Norms for Sit-Ups with Hands behind Neck (Muscular Endurance) for Ages Nine through Seventeen+

Percentile	Age							
	9–10	11	12	13	14	15	16	17+
Males								
95	47	48	50	53	55	57	55	54
75	38	40	42	45	47	48	47	46
50	31	34	35	38	41	42	41	41
25	25	26	30	30	34	37	35	35
5	13	15	18	20	24	28	28	26
Females								
95	45	43	44	45	45	45	43	45
75	34	35	36	36	37	36	35	35
50	27	29	29	30	30	31	30	30
25	21	22	24	23	24	25	24	25
5	10	9	13	15	16	15	15	14

Source: Adapted from AAHPERD, *Youth fitness test manual*, Reston, Va.: American Alliance for Health, Physical Education, Recreation and Dance, 1976.

TABLE 13.6 Norms for Sit-Ups Test with Hands behind Neck (Muscular Endurance) for Ages Twenty through Sixty-Nine

Performance Level	Age				
	20–29	30–39	40–49	50–59	60–69
Males					
Above average	43 and above	35 and above	30 and above	25 and above	20 and above
Average	37 to 42	29 to 34	24 to 29	19 to 24	14 to 19
Below average	36 and below	28 and below	23 and below	18 and below	13 and below
Females					
Above average	39 and above	31 and above	26 and above	21 and above	16 and above
Average	33 to 38	25 to 30	19 to 25	15 to 20	10 to 15
Below average	32 and below	24 and below	18 and below	14 and below	9 and below

Source: Adapted from *Physical fitness assessments and norms*, Dallas, Tex.: The Cooper Institute, 2004.

and the heels between 12 and 18 inches from the buttocks. The arms are crossed on the chest with the hands on opposite shoulders. A test partner holds the feet of the test performer to keep them in contact with the mat. On the signal "Go," the test performer (1) curls to a sitting position and touches the thighs with the elbows while maintaining arm contact with the chest and keeping the chin tucked on the chest (see figure 13.2), (2) curls back to the floor until the midback contacts the mat, and (3) continues to perform as many sit-ups as possible in 60 seconds. The test administrator should use the signal "Ready, Go" to begin the test, and the word "Stop" to conclude the test at the end of 60 seconds. Pausing between sit-ups is permitted.

TABLE 13.7   Norms for Sit-Ups Test with Hands Cupped behind Ears (Muscular Endurance) for Ages below Twenty through Sixty-Plus

Performance Level	Age					
	<20	20–29	30–39	40–49	50–59	60+
Males						
Excellent	51–55	47–52	43–48	39–43	35–39	30–35
Good	47–50	42–46	39–42	34–37	28–33	22–28
Fair	41–46	38–41	35–37	29–32	24–27	19–21
Females						
Excellent	46–54	44–49	35–40	29–34	24–29	17–26
Good	36–40	38–42	29–33	24–28	20–22	11–15
Fair	32–35	32–37	25–28	20–23	14–19	6–10

Source: Adapted from *Physical fitness assessments and norms*, Dallas, Tex.: The Cooper Institute, 2004.

Table 13.4 includes norms for this sit-ups test for ages five through college-age.

A second type of sit-ups test is administered in a similar procedure, except the hands are interlocked behind the performer's neck, the elbows are touched to the knees, and the performer must return to the full lying position before starting the next sit-up (see figure 13.3). The performer should be cautioned not to use the arms to thrust the body into a sitting position. Table 13.5 includes norms for ages nine through seventeen-plus, and table 13.6 includes norms for ages twenty through sixty-nine for this sit-ups test.

The third sit-ups test is administered in the same way as the second type test, except the hands are cupped behind the ears. Table 13.7 includes norms for ages below twenty through sixty-plus.

Scoring. The score for all three tests is the number of sit-ups correctly performed during the 60 seconds. Incorrect performance for the modified sit-ups test includes failure to curl up, failure to keep the arms against the chest, failure to touch the thighs with the elbows, and failure to touch the midback to the mat. The distance between the heels and the buttocks should be monitored continuously. Incorrect performance for the second and third types of sit-ups tests includes failure to keep the hands interlocked behind the neck, failure to touch the knees with the elbows, and failure to return to the full lying position. If partners are permitted to count the number of sit-ups, the test administrator should observe to be sure the partners are counting only sit-ups that are performed correctly.

♦ ♦ ♦   POINT OF EMPHASIS   ♦ ♦ ♦

- The sit-ups and curl-ups tests described in this chapter emphasize speed of performance. Similar tests are included as components of health-related fitness tests described in chapter 15. You will note, however, that a few of the tests in chapter 15 require that the sit-ups or curl-ups be performed at a specified cadence (e.g., 20 curl-ups per minute) rather than at maximum speed. Some exercise specialists believe that the speed procedure incorporates muscular power into the sit-ups and curl-ups tests whereas the cadence procedure better measures muscular endurance.

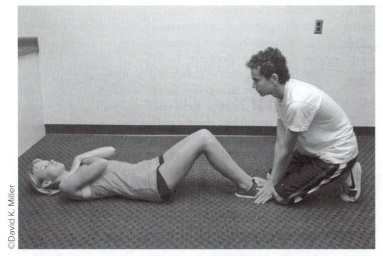

FIGURE 13.2   Modified sit-ups test.

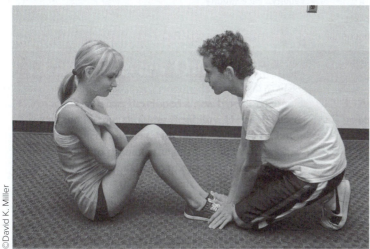

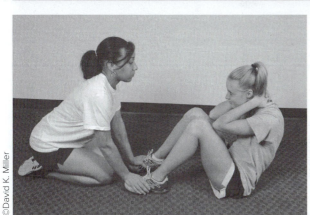

FIGURE 13.3   Sit-ups test (hands behind neck).

■ **Abdominal Curls**
(Robbins, Powers, and Burgess 1991)

Test Objective. To measure abdominal strength and endurance.
Age Level. Five through adulthood.
Equipment. Mats, tape, and stopwatch.
Validity. Logical validity.
Reliability. Not reported.
Norms. Table 13.8 provides norms for ages eighteen through thirty.
Administration and Directions. A strip of tape 3 inches wide is placed on the mat. The test performer assumes a supine position on the mat, with the fingertips at the edge of the strip. The knees are flexed, the feet are placed flat on the floor, and the heels are as close to the hips as possible. The test per-

Muscular Strength, Endurance, and Power   **169**

TABLE 13.8 Norms for Abdominal Curls for Ages Eighteen through Thirty

	Males	Females
Excellent	96 and above	89 and above
Good	82–95	76–88
Average	68–81	63–75
Poor	54–67	49–62
Very poor	53 and below	48 and below

Source: Robbins, G., Powers, D. and Burgess, S. *A wellness way of life*, 2d ed., Dubuque, Iowa: Brown & Benchmark Publishers, 1994.

former curls forward until the fingertips move forward 3 inches and curls backward until the shoulder blades touch the mat. The shoulder blades should lift from the mat with each curl, but the lower back should stay on the mat. The feet should not lift off the mat, and the feet *should not* be held down by a partner.

Scoring. The test score is the number of curls that can be performed in 1 minute.

■ One-Minute Curl-Up
(The Cooper Institute 2004)

Test Objective. To measure abdominal strength and endurance.
Age Level. Five through sixty-plus.
Equipment. Mats, ruler, tape, and stopwatch.

Validity. Face validity.
Norms. Table 13.9 provides norms for ages eighteen through sixty-plus.
Administration and Directions. The test administration and directions for the abdominal curl test described previously are followed except the test performer's feet are held in place by another individual.

■ Pull-Ups for Strength
(Johnson and Nelson 1986)

Test Objective. To measure arm and shoulder girdle strength.
Age Level. Twelve through college-age.
Equipment. A horizontal bar; 2½-, 5-, 10-, and 25-pound weight plates; a rope or strap to secure the weights to the waist of the test performer; and a chair.
Validity. Face validity.
Reliability. .99.
Objectivity. .99.
Norms. Johnson and Nelson provide norms for college males.
Administration and Directions. The horizontal bar is raised to a height so that the test performer's feet will be off the floor. The test performer (1) secures the desired amount of weight to the waist and steps on the chair (the test administrator should assist when the performer steps to and from the chair), (2) grasps the bar with the overhand grip (palms forward) and assumes a straight-arm hang (chair is removed), and (3) pulls upward until the chin is above the bar (chair is replaced under the feet). The

TABLE 13.9 Norms for Abdominal Curls for Ages Eighteen through Sixty-Plus

Performance Level	Age				
	18–29	30–39	40–49	50–59	60+
Males					
Advanced	>50	>45	>40	>35	>30
Intermediate	30–50	22–45	21–40	18–35	15–30
Beginner	<30	<22	<21	<18	<15
Females					
Advanced	>45	>40	>35	>30	>25
Intermediate	25–45	20–40	18–35	12–30	11–25
Beginner	<25	<20	<18	<12	<11

Source: Adapted from *Physical fitness assessments and norms*, Dallas, Tex.: The Cooper Institute, 2004.

performer may step down and readjust the weights before repeating the test.

Scoring. Two pull-ups are permitted, and the greatest amount of weight lifted is recorded. The test score is the amount of weight lifted divided by body weight. The test performer who cannot lift more than his or her own body weight receives a score of zero. No swinging action to move upward is permitted.

■ Pull-Ups for Endurance
(AAHPERD 1976a)

Test Objective. To measure arm and shoulder girdle strength and endurance.
Age Level. Nine through college-age.
Equipment. Metal or wooden bar approximately 1½ inches in diameter (inclined ladder may be used).
Validity. Face validity.
Reliability. .87.
Norms. Table 13.10 provides norms for males ages nine through seventeen-plus.
Administration and Directions. The test performer hangs from the bar using the overhand grip (palms forward) with the legs and arms fully extended. The feet should not touch the floor. The performer pulls upward until the chin is over the bar and then lowers the body to a full hang position. The pull-up is repeated as many times as possible.
Scoring. Only one trial is administered, unless it is obvious the performer can do better with a second attempt. The score is the number of completed pull-ups. The knees must not be flexed, and kicking, swinging, and snap-up motions are not permitted. The test administrator may prevent these actions by holding an extended arm across the front of the performer's thighs.

A test using the reverse grip (palms facing the body) is also administered to measure arm and shoulder girdle strength and endurance. This is an acceptable grip, but because the test performers will be able to complete more repetitions with this grip, the AAHPERD norms should not be used for scoring.

■ Modified Pull-Ups for Endurance

Note: Though designed for females, this test may be administered to males who are unable to perform the pull-ups previously described.
Test Objective. To measure arm and shoulder girdle endurance.
Age Level. Ten through college-age.
Equipment. Horizontal bar.
Validity. Face validity.
Norms. None.
Administration and Directions. The bar is adjusted to the height of the base of the performer's sternum when the performer is standing erect. The performer (1) grasps the bar with an overhand grip (palms forward) and slides the feet under the bar until the arms are straight and the angle between the arms and trunk is 90°, (2) keeps the body rigid and straight and brings the chin over the bar, and (3) completes as many pull-ups as possible (see figure 13.4).
Scoring. Only one trial is permitted, and the score is the number of correct pull-ups completed.

■ Baumgartner Modified Pull-Ups
(Baumgartner and Jackson 1982; Baumgartner et al. 1984)

Test Objective. To measure arm and shoulder girdle strength, endurance, or both.
Age Level. Elementary school through college.

TABLE 13.10 Norms for Pull-Ups Test for Males Ages Nine through Seventeen+

Percentile	Age							
	9–10	11	12	13	14	15	16	17+
95	9	8	9	10	12	15	14	15
75	3	4	4	5	7	9	10	10
50	1	2	2	3	4	6	7	7
25	0	0	0	1	2	3	4	4
15	0	0	0	0	1	1	3	2

Source: Adapted from AAHPERD, *AAHPERD youth fitness test manual*, Reston, Va.: American Alliance for Health, Physical Education, Recreation and Dance, 1976.

FIGURE 13.4 Modified pull-ups for females.

Equipment. The necessary equipment is sold commercially, or it may be constructed locally with inexpensive parts. The equipment consists of an inclined board with a rail system for a scooter board to slide on (see figure 13.5).

Validity. Face validity and construct validity, since males performed significantly better than females.

Reliability. Reliability coefficients of .89 to .98 have been reported.

Norms. Table 13.11 reports norms for ages six through college-age.

Administration and Directions. The test performer lies prone on the scooter board and grasps the bar with an overhand grip, hands shoulder-width apart. The arms should be fully extended. The test is then performed like the regular pull-ups test, pulling the chin over the bar and returning to a straight-arm hanging position. The performer should pull evenly with both arms and not drag the toes.

Scoring. The score is the completed number of repetitions.

■ **Modified Pull-Ups**
(Pate et al. 1987)

Test Objective. To measure upper body muscular strength and endurance.

Age Level. Five through eighteen.

Equipment. Modified pull-up stand or a low pull-up bar that allows for adjustment of height and elastic bands.

Administration and Directions. The test performer lies on the back with the shoulders between the uprights and reaches straight up as high as possible (head and shoulders remain flat on floor). The tester sets the bar approximately 2 inches above the performer's outstretched hands and places the elastic band 7 to 8 inches below the bar. The performer raises the body high enough to grasp the bar with the palms forward (see figure 13.6a). In the starting position, the heels are on the floor, the buttocks are off the floor, and the arms and legs are straight. The pull-up is completed when the chin is hooked over the elastic band (see

FIGURE 13.5 Baumgartner modified pull-ups test.

TABLE 13.11 Norms for Baumgartner's Modified Pull-Ups Test

Performance Level	Age									
	6	**7**	**8**	**9–11**	******	**14**	**15**	**16**	**17–18**	**College**
					Males					
Above average	18 and above	23 and above	26 and above	32 and above		30 and above	31 and above	35 and above	33 and above	34 and above
Average (40% to 60%)	13 to 17	18 to 22	19 to 25	25 to 31		25 to 29	27 to 30	30 to 34	29 to 32	28 to 33
Below average	12 and below	17 and below	18 and below	24 and below		24 and below	26 and below	29 and below	28 and below	27 and below

Performance Level	Age						
	6	**7**	**8**	**9–11**	******	**14–15**	******	**College**
					Females		
Above average	18 and above	21 and above	19 and above	24 and above		14 and above		13 and above
Average (40% to 60%)	13 to 17	15 to 20	14 to 18	18 to 23		10 to 13		10 to 12
Below average	12 and below	14 and below	13 and below	17 and below		9 and below		9 and below

**Norms not reported for males ages twelve through thirteen or for females ages twelve through thirteen and sixteen through eighteen.

Source: Adapted from Jackson, A. et al., "Baumgartner's modified pull-up test for male and female elementary school aged children," *Research Quarterly for Exercise and Sport*, vol. 53, 1982, 163–164; and Baumgartner, T. A. et al., "Equipment improvements and additional norms for the modified pull-ups test," *Research Quarterly for Exercise and Sport*, vol. 55, 1985, 64–68.

figure 13.6b). The performer returns to the full extension of the arms and repeats as many times as possible. The body is to remain straight throughout the test.

Scoring. The score is the completed number of repetitions. No norms have been reported.

■ **Flexed-Arm Hang**
(AAHPERD 1976a)

Test Objective. To measure arm and shoulder girdle endurance.
Age Level. Nine through college-age.
Equipment. A horizontal bar 1½ inches in diameter and a stopwatch.
Validity. Face validity.
Reliability. .90.
Objectivity. .99.

Norms. Table 13.12 provides norms for females ages nine through seventeen-plus.
Administration and Directions. The bar should be at a height that does not allow the test performer to touch the floor from the flexed-arm position. With the assistance of two spotters and using an overhand grip, the performer raises the body off the floor so that the chin is above the bar and the elbows are flexed. This position is held for as long as possible.
Scoring. The score is the number of seconds the proper position is maintained. The test administrator should begin the time as soon as the performer is in the flexed-arm position and should stop the time when the chin touches the bar, tilts backward, or drops below the bar. Though developed for females, this test may be used for males who are unable to perform the pull-ups test.

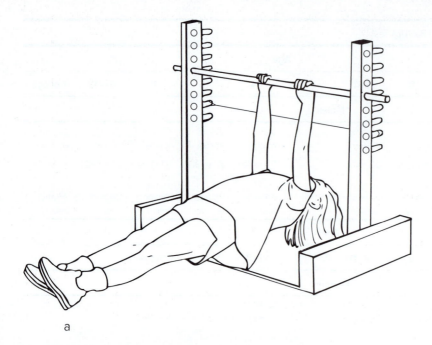

a

FIGURE 13.6 Modified pull-ups.

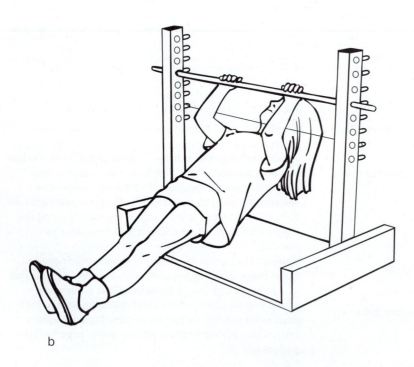

b

TABLE 13.12 Norms in Seconds for Flexed-Arm Hang for Females Ages Nine through Seventeen+

Percentile	Age							
	9–10	11	12	13	14	15	16	17+
95	42	39	33	34	35	36	31	34
75	18	20	18	16	21	18	15	17
50	9	10	9	8	9	9	7	8
25	3	3	3	3	3	4	3	3
15	1	2	1	1	2	2	1	2

Source: Adapted from AAHPERD, *AAHPERD youth fitness test manual*, Reston, Va.: American Alliance for Health, Physical Education, Recreation and Dance, 1976.

■ Dip for Strength
(Johnson and Nelson 1986)

Test Objective. To measure arm and shoulder girdle strength.
Age Level. Twelve through college-age.
Equipment. Parallel bars, weight plates, straps, and a chair.
Validity. Face validity.
Reliability. .98.
Objectivity. .99.
Norms. Johnson and Nelson (1986) provide norms for college males.
Administration and Directions. The bars should be at a height that allows the test performer to be freely above the floor while in the lowered bent-arm support position. After securing the desired amount of weight to the waist, the test performer (1) steps on the chair and takes a secure grip on the bars (he or she should be assisted when stepping to and from the chair), (2) assumes a straight-arm support position (the chair is removed), (3) lowers himself or herself until the elbows form a right angle, and (4) pushes to a straight-arm support position (chair is replaced). The performer may step down and readjust the weights before attempting the exercise again.
Scoring. Two dips are permitted. The greatest amount of weight lifted is recorded. The test score is the amount of weight lifted divided by body weight. The test performer is not permitted to swing or kick in returning to the straight-arm support position.

■ Dips for Endurance
(Johnson and Nelson 1986)

Test Objective. To measure arm and shoulder girdle endurance.
Age Level. Ten through college-age.
Equipment. Parallel bars.

Validity. Face validity.
Reliability. .90.
Objectivity. Not reported.
Norms. None reported.
Administration and Directions. The bars should be at a height that allows the test performer to be freely above the floor while in the lowered bent-arm support position. The performer (1) jumps to a straight-arm support position between the bars, (2) lowers the body until the angle at the elbows is a right angle or less, and (3) completes the exercise as many times as possible.
Scoring. The score is the number of correct dips completed. Resting between dips and kicking or swinging are not permitted.

■ Push-ups in Rhythm
(President's Council on Physical Fitness and Sports 2012)

Test Objective. To measure upper body strength/endurance.
Age level. Six through seventeen.
Equipment. None required.
Validity. Face validity.
Reliability and Objectivity. Not reported.
Norms. Table 13.13 reports the 50th and 85th percentiles for males and females ages six through seventeen.
Administration and Directions. The test performer (1) lies face down on the floor with the body straight, arms bent, and hands flat on the floor beneath the shoulders; (2) uses the toes as the pivot point and pushes upward to a straight-arm position; (3) lowers the body until there is a 90° angle at the elbows; (4) a partner holds her or his hands at the point of the 90° angle so that the test performer goes down until the shoulders touch the partner's hands; (5) the push-ups are done to a metronome, with one complete push-up every 3 seconds; and (6) the

TABLE 13.13 Percentile Norms for Push-ups in Rhythm for Ages Six through Seventeen

Percentile	Age											
	6	7	8	9	10	11	12	13	14	15	16	17
Males												
50	7	8	9	12	14	15	18	24	24	30	30	37
85	9	14	17	18	22	27	31	39	40	42	44	53
Females												
50	6	8	9	12	13	11	10	11	10	15	12	16
85	9	14	17	18	20	19	20	21	20	20	24	25

Source: Adapted from the *President's Council on Physical Fitness and Sports, President's challenge physical fitness program*, Washington, D.C.: President's Council on Physical Fitness and Sports, 2012.

push-ups are continued until the performer can do no more in rhythm (cannot perform the last three in rhythm).

Score. The score is the maximum number of push-ups that can be completed in rhythm.

■ **Push-Ups**

(Johnson and Nelson 1986)

Test Objective. To measure arm and shoulder girdle endurance.

Age Level. Ten through adulthood.

Equipment. None required; mats may be used.

Validity. Face validity.

Objectivity. .99.

Norms. Table 13.14 reports norms for males and females (modified push-ups) ages twenty through sixty-nine. The *ACSM's Health-Related Physical Fitness Assessment* and the physical fitness assessment of *CSEP-Physical Activity Training for Health* (CSEP-PATH) described in chapter 15 also include norms for males and females ages twenty through sixty-nine. (With these tests, performer must touch mat with the chin.)

Administration and Directions. The test performer (1) lies face down on the floor with the body straight, arms bent, and hands flat on the floor beneath the shoulders; (2) uses the toes as the pivot point and pushes upward to a straight-arm position; (3) lowers the body until the chest touches the floor; and (4) repeats the exercise as many times as possible without rest. The body must stay rigid (not sag or pike upward) throughout the test. A sponge that is 2 inches high may be placed on the floor for the performer to touch with the chest. This particular test procedure does not require that the push-ups be performed in a cadence or rhythmic pace. Some fitness

tests (e.g., Fitnessgram) require that the push-ups be performed in such a way.

Scoring. The score is the number of correct push-ups completed.

■ **Modified Push-Ups**

Test Objective. To measure arm and shoulder girdle endurance.

Age Level. Ten through adulthood.

Equipment. None required; mats may be used.

Validity. Face validity.

Reliability. .93 (Johnson and Nelson 1986).

Objectivity. Not reported.

Norms. Table 13.14 provides norms for females ages twenty through sixty-nine. The *ACSM's Health-Related Physical Fitness Assessment* and *CSEP-Physical Activity Training for Health* (CSEP-PATH) described in chapter 15 also include norms.

Administration and Directions. The test performer (1) lies face down on the floor with the body trunk straight, knees bent at right angles, arms bent, and hands flat on the floor beneath the shoulders; (2) uses the knees as the pivot point and pushes upward to a straight-arm position (see figure 13.7); (3) lowers the body until the chest touches the floor; and (4) repeats the exercise as many times as possible without rest. The body trunk must remain straight throughout the test. Modified push-ups also may be performed with a bench. The push-up is performed in the same manner as regular push-ups (weight supported on hands and toes) except the hands are placed on a bench that is approximately 15 inches high and 15 inches long.

Scoring. The score is the number of correct push-ups completed.

TABLE 13.14 Norms for Push-Ups Test (Muscular Endurance) for Ages Twenty through Sixty-Nine

Performance Level	Age				
	20–29	30–39	40–49	50–59	60–69
Males					
Above average	45 and above	35 and above	30 and above	25 and above	20 and above
Average	35 to 44	25 to 34	20 to 29	15 to 24	10 to 19
Below average	34 and below	24 and below	19 and below	14 and below	9 and below
Females **(Modified Push-Ups)**					
Above average	34 and above	25 and above	20 and above	15 and above	5 and above
Average	17 to 33	12 to 24	8 to 19	6 to 14	3 to 4
Below average	16 and below	11 and below	7 and below	5 and below	2 and below

Source: Adapted from Pollock, M. L., Wilmore, J. H. and Fox, S. M., *Health and fitness through physical activity*, New York: John Wiley & Sons, 1978.

©David K. Miller

FIGURE 13.7 Modified push-ups.

Tests of Muscular Power

Two types of muscular power may be measured: athletic power and work power. The distance the body or an object can be propelled through space indicates athletic power (vertical jump and medicine ball put when all of the body is used to propel the ball). If work power is to be measured, extraneous movements are controlled or eliminated, so that maximum effort must be put forth by the muscle groups being tested. For example, if the vertical jump is used to measure work power, the test performer is not permitted to swing the arms. Because power is rarely measured to determine the health or physical fitness status of an individual, only three power tests will be presented.

■ Vertical Jump (Athletic Power)
(Sargent 1921)

Test Objective. To measure explosive leg power.

Age Level. Nine through adulthood.

Equipment. A yardstick or measuring tape, chalk, and a wall of sufficient height.

Validity. .78 using a criterion test of four power events in track and field.

Reliability. .93.

Objectivity. Coefficients >.90 have been reported.

Norms. Table 13.15 reports norms for ages ten through seventeen-plus, and table 13.16 reports norms for ages twenty through fifty-nine. Norms for ages fifteen through sixty-nine also are included with the Canadian Physical Activity, Fitness & Lifestyle Appraisal (see chapter 15).

Administration and Directions. A yardstick or tape measure is taped to the wall to measure the distance between two chalk marks. The test performer (1) stands with the dominant side toward the wall and feet flat on the floor; (2) holding a piece of chalk (1 inch in length) in the dominant hand, reaches as high as possible and makes a mark on the wall; and (3) jumps as high as possible and makes another mark at the height of the jump. Three trials are administered. (Rather

TABLE 13.15   Norms in Inches for the Vertical Jump for Ages Ten through Seventeen+

Percentile	Age							
	10	11	12	13	14	15	16	17+
	Males							
95	15.5	16.5	17.5	19.0	20.5	21.5	22.5	24.0
75	12.5	13.5	14.5	16.0	17.5	18.5	19.5	21.0
50	11.0	12.0	13.0	14.5	16.0	17.0	18.0	19.5
25	9.0	10.0	11.0	12.5	14.0	15.0	16.0	17.5
5	6.0	7.0	7.0	8.5	10.0	11.0	12.0	13.5
	Females							
95	14.0	14.5	15.0	15.5	16.0	17.0	17.0	17.0
75	11.5	12.0	12.5	13.0	13.5	14.5	14.5	14.5
50	10.0	10.5	11.0	11.5	12.0	13.0	13.0	13.0
25	8.5	9.0	9.5	10.0	10.5	11.5	11.5	11.5
5	6.0	6.5	7.0	7.5	8.0	9.0	9.0	9.0

Source: Adapted from *Physical fitness—motor ability test*, Austin, Tex.: Texas Governor's Commission on Physical Fitness, 1973.

than using a piece of chalk to make the mark, chalk can be placed on the fingertips.) All test performers should practice the jump until it can be executed correctly before attempting the test.

Scoring. For each jump the score is the distance between the two chalk marks, measured to the nearest half inch. The greatest distance is the test score.

■ **Standing Broad Jump (Athletic Power)**
(AAHPERD 1976a)

Test Objective. To measure explosive leg power.

Age Level. Six through college-age.

Equipment. A yardstick, tape, and tape measure; mat is optional.

Validity. Face validity.

Reliability. Coefficients ranging from .83 to .99 have been reported.

Norms. Table 13.17 reports norms for ages nine through seventeen-plus.

Administration and Directions. A tape measure should be taped to the floor or mat close to and parallel with the area where the jump will be performed. The test performer (1) stands behind the restraining line with the feet parallel and several inches

TABLE 13.16   Norms in Inches for Vertical Jump for Ages Twenty through Fifty-Nine

Percentile	Age			
	20–29	30–39	40–49	50–59
	Males			
95	26.5	25	22	21
75	23	21	18	16.5
50	20.5	19.5	16	14
25	18	17	14	12
5	13.5	14.5	11	9.5
	Females			
95	19	17	13.5	NA
75	17	15	12.5	NA
50	15	12.5	10	NA
25	13	11	8.5	NA
5	11.5	9	7	NA

Source: Adapted from *Physical fitness assessments and norms*, Dallas, Tex.: The Cooper Institute, 2004.

TABLE 13.17 Norms in Feet and Inches for Standing Broad Jump for Ages Nine through Seventeen+

Percentile	Age							
	9–10	11	12	13	14	15	16	17+
Males								
95	6′ 0″	6′ 2″	6′ 6″	7′ 1″	7′ 6″	8′ 0″	8′ 2″	8′ 5″
75	5′ 4″	5′ 7″	5′ 9″	6′ 3″	6′ 8″	7′ 2″	7′ 6″	7′ 9″
50	4′ 11″	5′ 2″	5′ 5″	5′ 9″	6′ 2″	6′ 8″	7′ 0″	7′ 2″
25	4′ 6″	4′ 8″	5′ 0″	5′ 2″	5′ 6″	6′ 1″	6′ 6″	6′ 6″
5	3′ 10″	4′ 0″	4′ 2″	4′ 4″	4′ 8″	5′ 2″	5′ 5″	5′ 3″
Females								
95	5′ 10″	6′ 0″	6′ 2″	6′ 5″	6′ 8″	6′ 7″	6′ 6″	6′ 9″
75	5′ 2″	5′ 4″	5′ 6″	5′ 9″	5′ 11″	5′ 10″	5′ 9″	6′ 0″
50	4′ 8″	4′ 11″	5′ 0″	5′ 3″	5′ 4″	5′ 5″	5′ 3″	5′ 5″
25	4′ 1″	4′ 4″	4′ 6″	4′ 9″	4′ 10″	4′ 11″	4′ 9″	4′ 11″
5	3′ 5″	3′ 8″	3′ 10″	4′ 0″	4′ 0″	4′ 2″	4′ 0″	4′ 1″

Source: Adapted from AAHPERD, *AAHPERD youth fitness test manual*, Reston, Va.: American Alliance for Health, Physical Education, Recreation and Dance, 1976.

apart, (2) bends the knees and swings the arms forward, and (3) jumps forward as far as possible. The test administrator marks the landing point of the nearest heel to the restraining line with the yardstick (yardstick is placed perpendicular to tape measure). All test performers should be permitted to practice the jump until they can perform it correctly. Three trials are administered.

Scoring. The score is the number of inches between the restraining line and the nearest heel on landing. If the test performer falls backward on landing, the measurement is made from the restraining line to the nearest part of the body touching the floor or mat.

■ **Medicine Ball Put (Work Power)**
(Clemmons, Campbell, and Jeansonne 2010)

Test Objective. To measure upper body power.
Age Level. High school through adulthood.
Equipment. Tape measure, 6 and 9 kg medicine ball, and a 45° inclined bench.
Validity. Concurrent validity coefficients (bench press power test) of .79 and .86 were found for college-age females and males, respectively.

Reliability. Coefficients of .94 and .92 were found for college-age females and males, respectively.
Norms. None reported.
Administrations and Directions. A measuring tape is placed on the floor with the near end positioned under the frame of the bench to anchor it. The tip (0″) of the tape should be in line with (approximately beneath) the posterior portion of the medicine ball as it rests on the test performer's chest in the ready position. The tape should extend outward at least 25 feet. Extending one foot from each side of the measuring tape, a border should be created with marking tape (e.g., duct tape) that provides a region of 2 feet within which the ball must land. The test performer (1) assumes a reclining position on the bench; (2) holds the ball with both hands, resting it on the chest; (3) when ready, the performer thrusts the ball forward as far as possible. The ball must land in the 2 feet region to be an accepted throw.
Scoring. The score is the distance of the throw measured to the nearest inch. The best of two throws is the recorded score. A recovery period (less than two minutes) should be provided between trials. Any throws outside the 2 feet region are not recorded and must be repeated after an adequate recovery period. Covering the ball in gymnastics chalk before each attempt will facilitate accurate measurement of throws. The near edge of the

chalk mark toward the bench should be used for the measurement.

Note: If no bench is available, the test may be conducted with the test performer on the knees or sitting in a chair with the back firmly against the chair back.

Exercises to Develop Muscular Strength and Endurance

The following exercises require no special equipment and, with a few exceptions, can be performed by children through adults. Avoiding extreme soreness or injury when the following, and similar, exercises are performed requires that certain guidelines be observed:

1. Perform stretching and warm-up exercises before attempting muscular effort.

2. Since some exercises are more difficult than others, perform the ones that provide a mild overload and gradually progress to the more difficult ones.

3. Unless otherwise indicated, begin with ten repetitions and add two or three repetitions each week until the desired number is reached. If unable to perform ten repetitions, begin with a lower number.

4. Perform the exercises 3 to 5 days per week.

Posterior Upper Arms, Shoulders, Chest, and Upper Back

Chair Push-Up. (1) Place hands shoulder-width apart with fingertips forward on chair or bench, feet on the floor, and weight supported on the toes; (2) straighten arms with chin up and chest forward; (3) bend arms and lower chest within 1 to 2 inches of chair; and (4) push back to starting position.

Modified Push-Up. Perform in same manner as modified push-up test (figure 13.7).

Push-Up. Perform in same manner as push-up test.

Advanced Push-Up. Perform in same manner as regular push-up, but place feet on a bench or chair.

Anterior Upper Arms, Shoulders, Chest, and Upper Back

Modified Pull-Up. Perform in same manner as modified pull-up tests (figures 13.4 and 13.5).

Pull-Up. Perform in same manner as pull-up test.

Pull-Up with Weight. (1) Fill two plastic milk or bleach bottles with equal amounts of water or sand, and tie a bottle to each end of a rope that is 24 to 36 inches long; (2) hang the bottles around the shoulders so that they are in front of the body (may place padding between the rope and neck); and (3) perform the pull-ups.

Arm Curls. (1) Fill two plastic milk or bleach bottles with equal amounts of water or sand, and tie a bottle to each end of a bar or heavy stick that is approximately 36 to 40 inches long; (2) stand erect with arms fully extended downward and grasp bar with palms up and shoulder-width apart; (3) raise bar to chest by bending arms (elbows should remain at sides and back should remain straight); and (4) perform two or three sets of six to ten repetitions.

Abdomen

To perform these exercises, lie on the back with the knees bent and feet flat on the floor.

Trunk Curl. (1) Clasp hands on top of head (placing the hands behind head may cause the head to jerk forward, straining the neck muscles); (2) roll head and shoulders forward and upward enough to feel tension; and (3) return to starting position.

Reverse Sit-Up. (1) Place arms at sides and lift knees to chest, raising hips off the floor, and (2) return to starting position.

Assisted Flexed-Knee Sit-Up. Perform sit-up with hands under thighs to help pull the upper body up to position where no resistance is encountered.

Flexed-Knee Sit-Up. Perform sit-up with arms at sides, arms folded across chest, or hands clasped on top of head.

Sit-Up with Feet Elevated. Begin in same position as previous sit-ups but place feet on seat of chair, bed, or bench; knees remain bent, and arms may be placed in any position.

Lateral Trunk

Side Bender. (1) Stand with feet shoulder-width apart and hands clasped behind head, and (2) alternate bending to right and left while maintaining straight back and legs. Perform the same number of repetitions for each side. This exercise may be made more difficult by extending arms overhead or extending at sides, holding a weight in each hand.

Lower Back and Buttocks

Back Tightener. (1) Lie facedown with hands behind lower back, and (2) raise head and chest slightly off floor, tensing lower back and buttocks muscles. Do not overextend.

Leg Raise. (1) With body supported on hands and knees, extend and raise one leg behind the body. (2) Perform the same number of repetitions with each leg. Wearing heavy shoes or adding weight to ankles will increase resistance.

Back Leg Raise. (1) Lie facedown, hands clasped behind head, and (2) lift straight legs a few inches off floor. Hold head and chest down.

Back Extension. (1) Lie on a bench facedown and extend body from waist up over the edge of bench (it will be necessary to strap feet down or have someone hold them). (2) With hands clasped behind head, lift head and trunk. Do not overextend.

Lateral Hips and Thighs

Side Leg Raise. (1) Using the arms to maintain balance, lie on right side with legs straight; (2) lift left leg straight up from side as high as possible; (3) return to starting position; and (4) perform the same number of repetitions with each leg. Wearing heavy shoes or adding weight to ankles will increase resistance.

Leg Raise. (1) Lie on back with arms at sides and lift legs until they are perpendicular to floor; (2) open legs to a wide V-shape; and (3) close the V and return to starting position. May use heavy shoes or weights for added resistance.

Upper Legs

Two-Leg Squat. (1) Stand with feet 12 inches apart, with arms extended in front and parallel to floor; (2) squat until knees are bent at a 90° angle (do not go beyond this point;

place a chair behind the legs to prevent squatting past 90°); and (3) return to standing position.

Single Leg Knee Dip (with Assistance). (1) Stand facing a partner and hold right hands as if shaking hands (if necessary may use table or chair); (2) keeping left leg extended in front, squat down on right foot until knee is at a 90° angle (partner remains standing); (3) grab partner's hand with both hands to return to standing position; and (4) perform the same number of dips with each leg, though attempt no more than five to seven dips when first performing this exercise. Using partner's hand only for balance throughout exercise will increase difficulty.

Lower Legs

Heel Raises. (1) Stand on a board, book, or something similar, with heels resting off the edge; (2) using arms for balance, rise up onto toes; and (3) return to starting position. Hanging weights around shoulders will increase resistance.

Jumps in Place. (1) With feet parallel, 12 inches apart, jump in place. (2) Maintain a steady pace. Do not attempt to jump too high, and try to perform on a soft surface (mats, or wood floor with carpet).

Review Problems

1. Review additional muscular strength, endurance, and power tests found in other textbooks. Note the groups for whom the tests are intended and the validity, reliability, and objectivity coefficients.

2. Administer one of the muscular strength and one of the endurance tests described in this chapter to several of your classmates. Ask them to provide constructive criticism of your test administration.

3. Interview individuals responsible for weight-training programs at fitness or wellness centers. Inquire about tests that are used to measure muscular strength and endurance, interpretation of test results, and programs prescribed for development of muscular strength and endurance.

4. A physical education teacher administered the modified sit-ups test to students in the second grade.

The scores listed below are for the fifty girls in the second grade. Determine the mode, median, mean, and standard deviation for the scores. Refer to table 13.5, and compare the group with national norms.

15	34	20	31	22
29	16	39	27	31
23	33	24	30	32

21	35	15	38	20
37	18	21	33	22
29	37	40	22	6
19	18	24	30	22
20	29	18	28	14
36	22	18	29	28
25	18	38	17	31

Chapter Review Questions

1. What is the definition of muscular strength? What is the difference between dynamic strength and static strength?

2. How is dynamic strength measured with weight-training equipment?

3. What is muscular endurance? What is the difference between dynamic endurance and static endurance?

4. How is dynamic muscular endurance measured with weight-training equipment?

5. What is the difference between relative and absolute muscular endurance tests?

6. What is muscular power?

7. Why should muscular strength and muscular endurance be measured in health promotion?

8. What are your responsibilities after the measurement of muscular strength and endurance? How do the programs for development of muscular strength and endurance differ for children and adults?

14 Anthropometry and Body Composition

After completing this chapter, you should be able to

1. Define the terms *anthropometry, somatotype, body composition, overfat, obese,* and *lean body weight.*

2. State why body structure and composition should be measured.

3. Describe responsibilities after the measurement of body structure and composition.

4. Describe the major characteristics of Sheldon's classification of body types.

5. Correctly interpret height–weight tables.

6. Classify body frames.

7. State the problems associated with the use of height–weight tables to determine desirable weight.

8. Describe eight acceptable sites for skinfold measurements.

9. Perform skinfold measurements, estimate percent body fat, and advise individuals of optimal percent fat ranges.

10. Calculate an individual's desirable body weight on the basis of an acceptable percent body fat.

11. Determine body mass index (BMI) and waist-to-hip ratio and advise individuals of BMI values and waist-to-hip ratios associated with the lowest risk of health problems.

12. Contrast the use of skinfold measurements, BMI, waist circumference, and waist-to-hip ratio (i.e., the appropriate use of each).

Anthropometry, the measurement of the structure and proportions of the body, is one of the earliest forms of measurement in physical education. It may include measurement of height and weight; measurement of circumferences, diameters, and lengths of body segments; and **somatotyping** (body typing).

Body composition refers to the component parts of the body. Though there are many component parts, for measurement purposes body composition is interpreted as referring to body fat weight and lean body weight. Because **lean body weight** is found by subtracting the weight of body fat from the total body weight, it is often interpreted as fat-free weight. Technically, however, it includes a small amount of essential lipid that is associated with a variety of tissues in the body, such as the nerve sheaths, the brain, and the cell membranes. Depending on body size, about 1.5% to 3% of the weight of the lean body is essential lipids, and 40% to 50% is composed of muscle weight or mass. Organs and tissues, such as skin and bones, make up the remaining portion.

Overfat is indicated when individuals have a higher percentage of body fat than is desirable. All experts do not agree on the exact ranges of desirable percent body fat. Anyone with a body mass index (BMI) between 25 and 29 is considered overfat. Individuals are considered **obese** when their percent body fat increases their risk of mortality and morbidity. Again, not all experts agree on the percent body fat that classifies an individual as obese. Anyone with a BMI of 30 or higher is considered obese. Acceptable ranges of percent body fat and application of the BMI for children and adults will be discussed later in the chapter.

Why Measure Body Structure and Composition?

Research involving somatotyping requires accurate body type classification, but understanding the concept of somatotyping and being able to roughly determine body types can be of value to coaches, physical education teachers, and fitness instructors. The values found in most weight tables are grouped into height and body type categories. Estimation of desirable weight through a height–weight table is not ideal, because no estimation of percent body fat can be made. If this method is used, however, individuals should realistically determine their body type. In addition, body type classification may be useful when planning obtainable fitness goals. For example, individuals with a thick abdomen, wide hips, heavy buttocks, and short, heavy legs (endomorphic body type characteristics) usually do not perform as well on running tests as individuals with a slender abdomen and hips and lean or muscular legs. This does not mean that certain individuals are to avoid running for health benefits, but it does mean that their running goals should be realistic in terms of their body type.

Height and weight measurements may be recorded for diagnostic purposes. Great differences exist in the physiological maturity of boys and girls, and not all individuals of the same age are expected to have identical heights and weights. The recording of these variables during the growing and developing years may serve to prevent the occurrence of long-term health problems. Young people who significantly deviate from either height or weight range, or both, for their ages probably should be observed to determine that no health problems exist. (This determination should be done in a way that is not embarrassing to the individuals.) Height and weight measurements also may be used for homogeneous grouping of youth for sports participation. Classification indexes based on height, weight, and age were developed in the 1930s for this purpose, but currently, they are not extensively used.

The measurement of body composition is an important consideration for everyone who promotes good health. It is estimated that more than 36% of Americans aged twenty years and older are obese and an additional 34% of this age group are overfat. (Some sources estimate an even higher percentage for overfat or obese.) This excess fat is not limited to the adult population. Among children and teens ages two through nineteen, 17% are obese and 33% are either overfat or obese. There is a strong correlation between obesity and increased risk of chronic diseases such as coronary artery disease, diabetes, hypertension, hyperlipidemia, and certain cancers. Unless something is done to aid individuals in the management of their body fat, there will be an increase in the occurrence of these health problems.

In an effort to combat overfatness, millions of Americans undertake weight-loss diets. They fail, however, to understand the difference between the loss of body fat and lean body weight and the role of exercise in weight management. In addition, they mistakenly use weight as indicated on scales to determine the success or lack of success of their diet. Physical educators need to assume a leadership role in counseling individuals who are attempting to lose weight. We should be prepared to measure body composition and to advise individuals how to correctly lose body fat.

Furthermore, some people attempt to lose weight, though their percent body fat is acceptable. For example, some athletes, especially amateur wrestlers and gymnasts, have unrealistic images of what their weight should be, and they do not realize the implications of changes in their body composition. Many distance runners also attempt to get their weight too low, in the belief that their running times will improve. This problem is not limited to athletes, however. Other individuals create health problems for themselves because they have an incorrect perception of a slender body. Underweight individuals with too little body fat tend to be malnourished. These individuals are at greater risk for fluid-electrolyte imbalances, osteoporosis, bone fractures, muscle atrophy, cardiac arrhythmias, kidney problems, and other health risks. Many of these people have emotional problems and need professional counseling to overcome those problems, but possibly some would discontinue efforts to lose weight if they understood the relationship between body fat and good health.

Responsibilities after Measurement

After measuring for body structure and/or composition, your efforts probably will be focused on working with individuals who need to reduce their percent body fat. With children, the support and cooperation of their parents are essential. The advice and assistance of a nutritionist may also be necessary. With all individuals, children and adults, the best approach to reduction of body fat is through a program involving increased physical activity and a modest decrease in caloric intake. Attempts at extreme changes in physical activity and eating habits often are doomed for failure. A permanent change in eating behavior is more easily achieved with only a modest decrease in caloric intake than with a great decrease in caloric intake. With adults, when exercise and diet changes are combined, 80% to 95% of the weight loss is through loss of fat tissue. If weight loss is accomplished strictly through dieting, 30% to 45% of the weight reduction is through loss of lean tissue. Unsound gimmicks or diets should be avoided, and weight reduction goals should be realistic. Weight reduction should be gradual, with a loss of no more than 1 to 2 pounds/week. For weight reduction purposes, exercise does not have to be intense. For example, walking a mile expends almost the same number of calories as running a mile.

If possible, percent body fat should be monitored during weight loss to be sure the body composition is not being altered in the wrong way. However, just as in weight reduction, expected changes in percent body fat should be realistic. A 1% to 2% loss of percent body fat every 6 to 8 weeks is a reasonable goal for most individuals.

◼ ARE YOU ABLE TO DO THE FOLLOWING?

- Define *anthropometry, somatotype, body composition, overfat, obese,* and *lean body weight.*

- State why body structure and composition should be measured.

- Describe responsibilities after the measurement of body structure and composition.

Body Type Classification (Somatotyping)

There are several methods of body type classification, but the classification described by Sheldon, Stevens, and Tucker (1970) is the best known. Sheldon's morphological classification includes the ectomorph, the mesomorph, and the endomorph. An **ectomorph** is a slender person with a light frame—the arms and legs are slender and long, the neck appears long, and muscle tissue has little definition. A **mesomorph** is an athletic-looking individual—the

shoulders are broad, the hips are narrow, and muscle tissue is predominant. An **endomorph** is a thick individual—the arms and legs are short compared with the torso, the chest and waist are about the same size, and the neck is thick.

Three numbers are used to designate the components of each of the three types, with 7 as the highest and 1 as the lowest rating for each. The first number refers to endomorphic, the second to mesomorphic, and the third to ectomorphic characteristics. The rating 7-1-1 designates a pure endomorph; 1-7-1, a pure mesomorph; and 1-1-7, a pure ectomorph. Such extreme ratings are rare, however; usually, at least two components of each type are present in an individual. A 2-5-4 designation indicates a less than average number of endomorphic characteristics, a more than average number of mesomorphic characteristics, and an average number of ectomorphic characteristics. Simplified modifications of Sheldon's classification have been developed, but unless you are involved in research, rarely will it be necessary for you to use a numbering system to designate body types.

By knowing the major characteristics of each body type, one can estimate the two dominant body types of each individual and put the estimate to practical use. For example, a relationship exists between somatotype and certain sports. A football lineman with a low center of gravity and wide hips and shoulders has an advantage in blocking. Football linemen, therefore, usually rate high on the mesomorph and endomorph scales and low on the ectomorph scale. On the other hand, individuals who play center on college or professional basketball teams, as well as long-distance runners, rate high on the ectomorph scale. When advising individuals about the relationship of physical activity and body types, you should emphasize that training may result in improved performance, but it will not result in a change of body type.

Height–Weight Tables

In 1959, the Metropolitan Life Insurance Company published height–weight tables that provided the desirable weight for males and females (see table 14.1). In 1983, the company released revised tables that were said to represent the weights associated with the lowest death rates among approximately 4,200,000 people observed for 22 years. These tables continue to be used in some settings as guidelines for desirable weight (see table 14.2).

TABLE 14.1 1959 Metropolitan Life Insurance Company Table of Desirable Weights (in Pounds) for Men and Women of Ages Twenty-Five and Over (Indoor Clothing)

Height (with Shoes on; 1-Inch Heels)	Small Frame (lb)	Medium Frame (lb)	Large Frame (lb)
Men			
5 ft 2 in.	112–120	118–129	126–141
5 ft 3 in.	115–123	121–133	129–144
5 ft 4 in.	118–126	124–136	132–148
5 ft 5 in.	121–129	127–139	135–152
5 ft 6 in.	124–133	130–143	138–156
5 ft 7 in.	128–137	134–147	142–161
5 ft 8 in.	132–141	138–152	147–166
5 ft 9 in.	136–145	142–156	151–170
5 ft 10 in.	140–150	146–160	155–174
5 ft 11 in.	144–154	150–165	159–179
6 ft 0 in.	148–158	154–170	164–184
6 ft 1 in.	152–162	158–175	168–189
6 ft 2 in.	156–167	162–180	173–194
6 ft 3 in.	160–171	167–185	178–199
6 ft 4 in.	164–175	172–190	182–204
Women			
4 ft 10 in.	92–98	96–107	104–119
4 ft 11 in.	94–101	98–110	106–122
5 ft 0 in.	96–104	101–113	109–125
5 ft 1 in.	99–107	104–116	112–128
5 ft 2 in.	102–110	107–119	115–131
5 ft 3 in.	105–113	110–122	118–134
5 ft 4 in.	108–116	113–126	121–138
5 ft 5 in.	111–119	116–130	125–142
5 ft 6 in.	114–123	120–135	129–146
5 ft 7 in.	118–127	124–139	133–150
5 ft 8 in.	122–131	128–143	137–154
5 ft 9 in.	126–135	132–147	141–158
5 ft 10 in.	130–140	136–151	145–163
5 ft 11 in.	134–144	140–155	149–168
6 ft 0 in.	138–148	144–149	153–173

Source of basic data: Society of Actuaries, *Build and blood pressure study*, New York: Metropolitan Life Insurance Company, 1959.
Note: For those between 18 and 25, subtract 1 pound for each year under 25.

TABLE 14.2 1983 Metropolitan Height and Weight Tables for Men and Women of Ages Twenty-Five through Fifty-Nine

Height (with Shoes on; 1-Inch Heels)	Small Frame (lb)	Medium Frame (lb)	Large Frame (lb)
Men (Indoor Clothing Weighing 5 lb)			
5 ft 2 in.	128–134	131–141	138–150
5 ft 3 in.	130–136	133–143	140–153
5 ft 4 in.	132–138	135–145	142–156
5 ft 5 in.	134–140	137–148	144–160
5 ft 6 in.	136–142	139–151	146–164
5 ft 7 in.	138–145	142–154	149–168
5 ft 8 in.	140–148	145–157	152–172
5 ft 9 in.	142–151	148–160	155–176
5 ft 10 in.	144–154	151–163	158–180
5 ft 11 in.	146–157	154–166	161–184
6 ft 0 in.	149–160	157–170	164–188
6 ft 1 in.	152–164	160–174	168–192
6 ft 2 in.	155–168	164–178	172–197
6 ft 3 in.	158–172	167–182	176–202
6 ft 4 in.	162–176	171–187	181–207
Women (Indoor Clothing Weighing 3 lb)			
4 ft 10 in.	102–111	109–121	118–131
4 ft 11 in.	103–113	111–123	120–134
5 ft 0 in.	104–115	113–126	122–137
5 ft 1 in.	106–118	115–129	125–140
5 ft 2 in.	108–121	118–132	128–143
5 ft 3 in.	111–124	121–135	131–147
5 ft 4 in.	114–127	124–138	134–151
5 ft 5 in.	117–130	127–141	137–155
5 ft 6 in.	120–133	130–144	140–159
5 ft 7 in.	123–136	133–147	143–163
5 ft 8 in.	126–139	136–150	146–167
5 ft 9 in.	129–142	139–153	149–170
5 ft 10 in.	132–145	142–156	152–173
5 ft 11 in.	135–148	145–159	155–176
6 ft 0 in.	138–151	148–162	158–179

Source of basic data: Society of Actuaries and Association of Life Insurance Medical Directors of America, *1979 build study*, New York: Metropolitan Life Insurance Company, 1980.

However, when the new tables were released, the American Heart Association (AHA) encouraged Americans to continue to use the 1959 recommendations (see table 14.1). The AHA took this position because the new tables list average weight range increases of 13 pounds for short men and 10 pounds for short women, small increases for medium-height men and women, and insignificant increases for tall men and women. The AHA noted that merely looking at death rates obscured health risks associated with the increased weights. The AHA also stated that few health problems are improved by gaining weight, pointing out that the incidence of heart disease, high blood pressure, and diabetes increases in relation to weight gained. Also, the new acceptable weights most likely are skewed upward by the fact that cigarette smokers, who tend to be thinner than nonsmokers and who die at significantly younger ages, were not taken into account in calculating the new tables. Another controversy occurred in 1990 when the U.S. Departments of Agriculture and Health and Human Services released its booklet *Nutrition and Your Health: Dietary Guidelines for Americans.* The nutritional guidelines provided in this booklet were endorsed by nutritionists and the medical community, but the suggested weights for Americans were not accepted by all. Many medical personnel believed that the booklet's weight chart permitted too much weight gain during the aging process. The arguments against the chart were the same as those opposing the 1983 charts of the Metropolitan Life Insurance Company.

The major problem associated with the use of height–weight tables is that they reveal nothing about body composition. Two individuals may be the same height and weight but have entirely different body composition. One individual may be overfat; the other individual may be very muscular. With this limitation, however, the tables have value as a screening device. If individuals are more than 10% below the midpoint of the weight range for their height and weight, they may be underweight. If individuals are more than 10% above the midpoint of the weight range, they may be overfat. For such individuals, an appropriate method for determination of body composition should be performed before any decision is made about their fatness or leanness.

A major drawback to all height–weight tables is that some individuals do not correctly determine their frame size when selecting an appropriate weight range. Many small- or medium-framed overfat individuals consider themselves large-framed and do not realistically examine their weight problem. On the other hand, some medium- or large-framed individuals with an acceptable percent body fat view themselves as small-framed and mistakenly attempt to lose weight. Determination of body frame is best performed by trained personnel, but the following practical methods may be used.

Elbow Breadth

Extend the right arm and bend the forearm upward at a 90° angle. Keep the fingers straight and turn the palm away from the body. Place the thumb and index finger of the left hand on the two prominent bones on either side of the right elbow, and measure the space between the thumb and index finger of the left hand with a ruler or tape measure. Record the measurement and compare with the standards in table 14.3.

Ankle Girth

Pulling the tape as snug as possible, measure the girth of the right ankle at the smallest point, just above the bony prominences. Record the measurement and compare with the standards in table 14.4.

■■■ ARE YOU ABLE TO DO THE FOLLOWING?

- Describe the major characteristics of Sheldon's classification of body types.

- Correctly interpret height–weight tables and classify body frames.

- State the problems associated with the use of height–weight tables to determine desirable weight.

Body Composition

Several methods are available for measurement of body composition. Some methods are expensive and are limited to research or medical purposes. Regardless of the method used, you as the test administrator should be sensitive to the feelings of the individual being measured. You should seek to establish a testing environment that will avoid causing anyone to be uncomfortable or embarrassed.

TABLE 14.3   Standards for Estimating Medium Frame Using Elbow Breadth and Height

Males		Females	
Height (Inches)*	**Elbow Breadth** (Inches)**	**Height (Inches)***	**Elbow Breadth** (Inches)**
61 to 62	2½ to 2⅞	57 to 58	2¼ to 2½
63 to 66	2⅝ to 2⅞	59 to 62	2¼ to 2½
67 to 70	2¾ to 3	63 to 66	2⅜ to 2⅝
71 to 74	2¾ to 3⅛	67 to 70	2⅜ to 2⅝
75 and above	2⅞ to 3¼	71 and above	2½ to 2¾

*Height without shoes.
**Measurements lower than those listed indicate a small frame, and higher measurements indicate a large frame.
Source of basic data: *Society of Actuaries and Association of Life Insurance Medical Directors of America, 1979 build study*, New York: Metropolitan Life Insurance Company, 1980.

TABLE 14.4   Standards for Estimating Body Frame Size from Ankle Girth (Inches)

Sex	Small	Medium	Large
Male	Less than 8	8 to 9.25	More than 9.25
Female	Less than 7.5	7.5 to 8.75	More than 8.75

Source: Johnson, P. B. et al., *Sport, exercise and you*, New York: Holt, Rinehart & Winston, 1975.

Bioelectrical Impedance Analysis (BIA)

Bioelectrical impedance analysis (BIA), a method that is popular in health promotion environments, is based on the difference between the resistance of lean tissue to an electrical current and the resistance of fat tissue. With this method, a tiny electrical current is sent through the body. Since electrolytes in water are an excellent conductor of electricity, the amount of water in the body affects the flow of the current. Lean tissue contains mostly water (70% or more), whereas fat tissue is less than 20% water. The less the recorded resistance, the greater is the water content and hence the greater the lean tissue.

The early versions of this method required that electrodes be attached to the body (ankle and wrist sites). However, a variety of BIA devices are now sold for commercial and home use. One type of device permits the person to stand barefooted on a bathroom scalelike instrument. Another type requires that the person hold handgrips while extending the arms. Both of these devices are less expensive than the top-rated calipers.

BIA offers a fast, noninvasive technique for body composition analysis. The use of BIA instruments does not require a high degree of technician skill, and the more recent instruments have approximately the same standard error for estimating percent body fat as the standard error for skinfold measurements (about ±3.5%). A major source of error for BIA is the state of hydration of the tested

+ + +   **POINT OF EMPHASIS**   + + +

- You should always be aware of the standard error of estimate for the technique you are using to estimate an individual's body composition. For example, imagine that you estimate an individual to have a percent body fat of 18, and you use a technique that has a 4% standard of estimate. Your interpretation is that the individual could possibly have a percent body fat in the range of 14 to 22.

person. Conducting a BIA soon after a meal decreases the resistance and probably will underestimate the percent body fat. Dehydration, however, increases resistance and overestimates the percent body fat.

Air Displacement Plethysmography (BOD POD)

Air displacement plethysmography is a method used in clinical and laboratory settings to measure body volume (used to estimate percent body fat). The procedure is based on the same principle as underwater weighing but uses air instead of water. Body volume is determined by comparing the initial volume of an empty chamber (marketed commercially as BOD POD) and the volume with the person inside. For the measurement, the individual must wear a tight-fitting swimsuit. After being weighed on an electronic scale, the individual sits inside the chamber (figure 14.1) for 3 to 5 minutes. The individual breathes into an air circuit to compute pulmonary gas volume, which is used to determine the correct body volume.

The BOD POD is expensive, but it provides a quick method to determine percent body fat. Because they fear immersion, some individuals prefer the BOD POD to underwater weighing. The BOD POD, developed with funding provided by the National Institutes of Health (NIH), is being used in university laboratories. Some research found the BOD POD to have a standard error of less than 2%, but other research has produced mixed results.

Dual-Energy X-Ray Absorptiometry (DXA)

Dual-energy X-ray absorptiometry (DXA) provides estimates of bone mineral, fat, and lean soft-tissue mass. With DXA, two distinct low-energy X-ray beams (with low radiation) penetrate bone and soft-tissue areas. For the procedure, the individual lies supine on a table while detector probes pass slowly across the body. The entire scan takes approximately 12 minutes. Computer software produces an image and estimates of bone mineral content, fat tissue, and lean soft tissue. Analysis also includes selected trunk and limb regions for tissue composition. Although it is an expensive procedure, research has shown DXA to have a degree of agreement with underwater weighing in the

FIGURE 14.1 Air displacement plethysmography (BOD POD) testing. (Photo courtesy of Life Measurement Inc. Used with permission.)

Photo provided courtesy of COSMED USA, Inc.—Concord, CA

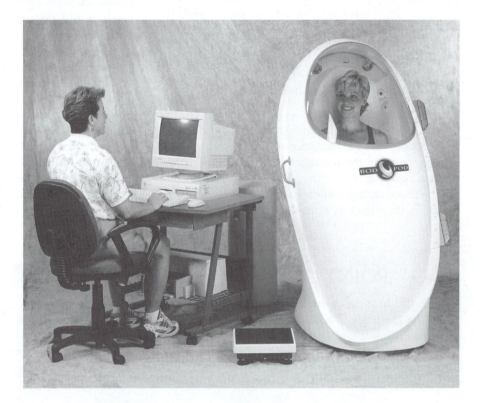

estimate of percent body fat (standard error of less than 2%). Because DXA is fast, safe, and noninvasive, its use in the laboratory setting is increasing.

Underwater Weighing

Underwater weighing, illustrated in figure 14.2, is the most popular laboratory method to estimate percent body fat. With a standard error of estimate of $\pm.8$ to $\pm1.2\%$, it is considered a very valid method. The objective of underwater weighing,

also called hydrostatic weighing, is to determine body volume, which is then used to calculate body density. This method is based on the Archimedes principle for measuring the density of a body. According to the Archimedes principle, when a body (person) is submerged under water, the weight a body loses underwater equals the weight of the water it displaces. That is,

weight of the water displaced = weight of body in air
− weight of body under water

The weight of the water displaced divided by the density of the water equals the volume of the water, and the volume of the water equals the volume of the body submerged. For individuals, this volume is referred to as body volume. The density of the water, determined with the appropriate formula, is a function of its temperature. Before determining body density, residual lung volume (the amount of air remaining in the lungs after maximal exhalation) also must be measured. With body volume, water density, and residual lung volume determined, the appropriate mathematical equation is then used to calculate body density. After body density is calculated, another equation is used to estimate the percentage of body fat. Lean tissue (bone and muscle) has a greater density than fat tissue. Thus, the higher an individual's body density, the lower the person's percentage of body fat.

Obviously, the estimation of body fat through underwater weighing is costly and requires more time and trained personnel than other methods. Additionally, some individuals fear total immersion in the water, and it is not an acceptable method for individuals with certain medical conditions.

Skinfold Tests

The measurement of body composition may also be done through the measurement of subcutaneous body fat with skinfold calipers. The use of a skinfold caliper involves pinching a fold away from the underlying muscle and applying the caliper to the fold. All measurements are taken on the right side of the body, and they should not be taken immediately after exercise because the shift of body fluid to the skin will increase the skinfold size. The directions for skinfold testing are as follows:

1. Grasp the skinfold firmly between the thumb and index finger about ½ inch from the site at which the caliper is

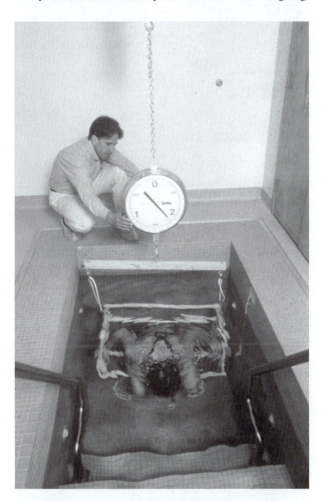

FIGURE 14.2 Underwater weighing technique. (Photograph provided by Richard G. Israel, Human Performance/Clinical Research Lab, Department of Health and Exercise, Colorado State University.)

Courtesy of Human Performance Clinical Research Laboratory, Department of Health and Exercise Science, Colorado State University

to be applied. Since the thickness of the fold reflects the percentage of body fat, it should be great enough to include two thicknesses of skin with intervening fat, but it should not include muscle or fascia. The test administrator may ask the subject to tense the underlying muscles to determine if muscle tissue is included in the fold.

2. While continuing to hold the fold, apply the caliper to the fold above or below the finger and slowly release the caliper grip so that full tension is exerted on the fold. The measurement is read to the nearest .5 millimeter about 1 to 2 seconds (no longer) after the grip is released.

3. Take a minimum of two measurements at each site, and if they vary by more than 1 millimeter, take a third measurement. Instructions for specific tests and/or type of skinfold caliper used sometimes differ in this step. For example, one test procedure may use the median score of three measurements, while another test may require that two consecutive measurements agree within .5 millimeters or less. Another test procedure may require that site measurements not vary from each other by more than ±10%. It is best to follow the instructions of the skinfold caliper and test procedure being administered. Take the measurements in rotational order (circuits) rather than taking consecutive readings at each site. Sometimes consecutive readings at the same site are smaller because of the compression of fat.

Skinfold measurements may be taken in several places, eight of which are described here. To ensure accuracy and consistency, you can mark the sites with a grease pencil. Figures 14.3 through 14.10 show the measurement sites.

1. Chest: a diagonal fold half the distance between the anterior axillary line and nipple for males; one-third of the distance between the anterior axillary line and nipple for females.

2. Axilla: a vertical fold on the midaxillary line at the level of the xiphoid process of the sternum.

3. Triceps: a vertical fold over the triceps muscle, halfway between the acromion and olecranon processes (arm should be extended and relaxed).

4. Subscapula: a diagonal fold beneath the inferior angle of the scapula.

5. Abdominal: a vertical fold approximately ½ to 1 inch to the right of the navel.

6. Suprailium: a slightly diagonal fold on the crest of the ilium at the anterior axillary line.

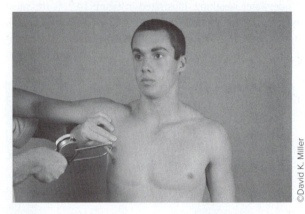

FIGURE 14.3   Caliper placement for chest skinfold measurement.

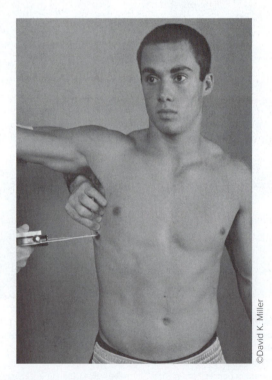

FIGURE 14.4   Caliper placement for axilla skinfold measurement.

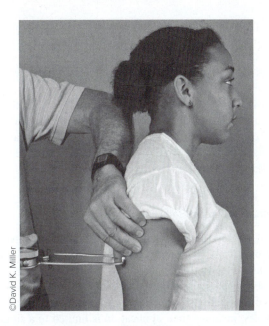

FIGURE 14.5   Caliper placement for triceps skinfold measurement.

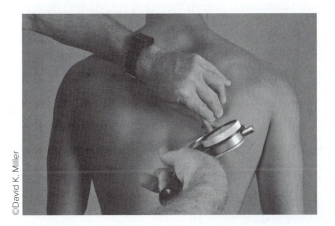

FIGURE 14.6   Caliper placement for subscapular skinfold measurement.

7. Thigh: a vertical fold on the anterior right thigh midway between the hip and knee joints (weight should be on left foot).

8. Calf: a vertical fold on the inside of the calf; right foot is placed flat on bench with knee flexed to 90°; vertical fold of skin is grasped just above the largest part of calf girth, and fold of skin is measured at the largest part of girth.

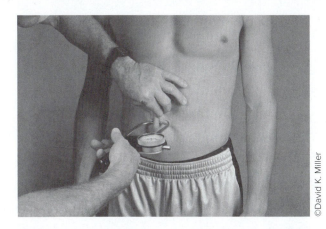

FIGURE 14.7   Caliper placement for abdominal skinfold measurement.

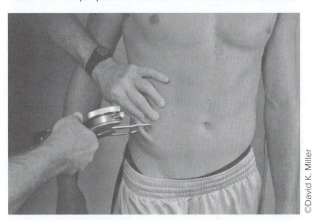

FIGURE 14.8   Caliper placement for suprailium skinfold measurement.

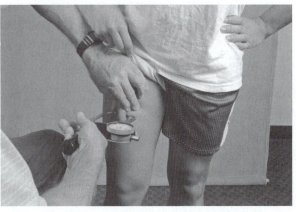

FIGURE 14.9   Caliper placement for thigh skinfold measurement.

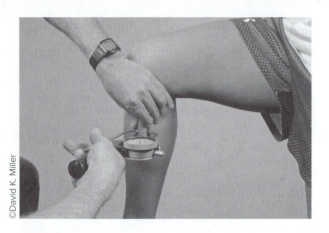

FIGURE 14.10   Caliper placement for calf skinfold measurement.

Skinfold measurements have a standard error of 3.5 to 4% and rarely are performed outside the laboratory setting for two reasons: the expense of the skinfold calipers and the lack of confidence in the reliability of the measurements. A study by Lohman and Pollock (1981) concluded that less expensive calipers may be suitable for a mass testing setting, if the test administrator is well trained. Differences between the scores of experienced and inexperienced testers occurred less often when an expensive metal caliper was used. However, Lohman and Pollack also found that when inexperienced testers were trained, similar scores were obtained when using a plastic caliper with a spring and a caliper with a uniform tension independent of skinfold thickness. The major requirement for a skinfold caliper is that it exert a constant force of 10 g/mm^2 at the skinfold site, regardless of the skinfold thickness. Inexpensive calipers are capable of exerting this force if the springs in them are not weakened.

Skinfold measurements can be reliable if testers are willing to practice performing the measurements. Consistency of measurement is obtained only through practice. Testers who are willing to measure many individuals can develop the skill to perform skinfold measurements with accuracy and consistency. You should seek to develop this skill.

Estimating Percent Body Fat

Many regression equations with functions to predict hydrostatically measured body density from skinfold measurements have been published. These equations are termed **population-specific** or **generalized.** Population-specific equations were developed from homogeneous samples, meaning their application is limited to a similar sample (e.g., age and gender). Generalized equations that can be used with samples varying in age and body fatness have been developed to eliminate that problem. The generalized equations were based on large heterogeneous samples. Regression models that account for age and the nonlinear relationship between skinfold fat and body density were then developed. The generalized approach makes it possible to use one equation rather than several, without a loss in prediction accuracy.

Computer and microcomputer programs are available, or may be developed, to determine body density and

---

♦ ♦ ♦   POINT OF EMPHASIS   ♦ ♦ ♦

- To estimate body composition, the body is divided into a fat component and a fat-free body component (lean body weight). Body density is measured to determine these components. Because of the relative proportion of water and mineral found in the fat-free body component, fat-free body density varies with age, gender, ethnicity, level of body fatness, and physical activity level. For example, in comparison to mature youth and young adults, children have a lower fat-free body density because they have a relatively lower mineral content and higher body water values. The same is generally true for older individuals because of their lower body mineral content. Tables 14.5 through 14.8 account for the difference in fat-free body density. You will note that for equal sum of skinfolds, the percent fat estimate increases as the age increases.

percent body fat after the skinfold measurements have been completed. However, computer-generated tables that provide percent body fat estimates have been developed, eliminating the need for calculations by the test administrator. Values published by Jackson and Pollock (1985) are presented in tables 14.5 through 14.8. Jackson and Pollock found that two different sums of three skinfolds for males and females were highly correlated with the sum of seven of the skinfolds previously described. For males, chest, abdomen, and thigh skinfolds were used, and for females, triceps, suprailium, and thigh skinfolds were used. The researchers also found that the sums of triceps, chest, and subscapular skinfolds for males and triceps, abdomen, and suprailium for females were similarly accurate. The test administrator has the option of using either combination, but the latter skinfolds may be more practical.

▓▓▓ ARE YOU ABLE TO DO THE FOLLOWING?

- List and describe eight sites for skinfold measurements.

- Perform skinfold measurements, estimate percent body fat, and advise individuals of optimal percent fat ranges.

Optimal Percent Body Fat and Desirable Body Weight

Health-related physical fitness tests, which include a body composition component, are included in chapter 15. Health standards for percent fat or sum of skinfold measurements for children and youth are provided with the tests; some tests include standards for adults. Though skinfolds are related to body fatness in children, the absolute amount of body fat cannot be accurately determined. The relation of skinfold fat to body fatness differs by sex and also changes as children mature. Therefore, a given skinfold thickness does not correspond to the same body fat content for seven-year-olds as it does for seventeen-year-olds.

What is a desirable percent fat for children and adults? As stated previously, being overfat, and certainly being obese, increases your risk of health problems. On the other hand, the loss of too much body fat may affect your health. Different optimal limits of percent body fat have been reported, but it is difficult to compare standards because studies do not always group age ranges in the same way. The FitnessGram (the Cooper Institute 2017), described in chapter 15, includes

the percent body fat Healthy Fitness Zone (HFZ) for males and females, ages five through seventeen and older. The highest acceptable percent body fat for males, 22.2, is at an age older than seventeen. The highest acceptable percent body fat for females, 30.4, is at age seventeen. The FitnessGram also reports that for a male older than seventeen, a percent body fat less than 7.0 is considered too lean. For a female older than seventeen, a percent body fat less than 16.5 is considered too lean. The YMCA Fitness Test (Golding 2000), also described in chapter 15, reports the "good" standard for percent fat for males, ages twenty-six to thirty-five, as 11% to 13%. For females of the same age group, the range is 18% to 20%. Ross and Jackson (1990) report that for the age group thirty to thirty-nine, the optimal range for percent fat is 12% to 22% for males and 16% to 26% for females. T.G. Lohman (1982) reports that a 10% to 22% fat content in men and a 20% to 32% fat content in women seems satisfactory. Lohman also reports that for the nonathlete, the percent body fat probably should be no lower than between 5% and 10% for males and between 15% and 18% for females.

In some sports, a low percent body fat is desirable. The average percent body fat for highly trained male endurance athletes (e.g., distance runners) is 4% to 10%. For highly trained female endurance athletes, it is 13% to 18%. The recommended minimal percent fat for male athletes is 3% to 7%, and for female athletes it is 10% to 18%.

Although they are not the same, the optimal percent body fat ranges for the tests reported in chapter 15 are considered acceptable by health experts. Your selection of one of these tests to use in a professional setting need not be determined by the percent fat standards. If your professional responsibilities are in the school environment and you perform skinfold measurements, you should use an acceptable standardized physical fitness test and its health-related percent fat standards. If your professional responsibilities are elsewhere and you choose not to use an acceptable standardized physical fitness test, table 14.9 provides more recently developed optimal percent body fat standards for various adult ages. The more an individual's percent body fat deviates from these percentages, the greater the health risks. Once the percent body fat has been estimated, desirable weight can be determined. The desired weight is calculated from lean weight.

A sample calculation is provided.

Given: Body weight = 200 pounds; %fat = 24%.

TABLE 14.5 Percent Fat Estimate for Men: Sum of Chest, Abdomen, and Thigh Skinfolds

Sum Skinfolds (mm)	Age to Last Year*								
	Under 22	23–27	28–32	33–37	38–42	43–47	48–52	53–57	Over 57
8–10	1.3	1.8	2.3	2.9	3.4	3.9	4.5	5.0	5.5
11–13	2.2	2.8	3.3	3.9	4.4	4.9	5.5	6.0	6.5
14–16	3.2	3.8	4.3	4.8	5.4	5.9	6.4	7.0	7.5
17–19	4.2	4.7	5.3	5.8	6.3	6.9	7.4	8.0	8.5
20–22	5.1	5.7	6.2	6.8	7.3	7.9	8.4	8.9	9.5
23–25	6.1	6.6	7.2	7.7	8.3	8.8	9.4	9.9	10.5
26–28	7.0	7.6	8.1	8.7	9.2	9.8	10.3	10.9	11.4
29–31	8.0	8.5	9.1	9.6	10.2	10.7	11.3	11.8	12.4
32–34	8.9	9.4	10.0	10.5	11.1	11.6	12.2	12.8	13.3
35–37	9.8	10.4	10.9	11.5	12.0	12.6	13.1	13.7	14.3
38–40	10.7	11.3	11.8	12.4	12.9	13.5	14.1	14.6	15.2
41–43	11.6	12.2	12.7	13.3	13.8	14.4	15.0	15.5	16.1
44–46	12.5	13.1	13.6	14.2	14.7	15.3	15.9	16.4	17.0
47–49	13.4	13.9	14.5	15.1	15.6	16.2	16.8	17.3	17.9
50–52	14.3	14.8	15.4	15.9	16.5	17.1	17.6	18.2	18.8
53–55	15.1	15.7	16.2	16.8	17.4	17.9	18.5	19.1	19.7
56–58	16.0	16.5	17.1	17.7	18.2	18.8	19.4	20.0	20.5
59–61	16.9	17.4	17.9	18.5	19.1	19.7	20.2	20.8	21.4
62–64	17.6	18.2	18.8	19.4	19.9	20.5	21.1	21.7	22.2
65–67	18.5	19.0	19.6	20.2	20.8	21.3	21.9	22.5	23.1
68–70	19.3	19.9	20.4	21.0	21.6	22.2	22.7	23.3	23.9
71–73	20.1	20.7	21.2	21.8	22.4	23.0	23.6	24.1	24.7
74–76	20.9	21.5	22.0	22.6	23.2	23.8	24.4	25.0	25.5
77–79	21.7	22.2	22.8	23.4	24.0	24.6	25.2	25.8	26.3
80–82	22.4	23.0	23.6	24.2	24.8	25.4	25.9	26.5	27.1
83–85	23.2	23.8	24.4	25.0	25.5	26.1	26.7	27.3	27.9
86–88	24.0	24.5	25.1	25.7	26.3	26.9	27.5	28.1	28.7
89–91	24.7	25.3	25.9	26.5	27.1	27.6	28.2	28.8	29.4
92–94	25.4	26.0	26.6	27.2	27.8	28.4	29.0	29.6	30.2
95–97	26.1	26.7	27.3	27.9	28.5	29.1	29.7	30.3	30.9
98–100	26.9	27.4	28.0	28.6	29.2	29.8	30.4	31.0	31.6
101–103	27.5	28.1	28.7	29.3	29.9	30.5	31.1	31.7	32.3
104–106	28.2	28.8	29.4	30.0	30.6	31.2	31.8	32.4	33.0
107–109	28.9	29.5	30.1	30.7	31.3	31.9	32.5	33.1	33.7
110–112	29.6	30.2	30.8	31.4	32.0	32.6	33.2	33.8	34.4
113–115	30.2	30.8	31.4	32.0	32.6	33.2	33.8	34.5	35.1
116–118	30.9	31.5	32.1	32.7	33.3	33.9	34.5	35.1	35.7
119–121	31.5	32.1	32.7	33.3	33.9	34.5	35.1	35.7	36.4
122–124	32.1	32.7	33.3	33.9	34.5	35.1	35.8	36.4	37.0
125–127	32.7	33.3	33.9	34.5	35.1	35.8	36.4	37.0	37.6

*Last calendar birthday.

Source: Jackson, A. S. and Pollock, M. L., "Practical assessment of body composition," *The Physician and Sports medicine*, vol. 13, no. 5, 1985, 76–90.

TABLE 14.6 Percent Fat Estimate for Women: Sum of Triceps, Suprailium, and Thigh Skinfolds

Sum of Skinfolds (mm)	Age to Last Year*								
	Under 22	**23–27**	**28–32**	**33–37**	**38–42**	**43–47**	**48–52**	**53–57**	**Over 57**
23–25	9.7	9.9	10.2	10.4	10.7	10.9	11.2	11.4	11.7
26–28	11.0	11.2	11.5	11.7	12.0	12.3	12.5	12.7	13.0
29–31	12.3	12.5	12.8	13.0	13.3	13.5	13.8	14.0	14.3
32–34	13.6	13.8	14.0	14.3	14.5	14.8	15.0	15.3	15.5
35–37	14.8	15.0	15.3	15.5	15.8	16.0	16.3	16.5	16.8
38–40	16.0	16.3	16.5	16.7	17.0	17.2	17.5	17.7	18.0
41–43	17.2	17.4	17.7	17.9	18.2	18.4	18.7	18.9	19.2
44–46	18.3	18.6	18.8	19.1	19.3	19.6	19.8	20.1	20.3
47–49	19.5	19.7	20.0	20.2	20.5	20.7	21.0	21.2	21.5
50–52	20.6	20.8	21.1	21.3	21.6	21.8	22.1	22.3	22.6
53–55	21.7	21.9	22.1	22.4	22.6	22.9	23.1	23.4	23.6
56–58	22.7	23.0	23.2	23.4	23.7	23.9	24.2	24.4	24.7
59–61	23.7	24.0	24.2	24.5	24.7	25.0	25.2	25.5	25.7
62–64	24.7	25.0	25.2	25.5	25.7	26.0	26.7	26.4	26.7
65–67	25.7	25.9	26.2	26.4	26.7	26.9	27.2	27.4	27.7
68–70	26.6	26.9	27.1	27.4	27.6	27.9	28.1	28.4	28.6
71–73	27.5	27.8	28.0	28.3	28.5	28.8	29.0	29.3	29.5
74–76	28.4	28.7	28.9	29.2	29.4	29.7	29.9	30.2	30.4
77–79	29.3	29.5	29.8	30.0	30.3	30.5	30.8	31.0	31.3
80–82	30.1	30.4	30.6	30.9	31.1	31.4	31.6	31.9	32.1
83–85	30.9	31.2	31.4	31.7	31.9	32.2	32.4	32.7	32.9
86–88	31.7	32.0	32.2	32.5	32.7	32.9	33.2	33.4	33.7
89–91	32.5	32.7	33.0	33.2	33.5	33.7	33.9	34.2	34.4
92–94	33.2	33.4	33.7	33.9	34.2	34.4	34.7	34.9	35.2
95–97	33.9	34.1	34.4	34.6	34.9	35.1	35.4	35.6	35.9
98–100	34.6	34.8	35.1	35.3	35.5	35.8	36.0	36.3	36.5
101–103	35.3	35.4	35.7	35.9	36.2	36.4	36.7	36.9	37.2
104–106	35.8	36.1	36.3	36.6	36.8	37.1	37.3	37.5	37.8
107–109	36.4	36.7	36.9	37.1	37.4	37.6	37.9	38.1	38.4
110–112	37.0	37.2	37.5	37.7	38.0	38.2	38.5	38.7	38.9
113–115	37.5	37.8	38.0	38.2	38.5	38.7	39.0	39.2	39.5
116–118	38.0	38.3	38.5	38.8	39.0	39.3	39.5	39.7	40.0
119–121	38.5	38.7	39.0	39.2	39.5	39.7	40.0	40.2	40.5
122–124	39.0	39.2	39.4	39.7	39.9	40.2	40.4	40.7	40.9
125–127	39.4	39.6	39.9	40.1	40.4	40.6	40.9	41.1	41.4
128–130	39.8	40.0	40.3	40.5	40.8	41.0	41.3	41.5	41.8

*Last calendar birthday.
Source: Jackson, A. S. and Pollock, M. L., "Practical assessment of body composition," *The Physician and Sports medicine*, vol. 13, no. 5, 1985, 76–90.

TABLE 14.7 Percent Fat Estimate for Men: Sum of Triceps, Chest, and Subscapular Skinfolds

Sum of Skinfolds (mm)	Age to Last Year*								
	Under 22	23–27	28–32	33–37	38–42	43–47	48–52	53–57	Over 57
8–10	1.5	2.0	2.5	3.1	3.6	4.1	4.6	5.1	5.6
11–13	3.0	3.5	4.0	4.5	5.1	5.6	6.1	6.6	7.1
14–16	4.5	5.0	5.5	6.0	6.5	7.0	7.6	8.1	8.6
17–19	5.9	6.4	6.9	7.4	8.0	8.5	9.0	9.5	10.0
20–22	7.3	7.8	8.3	8.8	9.4	9.9	10.4	10.9	11.4
23–25	8.6	9.2	9.7	10.2	10.7	11.2	11.8	12.3	12.8
26–28	10.0	10.5	11.0	11.5	12.1	12.6	13.1	13.6	14.2
29–31	11.2	11.8	12.3	12.8	13.4	13.9	14.4	14.9	15.5
32–34	12.5	13.0	13.5	14.1	14.6	15.1	15.7	16.2	16.7
35–37	13.7	14.2	14.8	15.3	15.8	16.4	16.9	17.4	18.0
38–40	14.9	15.4	15.9	16.5	17.0	17.6	18.1	18.6	19.2
41–43	16.0	16.6	17.1	17.6	18.2	18.7	19.3	19.8	20.3
44–46	17.1	17.7	18.2	18.7	19.3	19.8	20.4	20.9	21.5
47–49	18.2	18.7	19.3	19.8	20.4	20.9	21.4	22.0	22.5
50–52	19.2	19.7	20.3	20.8	21.4	21.9	22.5	23.0	23.6
53–55	20.2	20.7	21.3	21.8	22.4	22.9	23.5	24.0	24.6
56–58	21.1	21.7	22.2	22.8	23.3	23.9	24.4	25.0	25.5
59–61	22.0	22.6	23.1	23.7	24.2	24.8	25.3	25.9	26.5
62–64	22.9	23.4	24.0	24.5	25.1	25.7	26.2	26.8	27.3
65–67	23.7	24.3	24.8	25.4	25.9	26.5	27.1	27.6	28.2
68–70	24.5	25.0	25.6	26.2	26.7	27.3	27.8	28.4	29.0
71–73	25.2	25.8	26.3	26.9	27.5	28.0	28.6	29.1	29.7
74–76	25.9	26.5	27.0	27.6	28.2	28.7	29.3	29.9	30.4
77–79	26.6	27.1	27.7	28.2	28.8	29.4	29.9	30.5	31.1
80–82	27.2	27.7	28.3	28.9	29.4	30.0	30.6	31.1	31.7
83–85	27.7	28.3	28.8	29.4	30.0	30.5	31.1	31.7	32.3
86–88	28.2	28.8	29.4	29.9	30.5	31.1	31.6	32.2	32.8
89–91	28.7	29.3	29.8	30.4	31.0	31.5	32.1	32.7	33.3
92–94	29.1	29.7	30.3	30.8	31.4	32.0	32.6	33.1	33.4
95–97	29.5	30.1	30.6	31.2	31.8	32.4	32.9	33.5	34.1
98–100	29.8	30.4	31.0	31.6	32.1	32.7	33.3	33.9	34.4
101–103	30.1	30.7	31.3	31.8	32.4	33.0	33.6	34.1	34.7
104–106	30.4	30.9	31.5	32.1	32.7	33.2	33.8	34.4	35.0
107–109	30.6	31.1	31.7	32.3	32.9	33.4	34.0	34.6	35.2
110–112	30.7	31.3	31.9	32.4	33.0	33.6	34.2	34.7	35.3
113–115	30.8	31.4	32.0	32.5	33.1	33.7	34.3	34.9	35.4
116–118	30.9	31.5	32.0	32.6	33.2	33.8	34.3	34.9	35.5

*Last calendar birthday.

Source: Jackson, A. S. and Pollock, M. L., "Practical assessment of body composition," *The Physician and Sports medicine*, vol. 13, no. 5, 1985, 76–90.

TABLE 14.8 Percent Fat Estimate for Women: Sum of Triceps, Abdomen, and Suprailium Skinfolds

Sum of Skinfolds (mm)	Age to Last Year*								
	Under 22	23–27	28–32	33–37	38–42	43–47	48–52	53–57	Over 57
8–12	8.8	9.0	9.2	9.4	9.5	9.7	9.9	10.1	10.3
13–17	10.8	10.9	11.1	11.3	11.5	11.7	11.8	12.0	12.2
18–22	12.6	12.8	13.0	13.2	13.4	13.5	13.7	13.9	14.1
23–27	14.5	14.6	14.8	15.0	15.2	15.4	15.6	15.7	15.9
28–32	16.2	16.4	16.6	16.8	17.0	17.1	17.3	17.5	17.7
33–37	17.9	18.1	18.3	18.5	18.7	18.9	19.0	19.2	19.4
38–42	19.6	19.8	20.0	20.2	20.3	20.5	20.7	20.9	21.1
43–47	21.2	21.4	21.6	21.8	21.9	22.1	22.3	22.5	22.7
48–52	22.8	22.9	23.1	23.3	23.5	23.7	23.8	24.0	24.2
53–57	24.2	24.4	24.6	24.8	25.0	25.2	25.3	25.5	25.7
58–62	25.7	25.9	26.0	26.2	26.4	26.6	26.8	27.0	27.1
63–67	27.1	27.2	27.4	27.6	27.8	28.0	28.2	28.3	28.5
68–72	28.4	28.6	28.7	28.9	29.1	29.3	29.5	29.7	29.8
73–77	29.6	29.8	30.0	30.2	30.4	30.6	30.7	30.9	31.1
78–82	30.9	31.0	31.2	31.4	31.6	31.8	31.9	32.1	32.3
83–87	32.0	32.2	32.4	32.6	32.7	32.9	33.1	33.3	33.5
88–92	33.1	33.3	33.5	33.7	33.8	34.0	34.2	34.4	34.6
93–97	34.1	34.3	34.5	34.7	34.9	35.1	35.2	35.4	35.6
98–102	35.1	35.3	35.5	35.7	35.9	36.0	36.2	36.4	36.6
103–107	36.1	36.2	36.4	36.6	36.8	37.0	37.2	37.3	37.5
108–112	36.9	37.1	37.3	37.5	37.7	37.9	38.0	38.2	38.4
113–117	37.8	37.9	38.1	38.3	39.2	39.4	39.6	39.8	39.2
118–122	38.5	38.7	38.9	39.1	39.4	39.6	39.8	40.0	40.0
123–127	39.2	39.4	39.6	39.8	40.0	40.1	40.3	40.5	40.7
128–132	39.9	40.1	40.2	40.4	40.6	40.8	41.0	41.2	41.3
133–137	40.5	40.7	40.8	41.0	41.2	41.4	41.6	41.7	41.9
138–142	41.0	41.2	41.4	41.6	41.7	41.9	42.1	42.3	42.5
143–147	41.5	41.7	41.9	42.0	42.2	42.4	42.6	42.8	43.0
148–152	41.9	42.1	42.3	42.8	42.6	42.8	43.0	43.2	43.4
153–157	42.3	42.5	42.6	42.8	43.0	43.2	43.4	43.6	43.7
158–162	42.6	42.8	43.0	43.1	43.3	43.5	43.7	43.9	44.1
163–167	42.9	43.0	43.2	43.4	43.6	43.8	44.0	44.1	44.3
168–172	43.1	43.2	43.4	43.6	43.8	44.0	44.2	44.3	44.5
173–177	43.2	43.4	43.6	43.8	43.9	44.1	44.3	44.5	44.7
178–182	43.3	43.5	43.7	43.8	44.0	44.2	44.4	44.6	44.8

*Last calendar birthday.

Source: Jackson, A. S. and Pollock, M. L., "Practical assessment of body composition," *The Physician and Sports medicine*, vol. 13, no. 5, 1985, 76–90.

TABLE 14.9   Percent Body Fat Standards

| | | | Age | | | |
Percentile	20–29	30–39	40–49	50–59	60–69	70–79
			Males			
90 (Excellent)	7.9	12.4	15.0	17.0	18.1	17.5
75 (Good)	11.5	15.9	18.5	20.2	21.0	21.0
55 (Fair)	15.8	19.2	21.4	23.0	23.6	23.7
			Females			
90 (Excellent)	15.1	15.5	16.8	19.1	20.2	18.3
75 (Good)	17.6	18.3	20.6	23.6	24.6	23.7
55 (Fair)	20.6	22.0	24.6	27.6	28.3	27.6

Source: Adapted from American College of Sports Medicine, *ACSM's Health-Related Physical Fitness Assessment Manual*, 5th ed., Philadelphia: Wolters Kluwer Health, 2018. Orginal source: Cooper Institute, *Physical Fitness Assessment and Norms for Adults and Law Enforcement*, Dallas: Cooper Institute.

Calculation of fat weight (FW)

$$FW = body\ weight \times (\%\ fat \div 100)$$
$$= 200 \times (24\% \div 100)$$
$$= 200 \times .24$$
$$FW = 48\ pounds$$

Calculation of lean body weight (LBW)

$$LBW = body\ weight - FW$$
$$= 200 - 48$$
$$LBW = 152\ pounds$$

Calculation of desirable body weight (DBW)

$$DBW = \frac{LBW}{1.00 - (desired\ \%\ fat \div 100)}$$
$$= \frac{152}{1.00 - (19\% \div 100)}$$
$$= \frac{152}{1.00 - .19}$$
$$= \frac{152}{.81}$$
$$DBW = 187.7\ pounds$$

Because measurement errors may occur, when you are estimating percent body fat, it is best to determine desirable body weight ranges. Table 14.9 may be used to establish desirable body weight ranges that include the optimal percent body fat.

Cooper Method for Determining Ideal Weight

When body fat cannot be estimated through skinfold measurements, the Cooper (1982) method may be used to calculate the ideal weight for men and women. Men multiply their height in inches by 4, and then subtract 128. Women multiply their height in inches by 3.5, and then subtract 108. The resulting values will give men of average build a weight with roughly 15% to 19% body fat and women of average build a weight with roughly 18% to 22% body fat. Large-boned individuals should add 10% to the calculated figure to determine their ideal weight, and small-boned individuals should subtract 10%.

Body Mass Index (BMI)

The **body mass index** (BMI) provides an indication of the relationship of weight to height. It is used worldwide in health and disease studies, but its standard error is large. The error is especially large for children and the elderly because their muscle and bone weights in relationship to their heights can change rapidly. Because it does not provide an estimate of percent body fat, BMI is not a recommended procedure for determining body composition. The BMI has been found to correlate with health risks, however, and can be used as a screening tool when body fat estimates are not available. The BMI is computed with the following equation:

$$BMI = \frac{weight\ in\ kilograms}{(height\ in\ meters)^2}$$

(1 kilogram = 2.2046 pounds; 1 meter = 39.37 inches)

For adults, a BMI of 20 to 25 is generally associated with the lowest risk of health problems; health risks, including high blood pressure and diabetes, increase as the BMI exceeds 25. Adults with a BMI greater than 30 are considered obese, and anyone with a BMI greater than 40 is considered morbidly obese and in need of medical attention.

For children and adolescents (ages 2–19), the BMI is plotted on the Centers for Disease Control and Prevention growth chart. With the growth chart, it is possible to determine the BMI percentile for the age and sex of the individual. Children and adolescents with a BMI at or above the 85th percentile but below the 95th percentile (same age and sex) are considered overweight. Obesity is defined as a BMI at or above the 95th percentile. To determine if the child or adolescent has excess fat, additional testing for percent body fat may be needed.

Table 14.10 indicates classification of overweight and disease risk associated with BMI for adults.

Fat Distribution

Research shows that body shape, as well as body fat, is important to health. Excess body fat concentrated in the abdominal area may be a greater health risk than fat found around the thighs and hips. It appears that abdominal fat is more easily broken down than fat in other places. This broken-down fat goes straight to the liver, which may lead to dangerous elevations in blood fat and insulin levels.

A favorable **waist-to-hip ratio** may decrease the risk of diseases associated with excess weight. To determine the waist-to-hip ratio, perform the following steps:

1. Measure around the waist where it is the smallest; stand relaxed at end of normal expiration; do not pull in the stomach.

2. Measure the hips where they are the largest.

3. Divide the waist measurement by the hips measurement to obtain the waist-to-hip ratio.

You should be aware that different procedures may be described for measurement of waist circumference. For example, the *CSEP-Physical Activity Training for Health* (CSEP-PATH), described in chapter 15, requires that the tape be placed on the uppermost border of the iliac crest. Table 14.11 includes waist-to-hip ratios that indicate moderate health risks.

TABLE 14.10 Classification of Disease Risk Associated with Body Mass Index (BMI) and Waist Circumference

| Weight | BMI (kg/m²) | Disease Risk Associated with BMI and Waist Circumference | |
		Male, ≤40 in.; Female, ≤35 in.	Male, >40 in.; Female, >35 in.
Underweight	<18.5	No risks assigned	No risks assigned
Normal weight	18.5–24.9	No risks assigned	No risks assigned
Overweight	25.0–29.9	Increased	High
Obesity (class)			
I	30.0–34.9	High	Very high
II	35.0–39.9	Very high	Very high
III	≥40	Extremely high	Extremely high

Source: Adapted from *ACSM's guidelines for exercise testing and prescription*, Philadelphia: Wolter Kluwer Health, 2010.

TABLE 14.11   Moderate Risks Standards for Waist-to-Hip Circumference Ratio*

	Age				
	20–29	30–39	40–49	50–59	60–69
Male	.83–.88	.84–.91	.88–.95	.90–.96	.91–.98
Female	.71–.77	.72–.78	.73–.79	.74–.81	.76–.83

*Measurements lower than those listed indicate low risk, and higher measurements indicate high to very high risk.
Source: Adapted from *ACSM's health-related physical fitness assessment manual*, Philadelphia: Lippincott Williams & Wilkins, 2005.

▰▰ ARE YOU ABLE TO DO THE FOLLOWING?

- Calculate an individual's desirable weight on the basis of an acceptable percent body fat.

- Determine the body mass index (BMI) and waist-to-hip ratio and advise individuals of BMI values and waist-to-hip ratios associated with the lowest risk of health problems.

Review Problems

1. If skinfold calipers are available, perform skinfold measurements on several of your classmates. Use different types of calipers, if possible, on the same individuals and compare the results. Do you obtain similar measurements with different calipers?

2. Ask the directors of several local health or fitness clubs how they estimate percent body fat for their members.

Chapter Review Questions

1. Define the terms *anthropometry, somatotype, body composition, overfat, obese,* and *lean body weight.*

2. Why is the measurement of body structure and composition important in health promotion, and what are your responsibilities after their measurement?

3. How can you use body type classification in the promotion of an active lifestyle?

4. What are two major problems with the use of height–weight tables to determine desirable weight?

5. Describe two ways in which body frame can be determined.

6. List and describe eight acceptable sites for skinfold measurements.

7. Describe the correct procedure for performing skinfold measurements.

8. How is the BMI calculated? What is considered overfat and obese for adults and children, as determined through the BMI?

9. What information does the BMI provide and why is it used? What measure is not provided with the BMI?

10. What waist circumferences place males and females at greater risk for health problems?

11. How is the waist-to-hip ratio determined and why is it used in health promotion?

15 Physical Fitness

After completing this chapter, you should be able to

1. Define and measure *health-related physical fitness* and *skill-related physical fitness*.

2. State why physical fitness should be measured.

3. List six guidelines for the administration and use of physical fitness tests.

4. Contrast norm-referenced and criterion-referenced standards and state how both may be used appropriately in testing for physical fitness.

5. Describe responsibilities after the measurement of physical fitness and prescribe activities and exercises for the development of physical fitness.

The terms **fitness** and **physical fitness** are often used interchangeably. Though both terms involve quality of life, they do not mean the same thing. Fitness includes emotional, mental, spiritual, and social fitness, as well as physical fitness. Currently, a popular term for fitness is *wellness*. Everyone should be concerned with total fitness, but the responsibilities of physical educators are more related to physical fitness.

Different people and groups interpret physical fitness in different ways. It is sometimes defined as the capacity for sustained physical activity without excessive fatigue or as the capacity to perform everyday activities with reserve energy for emergency situations. By these definitions many persons incorrectly classify themselves as physically fit. It is especially incorrect to accept these definitions when the relations between inactivity and health are considered. Some individuals consider physical fitness synonymous with cardiorespiratory fitness, whereas other groups limit their perception of physical fitness to muscular strength and endurance.

When one is defining physical fitness, it may be best to describe two types of physical fitness: **health-related** and **skill-related.** Both types require regular exercise, and both require proper nutrition and rest. However, health-related physical fitness includes cardiorespiratory fitness, muscular strength, muscular endurance, flexibility, and body composition (leanness/fatness). Health-related physical fitness means the organic systems of the body are healthy and function efficiently, so you are able to engage in vigorous tasks and leisure activities. It exerts a positive influence on several risk factors associated with cardiovascular diseases, and it is effective in reducing the risk of back pain, diabetes, osteoporosis, and obesity. In addition, it is an effective way to manage emotional stress. In other words, health-related fitness enables you to look better, feel better, and enjoy a healthy, happy, and full life.

Skill-related physical fitness may provide the same benefits as health-related physical fitness, but it also includes motor skills required in sports and specific types of jobs. For this reason, skill-related fitness is sometimes referred to as athletic performance–related physical fitness, or motor fitness. In addition to the five health-related components—cardiorespiratory fitness, muscular strength, muscular endurance, flexibility, and body composition—skill-related physical fitness includes agility, balance, coordination, power, reaction time, and speed.

Exercise programs for the maintenance and development of health-related physical fitness are usually different from programs for skill-related physical fitness, particularly if the purpose of the program is to prepare the individual for athletic competition. Too often exercise programs for athletes place little emphasis on health-related components. In fact, because they have not made a commitment to health-related fitness, many athletes fail to continue an exercise program after they cease to participate in sports.

Why Measure Physical Fitness?

The relationship between good health and cardiorespiratory fitness, muscular strength, muscular endurance, flexibility, and body composition has been described previously. The development of these components should be a primary objective in all school physical education programs as well as all fitness programs. Physical educators should be prepared to measure them, interpret the test results, and prescribe the appropriate activities for the development of health-related physical fitness. In addition, test results can be used to teach the concepts of fitness, motivate for self-improvement, and help individuals plan fitness goals.

Though sports participation is not essential for a healthy lifestyle, many individuals enjoy taking part in sports, and the enjoyment is usually greater for individuals possessing skill-related physical fitness. The skills of agility, balance, coordination, power, reaction time, and speed are important components of sports performance. These motor skills also are related to the performance of many types of occupations and daily activities. Testing for skill-related physical fitness can serve to motivate high-ability individuals to perform at even higher levels. In addition, diagnostic testing will enable the physical educator to prescribe the appropriate activities for individuals who do not possess adequate skill-related fitness.

It is doubtful that performance on fitness tests should be used for grading purposes. A poor performance on a fitness test, resulting in an unwanted grade, may have a negative effect on an individual. Rather than being motivated to move toward an active lifestyle, the individual may become even more inactive. In the school environment, use fitness tests for the previously described reasons.

Guidelines for the Administration and Use of Fitness Tests

Fitness testing can be an important part of any school physical education or fitness programs. The following guidelines (Corbin 1987; Franks, Morrow, and Plowman 1988), however, should be observed when fitness tests are administered:

1. Measure fitness components that the public and research experts agree are the most important. Focus on health and self-improvement rather than on comparison with others.

2. In the school environment, fitness tests should be a part of the total educational program. Attention should be given to the knowledge and understanding of fitness concepts, and students should be held accountable for class work. Written test items should measure the students' understanding of the concepts.

3. Fitness test results should be kept confidential; careful attention should be given to ensure that the test results do not embarrass a student or threaten his or her self-image.

4. Teach students how to take fitness tests; give ample time for practice of the test components.

5. Fitness awards should encourage lifetime activity rather than a one-time performance.

6. Take care to provide necessary, sufficient, and valid information regarding test results to parents and students.

Norm-Referenced Standards versus Criterion-Referenced Standards

Although criterion-referenced standards and norm-referenced standards have been discussed previously, it is important to consider them again in the discussion of fitness testing. Both standards may be used appropriately. The discussion in this section is based on Going and Williams (1989) and Cureton and Warren (1990).

Recall that comparison of an individual's performance with that of other individuals having common characteristics is called norm-referenced measurement. Norm-referenced tests are well suited for the measurement of skill-related physical fitness if the goal is to motivate individuals to achieve a high level of fitness. On the other hand, the use of norm-referenced fitness standards with physically inactive and low-fit individuals may be inadvisable. When norm-referenced fitness standards (percentiles) are used without consideration of the absolute score, improvements in student performance may not be noted and individuals may be discouraged rather than encouraged to seek improvement.

Criterion-referenced standards are used when individual differences are unimportant and performance is judged relative to some standard that reflects a satisfactory level of the attribute being measured. In contrast to norm-referenced testing, a score higher than another score at or above the standard is not necessarily better. Criterion-referenced standards for health-related physical fitness tests purportedly represent the minimum level of an attribute or function that is consistent with good health. The standards are used as goals for low-fit individuals, and, unless limited physically, most individuals are capable of attaining the standards. A criticism of such standards, however, is that because they represent desired minimum levels of fitness, they do not serve to motivate individuals to seek a higher level of fitness.

Both types of standards are included in the tests described in this chapter. The purpose of testing should determine the test and standards that you choose to use.

Responsibilities after Measurement

With the administration of a health-related or skill-related physical fitness test, you may identify individuals who should seek to improve their status in one or more components of physical fitness. If so, an activity program that will develop each component should be designed. One particular type of activity or exercise will not develop all components of health-related or skill-related physical fitness. For example, running is an excellent activity for the development of cardiorespiratory fitness, but other activities must be performed to develop arm and shoulder strength and flexibility. The same is true of many cardiorespiratory fitness programs. Also, weight-lifting programs are excellent for muscular strength and endurance, but other types of programs are better for cardiorespiratory fitness. Activities and exercises that may be used to develop the components of health-related physical fitness as well as agility and balance have been described in previous chapters. By selecting appropriate activities for different ages, you can design a sound program to develop any or all of these components.

In the school environment, you may want to develop programs that students can follow outside of the school environment. For many students, the program probably should be highly organized, but students who are physically active will not need such an organized program. All students may be asked to maintain a journal of their daily physical activities. With this approach, programs can be individualized to meet the needs of each student. As a teacher, your goal should be to guide each student toward an active lifestyle.

ARE YOU ABLE TO DO THE FOLLOWING?

- Define *health-related* and *skill-related physical fitness* and state why they should be measured.

- List six guidelines for the administration and use of fitness tests.

♦ ♦ ♦ POINT OF EMPHASIS ♦ ♦ ♦

- Whether you are working with children, young people, or adults, a primary objective should be the promotion of an active lifestyle. For this reason, it may be more important to emphasize the individual and not the standards that you choose to use. Rather than rigidly adhering to norm-referenced or criterion-referenced standards, the best approach may be the comparison of individuals with themselves—that is, compare their test scores with their past and future scores and motivate them to work toward the standards.

- Contrast norm-referenced and criterion-referenced standards and state when each standard may be used appropriately.

- Describe responsibilities after the measurement of physical fitness.

Tests of Health-Related Physical Fitness

Establishing a single test battery that measures all components of health-related or skill-related physical fitness is difficult. Since there is no one item that measures total body muscular strength, muscular endurance, or flexibility, a decision must be made as to which parts of the body are to be measured for these components. Some tests include items that measure arm and shoulder girdle strength and endurance. Strength and endurance of the abdominal region and low-back–posterior-thigh flexibility are often included in these tests because of their importance in prevention of low-back disorders. Rather than selecting a single test battery, however, you may choose to measure physical fitness through a combination of test items presented in previous chapters. This approach is acceptable if you use items intended for the group (age and gender) you are testing.

When reviewing the health-related and skill-related physical fitness tests described in this chapter, you should be aware of the following considerations: (1) Some tests have similar items that may not be administered in the same way (i.e., sit-ups, push-ups, and sit and reach). If you plan to use the norms of a particular test, it is important to administer all items in the manner described in the test. (2) Some of the criterion-referenced standards vary for the health-related physical fitness test items. (3) Tests currently not promoted are included. These tests are presented because of the uniqueness of a component or components (you may choose to administer these components sometime in the future) and because norms are available.

Discussions about the possibility of a national youth fitness test have been held among representatives of various groups. Health-related physical fitness tests are similar because most experts agree upon the components of health-related physical fitness and the various test items that can be used to measure these components. There is not agreement upon the health-related standards, however. In addition, some groups feel that a physical fitness test should include both health-related and skill-related physical fitness items. Developing a national test requires agreement about these concerns as well as awards, computer software, promotion, and title.

■ FitnessGram
(The Cooper Institute 2017)

The FitnessGram is a comprehensive fitness-health battery for children and youth with software that generates reports for each individual's performance on all test components. The Presidential Youth Fitness Program (PYFP) includes the FitnessGram to assess the health-related fitness of students in grades K–12.

For all test items, the test performer may be classified in the Health Fitness Zone (HFZ) or the Needs Improvement Zone (NIZ). The HFZ indicates the child or youth has a fitness level that provides important health benefits. The NIZ indicates the child or youth may be at risk if the level of fitness remains the same over time. Aerobic capacity and body composition also include the Needs Improvement-Health Risk Zone (NI-HRZ) which indicates the test performer has current or future health risks. Additionally, body composition includes a fourth option, the Very Lean Zone (VLZ), because of risks associated with being too lean. The lower end (good) standards of the HFZ are provided in table 15.1.

ActivityGram may also be used with FitnessGram software. The student is asked to complete a three-day record of physical activity and a short survey about physical activity. The software provides a detailed assessment of the student's physical activity.

Age Level. Five through seventeen-plus.

Equipment. Flat, nonslippery surface at least 20 meters long; a computer, laptop, or handheld music device connected to speakers; a measuring tape; marker cones; pencil; appropriate scoring sheets; stopwatch; a digital scale; stadiometer (recommended for height measurement); bioelectrical impedance analysis device or skinfold calipers; gym mat; measurement strips; yardstick; ruler; modified pull-up stand (if modified pull-up administered); horizontal bar (if flexed arm hang administered); and sit and reach box or a sturdy box with a height of 12 inches and measuring scale placed on top of the box.

Test Components

1. Aerobic capacity: Three test options are provided. The FitnessGram software or the web resource is used to determine the aerobic capacity. Because criterion-referenced standards are not available for ages 5–9,

TABLE 15.1 The FitnessGram—Lower End (Good) Standards of the Healthy Fitness Zone

Test Item	5	6	7	8	9	10	11	12	13	14	15	16	17	17+
Males														
Aerobic capacity ($\dot{V}O_2$ max)*						40.2	40.2	40.3	41.1	42.5	43.6	44.1	44.2	44.3
PACER, 1-mile run, walk test														
Percent fat**	18.8	18.8	18.8	18.8	20.6	22.4	23.6	23.6	22.8	21.3	20.1	20.1	20.9	22.2
Body mass index**	16.8	17.1	17.6	18.2	18.9	19.7	20.5	21.3	22.2	23	23.7	24.5	24.9	24.9
Curl-up	2	2	4	6	9	12	15	18	21	24	24	24	24	24
Trunk lift (in.)	6	6	6	6	6	9	9	9	9	9	9	9	9	9
Push-up	3	3	4	5	6	7	8	10	12	14	16	18	18	18
Modified pull-up	2	2	3	4	5	5	6	7	8	9	10	12	14	14
Flexed-arm hang (sec)	2	2	3	3	4	4	6	10	12	15	15	15	15	15
Back-saver sit and reach***	8	8	8	8	8	8	8	8	8	8	8	8	8	8
Shoulder stretch****														
Females														
Aerobic capacity ($\dot{V}O_2$ max)*						40.2	40.2	40.1	39.7	39.4	39.1	38.9	38.8	38.6
PACER, 1-mile run, walk test														
Percent fat**	20.8	20.8	20.8	20.8	22.6	24.3	25.7	26.7	27.7	28.5	29.1	29.7	30.4	31.3
Body mass index**	16.8	17.2	17.9	18.6	19.4	20.3	21.2	22.1	22.9	23.6	24.3	24.8	24.9	24.9
Curl-up	2	2	4	6	9	12	15	18	18	18	18	18	18	18
Trunk lift (in.)	6	6	6	6	6	9	9	9	9	9	9	9	9	9
Push-up	3	3	4	5	6	7	7	7	7	7	7	7	7	7
Modified pull-up	2	2	3	4	4	4	4	4	4	4	4	4	4	4
Flexed-arm hang (sec)	2	2	3	3	4	4	6	7	8	8	8	8	8	8
Back-saver sit and reach***	9	9	9	9	9	9	10	10	10	10	12	12	12	12
Shoulder stretch****														

*For ages 5–9, time standards are not recommended; completion of distance is recognized.
**Only upper limit of percent fat and body mass index are shown in table.
***Must meet the standard on both the right and left sides.
****"Y" must be recorded on both right and left sides.

Source: The Cooper Institute, *FitnessGram Administration Manual: The Journey to MyHealthy Zone*, 5th ed., Champaign, Il.: Human Kinetics, 2017.

aerobic capacity scores and feedback are not provided for these ages. For these students, the goal is to complete the test at a comfortable pace.

The PACER. The test objective is to run as long as possible back and forth across a 20-meter distance at a specified pace that gets faster each minute (initial pace is easy but progresses to a harder pace). Two lines, 20 meters apart, are marked on the floor. On the start command, participants run across the area and touch the line by the time a beep sounds. At the sound of the beep, they run back to the starting line. Participants who get to a line before the beep must wait for the beep before running in the other direction. The participants continue in this manner until they can no longer reach a line before the beep sounds. The first time a participant does not reach the line by the beep, the participant reverses direction immediately, returns to the previous line, and attempts to get back on pace with the next beep. The participant is allowed to catch up with the pace, but the test is completed when the participant fails to reach the line by the beep for the second time. Set to music, this test can provide a valid, fun alternative to the distance run for measuring aerobic capacity. The PACER is recommended for all ages, but its use is strongly encouraged for grades K–3. Typically, in these grades, the test will last only a few minutes. A lap is one 20-meter distance (from one end to the other). The number of laps completed and the student's age are used to estimate aerobic capacity.

15-meter distance. As some gymnasiums are not 20 meters in length, an alternative 15-meter PACER test is available. The test procedures are the same, but the number of laps are different.

1-mile run/1-mile run (alternative). Students are instructed to run 1 mile as fast as possible. Performance standards for students in grades K–3 have purposely not been established. These students are instructed to complete the distance at a comfortable pace. The student' age, sex, BMI, and run time (minutes and seconds) are used to estimate aerobic capacity.

Walk test (alternative). This test is to be used with participants ages thirteen years and older. The participants are instructed to walk 1 mile as quickly as possible while maintaining a constant walking pace the entire distance. At the conclusion of the 1-mile walk, the participant's heart rate is counted for 60 seconds. The heart rate, BMI, and walk time (minutes and seconds) are used to estimate aerobic capacity.

2. Body composition: Body composition may be determined with bioelectrical impedance analysis (BIA), skinfold measurements, or body mass index (BMI). The sum of the triceps and medial-calf skinfold measurements is used for grades K–12. For college students, the formula to calculate percent body fat includes the abdominal skinfold measurement as well as the triceps and calf skinfold measurements. Each measurement should be taken three times, with the recorded score being the middle measurement value. Body mass index is calculated with the following formula: Weight (kg)/Height (m)^2.

3. Abdominal strength and endurance: The curl-up. The test performer lies in a supine position on a mat, knees bent at an angle of approximately 140°, feet flat on the floor, legs slightly apart, and arms straight and parallel to the trunk, with palms of hands resting on the mat. After the test performer assumes the correct position, the measuring strip (30 to 35″ × 3″ for ages 5–9 and 30 to 35″ × 4 1/2″ for ages 10–17) is placed under the knees on the mat so that the fingertips are just resting on the edge of the measuring strip. Keeping the feet in contact with the mat, the test performer curls up slowly until the fingertips reach the other side of the measuring strip and then curls back down until the head touches the mat. Movement should be slow and controlled to the specified cadence of about twenty curl-ups per minute (one curl every 3 seconds). The teacher should call a cadence or use a prerecorded cadence. The test is completed when the student can no longer continue or performs a maximum number of seventy-five curl-ups. A test partner should count the curls and judge if the head makes contact with the mat.

4. Trunk extensor strength and flexibility: Trunk lift. The student being tested lies on the mat in a prone position, with the toes in a pointed position and the hands placed under the thighs. A coin or other marker is placed on the mat in line with the student's eyes. The student lifts the upper body off the mat, in a very slow

and controlled manner, to a maximum height of 12 inches. During the upper body lift, the student's focus should be on the coin. The position is held long enough to allow the tester to measure the distance of the student's chin from the floor. The score is recorded to the nearest inch, and distances above 12 inches are recorded as 12 inches.

5. Upper body strength and endurance: Several test items are available to measure this component. Both extensor and flexor muscles should be measured.

   Push-up. The student performs as many push-ups as possible at a rate of twenty per minute (one push-up every 3 seconds and elbow angle of 90°).

   Modified pull-up. The necessary equipment and test procedure are shown in figure 13.6. The student attempts to perform as many modified pull-ups as possible.

   Flexed-arm hang. The student attempts to hang the chin above the bar as long as possible.

6. Flexibility: Two items are used to measure different body areas. As flexibility is generally not a problem with children and youth, the measurement of flexibility is optional in the FitnessGram.

   Back-saver sit and reach. This item is similar to the traditional sit and reach except that it is performed on one side at a time. Measurement of only one side prevents possible hyperextension at the knees. The test may be performed with the sit and reach box described in chapter 12 or with a sturdy box (12 inches high) and a measuring scale (yardstick) placed on top of the box. With the shoes removed, the student sits down at the test box. One leg is fully extended with the foot flat against the end of the box. The other knee is bent, with the sole of the foot flat on the floor and 2 to 3 inches to the side of the straight knee. The arms are extended forward over the measuring scale with the hands placed one on top of the other. With palms down, the student reaches directly forward with both hands along the scale four times and holds the position of the fourth reach for at least 1 second. After measuring one side, the student switches the position of the legs and reaches again. If necessary, the student may allow the bent knee to

move to the side as the body moves by it, but the sole of the foot must remain on the floor. The recorded score is the nearest .5 inch reached on each side to a maximum of 12 inches. To be in the HFZ, the standard must be met on both sides.

Shoulder stretch. To test the right shoulder, the student reaches with the right hand over the right shoulder and down the back as if to pull up a zipper. At the same time, the left hand is placed behind the back and reaches up, trying to touch the fingers of the right hand. A partner observes if fingers touch. The left shoulder is measured by the movement of the arms reversing. The test is scored as "Y" or "N" for each shoulder; the fingers must touch for a "Y" score. Figure 12.8 provides an illustration of this test.

■ **AAHPERD Health-Related Physical Fitness Test for College Students**
(AAHPERD 1980a; Pate 1985)

The AAHPERD Health-Related Fitness Test was developed originally for use with students ages six to seventeen. The American Alliance for Health, Physical Education, Recreation and Dance (AAHPERD), now known as the Society of Health and Physical Educators (SHAPE America), no longer promotes the Health-Related Fitness Test. However, as college-student norms were developed for this test in 1985, it is a useful test for individuals 18–23 years old. Table 15.2 reports percentile norms for the test.

Age Level. College-age.

Equipment. Stopwatch, any flat measured area, skinfold caliper, and sit and reach box.

Test Components

1. Cardiorespiratory functional capacity and endurance: 1-mile run or 9-minute run. The test performers are instructed to run 1 mile as fast as possible or to cover as much distance as possible in 9 minutes.
2. Body composition: The sum of the triceps and subscapular skinfold measurements.
3. Abdominal muscular strength and endurance: Modified sit-ups (arms crossed on chest). This test is described in chapter 13.
4. Flexibility (extensibility) of the low back and hamstrings: Sit and reach. The sit and reach box and test procedure are described in chapter 12. The score is recorded to the nearest 1/4 inch.

TABLE 15.2 College-Age Norms for the AAHPERD Health-Related Physical Fitness Test

Percentile	1-mile run (min:sec)	9-Minute Run (Yards)	Sum of Skinfolds (mm)	Percent Fat	Sit-Ups	Sit and Reach (Inches)
Males						
95	5:30	2,640	12	3.9	60	17.75
75	6:12	2,349	16	6.6	50	15.50
50	6:49	2,200	21	9.4	44	13.50
25	7:32	1,945	26	13.1	38	11.50
5	9:47	1,652	40	20.4	30	7.50
Females						
95	7:02	2,230	17	13.7	53	18.50
75	8:15	1,870	24	19.0	42	16.25
50	9:22	1,755	30	22.8	35	14.50
25	10:41	1,460	37	27.1	30	12.50
5	12:43	1,101	51	33.7	21	9.50

Source: Adapted from AAHPERD, *Norms for college students—Health-related physical fitness test*, Reston, Va.: American Alliance for Health, Physical Education, Recreation and Dance, 1985.

■ YMCA Fitness Test
(Golding 2000)

The YMCA Fitness Test is administered as part of a health-related physical fitness program sponsored by the YMCA. A health screening is required before the test is administered. An exercise program based on results of the test items is prescribed. Table 15.3 reports norms for the "Good" rating on the test items. The reference includes norms from the range of "Very Poor" to "Excellent."

Age Level. Eighteen through sixty-five-plus.

Equipment. Skinfold caliper, bicycle ergometer, 12-inch-high sturdy bench, yardstick, barbell, weights, metronome, and mat.

Test Components

1. Body composition: Both men and women use the sum of four skinfold sites—abdomen, ilium, triceps, and thigh. Three sites should be used only if the thigh skinfold cannot be measured accurately.
2. Cardiorespiratory endurance: The bicycle ergometer is used to measure this component. Maximal physical working capacity (PWC) and maximal oxygen uptake ($\dot{V}O_2$max) are predicted from the performer's response to a submaximal workload.

The 3-minute step test (described in chapter 11) may be used as a substitute for the bicycle ergometer test. The individual steps up and down on a 12-inch bench for 3 minutes at a rate of 24 steps per minute. The score is the total 1-minute postexercise heart rate (count must begin within 5 seconds after completion of the test).

3. Trunk flexion: Sit and reach. A yardstick is placed on the floor with tape across it at right angles to the 15-inch mark. The performer sits with the yardstick between the legs, with the zero (0) mark toward the body, and extends the legs with the feet approximately 12 inches apart. The heels of the feet should nearly touch the edge of the taped line. With one hand on top of the other, the individual reaches forward as far as possible and holds the position momentarily. The score (to the nearest 1/4 inch) is the best of three trials.
4. Muscular strength and endurance:

   Bench press. The metronome is set for 60 beats per minute (bpm), and individuals must repeat the up-and-down movement with each click. Males use an 80-pound barbell, and females use a 35-pound barbell. The score is the number of successful repetitions. The test is terminated when full extension cannot be completed or when the individual cannot keep up with the cadence. For

TABLE 15.3 Standards for the Rating of "Good" for the YMCA Fitness Test

Test Item	Age					
	18–25	**26–35**	**36–45**	**46–55**	**56–65**	**65+**
Males						
% Fat	8–10	11–13	16–18	18–20	19–21	19–21
3-min step test (heart rate)	79–84	79–85	86–94	89–96	89–97	89–95
PWC max (kgm)	1,750–1,945	1,665–1,820	1,565–1,725	1,385–1,520	1,240–1,400	1,045–1,175
$\dot{V}O_2$max (ml/kg)	53–60	50–54	44–49	40–43	37–39	33–36
Flexibility (in.)	20–21	18–19	17–19	16–17	15–17	13–15
Bench press (repetitions)	34–41	26–30	24–28	20–22	14–20	10–14
Half sit-ups	61–72	41–45	36–40	29–33	26–29	22–26
Females						
% Fat	18–20	19–21	20–23	23–25	24–26	22–25
3-min step test (heart rate)	88–97	91–97	93–101	96–102	97–103	93–100
PWC max (kgm)	1,175–1,320	1,115–1,245	1,035–1,135	930–1,045	840–970	640–725
$\dot{V}O_2$max (ml/kg)	48–54	46–51	39–44	35–39	32–36	28–31
Flexibility (in.)	21–23	20–22	19–21	18–20	18–19	18–19
Bench press (repetitions)	28–32	25–29	21–25	20–22	16–20	12–14
Half sit-ups	37–41	33–37	27–30	22–25	18–21	18–22

Source: Adapted from Golding, L. A. ed., *YMCA fitness testing and assessment manual*, 4th ed., Champaign, Ill.: Human Kinetics, 2000.

safety, at least one spotter should be present during the test.

Half sit-ups. The performer lies supine on the floor with the knees bent at right angles, hands pronated, and the fingertips on a 6-inch strip of tape that is perpendicular to the body. A second 6-inch strip of tape is placed on each side of the body, 3.5 inches apart from the first and toward the feet. The performer curls up so that the fingertips of each hand reach the second strip of tape and then returns to the start position. The shoulders must touch the floor. The score is the number of repetitions performed in one minute.

■ ACSM's Health-Related Physical Fitness Assessment
(American College of Sports Medicine 2018)

The *ACSM's Health-Related Physical Fitness Assessment Manual* includes measurement of body composition, muscular fitness, flexibility, and cardiorespiratory fitness. For each component,

several measurement procedures are described. The manual also includes preassessment screening procedures and risk factor assessments.

Age Level. Twenty through adulthood.

Equipment. Underwater weighing facility (optional), bioelectrical impedance analyzer (optional), skinfold measurement calipers, handgrip dynamometer, leg and back strength dynamometer, free weights and weight bench, mat, tape, metronome, goniometer, sit and reach box, yardstick, flat measured surface, and stopwatch.

Test Components

1. Body composition: Underwater weighing, bioelectrical impedance analysis, or skinfold measurements may be used. Three options may be used for skinfold measurements: One uses seven skinfold sites and two use different combinations of three sites.

   Seven sites for males and females: chest, midaxillary, triceps, subscapular, abdomen, suprailiac, thigh.

Sites for males: chest, abdomen, thigh or chest, triceps, subscapular.

Sites for females: triceps, suprailiac, thigh or triceps, suprailiac, abdomen.

The ASCM percent body fat standards are included in table 14.9.

2. Muscular fitness:

Grip strength and back strength. The grip strength of both hands are measured with a hand dynamometer. Back strength is measured with a dynamometer.

1-repetition maximum (RM) bench press (muscular strength).

1-repetition maximum (RM) leg press (muscular strength).

Both tests are described in chapter 13, and tables 13.1 and 13.2 include standards for the tests.

Push-up (muscular endurance). The maximum number of push-ups performed consecutively without rest is counted. Males use the toes as the pivot point, and females use the knees. Both males and females must touch the chin to the mat. Table 15.4 includes standards for this test.

Partial curl-up (muscular endurance). Individual lies supine with knees bent at 90° and arms extended at sides with fingers touching a piece of masking tape. A second piece of masking tape is placed beyond the first. The tapes should be 12 cm apart for individuals less than 45 years of age and 8 cm apart for individuals 45 years or older. A metronome is set at 40 beeps per minute. At first beep, the individual slowly lifts shoulder blades off the mat until finger tips touch the second piece of tape. On next beep, the individual slowly returns the shoulder blades to the mat by flattening the lower back. The curl-ups are repeated in time with the metronome (20 curls per minute). Without pausing, as many curl-ups as possible are completed to a maximum of 75. Table 15.4 includes standards for this test.

3. Flexibility: Manual provided standards for range of motion measured at six sites (shoulder girdle, elbow, trunk, hip, knee, and ankle) with a goniometer.

Sit and reach. The YMCA sit and reach test or the *CSEP-Physical Activity Training for Health (CSEP-PATH)* sit and reach test may be used. Both tests are described in this chapter. Tables 15.3 and 15.8 includes standards for the tests.

4. Cardiorespiratory fitness: Assessment of cardiorespiratory fitness may be done with the Queens College Step Test, 1-mile walk test, 1.5-mile run test, or 12-minute run test. These tests with standards are described in chapter 11. The manual also includes procedures for testing with a cycle ergometer and treadmill.

■ **CSEP-Physical Activity Training for Health (CSEP-PATH)**
(Canadian Society for Exercise Physiology 2013)

Note: Because several test items are unique, the *CSEP-Physical Activity Training for Health (CSEP-PATH)* is described in greater detail than the other tests presented in this chapter.

The CSEP-PATH manual is a straightforward and systematic approach outlining the proper procedures for the appraisal and counseling of persons aged fifteen to sixty-nine, emphasizing the health benefits of physical activity. The topics of understanding behavior change, helping people change, healthy physical activity participation, healthy lifestyle, basic exercise physiology, and health-related fitness are covered. The manual includes appraisal tools, case studies, and references.

TABLE 15.4 Standards for the ACSM Push-Up and Partial Curl-Up Tests

Test Item	Age				
	20–29	30–39	40–49	50–59	60–69
Males					
Push-up (good–very good)	28–35	21–29	16–24	12–20	10–17
Partial curl-up (average–above average)	31–56	36–69	51–75	35–60	19–33
Females					
Push-up (good–very good)	20–29	19–26	14–23	10–20	11–16
Partial curl-up (average–above average)	32–45	28–43	28–42	16–30	19–30

Adapted from American College of Sports Medicine. 2018. ACSM's health-related physical fitness assessment manual. 5th ed. Philadelphia: Wolters Kluwer.

The health-related fitness appraisal includes muscular power as a component of musculoskeletal fitness, and all appraisal measurements are reported in metric values. Preappraisal screening procedures described in the manual include measurement of resting heart rate, blood pressure, and utilization of the Get Active Questionnaire.

Age Level. Fifteen through sixty-nine.

Equipment. Tape measure, weight scale, skinfold caliper, stethoscope, ergometer steps, mCAFT CD or cassette player, stopwatch, masking tape, heart rate monitor, hand dynamometer, metric ruler, flexometer, gym mat, metronome, and chalk.

Test Components

1. Body composition: Standing height (m) without shoes, weight (kg) without shoes and in light clothing, and waist circumference (cm) are measured. The waist circumference is measured at the top of the iliac crest. The test administrator should locate the uppermost lateral border of the right iliac crest and draw a horizontal line from the landmark to the midline of the body. The measuring tape is then placed directly around the abdomen so that the level of the inferior edge of the tape is at the level of the horizontal line. The tape should be positioned in a horizontal plane around the abdomen. At the end of a normal expiration, the tape should be snug but not cause indentation to the skin. The measurement should be to the nearest .5 cm. A table is provided in the manual so that the individual's health risk may be estimated with the BMI and waist circumference.

Males and females, ages 20–65, have the least health risk with a BMI of 18.5–24.9. Males with a waist circumference 90 cm or more are placed in the appropriate health risk rating. The same is done for females with a waist circumference 80 cm or more.

2. Aerobic fitness: The Modified Canadian Aerobic Fitness Test (mCAFT), a step test, is used to measure this component. It is recommended that high-quality heart rate monitors be used, but the postexercise heart rate can be determined with a stethoscope or by palpation at the radial artery. Figure 15.1 shows the ergometer steps that are used to administer the mCAFT. The manual provides guidelines for construction of the steps. For the test, performers complete one or more stepping sessions of 3 minutes at predetermined cadences based on their age and gender. All test performers begin the stepping sequence on double 20.3 cm steps and complete as many progressively more demanding 3-minute sessions as necessary to equal or exceed the ceiling postexercise heart rate. The ceiling is set at 85% of the predicted maximal heart rate for their age: $.85 \times (220 - \text{age})$. Individuals with a high level of fitness may complete the test with a single-step sequence using a step 40.6 cm in height (stages 7 and 8 for males and stage 8 for females). The starting stages and the step cadences for each stage are shown in table 15.5. The test is structured so that in the first 3 minutes most individuals step at an intensity equal to 65% to 70% of the average aerobic power of a person ten years older. Instruction and time signals are given on the CD provided with the manual. These instructions tell when to start and stop exercising

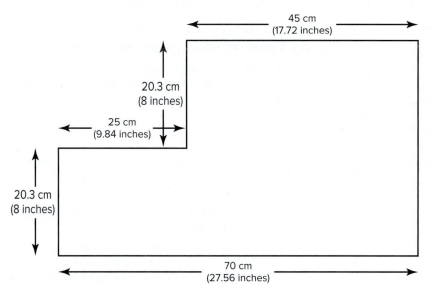

FIGURE 15.1 Ergometer steps for mCAFT.

TABLE 15.5 Starting Stages and Cadence for the Modified Canadian Aerobic Fitness Test (mCAFT)

Starting Stage

Age	Males	Females
60–69	1	1
50–59	2	1
40–49	3	2
30–39	3	3
20–29	4	3
15–19	4	3

Cadence for Stages (footplants/min)

Stage	Males	Females
1	66	66
2	84	84
3	102	102
4	114	114
5	132	120
6	144	132
7	118*	144
8	132*	118*

*Single step (40.6 cm).

Source: Adapted from Canadian Society for Exercise Physiology, *CSEP-Physical Activity Training for Health (CSEP)* Ottawa, Ontario: Canadian Society for Exercise Physiology, 2013.

and how to count the 10-second measurement of the postexercise heart rate.

Before beginning the test, test performers should have completed all preappraisal screening items. The test performers also should perform mild calf stretches before and after the stair stepping. After a demonstration, the test performers are permitted to practice the stepping sequence.

At the conclusion of the initial 3-minute session, the test performers cease to step and remain motionless, while standing. The heart rate monitor is immediately read. If a heart rate monitor is not used, the postexercise heart rate is counted for 10 seconds with a stethoscope placed either on the sternum or over the second intercostal space on the left side. The heart rate also may be determined by palpation at the radial artery. The determination of an accurate postexercise heart rate is the critical measurement for deciding if the performers should continue to the next 3-minute session of stepping. They *do not* continue if the heart rate is *equal to or above* the ceiling postexercise heart rate (85% of predicted maximal heart rate). If the heart rate is below the ceiling heart rate, the performers immediately begin the next 3-minute session. This process is continued until the ceiling heart rate is reached. After the performer has completed the test, the heart rate and blood pressure should be monitored for a specified period of time.

For both step sequences, the performer may start with either foot, but the instructions have the performer starting with the right foot. Test performers should feel free to stop stepping if they experience discomfort at any time.

Two-step sequence. Stand in front of the first step with feet together.

1. Place the right foot on the *first* step.
2. Place the left foot on the *second* step.
3. Place the right foot on the *second* step so the feet are together.
4. Start down with the left foot to the *first* step.
5. Place the right foot on the *ground* level.
6. Place the left foot on the *ground* level so that both feet are together.
7. Stop stepping at any time if you experience discomfort.

One-step sequence. Stand at the back or side of the top step with feet together.

1. Place the right foot on the *top* step.
2. Place the left foot on the *top* step so feet are together.
3. Place the right foot on *ground* level.
4. Place the left foot down on *ground* level so feet are together.

The aerobic fitness score is determined by using the oxygen cost of the step test and the performer's weight and age in this equation:

$$[17.2 + (1.29 \times O_2 \text{ cost}) - (.09 \times \text{wt in kg}) - (.18 \times \text{age in years})]$$

Table 15.6 reports the oxygen cost of the test (in milliliters per kilogram body weight per minute), and table 15.7 reports the health benefit zone for the score.

3. Musculoskeletal fitness: Five components of musculoskeletal fitness are appraised.

Grip strength. The grip strength of both hands is measured with a hand dynamometer. The grip is taken between the fingers and the palm at the base of the thumb, and the

TABLE 15.6 Oxygen Cost and Stepping Cadence for Stages of the Modified Canadian Aerobic Fitness Test

Males								
Stage	1	2	3	4	5	6	7	8
Stepping cadence	66	84	102	114	132	144	118*	132*
O_2 cost (ml)	15.9	18.0	22.0	24.5	29.5	33.6	36.2	40.1

Females								
Stage	1	2	3	4	5	6	7	8
Stepping cadence	66	84	102	114	120	132	144	118*
O_2 cost (ml)	15.9	18.0	22.0	24.5	26.3	29.5	33.6	36.2

*Single step (40.6 cm).

Source: Adapted from Canadian Society for Exercise Physiology, *CSEP-Physical Activity Training for Health (CSEP-PATH)* Ottawa, Ontario: Canadian Society for Exercise Physiology, 2013.

TABLE 15.7 Health Benefit Zones for Aerobic Fitness Scores (CSEP-Physical Activity for Health [CSEP-PATH])

Zone	Age					
	15–19	20–29	30–39	40–49	50–59	60–69
Males						
Excellent	57.4+	55.6+	48.8+	47.0+	41.8+	38.4+
Very good	52.4–57.3	50.6–55.5	45.4–48.7	42.7–46.9	36.5–41.7	32.8–38.3
Good	48.8–52.3	47.2–50.5	40.1–45.3	35.5–42.6	30.1–36.4	28.7–32.7
Fair	43.6–48.7	41.6–47.1	33.7–40.0	31.9–35.4	26.0–30.0	23.5–28.6
Poor	<43.6	<41.6	<33.7	<31.9	<26.0	<23.5
Females						
Excellent	49.0+	47.2+	45.4+	40.0+	36.6+	35.8+
Very good	43.7–48.9	42.0–47.1	40.1–45.3	35.1–39.9	34.0–36.5	32.8–35.7
Good	39.5–43.6	37.8–41.9	36.0–40.0	31.9–35.0	31.0–33.9	29.6–32.7
Fair	36.8–39.4	35.0–37.7	33.0–35.9	27.1–31.8	24.6–30.9	23.5–29.5
Poor	<36.8	<35.0	<33.0	<27.1	<24.6	<23.5

Source: Adapted from Canadian Society for Exercise Physiology, *CSEP-Physical Activity Training for Health (CSEP-PATH)* Ottawa, Ontario: Canadian Society for Exercise Physiology, 2013.

dynamometer is held in line with the forearm at the level of the thigh, away from the body. During the test neither hand nor the dynamometer should touch the body or any other object. Alternating hands, two trials per hand are administered. The grip score is recorded to the nearest kilogram, and the maximum score for each hand is combined for the test score.

Push-ups. Individuals who have lower-back problems should not perform the push-up test. Males perform the push-up with the weight on the toes and hands. Females perform the push-up with the weight on the knees and hands. In the down movement, both males and females must touch the mat with their chin. The maximum number of the push-ups are performed consecutively and without a time limit.

The test is stopped when the performer is seen to strain forcibly or is unable to maintain the proper push-up over two consecutive repetitions.

Sit and reach. The test procedure is very similar to the sit and reach test with the sit and reach box. The Modified Wells and Dillon Flexometer is used, however, rather than the sit and reach box. Before performing this item, all individuals should be permitted to warm up. Without shoes, the test performer sits with the legs fully extended and the soles of the feet placed flat against the flexometer. The flexometer should be adjusted to a height that enables the balls of the feet to be against the upper crossboards. The inner edges of the soles are placed 2 cm from the edge of the scale. The test performer assumes a position with the knees fully extended, arms evenly stretched, and palms down. The performer bends, reaches forward, and pushes the sliding marker along the scale with the fingertips as far forward as possible. The position of maximum flexion must be held for approximately 2 seconds. The test is performed twice, and the maximum reach, recorded to the nearest .5 cm, is the score.

Vertical jump. This test, described in chapter 13, is scored as a straight height jump and peak leg power. The highest jump of three trials, recorded to the nearest .5 cm, is the jump score. A rest period of 10 to 15 seconds is recommended between trials. Peak leg power, recorded as kilogram-meters per second, is determined with this formula:

$$\text{peak leg power (W)} = [60.7 \times \text{jump height (cm)}] \\ + [45.3 \times \text{weight (kg)}] - 2{,}055$$

Back extension. Prior to performing this test, it should be determined that the test performer has no current back pain or discomfort. The performer should be asked to (1) lie face down on a mat and conduct a single straight-leg extension with the right leg and then with the left leg and (2) followed by a single straight-leg extension with the right leg combined with an extension of the left arm and then repetition the same movements with the left leg and right arm. If no discomfort or pain is experienced, the test may be administered.

The portable steps used in the step test previously described may be used for this measurement. A bench or training room table also may be used. For comfort of the test performer, a mat should be placed on top of the portable steps. The performer lies face down on the top step with the legs on the steps and the iliac crest positioned at the step edge. This position places the upper body beyond the edge with no support. The test administrator should secure the performer's legs by holding the lower thighs or upper calves. Prior to beginning the test, the performer should support the upper body by extending the arms and placing the hands on the floor. To begin the test, the performer raises and crosses the arms on the chest and maintains the horizontal position with no rotation or lateral shifting. To add support for the lower spine, the performer should maintain contraction of the abdominal muscles throughout the test. The score is the number of seconds the position is held, up to a maximum of 180 seconds. The test should be terminated if pain or discomfort is experienced.

One-leg stance (balance). Test performer stands barefoot beside a sturdy chair for safety in the event balance is lost. With eyes open, performer crosses hands in front of chest and places hands on opposite shoulders, stands on leg of choice, and lifts the other foot so that it is near the ankle of standing leg (should not touch ankle). Time begins when the foot is raised from the floor. The position is held for a maximum of 45 seconds. Time ends when the arms are moved, the raised foot is moved toward the standing leg or touches the floor, the weight-bearing foot is moved, or a maximum of 45 seconds is recorded. The test is repeated on the other leg. The same test is then administered with the eyes closed. No health benefit rating is provided in the manual. The best time for the eyes-open test and the best time for the eyes-closed test, however, may be compared with age group and gender values provided in the manual.

Table 15.8 reports the "Good" health benefit zone for the grip strength, push-ups, sit and reach, peak leg power, and back extension. Scores above the "Good" zone are "Very Good" or "Excellent." Scores below are "Fair" or "Needs Improvement." The manual provides an interpretation of the zones.

Tests of Skill-Related Physical Fitness

Rarely does a single test battery include all components of skill-related physical fitness. Also, skill-related physical fitness components (the five health-related components and agility, balance, coordination, power, reaction time, and speed) are often measured as they relate to a particular sport. If you prefer to measure these components for a sport, various web sites provide such tests. However, remember to administer components that are appropriate for the group being tested.

■ AAU Physical Fitness Test
(Amateur Athletic Union 1994)

The Amateur Athletic Union (AAU) no longer promotes the AAU Physical Fitness Test. The test is presented, however, because of the uniqueness of some test items and the availability of test standards. Table 15.9 reports the criteria for

TABLE 15.8 "Good" Health Benefit Zones for Musculoskeletal Fitness (CSEP-Physical Activity Training for Health (CSEP-PATH))

	Age					
	15–19	**20–29**	**30–39**	**40–49**	**50–59**	**60–69**
Males						
Grip strength* (kg)	90–97	95–103	95–103	88–96	84–91	84–90
Push-ups	23–28	22–28	17–21	13–16	10–12	8–10
Sit and reach (cm)	29–33	30–33	28–32	24–28	24–27	20–24
Peak leg power (Watts)	3,858–4,184	4,297–4,639	3,967–4,388	3,242–3,699	2,967–3,566	2,843–3,290
Back extension (sec)	119–134	99–132	91–108	71–83	54–87	52–77
Females						
Grip strength* (kg)	53–59	58–62	58–62	54–60	49–53	45–47
Push-ups	18–24	15–20	13–19	11–14	7–10	5–11
Sit and reach (cm)	34–37	33–36	32–35	30–33	30–32	27–30
Peak leg power (Watts)	2,399–2,794	2,478–2,803	2,335–2,549	2,101–2,287	1,701–2,160	1,317–1,717
Back extension (sec)	122–140	102–135	112–140	80–114	47–74	19–39

*Combined right and left hand

Source: Adapted from Canadian Society for Exercise Physiology, *CSEP-Physical Activity Training for Health (CSEP-PATH)* Ottawa, Ontario: Canadian Society for Exercise Physiology, 2013.

Outstanding Achievement and Attainment standards. The Outstanding Performance standard is at the eightieth percentile, and the Attainment standard is at the forty-fifth percentile.

Age Level. Six through seventeen.

Equipment. Stopwatch, flat running surface, mat, tape measure, yardstick, horizontal bar, fifteen objects (tennis balls, beanbags, blocks, etc.), two chairs or traffic cones, one collection box, one large object-supply box, and three blocks or erasers.

Test Components

1. Cardiorespiratory endurance: Two test options are provided.

   Distance run. 1/4 mile for ages six and seven, 1/2 mile for ages eight and nine, 3/4 mile for ages ten and eleven, and 1 mile for ages twelve through seventeen.

   Hoosier endurance shuttle run. Two chairs are placed 20 yards apart. The performer runs from chair 1 and picks up an object placed by the helper on the seat of chair 2 and then returns by running around chair 1 and dropping the object in the container behind the chair. This action is repeated for 6 minutes. Count each object placed in the container, including the last object picked up, even if the runner has not reached the container. No partial credit should be given to the runner if an object has not been picked up. The scorekeeper must keep count of the number of objects removed from the container. The score is the number of objects collected in 6 minutes.

2. Trunk strength and endurance: 1-minute bent-knee sit-ups. Sit-ups are performed with arms crossed on the chest and partner holding feet. The arms remain in contact with the chest while touching the thighs with the elbows. The performer must return to the starting position after each sit-up.

3. Flexibility of hamstrings and lower back: Sit and reach test. A yardstick or tape measure is placed on the floor. The test performer sits near the zero (0) end of the tape and straddles the measuring tape, with the heels 12 inches apart, even with the 15-inch mark of the tape. With the legs straight and flat on the floor, and hands overlapped and facing the floor, the performer slides the hands as far as possible along the tape without bending the knees. Another person should hold the ankles for stability. The score is the farthest point touched by the tip of the fingers in the best of three trials.

4. Upper-body strength and endurance: Pull-ups (palms may face toward or away from body). The performer pulls the

TABLE 15.9 Awards Performance Criteria for AAU Physical Fitness Test

Event	Level of Performance	6	7	8	9	10	11	12	13	14	15	16	17
		Girls											

Age Level — Girls

Required:

Event	Level of Performance	6	7	8	9	10	11	12	13	14	15	16	17
1a. Endurance run (fractions of mile) (min:sec)	Attainment	¼ mi 2:30	¼ mi 2:24	½ mi 5:02	½ mi 4:57	¾ mi 7:30	¾ mi 7:25	1 mi 9:54	1 mi 9:50	1 mi 9:50	1 mi 9:50	1 mi 9:54	1 mi 9:51
	Outstanding achievement	2:05	2:00	4:06	4:04	6:10	6:06	8:15	8:04	8:08	8:00	8:07	8:16
OR 1b. Hoosier endurance shuttle run (no. of objects)	Attainment	20	21	22	22	23	23	23	23	23	23	23	24
	Outstanding achievement	23	24	25	25	26	26	26	26	26	26	27	27
2. Bent-knee sit-ups (1-minute time limit)	Attainment	22	25	29	31	32	33	35	35	36	35	35	36
	Outstanding achievement	31	34	38	39	40	42	43	45	45	44	44	44
3. Sit and reach (in.)	Attainment	17	17	17	17	17	17	19	20	20	20	20	20
	Outstanding achievement	19	20	20	21	21	21	21	23	23	23	23	24
4a. Pull-ups*	Attainment	1	1	1	1	1	1	1	1	1	1	1	1
	Outstanding achievement	1	1	2	2	2	2	2	1	1	1	1	1
OR 4b. Flexed-arm hang (seconds & tenths)	Attainment	6.0	7.0	8.0	8.5	10.0	12.4	15.0	15.9	13.0	12.0	10.2	8.1

Optional:

Event	Level of Performance	6	7	8	9	10	11	12	13	14	15	16	17
1. Long jump (feet & inches)	Attainment	3'4"	3'8"	3'11"	4'2"	4'5"	4'9"	5'1"	5'3"	5'5"	5'4"	5'5"	5'6"
	Outstanding achievement	4'0"	4'3"	4'6"	4'11"	5'1"	5'4"	5'9"	5'11"	6'0"	6'1"	6'1"	6'2"
2. Push-ups (modified) (30-second time limit)	Attainment	14	15	17	21	21	21	21	22	22	21	21	23
	Outstanding achievement	20	22	24	26	27	28	28	32	32	29	30	31
3. Phantom chair (isometric leg squat) (min:sec)	Attainment	:38	:50	1:02	1:02	1:03	1:03	1:04	1:05	1:09	1:02	1:02	1:05
	Outstanding achievement	1:16	1:30	1:54	2:00	2:06	2:10	2:15	2:20	2:23	2:02	2:02	2:00
4. Shuttle run** (seconds & tenths)	Attainment	14.2	13.5	13.1	12.2	12.2	11.8	11.6	11.2	11.2	11.2	11.2	11.1
	Outstanding achievement	12.9	12.5	12.0	11.5	11.3	10.9	10.5	10.3	10.4	10.4	10.4	10.2
5. Sprint (in yards) (seconds & tenths)	Attainment	50 yd 10.5	50 yd 10.0	50 yd 9.2	50 yd 9.1	50 yd 8.8	50 yd 8.5	50 yd 8.4	100 yd 15.8	100 yd 15.4	100 yd 15.5	100 yd 15.6	100 yd 15.7
	Outstanding achievement	9.6	9.0	8.8	8.4	8.0	7.8	7.8	14.4	14.1	14.1	14.2	14.2

*Standards for these items are based on data from the 1985 School Population Fitness Survey conducted by the University of Michigan Institute for Social Research.

**Should be conducted on gym floor or other clean, firm surface.

Source: The Amateur Physical Fitness Program. 1994.

TABLE 15.9 *Continued*

Event	Level of Performance	6	7	8	9	10	11	12	13	14	15	16	17
		Boys											
Required:													
1a. Endurance run (fractions of mile) (min:sec)	Attainment	¼ mi 2:23	¼ mi 2:13	½ mi 4:31	½ mi 4:20	¾ mi 6:35	¾ mi 6:27	1 mi 8:34	1 mi 7:54	1 mi 7:33	1 mi 7:27	1 mi 7:21	1 mi 7:08
	Outstanding achievement	2:00	1:52	3:41	3:42	5:30	5:19	7:10	6:45	6:28	6:18	6:14	6:12
OR 1b. Hoosier endurance shuttle run (no. of objects)	Attainment	21	23	23	24	25	25	25	25	26	26	26	26
	Outstanding achievement	25	26	26	27	28	29	29	29	29	30	30	30
2. Bent-knee sit-ups (1-minute time limit)	Attainment	22	27	31	34	36	38	40	41	44	44	44	46
	Outstanding achievement	31	36	39	43	45	48	49	51	53	53	53	55
3. Sit and reach (in.)	Attainment	15	15	15	15	15	15	15	15	16	17	17	17
	Outstanding achievement	17	18	18	18	18	18	18	18	19	20	20	20
4a. Pull-ups	Attainment	2	2	2	2	2	3	3	4	5	6	7	8
	Outstanding achievement	4	4	4	4	4	5	7	8	9	10	10	11
OR 4b. Flexed-arm hang* (seconds & tenths)	Attainment	5.0	7.0	9.0	8.0	10.0	10.0	10.0	12.0	17.0	28.0	25.0	29.0
Optional:													
1. Long jump (feet & inches)	Attainment	3'7"	4'0"	4'3"	4'7"	4'11"	5'1"	5'4"	5'10"	6'4"	6'7"	6'11"	7'3"
	Outstanding achievement	4'2"	4'6"	4'10"	5'3"	5'6"	5'9"	6'1"	6'7"	7'3"	7'5"	7'8"	8'0"
2. Isometric push-up (seconds & tenths)	Attainment	15.1	16.0	18.5	22.7	21.0	23.4	28.5	33.0	35.0	40.8	44.9	47.0
	Outstanding achievement	32.4	35.5	38.0	45.5	47.0	50.5	53.0	55.0	58.3	60.0	68.0	70.0
3. Phantom chair (isometric leg squat) (min:sec)	Attainment	:34	:53	1:02	1:06	1:06	1:16	1:20	1:22	1:24	1:25	1:30	1:30
	Outstanding achievement	1:07	1:30	2:00	2:08	2:37	2:43	2:59	3:02	3:00	3:28	3:00	3:00
4. Shuttle run** (seconds & tenths)	Attainment	13.6	13.1	12.5	12.0	11.8	11.2	11.1	10.6	10.2	9.9	9.7	9.6
	Outstanding achievement	12.6	12.0	11.6	11.4	10.8	10.4	10.2	9.8	9.5	9.1	9.1	8.7
5. Sprint (in yards) (seconds & tenths)	Attainment	50 yd 10.3	50 yd 9.8	50 yd 9.4	50 yd 9.0	50 yd 8.5	50 yd 8.3	50 yd 8.2	100 yd 14.8	100 yd 13.9	100 yd 13.2	100 yd 13.1	100 yd 12.6
	Outstanding achievement	9.3	8.9	8.5	8.4	7.6	7.5	7.4	13.4	12.6	12.2	12.2	11.9

*Standards for these items are based on data from the 1985 School Population Fitness Survey conducted by the University of Michigan Institute for Social Research.

**Should be conducted on gym floor or other clean, firm surface.

body up until the chin is raised above the bar. The body then is lowered until the arms are fully extended. Swinging, kicking, and resting are not permitted. The score is the number of complete pull-ups. Both males and females must do pull-ups to qualify for the Outstanding award. Participants who are unable to perform one pull-up are permitted to substitute the flexed-arm hang for this event but do not qualify for the Outstanding award. Such participants, however, are eligible for the Attainment or Participation award.

The following are optional test items:

1. Explosive leg strength and efficiency of control of body mass in space: Standing long jump. Three trials.
2. Upper-body static endurance (males): Isometric push-ups. The test performer takes the resting push-up position. On the command to begin, the body is pushed up until the elbows are bent at a 90° angle. The score is the time this position can be held.
3. Upper-body strength and endurance (females): Modified push-ups with 30-second time limit.
4. Static leg endurance: Isometric leg squat (phantom chair). With back flat against wall, the performer slides down the wall until the knees form a 90° angle. The feet should point directly forward and must be flat on the floor, and the arms should hang at the sides. The score is the length of time this position can be held.
5. Agility and quickness: Shuttle run. Two lines are placed 30 feet apart with masking tape. One block is placed at the starting line and two blocks at the parallel line. On the command to begin, the test performer runs to the line with two blocks; picks up a block; runs back to the

starting line and places the block on the starting line; picks up the block originally placed on the starting line; runs back to the parallel line and places the block on the line; picks up the third block; and returns as rapidly as possible across the starting line. The score is in seconds and tenths.
6. Speed, quickness, and anaerobic capacity: Sprint. 50 yards for ages six through twelve; 100 yards for ages thirteen through seventeen.

Review Problems

1. Review additional health-related and skill-related physical fitness tests in other sources. Do the tests include any components not reported in this textbook? If they do, do you consider them as components of health-related or skill-related physical fitness?

2. Interview several teachers in the local school system about their use of health-related and skill-related physical fitness tests. Ask which tests they prefer, and why.

3. Administer the AAHPERD Health-Related Physical Fitness Test for College Students to several of your classmates. Ask them to provide constructive criticism of your test administration.

4. Design programs to develop health-related physical fitness for the age groups sixteen through eighteen and fifty through fifty-nine.

Chapter Review Questions

1. What are the components of health-related physical fitness and skill-related physical fitness?

2. What are the differences between programs designed to develop health-related physical fitness and programs for skill-related physical fitness?

3. Why is it important that health-related physical fitness be measured? In your responsibilities after

measurement, what must you consider about each component of health-related physical fitness?

4. When is it appropriate to use norm-referenced standards and criterion-referenced standards?

5. When may it be appropriate not to use norm-referenced or criterion-referenced standards?

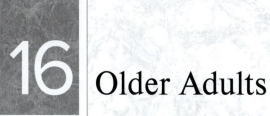

16 Older Adults

After completing this chapter, you should be able to

1. Define *functional fitness*.

2. State why the functional fitness of older adults should be measured.

3. Describe the pre-test/pre-activity screening process for older adults.

4. Measure the functional fitness of older adults.

5. Describe responsibilities after the measurement of functional fitness of older adults and prescribe appropriate activities and exercise.

Functional fitness is the physical capacity to perform ordinary daily activities safely and independently without undue fatigue (Osness et al. 1996; Rikli and Jones 1999a). In the United States, more of us are living longer, and as we age we hope to maintain a high level of functional fitness. At the beginning of the twentieth century, approximately 4% of the U.S. population were individuals over sixty-five years of age. By the year 2030, nearly 20% of the U.S. population will be sixty-five or older (U.S. Bureau of the Census 2008). As the number of individuals over the age of sixty-five increases, so will the number of the oldest old (eighty-five and older); in this latter group, we can expect an increase in the number of individuals who are unable to function effectively in society.

Why Measure Functional Fitness?

Although a sedentary lifestyle is often directly related to chronic diseases associated with aging, the activity level of many individuals declines with age even if they have no chronic disease. Regrettably, largely because of a sedentary lifestyle, many older individuals must exert maximum effort just to perform daily physical activities. Research indicates that much of the age-related physical decline in our older years may be prevented through an active lifestyle. Research

also indicates that older individuals can experience health benefits when changing from a sedentary lifestyle to an active lifestyle. To ensure the quality of life they desire, we must encourage the older population to be physically active. Before older individuals initiate such a program, however, it is important to identify any physical limitations (cardiorespiratory fitness, muscular strength and endurance, flexibility, and so on) that could place them at risk of bodily harm. In addition to identifying at-risk individuals, proper measurement and assessment can serve to do the following:

- Identify physical weaknesses or deficiencies that will limit success with the initiation of an active lifestyle.

- Identify physical abilities in which further decline may be prevented or reduced.

- Provide a baseline for evaluating improvement in physical performance.

- Provide feedback to individuals about their limitations and motivate them to initiate an active lifestyle.

- Provide data for evaluation of program effectiveness.

Responsibilities after Measurement

Your measurement of functional fitness should identify any physical limitations that place older adults at risk. Your challenge is to design the appropriate physical activity program that will improve their functional fitness. You can do this by helping them improve their cardiorespiratory fitness, muscular strength and endurance, flexibility, agility, and balance. You probably will find that older individuals exhibit wide variations in their level of functional fitness, but regardless of their physical health, regular physical activity can provide benefits for them. As you prepare their activity programs, you should consider individual differences in health status, physical fitness, and previous lifestyle. Even though there are no exercise or activity guidelines that can be applied to all older adults, there are general guidelines that you may observe. These guidelines are described at the conclusion of the chapter.

■■■■ ARE YOU ABLE TO DO THE FOLLOWING?

- Define *functional fitness* and state why the functional fitness of older adults should be measured.

- Describe responsibilities after the measurement of functional fitness.

Testing Guidelines

The pre-test/pre-activity screening is somewhat different from the screening performed for younger adults. As with other adults, an activity readiness questionnaire, such as PAR-Q+, should be administered. (The screening procedure and PAR-Q+ are described in chapter 11.) Since you are measuring a different type of fitness, however, the

Cooper Institute (2004b) also recommends that you ask older adult test participants to do the following:

- Walk about 8 feet.

- Stand and sit in a chair several times.

- Reach upward, backward, and across the body.

- Flex and extend the knee.

- Rotate the feet at the ankle joints.

- Hold and work with small objects.

- Stand while you observe their posture.

As they perform these movements, you may ask them to comment on their level of discomfort. An index of pain such as the following may be used:

1. Little or no joint discomfort.

2. Mild joint discomfort.

3. Moderate joint discomfort.

4. Severe joint pain.

5. Too painful to perform movement.

Tests of Functional Fitness

Many older individuals are capable of completing some of the physical performance test items presented in previous chapters. Norms for sixty and older individuals are available for such test items as sit-ups, abdominal curls, bench press, push-ups, 12-minute run, and step tests. In addition, the *ACSM's Health-Related Physical Fitness Assessment Manual* (2018), *CSEP-Physical Activity Training for Health (CSEP-PATH)* (2013), and the YMCA Fitness Test include norms for adults sixty and over. Some individuals will be better served,

◆ ◆ ◆ POINT OF EMPHASIS ◆ ◆ ◆

- There is more variability, both mentally and physically, among older adults than any other groups in our population. All individuals do not age in the same way. If you have responsibilities with the older population, you should be prepared to recognize and work with these individual differences.

however, by attempting the items presented in this chapter. These test items can be administered without costly laboratory equipment and are related to the daily functions of life.

■ Functional Fitness Assessment for Adults over Sixty Years
(Osness et al. 1996)

Test Objectives. To evaluate the ability of adults to carry on certain daily activities.

Age Level. Over sixty.

Equipment. Weight scale, tape measure, chair with arms (16-inch seat height), masking or duct tape, two cones, stopwatch, three unopened 12-ounce soda pop cans, a table, four 8-pound weights (or a half-gallon plastic milk bottle with handle), one-gallon plastic milk bottle with handle, sand, water, and normal chair with arms.

Validity. Assumed for ponderal index, sit and reach, and agility course; soda pop was validated using typical laboratory procedures for reaction time ($r = .59$), hand steadiness ($r = .399$), and hand–eye coordination ($.349$); arm-curl was validated using a cybex protocol elbow curl ($r = .82$); and 880-yard walk was validated by measurement of maximal oxygen intake per minute ($r = .615$).

Reliability. Test-retest studies were done in multiple laboratories; only one correlation value for each item is included in this test description.

Ponderal index: men and women ($r = .994$)

Sit and reach: men ($r = 0.988$); women ($r = .978$)

Agility course: men and women ($r = .995$)

Soda can: men ($r = .911$); women ($r = .853$)

Arm-curl: men and women ($r = .833$)

880-yard walk: men ($r = .82$)

Norms. Table 16.1 reports average standards for ages sixty through ninety.

Test Components

1. Ponderal index. Body weight is recorded to the closest pound and height is recorded in feet and inches to the nearest ½ inch; shoes and heavy garments should be removed. The measured weight in pounds is marked on the right scale of figure 16.1, and the measured height is marked on the left scale of figure 16.1. A straightedge is used to connect these two points. The point of intersection on the center scale is the ponderal index. The higher the ponderal index, the greater the degree of leanness. Record the ponderal index to the nearest .1 of one unit.

2. Trunk/leg flexibility: Sit and reach. This test procedure is similar to the sit and reach test item included in the YMCA Physical Fitness Test. A yardstick is taped to the floor with a perpendicular line over the 25-inch mark. The test performer, with shoes removed, sits with the legs extended flat on the floor and the heels at the 25-inch mark. The yardstick should be between the legs, with the zero (0) point toward the performer. With the feet spread about 12 inches apart and one hand placed directly on top of the other, the performer slowly reaches forward, sliding the hands along the yardstick as far as possible. The performer must hold the final position for at least 2 seconds. The test administrator should place a hand on top of one of the performer's knees to ensure that the knees are not raised during the test. Two practice trials are permitted, and the best of two test trials is recorded. The score is recorded to the nearest ½ inch.

3. Agility/dynamic balance. The agility course is marked as illustrated in figure 16.2. The test performer sits in the chair, with heels on the floor. On the signal "Ready, go," the performer stands up, moves to the right, goes to the inside and around the cone (counterclockwise), returns to the chair, sits down, and raises the feet from the floor. Without hesitating, the test performer immediately stands up, moves to the left, again going to the inside and around the cone (clockwise), returns to the chair, and sits down, completing one circuit. The performer immediately stands up and completes the circuit a second time. The two circuits complete one trial. After a 30-second rest, a second trial is administered. A practice trial is administered to acquaint the performer with the test. Each trial is scored to the nearest 0.1 second. The score is the time for the best trial.

4. Coordination: Soda can test. Place a 30-inch strip of ¾-inch masking tape on a table. The tape should be about 5 inches from the edge of the table. Starting at 2½ inches from either end of the tape, place a strip of tape (approximately 3 inches long) across the 30-inch strip of tape. Now place a second 3-inch strip exactly 5 inches from the first strip. Place additional strips until six 3-inch strips are placed across the 30-inch tape, 5 inches apart. For the purpose of the test, the 3-inch strips of tape are numbered 1 to 6. The preferred hand is used for the test. If the right hand is preferred, an unopened (12-ounce) soda can is placed on tapes 1, 3, and 5. To start the test, the performer places the right hand, with the thumb up, on can number 1. On the starting command, the test performer lifts the first can, turns it over and places it on tape number 2, then turns can 2 and places it on tape 4, and places can 3 on tape 6. The test performer immediately returns all three cans to their original places, beginning with can

TABLE 16.1 Average Standards for Functional Fitness Assessment for Adults over Age Sixty

	Age					
	60–64	**65–69**	**70–74**	**75–79**	**80–84**	**85–90**
	Men					
Ponderal index (P.I. units)	12.36–11.48	12.37–11.41	12.67–11.39	12.57–11.29	12.16–11.06	12.56–11.20
Flexibility (inches and hundredths of inches)	24.90–14.90	24.88–14.80	23.97–11.75	24.12–12.94	22.32–14.42	19.02–13.38
Agility/balance (seconds and hundredths of seconds)	19.22–31.50	18.46–35.52	15.11–41.31	23.42–40.08	23.35–41.85	17.07–50.05
Coordination (seconds and hundredths of seconds)	8.98–14.34	10.13–14.83	9.51–16.57	11.08–15.82	11.09–17.35	10.17–16.97
Strength/endurance (repetitions)	29.15–18.23	28.38–14.56	26.90–15.38	24.24–16.06	23.14–17.92	22.92–12.72
Aerobic fitness (minutes and hundredths of minutes)	5.84–8.40	6.30–9.34	7.07–9.61	5.99–13.47	6.69–9.49	8.15–10.89
	Women					
Ponderal index (P.I. units)	12.49–10.89	12.63–11.01	12.60–11.06	12.61–11.23	12.89–10.99	12.81–12.01
Flexibility (inches and hundredths of inches)	28.25–18.21	29.72–17.43	28.35–16.85	29.23–16.59	26.77–14.99	25.74–13.32
Agility/balance (seconds and hundredths of seconds)	19.54–30.40	21.13–33.61	21.99–36.09	23.40–44.64	21.99–52.19	29.59–57.91
Coordination (seconds and hundredths of seconds)	8.92–15.31	9.18–16.04	9.20–16.66	8.99–18.13	10.74–18.34	12.41–18.95
Strength/endurance (repetitions)	27.98–15.58	27.94–14.48	26.85–14.73	22.87–12.53	22.48–12.70	20.97–11.43
Aerobic fitness (minutes and hundredths of minutes)	6.88–10.00	6.69–10.83	6.72–11.46	8.10–11.84	8.36–13.06	8.28–12.48

Source: Adapted from Osness, W. H. et al., *Functional fitness for adults over 60 years*, 2d ed., Dubuque, Iowa: Kendall/Hunt Publishing, 1996.

1. On the "return trip," the cans are grasped with the hand in a thumb-down position. Upon completion of the return trip, without hesitation, the performer completes the entire process again. The trial consists of lifting, turning, and moving the cans a total of 12 times. After two practice trials, two test trials are performed. Each test trial is scored to the nearest 0.1 second; the best time is recorded as the score.

5. Strength/endurance. A 4-pound weight is used for women, and an 8-pound weight is used for men. As an alternative to weights, a 1-gallon plastic milk bottle filled with sand or water to the proper weight may be used. The test performer sits in a chair with the back straight against the chair and the nondominant hand at rest in the lap. The dominant arm hangs to the side. The weight is held in the dominant hand in a thumb-up position. The test administrator places a hand on the biceps of the test performer's dominant arm. On the signal to start, the test performer lifts the weight through the biceps' full range of motion until the lower arm touches the hand of the test administrator. The score

Height
in.

80
79
78
77
76
75
74
73
72
71
70
69
68
67
66
65
64
63
62
61
60
59
58
57
56

$H\!\!\diagup\!\!\sqrt[3]{W}$

16.0
15.5
15.0
14.5
14.0
13.5
13.0
12.5
12.0
11.5
11.0
10.5
10.0
9.5
9.0

Weight
lb

90
95
100
105
110
115
120
125
130
135
140
145
150
155
160
165
170
175
180
185
190
195
200
210
220
230
240
250
260
270
280
290
300

FIGURE 16.1 Nomogram for ponderal index.

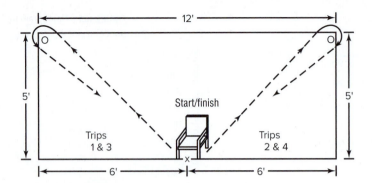

FIGURE 16.2 Agility course.

12'

5'

Start/finish

5'

Trips
1 & 3

Trips
2 & 4

6'

6'

is the number of repetitions that can be completed in 30 seconds.

6. Aerobic fitness: 880-yard walk. The test performer walks 880 yards as fast as possible. A measured, suitable test area is needed. One trial is administered, with the time recorded in minutes and seconds. The score is recorded to the nearest second (but must be converted to hundredths of a minute to compare with standard score). Individuals should be screened for cardiovascular or orthopedic problems. Individuals with the following conditions should consult their physician before attempting this test item:

- Significant orthopedic problems that may be aggravated by prolonged continuous walking.

- History of cardiac problems that can be negatively influenced by physical exertion.

- Lightheadedness while physically active or history of uncontrolled hypertension.

■ **Functional Fitness Test for Community-Residing Older Adults (Senior Fitness Test)**
(Rikli and Jones 1999a; Rikli and Jones 1999b)

Test Objectives. To assess the major underlying physical parameters associated with functional mobility in independent older adults.

Age Level. Sixty to ninety-plus.

Equipment. Straightback or folding chair (without arms and seat height approximately 17 inches), stopwatch, 5- and 8-pound weights, long measuring tape, cones, Popsicle sticks, chalk, masking tape, tape measure or 30-inch piece of cord, and 18-inch ruler.

Validity. Criterion validity was estimated for the 30-second chair stand (.77), arm-curl (men = .81; women = .78);

6-minute walk (.78); 2-minute step (.73); and chair sit and reach (.83). The back scratch was considered to be the best measure of overall shoulder flexibility, and the 8-foot up-and-go was considered to be a good measure of combined physiological attributes.

Reliability. Reliability values were as follows: 30-second chair stand (.89), arm-curl (.81), 6-minute walk (.94), 2-minute step test (.90), chair sit and reach (.95), back scratch (.96), and 8-foot up-and-go (.95).

Norms. Table 16.2 reports percentile norms for ages sixty through ninety-four.

Test Components

1. Lower body strength: 30-second chair stand. The test performer sits in the middle of the chair, with back straight, feet flat on the floor, and arms crossed at the wrists and held against the chest. The chair should be placed against a wall or in some other way stabilized so that it does not move during the testing. On the signal "Go," the performer rises to a full stand and then returns to a fully seated position. The test performer is to stand up and sit down as many times as possible in 30 seconds. After a demonstration by the test administrator, a practice trial of one to three repetitions should be done. The score is the total number of stands performed correctly in 30 seconds. If the test performer is more than halfway up at the end of 30 seconds, it counts as a full stand.

2. Upper body strength: Arm-curl. A 5-pound dumbbell is used for women, and an 8-pound dumbbell is used for men. The test performer sits in a chair, with back straight, feet flat on the floor, and the dominant side of the body close to the edge of the chair. The weight is held in the dominant hand (handshake grip), with the arm down beside the chair, perpendicular to the floor. On the signal "Go," the test performer turns the palm up while curling

TABLE 16.2   Percentile Norms for Functional Fitness Test for Community-Residing Older Adults

Percentile	Men						
	Age						
	60–64	65–69	70–74	75–79	80–84	85–89	90–94
Chair stand (no. of stands)							
25	14	12	12	11	10	8	7
50	16	15	15	14	12	11	10
75	19	18	17	17	15	14	12
90	22	21	20	19	18	17	15
Arm-curl (repetitions)							
25	16	15	14	13	13	11	10
50	19	18	17	16	16	14	12
75	22	21	21	19	19	17	14
90	25	25	24	22	21	19	17
6-minute walk (yards)							
25	610	560	545	470	445	380	305
50	675	630	610	555	525	475	405
75	735	700	680	640	605	570	500
90	790	765	745	715	680	660	590
2-minute step (no. of steps)							
25	87	86	80	73	71	59	52
50	101	101	95	91	87	75	69
75	115	116	110	109	103	91	86
90	128	130	125	125	118	106	102
Chair sit and reach (inches)							
25	−2.5	−3.0	−3.5	−4.0	−5.5	−5.5	−6.5
50	0.5	0.0	−0.5	−1.0	−2.0	−2.5	−3.5
75	4.0	3.0	2.5	2.0	1.5	0.5	0.5
90	6.5	6.0	5.5	5.0	4.5	3.0	2.0
Back scratch (inches)							
25	−6.5	−7.5	−8.0	−9.0	−9.5	−10.0	−10.5
50	−3.5	−4.0	−4.5	−5.5	−5.5	−6.0	−7.0
75	0.0	−1.0	−1.0	−2.0	−2.0	−3.0	−4.0
90	2.5	2.0	2.0	1.0	1.0	0.0	−1.0
8-foot up-and-go (seconds)							
25	5.6	5.7	6.0	7.2	7.6	8.9	10.0
50	4.7	5.1	5.3	5.9	6.4	7.2	8.1
75	3.8	4.3	4.2	4.6	5.2	5.3	6.2
90	3.0	3.8	3.6	3.5	4.1	3.9	4.4
BMI (kg/m^2)							
25	24.6	24.7	24.0	23.8	23.8	23.3	22.4
50	27.4	27.5	26.6	26.4	26.1	24.9	24.9
75	30.2	30.3	29.2	29.0	28.4	26.5	27.4
90	32.8	32.9	31.6	31.4	30.5	28	29.6

TABLE 16.2 *Continued*

Percentile	Women						
	Age						
	60–64	65–69	70–74	75–79	80–84	85–89	90–94
Chair stand (no. of stands)							
25	12	11	10	10	9	8	4
50	15	14	13	12	11	10	8
75	17	16	15	15	14	13	11
90	20	18	18	17	16	15	14
Arm-curl (repetitions)							
25	13	12	12	11	10	10	8
50	16	15	15	14	13	12	11
75	19	18	17	17	16	15	13
90	22	21	20	20	18	17	16
6-minute walk (yards)							
25	545	500	480	430	385	340	275
50	605	570	550	510	460	425	350
75	660	635	615	585	540	510	440
90	710	695	675	655	610	595	520
2-minute step (no. of steps)							
25	75	73	68	68	60	55	44
50	91	90	84	84	75	70	58
75	107	107	101	100	91	85	72
90	122	123	116	115	104	98	85
Chair sit and reach (inches)							
25	−0.5	−0.5	−1.0	−1.5	−2.0	−2.5	−4.5
50	2.0	2.0	1.5	1.0	0.5	−0.5	−2.0
75	5.0	4.5	4.0	3.5	3.0	2.5	1.0
90	7.0	6.5	6.0	5.5	5.0	4.5	3.5
Back scratch (inches)							
25	−3.0	−3.5	−4.0	−5.0	−5.5	−7.0	−8.0
50	−0.5	−1.0	−1.5	−2.0	−2.5	−4.0	−4.5
75	1.5	1.5	1.0	0.5	0.0	−1.0	−1.0
90	4.0	3.5	3.0	3.0	2.5	2.0	2.0
8-foot up-and-go (seconds)							
25	6.0	6.4	7.1	7.4	8.7	9.6	11.5
50	5.2	5.6	6.0	6.3	7.2	7.9	9.4
75	4.4	4.8	4.9	5.2	5.7	6.2	7.3
90	3.7	4.1	4.0	4.3	4.4	5.1	5.3
BMI (kg/m²)							
25	22.8	23.0	23.1	22.5	22.0	19.5	21.1
50	26.3	26.5	26.1	25.4	24.7	21.8	24.1
75	29.8	30.0	29.1	28.3	27.4	24.3	27.1
90	33.0	33.2	31.9	31.0	30.0	26.8	29.5

Source: Adapted from Rikli, R. E. and Jones, C. J., "Functional fitness normative scores for community-residing older adults, ages 60–94," *Journal of Aging and Physical Activity*, vol. 7, 1999, 162–182.

the arm through a full range of motion and then returns to the starting position (arm fully extended). At the down position, the weight again should be in the handshake position. The test administrator's fingers should be on the performer's mid-biceps to prevent upper arm movement and to ensure that a full curl is made. After a demonstration by the test administrator, a practice trial of one or two repetitions is given to check for proper form. The score is the number of curls made in 30 seconds. If the arm is more than halfway up at the end of 30 seconds, it counts as a curl.

3. Aerobic endurance. There are two options for the aerobic endurance item.

   6-minute walk. The test area consists of a rectangle 20 yards long and 5 yards wide. The inside perimeter of the rectangle should be marked with cones or chairs, and the 20-yard sides should be marked into 5-yard segments. A complete trip around the rectangle is 50 yards. The test involves walking as fast as possible for 6 minutes. A Popsicle stick can be given to the test performer each time the start cone is passed to keep track of the distance walked. The score is the total number of yards walked in 6 minutes to the nearest 5 yards. The test should be discontinued if at any time the test performer shows signs of dizziness, pain, nausea, or undue fatigue.

   2-minute step-in-place (an alternative to the 6-minute walk). The proper (minimum) knee-stepping height for each test performer is at a level even with the midway point between the middle of the kneecap and the top of the iliac crest. This point can be determined with a tape measure. To monitor the correct knee-stepping height, stack books on an adjacent table or attach a ruler to a chair or wall with masking tape to mark the proper knee height. On the signal "Go," the test performer begins stepping in place, starting with the right leg. Although both knees must be raised to the correct height to be counted, only the number of times the right knee reaches the correct height is counted. A practice test should be administered before the test day so that the test performer is aware of the proper pace. The score is the number of times the right knee reaches the minimum height. To assist with the pacing, tell the test performer when 1 minute has passed and when there are 30 seconds to go.

4. Lower body flexibility (hamstrings): Chair sit and reach. The test performer sits on the front edge of a straightback or folding chair. The crease between the top of the leg and the buttocks should be even with the edge of the chair. One leg is bent, with the foot placed flat on the floor; the other leg (the preferred leg) is extended straight in front of the hip, with the heel on the floor and the foot flexed

approximately 90°. With the extended leg as straight as possible (but not hyperextended), the performer slowly bends forward at the hip joint, sliding the hands (one on top of the other, with the tips of the middle fingers even) down the extended leg in an attempt to touch the toes. The spine should remain as straight as possible, with the head in line with the spine, not tucked. The reach must be held for 2 seconds. Performers should exhale as they bend forward, should avoid bouncing or rapid forceful movements, and should never stretch to the point of pain. After a demonstration by the test administrator, the test performer is asked to determine the preferred leg (the one that results in a better score). After two practice trials, two test trials are administered. With an 18-inch ruler, the number of inches by which the performer is short of reaching the toe (minus score) or reaches beyond the toe (plus score) is recorded. The middle of the toe at the end of the shoe represents a zero (0) score. The score, recorded to the nearest ½ inch, is the best score of the two trials.

5. Upper body (shoulder) flexibility: Back scratch. In a standing position, the test performer places the preferred hand over the same shoulder and reaches down the middle of the back as far as possible (palm toward the back, fingers extended, and elbow pointed up). The hand of the other arm is placed behind the back (palm up), reaching up as far as possible in an attempt to touch or overlap the extended middle fingers of both hands. Without moving the performer's hands, the test administrator helps to see that the middle finger of each hand is directed toward the other middle finger. After a demonstration by the test administrator, the test performer is asked to determine which is the preferred hand (the one that results in a better score). Two practice trials are followed by two test trials. The score, measured with a ruler to the nearest ½ inch, is the distance of overlap (plus score) or the distance between the tips of the middle fingers (negative score). The best score of the two trials is recorded.

6. Agility/dynamic balance: 8-foot up-and-go. A straightback or folding chair (seat height approximately 17 inches) is positioned against a wall or in some other way secured so that it does not move during testing. A cone is placed in front of the chair, with the back of the cone 8 feet from the front edge of the chair. The test begins with the test performer fully seated in the chair (erect posture), hands on thighs, and feet flat on the floor (one foot slightly in front of the other). On the signal "Go," the test performer gets up from the chair (pushing off of thighs is permitted), walks (no running is permitted) as quickly as possible around the cone, and returns to the seated position in the chair. After a demonstration, the performer should walk

through the test one time for practice. Two test trials then are administered; the score is the elapsed time (nearest 0.1 second) from the signal "Go" until the performer returns to the seated position in the chair. The best score of the two trials is recorded.

7. Body composition: Body mass index. The body mass index (BMI) is a weight:height ratio that is correlated with body fat. It is determined by dividing weight (in kilograms) by height (in meters) squared: $BMI = kg/m^2$. An alternative formula consists of multiplying the weight (in pounds) by 703 and dividing by height (in inches) squared: $BMI = (pounds \times 703) / inches^2$. The following BMI ratings are generally used:

Below 20: may indicate loss of muscle mass and bone tissue, especially in older adults.

20–25: normal range.

Above 25: overweight; higher risk of health problems.

■ **Physical Fitness Assessment of Older Adults**
(The Cooper Institute 2004a)

The Cooper Institute uses this test to measure health-related physical fitness rather than functional fitness. With the exception of the one-mile walk, however, the test components are similar to those of the two tests described previously.

Test Objectives. To assess the health-related components of fitness and to provide a baseline score for designing an appropriate exercise prescription to improve or maintain each fitness component.

Age Level. Forty to seventy-nine.

Equipment. Wristwatch with a second hand or stopwatch, hand-grip dynamometer, 5-pound weight, 10-pound ankle weight, masking tape, yardstick, and measuring tape.

Validity and Reliability. Not reported, but items are the same or similar to items for which validity and reliability have been reported.

Norms. Table 16.3 reports average standards for ages sixty through seventy-nine.

Test Components

1. Aerobic capacity: One-mile walk. (If the individual is unable to walk a mile or is confined to a wheelchair, the arm-crank ergometer test may be used. Since it is a maximal test, however, it should be administered in a clinical setting only.) The test performer walks one mile briskly without stopping. A measured flat path or walkway one mile or longer is needed. The time is recorded in minutes and seconds.

2. Muscular strength: Hand-grip test. The test performer stands straight with the weight evenly distributed on both feet and holds a hand-grip dynamometer with the scale facing away from the face. With the arms hanging at the sides, the test performer squeezes the dynamometer with as much force as possible, being careful to squeeze only once. Alternating the hands, three trials are attempted with each hand. A pause of 10 to 15 seconds should be allowed between each trial. The score is the highest value for each hand.

3. Upper body muscular endurance: Arm curls. The test performer stands with the back against a wall. The arms are held against the sides with a 5-pound weight in the dominant hand. With the palm facing up and the upper arm immobile, the test performer raises the weight to the shoulder. Only the biceps muscle is used to move the weight. The score is the number of repetitions that can be completed in 30 seconds.

4. Lower body muscular endurance: Lower leg extension. The test performer sits on a table with the knees just over the edge and a 10-pound weight attached to the dominant leg. Keeping the other leg immobile, the test performer fully extends the weighted lower leg. The score is the number of repetitions that can be completed in 30 seconds.

5. Trunk and leg flexibility: Sit and reach test. A piece of masking tape approximately 12 inches long is placed on the floor. A yardstick is taped to the floor perpendicular to the masking tape, flush with the 15-inch mark. With the shoes off, the test performer sits on the floor, straddles the yardstick so that the "0" end is pointed toward the body, and arranges the feet as close together as possible in line with the 15-inch mark. With one hand on top of the other (tips of the middle fingers even), the test performer then leans forward with the legs straight and reaches as far forward along the yardstick as possible. The legs must remain straight, and the position must be held for one second. No bouncing is permitted. The best of three trials is recorded. The score is recorded to the nearest ¼ inch.

6. Shoulder flexibility: Back scratch. The test performer stands, places the right hand over the right shoulder with the palm of the hand against the back, and reaches down as far as possible. At the same time, the performer places the left hand behind the back at the waistline with the back of the hand against the back and reaches up as far as possible. The test is repeated over the left shoulder and the position of the hands is exchanged. The distance between the tips of the right and left middle fingers is recorded to the nearest ¼ inch. If the hands do not touch, the distance apart is recorded in negative inches. If the hands touch, the score is 0, and if the hands overlap, the score is recorded as positive inches.

TABLE 16.3 Average Standards (Unless Indicated Otherwise) for Physical Fitness Assessment of Older Adults Age Sixty through Seventy-Nine

	Age	
	60–69	**70–79**
Men		
Aerobic capacity (minutes and seconds)	15:13–16:18	15:49–18:48
Muscular strength (kg)	40 (right hand), 36 (left hand)	36 (right hand), 33 (left hand)
Upper body muscular endurance (repetitions)	27–31	25–28
Lower body muscular endurance (repetitions)	26–30	26–30
Trunk and lower leg flexibility (inches)*	14.5	14.5
Shoulder flexibility (inches)*	−3.00 (right), −5.75 (left)	−3.00 (right), −5.75 (left)
Body composition		
Waist circumference (inches)**	>40	>40
BMI**	≥25 overweight, ≥30 obese	≥25 overweight, ≥30 obese
Women		
Aerobic capacity (minutes and seconds)	16:19–17:30	20:01–21:48
Muscular strength (kg)	22 (right hand), 20 (left hand)	21 (right hand), 18 (left hand)
Upper body muscular endurance (repetitions)	20–22	19–21
Lower body muscular endurance (repetitions)	23–25	24–25
Trunk and lower leg flexibility (inches)*	17	17
Shoulder flexibility (inches)*	.50 (right), −1.75 (left)	.50 (right), −1.75 (left)
Body composition		
Waist circumference (inches)**	>35	>35
BMI**	≥25 overweight, ≥30 obese	≥25 overweight, ≥30 obese

*Represents "good" category and can serve as a goal to work toward.
**Indicates overweight or obesity condition.
Source: Adapted from the Cooper Institute, *Fitness specialist for older adults*, Dallas, Tex.: The Cooper Institute, 2004.

7. Body composition: BMI and waist circumference. The waist is measured at the umbilicus while the test performer stands straight with the abdomen relaxed and feet together. The measurement is taken at the end of a normal breath, and the tape should not compress the skin. The test performer's height and weight are taken without shoes. The height is recorded to the nearest ¼ inch and the weight is recorded to the nearest ½ pound. The following formula may be used to determine BMI:

$$\frac{\text{weight (lbs.)} \times 703}{\text{height (inches)}^2}$$

■ **Functional Assessments—Frail**
(The Cooper Institute 2004a)

The following battery of tests assesses simple skills used in daily living. No norms are provided. The first trial serves as a baseline score and subsequent tests show increase, decrease, or maintenance of the skill. If individuals demonstrate limitations in the skills, exercise and activity can then be prescribed to improve their functionality.

Age Level. For any adult who appears to have lost some mobility and functionality.

Equipment. Straight-backed, firm chair without armrests, stopwatch, tape, and small object.

Test Components

1. Lower body strength: Chair stand. A straight-back chair, without armrests, with the seat height at approximately 80% of the test performer's knee height is used. The performer sits upright in the chair with the knees flexed to 90 degrees, back against the chair, and arms crossed over the body. The feet may be in any position. On the word "Go," the test administrator starts the stopwatch and the test performer stands up as rapidly as possible. The stopwatch is stopped when the performer is fully erect and attains standing balance. The procedure is repeated two times, with a rest period of 15–60 seconds between trials. If the performer cannot rise after 30 seconds with the arms crossed over the chest, he or she is told to stand using the arms to assist, and the same procedure is followed. The test administrator should be prepared to prevent the performer from falling if balance is lost. The mechanism of the stand and the time taken to complete the procedure is recorded. The score is the best time of three trials.

2. Strength and endurance: Stair climb. The test performer stands at the bottom of stairs (similar to home stairs; 6 in. height, 10 in. depth) and on the signal to start, climbs the stairs as fast as possible, trying not to use the rails. After a 30-second rest, the performer walks down the stairs at a casual pace. The time to climb the stairs is recorded. Also, any unsteadiness, number of rest stops, and if the performer descends the stairs with one foot at a time are recorded.

3. Functional mobility and habitual gait speed: 6-meter gait walk. The test performer stands behind the starting line and on the signal to start, walks 6 meters, turns, and returns to the starting line as fast as possible. The best time for two trials is recorded. The time is recorded to the nearest tenth of a second.

4. Balance and flexibility: Reaching up. The shelf should be located next to a counter or other objects that the test performers can use to steady themselves. The test performer removes a light object from a shelf that is high enough to require stretching or standing on the toes. The ability to take down the object is recorded (e.g., without holding onto other objects and becoming unsteady, need to steady self by holding onto something, and unable to take down object).

5. Position change: Bending. The test performer picks up a small object from the floor. The ability to perform the task is recorded (e.g., successful without the need to use support, needs support, unable to get upright after bending, and unable to bend down).

6. Balance: Stance positions. The test performer maintains balance with the feet in three different positions. For the first two positions, the feet should not be touching each other.

   Parallel foot stance. Stand with the feet close together, side-by-side.

   Semi-tandem stance. Stand with the preferred foot halfway in front of the other; weight may be placed on back foot, if desired.

   Tandem stance. Stand with the heel of the preferred foot in front touching the toes of the other foot; weight may be placed on back foot, if desired.

   Arms may be used for balance, but they cannot be touching another object. The time that the position is held, up to 10 seconds, is recorded.

7. Upper body strength and endurance: Wheelchair mobility. Sitting in a wheelchair, on the signal to start, the test performer propels the wheelchair as fast as possible for 30 feet, turns the chair, and returns to the starting line. The best of two trials to the nearest tenth of a second is recorded.

Physical Activity for the Older Adult

The term *physical activity* may be defined in many different ways. In this discussion of the older adult, physical activity includes all movements associated with everyday life (e.g., work, routine activities, exercise activities, and recreational activities). Usually, older adults are retired or their work responsibilities require little physical activity. For this reason, it is important that the lifestyle of these individuals includes recreational activities, exercise, or other activities that require physical exertion.

The older adult can experience the benefits of physical activity in much the same way as younger individuals. It is the immediate benefits that encourage most individuals to maintain an active lifestyle. With an active lifestyle, older adults have the following benefits:

- Have a better self-image.

- Sleep better.

- Maintain appropriate body composition.

- Have better muscle tone and strength.

- Better manage stress.

- Are more likely to have a positive attitude and experience less depression.

- Experience fewer minor infectious ailments.

- Have more frequent bowel movements (less constipation).

These benefits can be experienced shortly after changing to an active lifestyle. Over the long term, the benefits include the following:

- Continuation of immediate benefits.

- Increased cardiorespiratory endurance.

- Increased muscle strength and endurance.

- Increased flexibility.

- Prevention of bone loss; decreased risk of osteoporosis.

- Prevention and/or postponement of declines in balance and coordination.

- Postponement of decline in speed of movement and reaction time.

- Improved mental health.

For most individuals, physical activity of mild to moderate intensity is not dangerous. Some individuals, however, should consult a physician before increasing their physical activity. The *ACSM's Health-Related Physical Fitness Assessment Manual* (2018), *CSEP-Physical Activity Training for Health (CSEP-PATH)* (2013), and PAR-Q+ in figure 11.1 provide screening procedures and questions that will help individuals determine whether medical clearance should be obtained.

Even though individual differences should be considered, general exercise guidelines for older adults are as follows.

Activity

Large-muscle, rhythmic activities provide cardiorespiratory benefits. Examples of such aerobic activities are bicycling, jogging, swimming, and walking.

Frequency

The activities should be performed a minimum of 2 or 3 times a week. After a period of adjustment to the activity, most individuals are able to exercise 4 to 6 days a week without any negative consequences.

Duration

Although a sedentary individual can benefit from any activity increase, the typical exercise session would be as follows:

Warm-up and stretching: 10 to 20 minutes

Aerobic activity: 20 to 30 minutes

Cool down: 5 to 10 minutes

Intensity

The program should be one of low to moderate intensity and related to the functional capacity of the individual.

These guidelines are primarily for aerobic activities. Flexibility and muscular fitness (strength and endurance) exercises also should be included in an exercise program for the older adult. Upper and lower body muscle groups can benefit from the use of hand and leg weights. As with aerobic activities, muscle fitness exercises should be related to the functional capacity of the individual. Also, it is often best to avoid the use of rigid guidelines when prescribing any exercise for the older adult. Many sedentary individuals can experience health benefits from 10- to 15-minute segments of mild activity.

Review Problems

1. Think of all the older adults age sixty and over that you know. How are they different in physical abilities?

2. Design an exercise program to improve the functional fitness of an older adult group.

Chapter Review Questions

1. What is the definition of functional fitness?

2. Why is it important to measure functional fitness with the older population?

3. How is pre-testing screening different for older adults as compared to younger adults?

4. What are your responsibilities after the measurement of functional fitness in older adults? What physical components will you work to improve to help them improve their functional fitness?

17 Special-Needs Populations

After completing this chapter, you should be able to

1. Define the term *special-needs populations,* and state what must be done in public physical education programs to meet the needs of special-needs populations.

2. Describe the role of physical performance measurement in special-needs physical education programs.

3. Justify the use of norm-referenced and criterion-referenced tests with special-needs populations.

4. Describe responsibilities after the measurement of special-needs populations.

5. Select appropriate perceptual-motor performance, motor performance, and physical fitness tests, and administer them to special-needs populations.

The term **special-needs populations** is used when referring to disabled or impaired individuals. Federal laws require all public agencies to ensure a continuum of alternative placements to meet children's needs for special education and related services; the children are to be educated in the least restrictive environment in which their educational needs can be met. Amendments to the original law emphasize that "least restrictive environment" should not always be interpreted to mean separate physical education programs for these students. Therefore, as a teacher, you should be prepared to make adaptations or modifications in the regular physical education program when possible. You should seek approaches to these adaptations that emphasize what the individuals can do; accentuate the positive. However, the adaptations will not be the same for everyone. Special needs vary for persons with different disabilities and with different degrees of the same disability. Your professional preparation should include one or two courses that promote a better understanding of the needs of disabled individuals and the means by which physical educators can provide appropriate and worthwhile programs for all disabled students. This chapter emphasizes the place of measurement and assessment in physical education programs for special-needs populations and provides examples of perceptual-motor performance, motor performance, and physical fitness tests that may be used for screening and diagnostic purposes. Many tests are available. Though a few tests are described in this chapter, you should review other available tests and select the one that best meets your needs.

No activities for development of perceptual-motor abilities, motor performance, and physical fitness will be described in this chapter. However, many activities or modifications of activities described in previous chapters can be used for such purposes. In addition, there are many types and degrees of disability, and the activities for development of perceptual-motor abilities, motor performance, and physical fitness may vary with the type of disability.

Why Measure Special-Needs Populations?

Several public laws have had instrumental influence on educational programs for individuals with disabilities, but the Individuals with Disabilities Education Act of 1990 (Public Law 101–476) and Individuals with Disabilities Education Improvement Act of 2004 (Public Law 108–446) include the most recent versions and amendments of these laws. This act expanded upon the previous Education for the Handicapped Act and amendments. The Individuals with Disabilities Education Act (IDEA) states that disabled students have a right to the following:

- A free and appropriate education.
- Physical education.
- Equal opportunity in athletics and intramurals.
- An individualized education program (IEP) designed to meet unique needs.
- Programs conducted in the least restrictive environment.
- Nondiscriminatory testing and objective criteria for placement.
- Due process.
- Related services to assist in special education.

All of the public laws related to educational programs for individuals with disabilities have implications for the role of physical education. However, the Education for All Handicapped Children Act of 1975, PL 94–142, emphasizes the importance of evaluation in the education of disabled children. The law establishes a framework in which evaluation is the key to the type of program provided. Not all aspects of the law pertaining to evaluation will be described here, but the major points are as follows:

1. Every state is required to develop a plan for identifying, locating, and evaluating all disabled students.

2. All disabled children and their parents are guaranteed procedural safeguards. Known as due process, this requirement means that parents and their children must be informed of their rights, and they may challenge educational decisions they feel are unfair. The law also includes the following requirements: the parents must give written permission for their child to be evaluated; the results of the evaluation must be explained to the parents; the parents may request that an independent evaluation be conducted outside the school; and if the parents and the school cannot agree on the evaluation findings, a special hearing must be held. All evaluation results must be kept confidential.

3. Standards for evaluation must be followed. Tests must be used that measure achievement level rather than impaired sensory, manual, or speaking skills, and more than one test procedure must be used to determine the student's educational status. Since many disabled students have communication problems, tests must be administered to test ability rather than communication skills. Finally, a multidisciplinary team of qualified professionals must administer the test and interpret the results.

If you assume a professional position that includes responsibilities with special-needs populations, you should be familiar with all aspects of IDEA and PL 94–142, as well as with all other public laws for disabled individuals.

Regardless of federal laws, individuals with disabilities should have the opportunity to participate in physical activity. If they follow a sedentary lifestyle, they will experience the same health risks as others; if they are physically active, they can gain very similar benefits as individuals without disabilities. Through physical activity, they can enhance the functioning and health of their hearts, lungs, muscles, and bones; improve their flexibility, mobility, and coordination; and lessen the negative effects of some

---

◆ ◆ ◆ POINT OF EMPHASIS ◆ ◆ ◆

- No single test is suitable for all special-needs populations. Many physical performance tests are available for special-needs populations, including sports-related tests. When selecting a test to administer, ask yourself:

  Why this test? How will I use this test?

conditions or slow the progression of others. In addition, physical activity can develop stamina to make the demands of their daily living easier. In other words, individuals with special needs can improve their quality of life through physical activity.

Norm-Referenced or Criterion-Referenced Tests

Should norm-referenced or criterion-referenced tests be used with special-needs populations? Really, it is not a choice of using only one or the other, for both norm-referenced and criterion-referenced tests are needed when working with disabled students. Norm-referenced tests serve the same purposes as they do for other populations: standardized norms are useful in screening for motor problems, comparing students with similar disabilities, program evaluation, and the placement of students. Criterion-referenced tests are especially useful in measuring student progress and for making instructional decisions about individual students. These tests also can be used for screening purposes when students are asked to perform certain basic skills.

As stated in other chapters, perhaps your most important use of tests will be in the comparison of individuals' current performance with past and future performances. This use will enable you to individualize your work with each student.

Responsibilities after Measurement

As there are many types and degrees of disability, no specific responsibilities after testing will be described. However, if your testing identifies abilities and fitness levels that can be improved, you should seek to help the students do so. Depending on the needs of each student, you may need the assistance of someone who is more familiar with a particular type of disability. Do not hesitate to seek such assistance.

▧ ARE YOU ABLE TO DO THE FOLLOWING?

- Define the term *special-needs populations,* and state what must be done in public physical education programs to meet the needs of special-needs populations.

- Describe the role of physical performance measurement in special-needs physical education programs.

- State why norm-referenced and criterion-referenced measurement should be used in physical education programs for special-needs populations.

- Describe responsibilities after the measurement of special-needs populations.

Perceptual-Motor Performance Tests

Perceptual-motor performance tests sample the ability of children to integrate sensory information with past experience to make decisions about movement. There is little doubt that perception is an important aspect of successful movement, so perceptual-motor performance tests can be valuable educational tools. However, they should not be interpreted as providing an overall measurement of motor ability. Rather, each item of the test battery should be used to measure a separate, specific factor. Components of perceptual-motor efficiency include balance, postural and locomotor awareness, visual perception, auditory perception, kinesthetic perception, tactile perception, body awareness, and laterality and directionality. Perceptual-motor programs for the disabled are important, but they should not be used in place of physical education programs. A strong physical education program is essential to every child's motor development. Some disabled children may need both programs.

Before any formal testing of disabled students, familiarize yourself with their basic motor behavioral patterns. You may obtain much information through the informal techniques of observation, self-testing, discussion with others, and rating scales and checklists. The preferred hand and foot should be determined, as well as any movement patterns that can be used in a positive way. Preliminary measurement of such skills as running, skipping, balancing, catching, throwing, striking an object, and kicking may be conducted with a rating scale by asking the students to perform these skills while you observe. This type of preliminary testing may prevent problems during the formal testing.

Many perceptual-motor tests are available, but only three are presented as examples to illustrate the types of test components that may be included in perceptual-motor tests. You should refer to other sources before selecting a test. The test you choose to administer will depend on your needs and the age group you wish to test.

Purdue Perceptual Motor Survey
(Roach and Kephart 1966)

Though referred to as a test, the Purdue Perceptual Motor Survey is a survey. The survey manual includes clear and precise instructions for scoring and administering each item as well as illustrations clarifying exactly what the child is expected to do. Forms for recording each child's performance are provided. The survey may be purchased from Merrill Publishing Co., Inc., P.O. Box 508, Columbus, OH 43216.

Age Level. Six through ten.

Equipment. Visual achievement forms, chalkboard, chalk, yardstick, and penlight.

Test Components

1. Balance and posture. Walking forward, backward, and sideward on a walking board and performing a series of jumping, hopping, and skipping tasks while maintaining balance.
2. Body image and differentiation. Identification of body parts, imitation of movement, and participation in various obstacle-course activities.
3. Perceptual-motor match. Drawing circles and lines on a chalkboard and performing eight rhythmic writing tasks.
4. Ocular control. Ocular-pursuit tasks involving individual eye movement and simultaneous eye movement.
5. Form perception. Drawing various geometric shapes on a sheet of paper.

Ayres Southern California Perceptual-Motor Tests
(Miller and Sullivan 1982)

To perform this test, the child must understand simple verbal directions. In addition, because five of the six items call for adequate motor responses, caution must be taken in testing children with neuromuscular impairment. The test battery can be administered in approximately 20 minutes. The test may be purchased from Western Psychological Services, Los Angeles, California.

Age Level. Four through eight.

Equipment. Watch, table, and chairs.

Test Components

1. Imitation of postures. Imitate twelve postures demonstrated by the instructor.
2. Crossing midline of body. Point at, or touch, the designated ear or eye, using the left or the right hand.
3. Bilateral motor coordination. Use the palms of the hands to gently slap or touch the thighs with a rhythmical motion.

4. Right-left discrimination. Identify own left and right sides, those of another pupil, or of various objects.
5. Standing balance, eyes open. Maintain balance while standing on one foot and then change to the other foot. Balance is timed for each foot.
6. Standing balance, eyes closed. Same as component 5, except the eyes are kept closed throughout.

Andover Perceptual-Motor Test
(Nichols, Arsenault, and Giuffre 1980)

The Andover Perceptual-Motor Test measures the basic perceptual-motor areas necessary for normal development and motor learning. The test should be used as a quick screening device, not as a diagnostic tool. It can be administered to a group of twenty-five children in two 30-minute class sessions.

Age Level. Four through seven.

Equipment. Primary balance beam, two 8-inch balls, marking tape, and dowel or stick.

Test Components

1. Balance. The ability to maintain static and dynamic balance.
2. Eye-hand coordination. The ability to coordinate the eyes and hands to accomplish a task.
3. Locomotion. The ability to ambulate the body through space; a combination of strength, coordination, and balance is needed to perform this item.
4. Spatial awareness. The ability to make spatial judgments and perceive the body in relation to other objects in space.
5. Rhythm. The ability to hear, interpret the sounds heard, and respond to what is interpreted.

Motor Performance Tests

For many years, educators have been interested in the relationship of age and motor performance. Because of this interest, many tests have been established to measure motor skills and to compare an individual's motor performance with that of other individuals of similar age. (Many of these tests have been described in previous chapters.) Motor performance tests also have been established to serve as screening instruments, to help identify individuals with motor deficiencies and those in need of special education.

However, these tests often are incorrectly used to measure individual growth and progress over a period of time. Some teachers mistakenly believe that test scores will improve if students participate in a variety of movement experiences. But you should not expect changes in test scores unless the students practice items or skills that are very similar to the test items. Because many motor performance skills are highly specific, transfer of learning does not always occur as a result of participation in general movement experiences. On the other hand, assuming that no improvement in motor performance has taken place if test scores do not change is also incorrect. The students may have improved in skills that are not measured by the test. In addition, a general background in motor performance serves as a foundation for the development of specific motor skills. There are many motor performance tests, but only four are presented as examples.

■ The Bruininks-Oseretsky Test of Motor Proficiency
(Arnheim and Sinclair 1985; Safrit 1986)

The Bruininks-Oseretsky Test of Motor Proficiency can be administered in two forms: as a complete form or as a short form. The complete form consists of eight subtests composed of forty-six separate items. Four subtests measure gross motor skills, three measure fine motor skills, and one measures both fine and gross motor skills. The complete test requires 45 to 60 minutes to administer. The short form also consists of eight subtests, but only fourteen items. The short form can be administered in 15 to 20 minutes. The division of the test into eight basic areas permits the teacher to be specific in determining where to place the emphasis in remedying the children's movement problems. No special training is required of test administrators. The test kit may be purchased from the American Guidance Service, Inc., 4201 Woodland Road, Circle Pines, MN 55014-1796.

Age Level. Four and a fourth through fourteen and a fourth.

Equipment. Balance beam, ball, mazes, scissors, balance rod, matchbook, coins, small boxes, thread, playing cards, matchsticks, ballpoint pen, and paper.

Test Components

Long Form

Subtest 1: Running speed and agility (one item).

Subtest 2: Balance (eight items).

Subtest 3: Bilateral coordination (eight items).

Subtest 4: Strength (three items).

Subtest 5: Upper-limb coordination (nine items).

Subtest 6: Response speed (one item).

Subtest 7: Visual-motor control (eight items).

Subtest 8: Upper-limb speed and dexterity (eight items).

Short Form

Subtest 1: Running speed and agility.

Subtest 2: Standing on preferred leg while making circles with fingers.
Walking forward heel-to-toe on balance beam.

Subtest 3: Tapping feet alternately while making circles with feet.
Jumping up and clapping hands.

Subtest 4: Standing broad jump.

Subtest 5: Catching a ball with both hands.
Throwing a ball at a target with preferred hand.

Subtest 6: Response speed.

Subtest 7: Drawing a line through a straight path with preferred hand.
Copying a circle on paper with preferred hand.
Copying a picture of overlapping pencils with preferred hand.

Subtest 8: Sorting shape cards with preferred hand.
Drawing dots in circles with preferred hand.

■ The Basic Motor Ability Tests
(Arnheim and Sinclair 1979)

The Basic Motor Ability Tests (BMATs) are a battery of eleven tests designed to evaluate the selected motor responses of small- and large-muscle control, static and dynamic balance, eye-hand coordination, and flexibility. Each of the eleven subtests requires little training to administer. One child can be tested in approximately 12 to 15 minutes, and a group of five children can be tested in about 25 minutes, by one test administrator.

Age Level. Four through twelve.

Equipment. ½-inch beads; 18-inch round shoelace with ¾-inch plastic tip; 4″ × 5″ beanbags; wastepaper basket, 14 inches high; table; chair; transfer board consisting of two 8-ounce margarine containers, 4 inches in diameter, attached to and positioned on the board 12 inches apart; 30 regular-sized marbles; yardstick; 4′ × 6′ mat; blindfold; stopwatch; balance board with width of 1¾ inches; basketball; 50-foot tape measure; two Nerf balls (3-inch diameter ball and 10-inch diameter ball); target consisting of four vertical lines, 1 inch wide and 8 feet high, which are connected at the top by a horizontal line 1 inch wide (vertical lines are 2 feet apart); playground ball, 10 inches in diameter; and four cones.

Test Components

Subtest 1: Bilateral eye-hand coordination and dexterity.
Bead stringing with 40-second time limit.

Subtest 2: Eye-hand coordination. Target throwing with beanbags and wastepaper basket.

Subtest 3: Speed of hand movement, crossing from one side of the body to the other. Transfer of marbles from one container to another; both hands are tested, with 20-second time limit for each hand.

Subtest 4: Flexibility of back and hamstring muscles. Sit and reach.

Subtest 5: Strength and power in the thigh and lower-leg muscles. Standing long jump.

Subtest 6: Speed and agility in changing from a prone to a standing position. Move from face-down to standing position and touch mark on wall; repeat cycle as many times as possible in 20 seconds.

Subtest 7: Static balance. Static balance on 1¾-inch balance board; performed with eyes open and blindfolded on preferred foot and other foot; maximum of 10 seconds per trial.

Subtest 8: Arm and shoulder girdle explosive strength. Two-hand chest pass with basketball; three trials.

Subtest 9: Coordination associated with striking. Ability to strike Nerf ball with hand and hit target drawn on wall; five swings with each arm.

Subtest 10: Eye-foot coordination. Ability to kick ball at target; five kicks with each foot.

Subtest 11: Agility. Rapidly move the body and alter direction; zigzag pattern around cones.

■ The Stott, Moyes, and Henderson Test of Motor Impairment
(Miller and Sullivan 1982)

The objective of the Stott, Moyes, and Henderson Test of Motor Impairment is to ascertain and assess motor impairment of functional or presumed neurological origin. The test was derived from the original Oseretsky test and the revised Lincoln-Oseretsky test. The revised form contains sets of five test items each, one set for each year, ages five through fourteen. It can be administered to most pupils in approximately 20 minutes. Test procedures are available from Brook Educational Publishing Ltd., P.O. Box 1171, Guelph, Ontario N1H6N3.

Age Level. Five through fourteen.

Equipment. See test items (equipment varies for each age).

Test Components
1. Control and balance of the body while immobile.
2. Control and coordination of the upper limbs.
3. Control and coordination of the body while in motion.

4. Manual dexterity with emphasis on speed.
5. Simultaneous movement and precision.

Age Five
1. Balancing on tiptoes; feet together, eyes open.
2. Bouncing a ball and catching it in two hands.
3. Jumping over a cord at knee height.
4. Posting coins into a bank box.
5. Placing counters simultaneously into a box.

Age Six
1. Balancing on one leg; eyes open.
2. Bouncing a ball and catching it in one hand.
3. Hopping forward for 5 yards, between two lines.
4. Threading beads onto a lace.
5. Tracing a circular track with a pencil.

Age Seven
1. Balancing on one foot with arms raised; eyes open.
2. Following a track of holes in a wooden board with a pencil.
3. Walking heel-to-toe along a line.
4. Placing pegs on a board, one by one.
5. Touching tips of the fingers in order.

Age Eight
1. Balancing on one foot with other foot placed on the knee; eyes open.
2. Throwing a ball at a wall and catching the rebound.
3. Jumping sideward, three jumps, with feet together.
4. Threading a lace through a series of holes in a wooden board.
5. Walking while balancing a bead on a board.

Age Nine
1. Balancing on a wide board; eyes open.
2. Catching a ball in one hand.
3. Jumping and clapping twice before landing.
4. Placing a wooden pin through a series of holes.
5. Placing pegs simultaneously into a board.

Age Ten
1. Balancing on a narrow board; eyes open.
2. Guiding a ball around an obstacle course on a table.
3. Jumping over a knee-height cord; taking off with two feet together and landing on one foot.
4. Placing matchsticks in four small boxes.
5. Placing holed-squares simultaneously on two rods.

Ages Eleven and Twelve
1. Balancing heel-to-toe on two narrow boards; eyes open.
2. Hitting a target with a ball.
3. Hopping sideward into two squares.
4. Piercing holes in paper track.
5. Placing pegs on a board and squares on pins, simultaneously.

Ages Thirteen and Fourteen

1. Balancing on the toes of one foot.
2. Moving a ring along a rod.
3. Jumping backward and forward inside large circles.
4. Moving a pen around a track.
5. Piercing holes simultaneously with two styluses.

■ Test of Gross Motor Development-2 (TGMD-2)
(Ulrich 2000)

The Test of Gross Motor Development-2 measures gross motor abilities that develop early in life. It is used to identify children who are significantly behind in their age-expected gross motor development. The test also may be used to plan an instructional program and assess individual progress in gross motor skill development. The test consists of two subtests. Subtest one includes six items that measure locomotor skills. Subtest two includes six items that measure object control skills. The test provides standards for successful performance of each item. For each item, the child is given 1 for a successful performance, 0 for a failed attempt. No partial marks are given.

Age Level. Three to ten–eleven.

Equipment. Flat running surface, 4-inch lightweight ball, 8- to 10-inch playground ball, basketball, tennis ball, soccer ball, softball, 4- to 5-inch square beanbag, plastic electrical tape, 2 traffic cones plastic bat, and batting tee.

Test Components
Locomotor Skills

1. Speed run 50 feet.
2. Gallop 30 feet.
3. Hop on one leg for 15 feet.
4. Run and leap from one foot to the other.
5. Horizontal jump (standing broad jump).
6. Slide sideways 30 feet.

Object Control Skills

1. Strike a stationary ball (t-ball batting).
2. Dribble a basketball.
3. Catch ball thrown from five yards away.
4. Kick soccer ball.
5. Throw a ball baseball pitcher style.
6. Roll a ball underhand (like bowling).

Physical Fitness Tests

The development of physical fitness is important for special-needs populations for the same reasons it is important for other individuals. All children should be instructed in the why and how of a healthy lifestyle, and they should be provided the opportunity for development of health-related and skill-related physical fitness.

There is another important reason why special-needs populations need to develop and maintain physical fitness: Poor physical fitness can limit a child's performance and slow the rate of improvement in motor performance. For example, scores on balance and agility tests may be influenced by a child's poor muscular endurance and cardiorespiratory fitness. Any individual whose fitness limitations restrict progress in motor development should be involved in a program to strengthen those weaknesses.

The health-related and skill-related physical fitness of many disabled individuals may be measured with the same tests or test items presented in chapter 15. Adjustments in the items may be necessary, depending on the type and degree of disability. For example, distance runs may be shortened. If it is necessary to reduce the distance to the point that it is no longer a valid measure of cardiorespiratory fitness, the run may be used as a motivational item. (When it is necessary to adjust a test item for an individual, it is important not to compare the resulting score with scores achieved by individuals who can perform the item without adjustments.)

■ The Brockport Physical Fitness Test
(Winnick and Short 1999)

In 1993, the U.S. Department of Education funded Project Target, a research study designed primarily to develop a health-related, criterion-referenced physical fitness test for persons with disabilities, ages ten to seventeen. The Brockport Physical Fitness Test (BPFT), the test developed through Project Target, is designed primarily for individuals with mental retardation, spinal cord injury, cerebral palsy, blindness, congenital anomalies, and amputations. The test, however, can be used for young people with other disabilities and in the general population. There are twenty-seven test items in the BPFT, but generally four to six items can be used to assess the health-related physical fitness of an individual. Guidelines are provided in the test manual as to which items should be administered to the different populations and how the items may be modified. The manual also includes standards for each age, gender, and population.

Age Level. Ten to seventeen.

Equipment. Audio cassette player, PACER audio cassette, measuring tape, marker cones, electronic heart monitor (recommended), stopwatch, skinfold caliper, barbells and weights, gym mat, chair, adjustable horizontal bar, grip dynamometer, sturdy armchair, yardstick, standard wheelchair ramp, sit and reach box, and sturdy table.

Test Components

1. Aerobic functioning: Four test options are provided.

   20-meter PACER. The procedure and scoring are the same as those for the PACER included in the FitnessGram described in chapter 15.

   16-meter PACER. The test procedure is the same as that of the 20-meter PACER. The shorter version is recommended particularly for individuals with mental retardation and mild limitations in physical fitness.

   Target aerobic movement test. This item measures the ability of the performer to exercise at or above a recommended target heart rate for 15 minutes. Test performers can engage in virtually any physical activity as long as the activity is of sufficient intensity to reach a minimal target heart rate and to sustain the heart rate in a target heart rate zone. One test trial is given; the score is pass/fail.

   1-mile run or walk. The test performers run or walk 1 mile in the shortest time possible. One test trial is administered, and the score is recorded in minutes and seconds.

2. Body composition: Two items are included.

   Skinfolds. Skinfold measurements are used to estimate body fat. The measurements may be taken at three sites: triceps, subscapular, or calf. With one exception, the directions for skinfold testing described in chapter 14 should be followed. Rather than always performing the measurements on the right side, however, the measurements should be taken on the individual's dominant or preferred side. Three measurements should be taken at each skinfold site used. The middle measurement value is recorded as the criterion score. If a skinfold reading at the same site differs from other readings by 2 mm or more, an additional measurement should be taken, and the measurement that is substantially different should be deleted.

   Body mass index. The body mass index (BMI) provides an indication of the appropriateness of an individual's weight for the individual's height. The BMI can be determined by using a chart in the test manual or by using the following equations:

   $$\text{BMI} = \text{body weight (kg)}/\text{height (m)}^2$$

   $$\text{BMI} = [\text{body weight (lb)} \times 704.5]/\text{height (in.)}^2$$

3. Musculoskeletal functioning—muscular strength and endurance: Sixteen items are provided.

Bench press. A 35-pound barbell is used to measure upper extremity strength and endurance. The test performer lies supine on a bench, with knees bent and feet flat on the floor or on rolled mats placed on each side of the bench. The performer grasps the bar, with the hands directly above the shoulders and the elbows flexed. On the start command, the performer raises the barbell to a straight-arm position and then returns to the ready position. This procedure is repeated without rest until the barbell cannot be raised or until 50 repetitions for males or 30 repetitions for females are completed. One repetition should be completed every 3 to 4 seconds. One trial is administered, and the score is the number of repetitions performed correctly, up to 50 for males and 30 for females.

Curl-up. This test measures abdominal strength and endurance. The procedure and scoring are the same as those for the FitnessGram curl-up described in chapter 15. One trial is administered.

Modified curl-up. This test is similar to the curl-up with the following exceptions:

- The hands are placed on the front of the thighs.

- As the test performer curls up, the hands slide along the thighs until the fingertips contact the patellae. The hands should slide approximately 4 inches to the patellae or beyond, if necessary.

- If necessary, the test administrators can place their hands on the performer's kneecaps to provide a reach target.

Dumbbell press. A 15-pound dumbbell is used to measure arm and shoulder strength and endurance. While seated in a wheelchair or a sturdy chair, the performer grasps the dumbbell with the dominant hand. The elbow should be flexed so that the weight is close to and in front of the dominant shoulder. On the start command, the performer extends the elbow and flexes the shoulder so that the weight is lifted straight up and above the shoulder. When the elbow is completely extended, the weight is returned to the starting position. One repetition should be performed every 3 to 4 seconds until the performer is no longer able to completely extend the elbow or until 50 repetitions are completed. One trial is administered, and the score is the number of presses performed correctly, up to 50.

Extended-arm hang. This test measures hand, arm, and shoulder strength and endurance. Using an overhand or pronated grip, the performer hangs from a bar or similar hanging apparatus for as long as possible, up to 40 seconds. The performer may jump to the hanging position, be lifted to it, or move to it from a chair. A fully extended position, with the feet clear off the floor, must be maintained throughout the test. The performer can be steadied to prevent swaying. One trial is administered, and the score is the elapsed time to the nearest second, up to 40 seconds.

Flexed-arm hang. This test measures hand, arm, and shoulder strength and endurance. Using an overhand grip, the performer maintains a flexed-arm position while hanging from a bar for as long as possible. The performer is assisted to a position where the body is close to the bar and the chin is clearly over, but not touching, the bar. The body must not swing, the knees must not be bent, and the legs must not kick. One trial is administered, and the score is the time to the nearest second that the flexed-arm position can be maintained.

Dominant grip strength. A grip dynamometer is used to measure hand and arm strength. The test performer is seated on a straight-back, armless chair, with the feet flat on the floor. The dynamometer is squeezed with the second finger on the adjustable handle. After the handle is adjusted to the correct position, the performer squeezes the handle as hard as possible. The hand grasping the dynamometer should be held away from the body and the chair during the test. Three trials are administered with at least 30 seconds allowed between trials. The middle score, recorded to the nearest kilogram, serves as the criterion score.

Isometric push-up. This test measures strength and endurance of the upper body. The test performer assumes a front-leaning rest position with the hands directly below the shoulders, arms extended, the whole body in a straight line, and toes touching the floor. The test is ended when the correct push-up position can no longer be held. One trial is administered, and the score, recorded to the nearest second, is the length of time the proper position is maintained.

Pull-up. This test measures upper-body strength and endurance. Using an overhand (pronated) grip, the performer completes as many pull-ups as possible. The body must not swing, the knees must not be bent, and the legs must not kick during the pull-up. One trial is administered, and the score is the number of pull-ups completed.

Modified pull-up. This test measures upper-body strength and endurance. The test performer completes as many pull-ups as possible using the apparatus illustrated in figure 13.6. There is no time limit, but the pull-ups should be continuous. One trial is administered, and the score is the number of correct pull-ups completed.

Push-up. This test measures upper-body strength and endurance. The test performer completes as many push-ups as possible at a cadence of one push-up every 3 seconds.

One trial is administered, and the score is the number of correct push-ups completed.

40-meter push or walk. This test measures whether the individual has the strength and endurance to traverse a distance of 40 meters without reaching a moderate level of exertion. The test performers walk or push their wheelchairs a distance of 40 meters with a 5-meter start zone at a speed that is comfortable for them. The test performers are encouraged to travel at the speed that they usually use to move around the community. To pass the test, performers must be able to cover the 40 meters in 60 seconds or less while keeping the heart rate below the criterion for moderate exercise intensity. The test is timed to the nearest second. As soon as a test performer crosses the finish line, the test administrator counts the performer's radial pulse for 10 seconds. For the correct level of exercise intensity, test performers who walk or push a wheelchair with their legs must have a post-test 10-second pulse rate of 20 beats or less. Individuals who push a wheelchair with their arms must have a post-test 10-second pulse of 19 beats or less. Two trials can be administered. If two trials are used, the performer's pulse must be at or near resting level before the second trial is administered. The test is scored on a pass/fail basis. Performers pass when they can cover the distance within 60 seconds at the acceptable pulse rate.

Reverse curl. This test measures hand, wrist, and arm strength. The test performer lifts a 1-pound dumbbell with the preferred arm while seated in a chair or wheelchair. The movement starts with the weight resting on the midpoint of the thigh while the performer is in a normal seated position. The fingers are wrapped around the weight, and the forearm is pronated. With the wrist extended, the individual flexes the elbow and lifts the weight until the elbow is flexed to at least 45° (the arm remains pronated throughout the movement). The weight is held in this position for 2 seconds and then returned to the starting position. The movement must be controlled and the downward movement must be slower than the gravitational pull. One trial is administered, and the test is passed if the performer can complete one correct reverse curl.

Seated push-up. This test measures upper-body strength and endurance. With the hands placed on the handles of push-up blocks, on the armrests of a wheelchair, or on the armrests of a chair, the performer attempts a seated push-up and holds it for 20 seconds. The buttocks are raised from the supporting surface by extension of the elbows. The extension position is maintained for as long as possible. One trial is administered, and the score is the time that the position is held, up to 20 seconds.

Trunk lift. This test measures trunk extension, strength, and flexibility. The procedure and scoring are the same as those for the FitnessGram trunk lift.

Wheelchair ramp test. This test measures upper-body strength and endurance. The test performers push their chairs up a standard wheelchair ramp. The test is not timed, and multiple trials are permissible. Going beyond the 8-foot line meets the minimal standard; the preferred standard is met when the performer either goes beyond the 15-foot line or makes it to the top of a longer ramp that the individual frequently encounters.

4. Musculoskeletal functioning–flexibility or range of motion: Five items are provided.

Modified Apley test. This test measures upper-body flexibility. The test performer attempts to reach back and touch with one hand the superior medial angle of the opposite scapula. One trial is administered for each arm. Scoring for this test is as follows:

3–touch the superior medial angle of opposite scapula

2–touch the top of the head

1–touch the mouth

0–unable to touch the mouth

Back-saver sit and reach. This test measures the flexibility of the hamstring muscles. The procedure and scoring are the same as those for the FitnessGram back-saver sit and reach described in chapter 15.

Shoulder stretch. This test measures upper-body flexibility. The procedure and scoring are the same as those for the FitnessGram shoulder stretch.

Modified Thomas test. This test measures the length of the performer's hip flexor muscles. A thin strip of masking tape is placed on a sturdy table 11 inches from one of the short edges. The test performer lies in a supine position on the table so that the head of the femur is level with the strip of the tape (i.e., the hip joint is 11 inches from the edge of the table). The lower legs are relaxed as they hang off the table. To test the right hip, the performer lifts the left knee toward the chest and, with the hands, pulls the knee toward the chest until the back is flat against the table. At that point, the test administrator observes the position of the performer's right thigh. A maximum score is earned if the performer can keep the thigh in contact with the table surface while the back is flat. The procedure is repeated on the opposite side of the body. One trial is administered for each leg. The test is scored from 0 to 3 points as follows:

3–The tested leg remains in contact with the surface of the table when the opposite knee is pulled toward the chest, and the back is flat.

2–The tested leg does not remain in contact with the surface of the table, but the height of the performer's leg above the edge of the table is less than 3 inches.

1–The tested leg lifts more than 3 inches but less than 6 inches above the edge of the table.

0–The tested leg lifts more than 6 inches above the edge of the table.

Target stretch test. This test is a screening instrument used to estimate the extent of movement in various joints. For each movement, the performer is asked to achieve the maximum movement extent, and the test administrator evaluates the movement limit against sketches included in the manual. The eight movements are wrist extension, elbow extension, shoulder extension, shoulder abduction, shoulder external rotation, forearm supination, forearm pronation, and knee extension.

■ **Kansas Adapted/Special Physical Education Test**
(Johnson and Lavay 1988)

The Kansas Adapted/Special Physical Education Test Manual was developed primarily to address the need for health-related physical fitness testing of children with special needs in the state of Kansas. It is based on the rationale that all children can benefit from a structured program of physical activity and no child should be excluded, regardless of his or her disability. After proper testing, the test results should be used to develop individualized physical activity programs.

Age Level. Five through twenty-one.

Equipment. Mat, tape measure or yardstick, 12-inch ruler, 12-inch-high solid bench or box, masking tape, stopwatch, bar and weights (35 pounds), and large enough area for adequate aerobic movement.

Test Components

1. Abdominal strength and endurance: Bent-knee sit-ups. Arms are crossed on the chest; individual may grasp the shirt. Feet are held by partner; elbows touch the thighs, and shoulder blades must touch the flat surface with each return to the start position. The exercise is continued until the performer stops for 4 seconds, quits, or completes 50 correctly executed repetitions. The test performer is encouraged by the tester and class through cheers, praise, and the act of rhythmically counting repetitions. Three tape reference lines can be placed on the mat or floor to help the teacher keep the performer's heels within 12 to 18 inches of the buttocks. Line one is for placement of the buttocks,

line two is 12 inches from line one, and line three is 18 inches from line one.

2. Flexibility of lower back and posterior thighs: Sit and reach. Tape a 12-inch ruler to the front edge of a 12-inch bench or box where the 6-inch mark is at the front edge and the ruler is at a right angle to the edge. The front edge of the bench or box (6-inch mark) is considered the zero (0) position. The test is administered in the same way as the standard sit and reach test. If the test performer has an impairment in the limbs, the best functioning limb should be used. The position must be held for 1 second, and the score is the best of five trials. If the performer is unable to reach the 6-inch mark, the score is recorded as a negative score.

3. Upper-body strength and endurance: Isometric push-up and bench press. The isometric push-up score is the length of time (nearest tenth of a second) that the correct up position of a push-up can be held. The bench press is recommended for individuals thirteen years of age or older. The test performer assumes a supine position on the bench, with the knees bent and the feet placed on the floor on each side of the bench. The performer grasps a 35-pound barbell with both hands directly above the shoulders and raises the barbell to a straight-arm "ready" position. On command, the barbell is lowered until it touches the chest; it then is raised to the straight-arm position at a 90° angle to the body. This action is repeated until either the barbell cannot be raised any longer or 50 repetitions for males and 30 repetitions for females have been completed correctly. The flexed-arm hang and pull-ups are tests that may be used also.

4. Cardiovascular endurance: Run, walk, propelling in wheelchair, stationary bicycle, or propelling on scooter board.

Performer may use any fashion to elevate heart rate above the resting heart rate. The major objective is for the test performer to reach and maintain a heart rate between 140 and 180 beats per minute for 12 minutes after a 6-minute warm-up. The tester monitors the performer's heart rate every 3 minutes by counting the pulse rate at the carotid artery for 6 seconds. If the pulse rate is above 18 beats, the performer is asked to slow down and is closely monitored for stress. If the performer's pulse rate is above 20 beats for two consecutive checkpoints, the performer is stopped and the test is terminated. All test performers should be allowed 6 minutes of warm-up activity before starting this test item. The performer's score is the number of minutes he or she performs the test, as indicated in table 17.1.

■ **AAHPERD Motor Fitness Test for the Moderately Mentally Retarded**
(Johnson and Londeree 1976)

The AAHPERD Motor Fitness Test for the Moderately Mentally Retarded is a modification of the AAHPERD Youth Fitness Test. It is intended to be used when testing mentally retarded children who are capable of learning (IQs ranging from 50 to 70). The test may include thirteen items, but six items are recommended as sufficient for testing the motor fitness of the moderately retarded. The remaining items of height, weight, sitting bob and reach, hopping, skipping, tumbling progression, and target throw may or may not be included depending on the testing situation.

TABLE 17.1 Scoring for the Cardiovascular Endurance Event of the Kansas Adapted/Special Physical Endurance Test

Time Interval	Heart Rate		
	Below 14	Between 14 and 18	Above 18
First 3 minutes	Allow to continue, but give no credit.	Credit for 3 minutes.	Ask to slow down; monitor closely; credit for 3 minutes.
Second 3 minutes	Allow to continue, but give no credit; encourage to speed up.	Credit for 3 minutes.	Ask to slow down; monitor closely; credit for 3 minutes.
Third 3 minutes	Allow to continue, but give no credit; encourage to speed up.	Credit for 3 minutes.	Ask to slow down; monitor closely; credit for 3 minutes.
Fourth 3 minutes	Give no credit.	Credit for 3 minutes.	Credit for 3 minutes.

Note: The test performer is stopped when the pulse rate is above 20 beats per minute for two consecutive checkpoints.

Source: Johnson, R. E. and Lavay, B., *Kansas adapted/special physical education test manual*, Topeka, Kans.: Kansas State Department of Education, 1988.

Age Level. Norms are published for boys and girls, ages six through twenty.

Equipment. Metal or wooden bar 1½ inches in diameter, tumbling mat, stopwatch, tape measure, softballs, and flat running surface.

Test Components

1. Arm and shoulder strength and endurance: Flexed-arm hang.
2. Abdominal strength and endurance: 30-second sit-ups.
3. Explosive leg power: Standing long jump.
4. Coordination: Softball throw for distance.
5. Speed: 50-yard dash.
6. Cardiorespiratory fitness: 300-yard run or walk.

■ Special Fitness Test for Mildly Mentally Retarded Persons
(AAHPERD 1976b)

The Special Fitness Test for Mildly Mentally Retarded Persons is a modification of the AAHPERD Youth Fitness Test. The norms are different, but the components are similar to those of the Motor Fitness Test for the Moderately Mentally Retarded.
Age Level. Eight through eighteen.
Equipment. Metal or wooden bar 1½ inches in diameter, tumbling mat, stopwatch, tape measure, softballs, and flat running surface.

Test Components

1. Arm and shoulder strength and endurance: Flexed-arm hang.
2. Abdominal strength and endurance: 1-minute straight-leg sit-ups.
3. Agility: Shuttle run.
4. Explosive leg power: Standing long jump.
5. Speed: 50-yard dash.
6. Coordination: Softball throw for distance.
7. Cardiorespiratory fitness: 300-yard run.

■ Fait Physical Fitness Test for Mildly and Moderately Mentally Retarded Students
(Fait and Dunn 1984)

The Fait Physical Fitness Test is suitable for use with the educable and a majority of the medium and high trainables, if they do not have other disabilities that prevent safe performance of the test.
Age Level. Nine through twenty.

Equipment. Horizontal bar or doorway bar, mat, and flat running surface.

Test Components

1. Speed: 25-yard run.
2. Static muscular endurance of the arm and shoulder girdle: Bent-arm hang.
3. Dynamic muscular endurance of the flexor muscles of the leg and of the abdominal muscles: Leg lift.
4. Static balance: Balance on one leg with eyes closed.
5. Agility: 20-second squat thrust.
6. Cardiorespiratory endurance: 300-yard run or walk.

■ Buell AAHPERD Youth Fitness Adaptation for the Blind
(Buell 1982)

This test for the blind is an adaptation from the AAHPERD Youth Fitness Test.
Age Level. Ten through seventeen.
Equipment. Horizontal bar or doorway bar, mat, stopwatch, tape measure, basketball, and flat running surface.

Test Components

1. Arm and shoulder girdle strength and endurance: Pull-ups (boys) and flexed-arm hang (girls).
2. Abdominal strength and endurance: 1-minute bent-knee sit-ups.
3. Leg power: Standing long jump.
4. Speed: 50-yard dash.
5. Cardiorespiratory function: 600-yard run or walk.
6. Upper-body power: Basketball throw.

The norms for pull-ups (boys), flexed-arm hang (girls), sit-ups, and standing long jump are the same as in the revised AAHPERD Youth Fitness Test (1976a). Separate norms were developed for the 50-yard dash and for the 600-yard run or walk. The shuttle run test was eliminated, and a basketball throw was added to measure upper-body power.

Review Problems

1. Ask physical education teachers in local schools to describe the tests they are using to screen special-needs populations.

2. Review in other sources additional perceptual-motor performance, motor performance, and physical fitness tests for special-needs populations.

Chapter Review Questions

1. What does the term *special-needs populations* mean?

2. What is the role of physical performance measurement in special-needs physical education programs?

3. Should you use norm-referenced or criterion-referenced measurement tests with special-needs populations?

4. What is your primary responsibility after the measurement of special-needs populations?

18 | Sports Skills

After completing this chapter, you should be able to

1. Measure sports skills.

2. Describe accuracy-based, repetitive-performance, total body movement, and distance performance tests.

3. State how sports skills tests may be used in physical education.

4. Describe responsibilities after the measurement of sports skills.

5. Locate and select individual, dual, and team sports skills tests.

Many sports skills tests are described in the professional literature you will read. Some of these tests are valid and reliable; others are not. No attempt is made in this chapter to describe all good sports skills tests, but a very adequate sampling is provided. Unless indicated otherwise, the described tests may be administered to both males and females. Strand and Wilson (1993) and Collins and Hodges (2001) are excellent sources for sports skills tests that may be used in the school environment.

Selection of any sports skills test should be based on the criteria described in chapter 5. In addition to selecting a good test, you should recognize that some tests measure only one aspect of a sport. When such a test is administered, no generalization should be made about an individual's overall skill in a particular sport.

Norms are available for many sports skills tests, but unless you want to make national comparisons, it may be more appropriate to develop local norms. Often local norms are more meaningful, owing to differences in movement experiences, the socioeconomic environment of the group being tested, and the group used to develop the test norms.

The tests presented in this chapter are grouped under particular sports. Such tests may also be placed into four groups or classifications. **Accuracy-based** skills tests involve throwing, serving, striking, or kicking an object toward a target for accuracy. Throwing a football or baseball, shooting basketball free throws, serving a tennis ball, and kicking soccer goals are examples of such tests. **Repetitive-performance** tests, also called wall volley tests, involve the continuous performance of an activity for a specified time period. The test performer is required to stroke, pass, throw, or kick an object at a wall for a specified time period. The number of successful trials is the unit of measurement. Basketball passes, volleyball volleys, soccer kicks, and racket sports strokes are examples of such tests. **Total body movement** tests, also called speed tests, require the test performer to move the whole body in a restricted designated area as quickly as possible. Basketball and soccer dribbling tests are examples of these tests. **Distance or power performance** tests require the test performer to throw, kick, or strike an object for maximum displacement or force. Baseball or softball throws, the golf drives, football punts, and soccer kicks are examples of these tests. Baumgartner et al. (2007) and Morrow et al. (2005) provide additional discussion about these groups of sports skills tests.

Why Measure Sports Skills?

Perhaps the most popular purpose of sports skills measurement is to determine an individual's progress or level of achievement in a particular sport. Other

- Some sports skills tests provide opportunities for administration under gamelike conditions. On some occasions you may not be able to administer such tests, but if your goal is to conduct authentic assessment, you should try to do so.

important purposes for the measurement of sports skills follow.

Classification   A skills test can be administered early in the instruction in a sport to classify all participants. This early test eliminates the need to observe the individuals for several group meetings before attempting to classify them.

Diagnosis   Determining the strengths and weaknesses of the students can aid in the planning of unit objectives and can help identify students who may need special attention.

Motivation   Used correctly, a skills test can motivate individuals to improve their abilities in a sport. The challenge of competing against one's own scores often is more motivating than the challenge of competing against others.

Practice   While performing the test items, the students are actually practicing the skills of the sport.

Program accountability   Test scores, as well as other information, can be used to demonstrate to the administration, parents, and the public the objectives and values of physical education. When no such information is available, the perception of physical education as a "play period" is reaffirmed.

For whatever purpose you measure sports skills, you should emphasize that test performers attempt to execute the correct form and technique during the test. Occasionally, acceptable scores may be obtained without good form, but if your goal is to assist individuals in improving their skill and performance, you should insist on good technique. Also, rather than always using sports skills tests, at times you may prefer to use checklist, rating chart, analytical, and holistic rubrics (described in chapter 7). With these instruments, correct form is emphasized and rewarded.

Responsibilities after Measurement

Your responsibilities after measurement are related to your purposes for measuring sports skills. If you measure students to determine their level of achievement for grading purposes, you must have a grading system. Ideally, your grading system should be in place before you test, but there may be occasions when this is not possible. For example, it may be your first time teaching a particular sport. Whatever grading system you use, it should meet the criteria described in chapter 7. Additionally, you must choose whether to use norm-referenced or criteria-referenced grading. As stated earlier, it may be more appropriate to use local norms rather than national norms. As you gain teaching experience, you will feel more comfortable with the norms you develop. If you measure students for classification purposes, you will use the test scores to place them in the appropriate groups. You first, however, must determine the test scores required for group placement. If you measure for diagnosis purposes, your responsibility is to provide guidance for students to improve their weaknesses and increase their strengths. If you measure for motivation, you should emphasize the positive aspects of the students' performances and provide challenges and means for improvement. One of the reasons for testing sports skills may be program accountability, but as a teacher, you should never allow this to be the only reason for testing.

▬▬▬ ARE YOU ABLE TO DO THE FOLLOWING?

- Describe accuracy-based, repetitive-performance, total body movement, and distance performance tests.

- State how sports skills tests may be used in physical education.

- Describe responsibilities after the measurement of sports skills.

Individual and Dual Sports

Archery

■ AAHPER Archery Test
(AAHPER 1967)

Test Objectives. To measure archery skill.
Age Level. Twelve through eighteen.
Equipment. Standard 48-inch target faces, bows ranging from 15 to 40 pounds in pull, matched arrows (eight to ten per person) 24 to 28 inches in length, and archery accessories (arm guards and finger tabs).
Validity. Face validity.
Reliability. No reliability estimate is provided, but the test manual states that no test item in the battery has a reliability less than .70.
Administration and Directions. No more than four archers should shoot at one target. Two ends of six arrows (total of twelve) are shot at distances of 10, 20, and 30 yards for boys and 10 and 20 yards for girls. All archers begin at the 10-yard distance and move to the 20-yard line when the two ends have been completed. This process is repeated for each line. However, individuals who do not score at least 10 points at one distance may not advance to the next distance. Each archer is given four practice shots at each distance.
Scoring. Standard target scoring is used, with the point values 9, 7, 5, 3, and 1 for the respective circles from the center outward. Arrows falling outside the outer circle or missing the target are scored 0. Arrows passing completely through or rebounding off the target are awarded 7 points.

Badminton

■ French Short-Serve Test
(Scott et al. 1941)

Test Objective. To measure the ability to serve accurately with a low and short placement (degree of serving skill should be developed before the test is administered).
Age Level. Junior high through college-age.
Equipment. Badminton racket, shuttles, rope to stretch above net, and floor marking tape.
Validity. When tournament rankings were used as a criterion, a coefficient of .66 was reported.
Reliability. For college women, coefficients of .51 to .89 were reported.
Administration and Directions. A rope is stretched 20 inches directly above and parallel to the net. A series of 2-inch lines in the form of arcs are placed at distances of 22, 30, 38, and 46 inches from the midpoint of the intersection of the center line and the short-service line of the right service court. Each measurement includes the width of the 2-inch lines. The test performer may stand anywhere in the right service area, diagonally opposite the target. Twenty legal serves (may be two groups of ten) are attempted at the target (see figure 18.1). To earn points, the serve must pass between the rope and net and land somewhere in the proper service court area for doubles play.
Scoring. The scorer stands in a position (center of left service court, facing the target) to determine if the shuttle passes between the rope and net and to determine the point value of each serve. A score is awarded to any legal serve that passes between the rope and net and lands in the proper service court for doubles play.

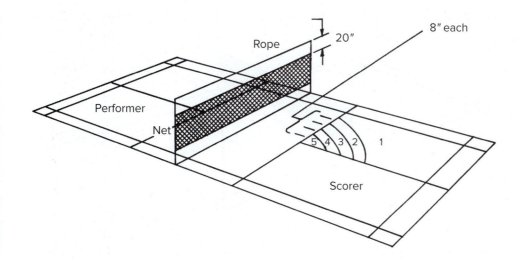

FIGURE 18.1 French short-serve test.

A score of 0 is recorded for any shuttle that does not pass between the rope and the net. The awarded points (5, 4, 3, 2, and 1) are based on the placement of the shuttle. Shuttles that land on a target line are awarded the point value of the higher area. If a shuttle hits the rope, the trial is not counted. Illegal serves may be repeated. The test score is the sum of the twenty serves.

Comment. The test performer should have the opportunity to practice this skill before attempting the test, because the reliability of the test is not as high for unskilled players. Drawing the target on the corner of a sheet or canvas for placement on the court will prevent the need of placing tape on the floor each time the test is administered.

■ Scott and French Long-Serve Test
(Scott and French 1959)

Test Objective. To measure the accuracy of the long serve.
Age Level. High school through college-age.
Equipment. Badminton racket, shuttles, and floor marking tape.
Validity. A coefficient of .54 was found by correlating the scores of college women with the subjective rating of judges.
Reliability. The internal consistencies of reliability estimates for college women were .77 and .68.
Administration and Directions. With the use of additional standards, a rope is stretched across the court 14 feet from and parallel to the net at a height of 8 feet. Floor markings are identical to those described for the French short-serve test, except for their location. The intersection of the long service line and the left side boundary line for singles is used for placement of the

target (see figure 18.2). Standing anywhere in the service court diagonally across from the target, the performer attempts twenty legal serves over the net and rope to the target area.
Scoring. A score (5, 4, 3, 2, or 1) is awarded to any legal serve that passes over the net and rope and lands in the target area. Serves that hit the rope are taken over, and shuttles that land on a target line are awarded the point value of the higher target. Illegal serves may be repeated. The test score is the sum of the twenty serves.
Comments. Any serve that lands beyond the back line receives 0 points. Because most opponents play serves that would land close to the back line, the test administrator may choose to develop a point system that includes an area 2 to 3 inches beyond the back line.

■ Poole Forehand Clear Test
(Poole and Nelson 1970)

Test Objective. To measure ability to hit the forehand clear from the backcourt, high and deep into the opponent's court.
Age Level. High school through college-age.
Equipment. Badminton rackets, shuttles, and floor marking tape.
Validity. When tournament play was used as a criterion measure, a coefficient of .70 was found.
Reliability. With the test-retest method, a coefficient of .90 was found.
Administration and Directions. The scoring zones are marked as shown in figure 18.3. A 15" × 15" square is drawn 11 feet from the net astride the center line (0 in figure 18.3).

FIGURE 18.2 Scott and French long-serve test.

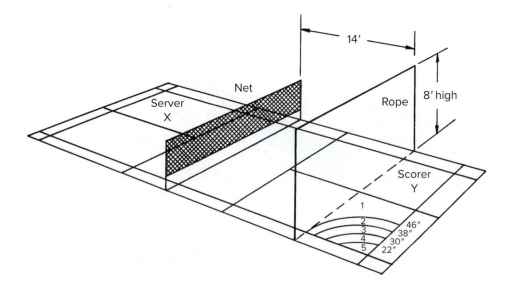

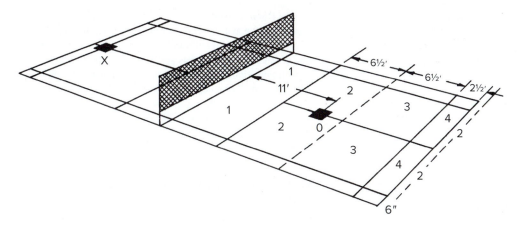

FIGURE 18.3 Poole forehand clear test.

Another square of equal size is drawn on the other side of the court at the intersection of the doubles long-service line and the center line (X in figure 18.3). If right-handed, the test performer stands with the right foot on the X square (left-handed, left foot) and a player stands at point 0 with a racket extended overhead. The performer places a shuttle, with the feather end down, on the forehand side of the racket, tosses the shuttle into the air, and hits it with an overhead forehand clear over the player's extended racket. The player calls out, "Low," if the shuttle fails to pass over the racket.

Scoring. The point value of the zone in which the shuttle lands is recorded, and the best ten of twelve shots are totaled for the test score. Shuttles landing on a target line are given the higher point value, and one point is deducted for any shuttle that fails to clear the extended racket of the player. The maximum score is 40.

Comments. The test performer should practice the tossing of the shuttle. The test also can be used to measure the backhand clear: The right-handed performer stands with the left foot in the X square, places the shuttle on the forehand side of the racket, tosses it into the air, and executes a backhand clear deep into the opponent's court.

Golf

Outdoor golf tests are preferable to indoor golf tests, and many such tests are available. In addition, it would not be difficult for you to devise accuracy tests for various clubs. Because of time and space limitations, however, it is sometimes necessary to administer indoor tests.

■ Clevett's Putting Test
(Clevett 1931)

Test Objective. To measure general golf putting ability.
Age Level. Junior high through college-age.
Equipment. Putters, golf balls, and smooth carpet, 20 feet long and 27 inches wide (marked as shown in figure 18.4).
Validity and Reliability. Not reported.
Administration and Directions. The carpet is placed on a level, smooth surface. It is divided into three equal 9-inch sections running the full length of the putting surface. Beginning 8 feet from the starting point, 48 scoring areas, each 9 inches square, are marked off. The square 10, or the imaginary hole, is located 15 feet from the starting line. Ten putts are attempted.

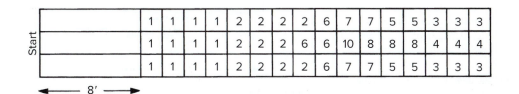

Start		1	1	1	1	2	2	2	2	6	7	7	5	5	3	3	3
		1	1	1	1	2	2	2	6	6	10	8	8	8	4	4	4
		1	1	1	1	2	2	2	2	6	7	7	5	5	3	3	3

← 8' →

FIGURE 18.4 Clevett's putting test.

Scoring. Each putt receives a numerical score based on the square on which the ball stops. The final score is the total points for the ten putts. Balls that stop on a line are given the higher point value. The test performer should be advised to putt too long rather than too short.

Comments. Cutting a hole in the 10 square makes the test more realistic. Also, with additional carpet, the distances can be varied.

■ The Green Golf Test
(Green, East, and Hensley 1987)

Test Objective. To measure the golf skills of putting, chipping, pitch shot, and approach shot.

Age Level. Originally designed for college students but may be used for individuals younger than college-age.

Equipment. Golf balls, golf clubs, flagsticks, measuring tape, and putting green.

Validity. A coefficient of .77 was found using a criterion measure of the score from two 18-hole rounds of golf.

Reliability. Coefficients ranged from .65 to .93 for each of the four test items.

Long Putt

Administration and Directions. Six golf balls are proportionally spaced around the cup on a circle with a 25-foot radius. The test performer starts at any one of the six positions, putts the ball as close to the hole as possible, and proceeds in a clockwise manner to the next ball. The balls are scored and removed from the green after each putt; one putt is permitted from each position.

Scoring. The score is the sum of the measured distance (to the nearest inch) from the cup for the six putts.

Chip Shot for 35 Feet

Administration and Directions. A flagstick is placed 10 feet from the edge of a flat green. At a distance of 35 feet from the flagstick, and using any iron, the test performer chips six balls toward the flagstick. The test performer is permitted to change clubs during the test period.

Scoring. The score is the sum of the measured distance (to the nearest foot) from the flagstick for the chip shots.

Pitch Shot from 40 Yards

Administration and Directions. From a distance of 40 yards and using either a 7-, 8-, or 9-iron, a pitching wedge, or a sand wedge, the test performer pitches six golf balls toward the flagstick.

Scoring. The score is the sum of the measured distance (to the nearest foot) from the flagstick for the six pitch shots.

Middle Distance Shot

Administration and Directions. Using any iron, the test performer hits four golf balls down a flat, open fairway toward a line of flags placed as targets across the fairway. The target flags are positioned 140 yards from the teeing area for males and 110 yards for females. The test performer is permitted to change clubs during the test period.

Scoring. The score is the sum of the measured perpendicular distance (to the nearest yard) from the line of flags for the four shots.

■ Indoor Golf Skill Test for Junior High School Boys (Grades 7–9)
(Shick and Berg 1983)

Test Objective. To measure golf skill with the 5-iron.

Equipment. Two 5-iron clubs (one right-handed and one left-handed), plastic golf balls, an orange cone, floor tape, tape measure, driving mat, and floor mat.

Validity. A coefficient of .84 was found using a criterion measure of the best of three scores on a par-3, nine-hole golf course.

Reliability. Coefficients of .97 and .91 were found for single test and test-retest administrations, respectively.

Administration and Directions. A target is placed on the floor of the testing area (see figure 18.5). Identifying the scoring areas with different colors will facilitate the scoring process. A mat is placed at the front edge of the target, and a driving

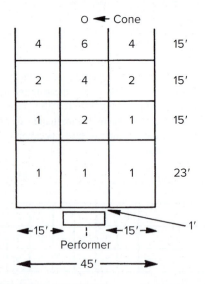

FIGURE 18.5 Indoor golf skill test.

mat is placed on the mat one foot from the target line. The test performer stands on the mat and hits the plastic ball as far as possible off the driving mat with a 5-iron, aiming for the orange cone. After two practice trials, twenty test trials are completed.

Scoring. Each trial score is the landing point of the ball on the target. Balls landing beyond the target but in line with the 4, 6, 4 target areas are given the point value of the closest target area. A topped ball that rolls through the scoring area is given one point. A ball landing on a target line is given the value of the highest adjacent target area. The test score is the sum of the twenty trial scores.

Handball

■ Tyson Handball Test
(Tyson 1970)

Test Objective. To measure essential handball skills.
Age Level. Originally designed for college males but may be administered to males and females in high school through college.
Equipment. Handballs, gloves, and stopwatch.
Validity. A coefficient of .92 was found for the three-item battery. Coefficients of .87, .84, and .76 were found for the 30-second volley, front-wall kill with the dominant hand, and back-wall kill with the dominant hand, respectively.
Reliability. Coefficients of .82, .82, and .81 were found for the items in their order of previous presentation.

30-Second Volley
Administration and Directions. Standing behind the short line holding a handball, the test performer puts the ball into play with a toss to the front wall and then volleys the ball against the front wall as many times as possible within the 30-second time period. Each return must be hit from behind the short line. Returns do not count when the short line is violated or the ball has bounced more than once. If the performer loses control of the ball, the test administrator quickly tosses him or her another ball. Either hand may be used.
Scoring. The item score is the total number of legal hits made in 30 seconds.

Front-Wall Kill with Dominant Hand
Administration and Directions. If right-handed, the test performer assumes a position in the doubles service box against the left sidewall, or if left-handed, the right sidewall. The test administrator stands in the middle of the service zone and begins the trial by tossing the ball against the front wall so that it rebounds to the right of the right-handed performer or to the left of the left-handed performer. As soon as the test administrator releases the ball, the performer is free to move, being sure to cross behind the

test administrator to get into a better position for hitting the ball. Five trials to place the ball in the target area on the front wall and floor are attempted (see figure 18.6).
Scoring. The item score is the total number of points accumulated on the five trials, with 25 points being the maximum.

Back-Wall Kill with Dominant Hand
Administration and Directions. The initial position of the test performer is the same as that for the front-wall kill item. The test administrator, however, is now positioned in the center of the court, 6 feet behind the short line. The test administrator tosses the ball to the front wall so that it rebounds and bounces 8 to 12 feet behind the short line and approximately 10 feet from the right sidewall for a right-handed performer, or 10 feet from the left sidewall for a left-handed person. For best results, the toss should be aimed for a spot between 15 and 18 feet high on the front wall. (A bad toss does not have to be played.) As the toss is made, the test performer may leave the starting position and move into a position that allows him or her to hit the ball with his or her dominant hand as the ball rebounds off the back wall. Five trials to place the ball in the target area on the front wall and floor are attempted (see figure 18.7).
Scoring. The item score is the points accumulated on the five trials, with 25 being the maximum.
Comments. The test administrator should practice the different tosses before administering the test items. Test performers should be aware that they do not have to return bad tosses.

Racquetball

■ Racquetball Skills Test
(Hensley, East, and Stillwell 1979)

Test Objective. To measure basic racquetball skills.
Age Level. High school through college-age.
Equipment. Rackets, four new racquetballs, colored floor marking tape, and stopwatch.
Validity. With instructor ratings as the criterion, concurrent coefficients of .79 and .86 were found for the short wall volley and the long wall volley, respectively.
Reliability. Test-retest coefficients ranging from .76 to .86 for the short wall volley and the long wall volley for college men and women were found.

Short Wall Volley Test
Administration and Directions. The test consists of two 30-second trials, preceded by a 30-second practice period. Holding two racquetballs, the test performer stands behind the short service line, drops a ball, and volleys it against the front wall for 30 seconds. All strokes must be made from behind the

FIGURE 18.6 Tyson front-wall kill with dominant hand test.

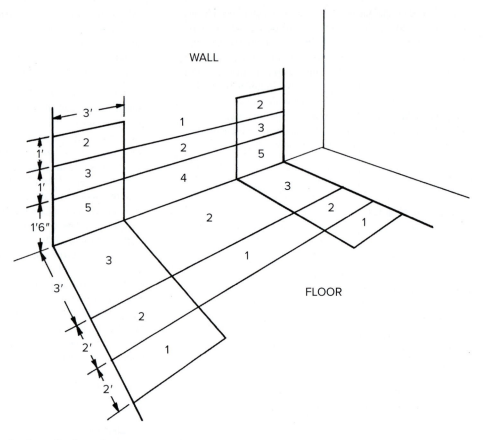

short line. The ball may be hit in the air or after bouncing one or more times, and any stroke may be used to keep the ball in play. If the ball does not return past the short line or if the performer misses it, the ball may be retrieved or a new ball may be put into play. The test administrator should be standing near the back wall with two additional racquetballs in the event they are needed. Each time a new volley is started, the ball must be put into play by being bounced behind the short line. The stopwatch is started when the performer drops the ball to begin the volley.

Scoring. The item score is the sum of the legal hits against the front wall for the two trials.

Long Wall Volley Test

Administration and Directions. The testing procedures for this item are the same as for the short wall volley test item, except the ball must be volleyed from behind a restraining line drawn 12 feet behind the short line. Two extra balls are placed in the crease of the back wall because the test administrator should not be in the court during this test.

Scoring. The scoring is the same as for the short wall test.

Tennis

■ Hewitt's Revision of the Dyer Backboard Tennis Test
(Hewitt 1965)

Test Objectives. To classify beginning and advanced tennis players by measuring rallying ability.

Age Level. High school through college-age.

Equipment. A smooth wall 20 feet high and 20 feet wide, tennis racket, at least one dozen new tennis balls, a basket, tape measure, stopwatch, and floor and wall marking tape.

Validity. Coefficients ranging from .68 to .73 for beginner classes and from .84 to .89 for advanced classes were found.

Reliability. With the test-retest method, coefficients of .82 and .93 were found for beginner and advanced classes, respectively.

Administration and Directions. A line 1 inch wide, 20 feet long, and at a height of 3 feet is placed on the wall. A restraining line 1 inch wide, 20 feet long, and 20 feet from the wall is placed on the floor. A basket of tennis balls is placed at one end of the restraining line. The test performer, standing

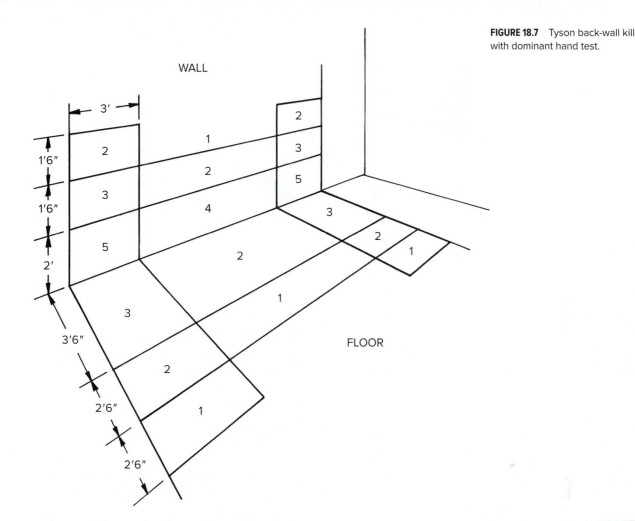

FIGURE 18.7 Tyson back-wall kill with dominant hand test.

behind the restraining line with two tennis balls and a racket, serves the ball against the wall. (Any type of serve is allowed.) The stopwatch is started when the ball hits above the net line on the wall. On the rebound, the performer begins a rally from behind the restraining line and attempts to hit the ball continuously against the wall so it hits on or above the line on the wall. If the ball gets away, the test performer may take another ball from the basket. Each time a new rally is started, the ball must be served. Three trials of 30 seconds each are given.

Scoring. One point is scored each time the ball hits on or above the wall line. If the test performer steps on or in front of the restraining line to hit a ball, the rally is continued but no point is scored. No points are scored on the serve. The test score is the average of the three trials.

■ **Hewitt Tennis Achievement Test**
(Hewitt 1966)

Test Objective. To measure the basic tennis skills of the service, forehand drive, and backhand drive.
Age Level. High school through college-age.
Equipment. Tennis rackets, thirty-six new tennis balls, court markings, poles or standards, and rope longer than width of court.
Validity. Coefficients ranging from .52 to .93 were found.
Reliability. Coefficients ranging from .75 to .94 were found.

Service Placement
Administration and Directions. A rope is placed 7 feet above the ground and parallel to the net. The right service court is marked as shown in figure 18.8. A 10-minute warm-up is

FIGURE 18.8 Hewitt service
placement and speed of
service tests.

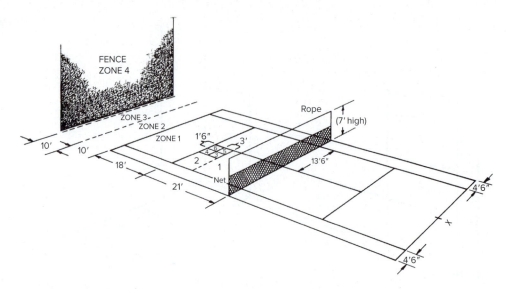

permitted. The test performer stands to the right of the center line behind the baseline and serves ten balls into the marked service court. The ball must be served between the rope and the net. Net balls and balls that hit the rope are repeated.

Scoring. The point value for the zone in which each ball lands is totaled for the ten trials. Balls going over the rope are given a score of 0.

Speed of Service

Administration and Directions. The court is divided into zones as shown in figure 18.8. The distance the ball bounces after it hits in the service area gives an indication of the speed the ball travels. The score is based on the zone in which the second bounce lands. Ten trials are given. This test can be conducted at the same time as the service placement test.

Scoring. The point value for the zone in which each ball bounces is totaled for the ten trials.

Forehand and Backhand Drive Tests

Administration and Directions. A rope is placed 7 feet above the ground and parallel to the net. The court is marked as shown in figure 18.9. The test performer stands at the center of the baseline. The test administrator is positioned, with a basket of balls, on the other side of the net at the intersection of the center line and the service line. The administrator hits five practice balls to the performer, who uses either the forehand or the backhand to return the balls. The balls hit by the administrator should land just beyond the service line. Twenty test trials are then administered the same way, the performer choosing which ten balls to hit with the forehand and which ten balls to hit with the backhand. If the drive goes between the net and the rope, points are scored, as indicated in figure 18.9. All net balls and those that hit the rope are repeated.

FIGURE 18.9 Hewitt forehand and backhand drive tests.

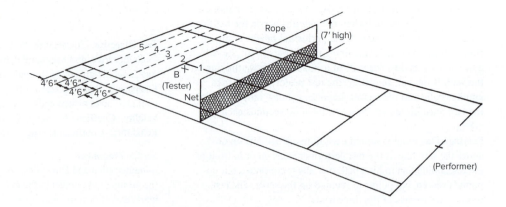

Scoring. The point value for the zone in which each ball lands is totaled for the twenty trials. Balls hit over the rope and landing in the scoring zones score one-half the regular value.

■ AAHPERD Tennis Skills Test
(AAHPERD 1989)

Test Objective. To measure the basic tennis skills of ground strokes (forehand and backhand) and the serve. A volley test is included as an optional item.

Age Level. Grade 9 through college.

Equipment. Tennis court, racket, twenty tennis balls, and tape or chalk.

Validity. Concurrent coefficients ranging from .65 to .91 were found for the three items.

Reliability. Coefficients ranging from .69 to .95 were found for the three items.

Ground Strokes

Administration and Directions. Lines are placed on the court as shown in figure 18.10. A 5-minute warm-up period is permitted. The test performer takes a position behind and at the center mark of the baseline. The test administrator is stationed with ten to twelve balls on the other side of the net, within approximately 3 feet of the net and along the center line. Using an overhand motion, the tester tosses twelve consecutive balls to the forehand and twelve consecutive balls to the backhand. The first two tosses to each side serve as practice. The ball should be tossed so that it lands beyond the service line on the desired side and within 6 feet of the test performer. The test performer may elect *not* to swing at no more than two tosses for each side. This decision must be made before attempting to stroke the ball. The performer should attempt to hit the ball over the net into the designated scoring area within the singles court.

Scoring. Each of the ten trials for both the forehand and backhand is scored for placement and power. The placement score is determined according to the target area in which the ball lands. The power score is determined according to the power zone in which the ball lands on the second bounce. Balls that are wide, long, or hit into the net receive a score of 0 for both placement and power. The total score is the sum of the placement and power scores for each of the scored trials.

Serve

Administration and Directions. Lines are placed on the court as shown in figure 18.11. A 5-minute warm-up is permitted. Two individuals may be tested simultaneously. A box of balls is placed several feet behind the center mark on the end of the court where the server is positioned. One server takes a position to serve to the

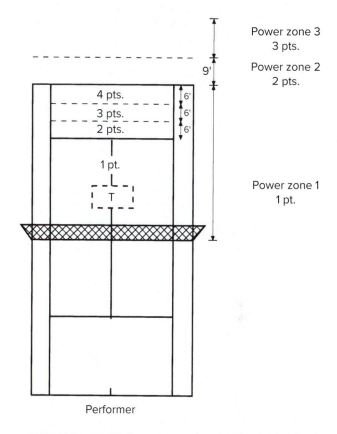

FIGURE 18.10 AAHPERD tennis ground stroke test—forehand and backhand drive.

deuce court; the other takes a position to serve to the ad court. Two practice serves are permitted. Four trials are attempted into the designated scoring area; each trial may consist of a second service attempt if the first serve is a fault. The first four trials are directed to the outside half of the designated service court, and the next four are directed toward the inside half. After each server has attempted eight scored trials to the designated service court, the servers trade positions and repeat the procedure (no additional warm-up serves are permitted). Let serves are reserved.

Scoring. Each of the sixteen service attempts is scored for both placement and power. The placement score is determined according to the target area within the service court in which the ball lands. Serves landing in the designated half of the court are awarded 2 points, serves landing elsewhere in the service court are awarded 1 point, and those landing outside of the service court are awarded 0 points. The power score is determined according to the power zone in which the ball lands on the second bounce. Serve balls that land outside the appropriate service court are scored 0 for power.

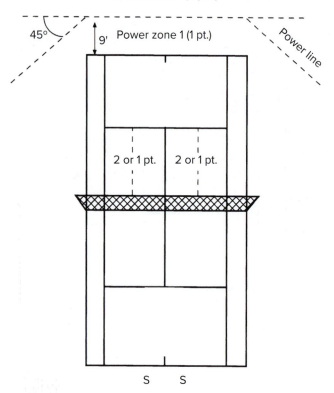

FIGURE 18.11 AAHPERD tennis serve test.

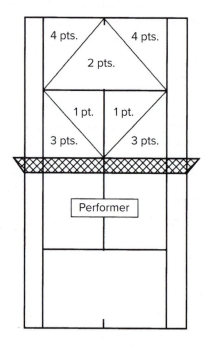

FIGURE 18.12 AAHPERD tennis volley test.

Volley (Optional Item)

Administration and Directions. Lines are placed on the court as shown in figure 18.12. A 5-minute warm-up period is permitted. The test performer takes a position 3 to 6 feet from the net in the center of the court. The tester is stationed with a box of tennis balls near the center of the baseline. Using a forehand stroke, the tester hits ten balls to the forehand side and ten balls to the backhand side of the performer. The first four balls to each side are for practice. The tester should hit the balls at a consistent, moderate speed, approximately 1 to 3 feet above the net (waist high to head high of the test performer). The performer may elect not to attempt to volley a total of two trials for each side. This decision must be made before attempting to return the ball. If the tester judges that an improper setup ball was responsible for a low score on a performer's attempt, the trial may be repeated.

Scoring. Each of the six designated trials for both the forehand and backhand is scored for placement. The placement score is determined according to the target area in which the ball

lands. Balls that are wide, long, or hit into the net receive a score of 0. The score is the sum of the scores for all twelve trials.

Team Sports

Basketball

■ **AAHPERD Basketball Skills Test**
(Hopkins, Shick, and Plack 1984)

Age Level. Ten through college-age.
Equipment. Basketballs, stopwatch, floor and wall marking tape, tape measure, and six cones.
Validity. Coefficients ranging from .37 to .91 for all ages and both sexes on individual test items and from .65 to .95 for test battery as a whole were found.
Reliability. With the test-retest method, coefficients ranging from .82 to .97 for all ages and both sexes on individual test items were found.

Speed Spot Shooting

Test Objectives. To measure skill in rapidly shooting from different positions and, to a limited extent, to measure agility and ball handling.

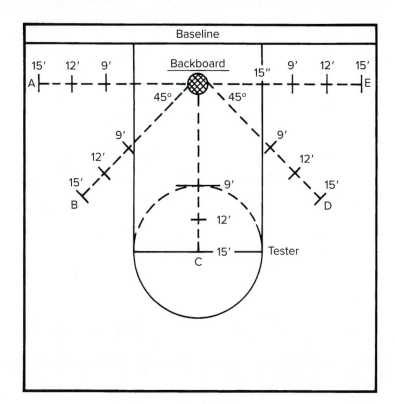

FIGURE 18.13 AAHPERD speed spot shooting test.

Administration and Directions. Floor markers are placed on the floor as shown in figure 18.13. The distances for spots B, C, and D are measured from the center of the backboard; those for spots A and E are measured from the center of the basket. For fifth and sixth graders, the shooting distance is 9 feet; for grades 7, 8, and 9, it is 12 feet; and for grades 10 through college, it is 15 feet. Holding a basketball, the test performer begins the test with one foot behind any one of the five markers. On the signal "Ready, Go," the performer shoots, retrieves the ball, and dribbles to and shoots from another spot. At least one shot must be taken from each of the five markers. A maximum of four layup shots may be attempted, but no two may be taken in succession. Three 60-second trials are administered, with the first being a practice trial.

Scoring. Two points are given for each shot made, and 1 point is given for each unsuccessful shot that hits the rim (from above). The item score is the sum of the scores for the two trials. The test administrator must record the number of layups attempted, the point value of the attempted shots, and if the performer attempts at least one shot from each of the five markers. No score is given for shots that follow ball-handling infractions such as traveling and double dribbling or for more than four layup attempts. If the performer fails to shoot from each of the five markers, the trial is repeated.

Passing

Test Objectives. To measure skill in chest passing and recovering the ball while moving.

Administration and Directions. A restraining line is drawn on the floor 8 feet from the wall and parallel to it, and squares are marked on the wall (as shown in figure 18.14). Only chest passes are permitted. Holding a basketball, the test performer stands behind the restraining line facing target A. On the signal "Ready, Go," the ball is passed to target A. The rebound is recovered while moving to be in line with target B. The ball is then passed to target B. This sequence is continued until target F is reached, where two passes are attempted. The performer then moves back toward target A. Three 30-second trials are taken, with the first being a practice trial.

Scoring. Each pass that lands in the target or on the target line earns 2 points. Passes hitting the wall between the targets earn 1 point. The item score is the sum of the two trials. No points are given if the performer's foot is on or over the line; if a second pass is made at targets B, C, D, or E; or if a pass other than a chest pass is used.

FIGURE 18.14 AAHPERD basketball passing test.

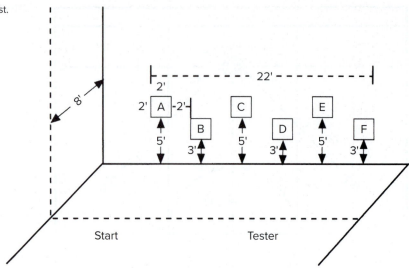

Start   Tester

Control Dribble

Test Objectives. To measure ball-handling skill (dribbling) while moving.

Administration and Directions. Six cones are placed as shown in figure 18.15. On the signal "Ready, Go," the test performer begins dribbling with the nondominant hand from the nondominant side of cone A to the nondominant side of cone B. For the remainder of the course, the performer may use the dominant hand, and hands may be changed when appropriate. Three timed trials are given, with the first being a practice trial.

Scoring. The trial score is recorded to the nearest one-tenth of a second. The item score is the sum of the two trials. The trial is retaken for ball-handling infractions, failure of the performer or ball to remain outside any cone, and failure to continue the test from the spot where loss of ball control occurred.

Defensive Movement

Test Objective. To measure basic defensive-movement skills.

Administration and Directions. The court is marked as shown in figure 18.16. The boundaries are the free throw line, the end line behind the basket, and the free throw lane lines. The middle lines on the free throw lane serve as markers for C and F. Marks A, B, D, and E must be made with floor tape. The test performer stands at point A, facing away from the basket. On the signal "Ready, Go," the performer slides to the left, without crossing the feet, to point B and touches the floor outside the lane with the left hand. Then, executing a drop step (changing defensive direction by moving the trailing foot in a sliding motion in the direction of the next move), the performer slides to point C and touches the floor outside the lane with the right hand, performs a drop step, and slides to point D. The test is

continued (as shown in figure 18.16) until both feet cross the finish line. Three timed trials are given, with the first being a practice trial.

Scoring. The trial score is recorded to the nearest one-tenth of a second. The item score is the sum of the two trials. The trial is repeated for crossing the feet during the slide or turn, running, failing to touch the hand to the floor outside the lane, and performing the drop step before the hand touches the floor.

Field Hockey

■ Chapman Ball Control Test
(Chapman 1982)

Test Objective. To measure the ability to combine quickness in stick movement with control of the force necessary to move the ball.

Age Level. High school through college-age.

Equipment. Hockey sticks, hockey balls, floor marking tape, and stopwatch.

Validity. Logical validity and, with a criterion measure of ratings of stickwork skills, concurrent validity coefficients of .63 and .64 were found.

Reliability. With single test administration, a coefficient of .89 was found.

Administration and Directions. A pattern is placed on the gymnasium floor (as shown in figure 18.17). The lines that divide the outer circle into three equal segments are ⅛ inch wide. (It is recommended that these segments be of a color

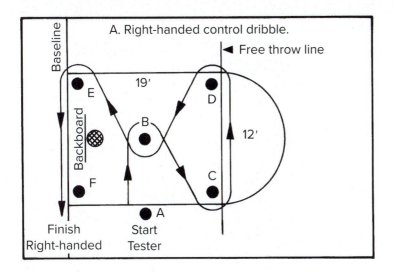

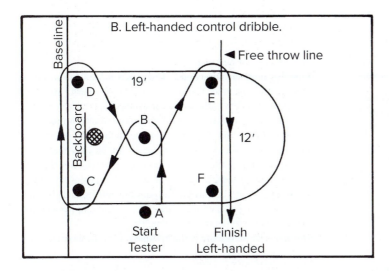

FIGURE 18.15   AAHPERD control dribble test.

that contrasts with both the hockey ball and the gymnasium floor.) The ball is placed just outside the outer circle, and on the signal "Ready, Go," the performer taps the ball through or into and out of the center circle with a hockey stick. Each time the ball is tapped through or out of the center circle, it must roll outside the outer circle. Three 15-second trials are given. It is recommended the test administrator be assisted by a separate timekeeper who can start and stop the trials at the end of 15 seconds. An alternative administration method is to tape-record the "go" and "stop" commands at 15-second intervals, so the test administrator does not have to observe the stopwatch and the test performer simultaneously. Test administration should include a demonstration of the scoring techniques, a brief practice period, and rest between all test trials. Providing two practice targets enables two performers to practice while a third is tested.

Scoring. One point is scored each time the ball is tapped (not pushed) through or into the center circle. A point also may be scored when the ball is tapped from the center circle to outside of the outer circle and if it passes through a different segment from the one it entered. Points can be scored only when the ball is tapped outside of the outer circle or from within the center circle. No points are scored when the ball is tapped while inside the outer circle or when it is tapped with the rounded side of the stick.

FIGURE 18.16   AAHPERD defensive-movement test.

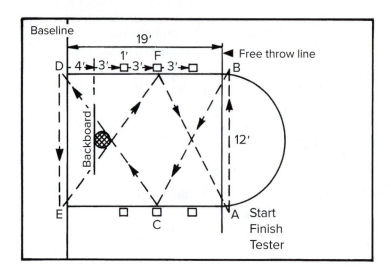

Football

■ AAHPER Football Skills Test
(AAHPER 1965)

The AAHPER football skills test includes ten items that measure different football skills. Eight items, which measure skills also used in touch or flag football, are described in this chapter. No validity or reliability coefficients were reported.

Test Objectives. Each item measures a single basic skill.

Age Level. Ten through eighteen; although designed for males, some of the items may be administered to females.

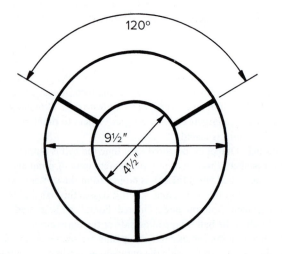

FIGURE 18.17   Chapman ball control test.

Equipment. Footballs, 8' × 11' canvas, five chairs, kicking tee, and tape measure.

Forward Pass for Distance

Administration and Directions. The pass is made from within a 6-foot restraining area. The contact point of the performer's first pass is marked with a metal or wooden stake. Three trials are given, and the stake is moved if the second or third pass is longer. If the test item is administered on a football field, the restraining area should be placed parallel to the yard lines. (Administration of the test on a football field facilitates the measurement process because it is necessary to measure only the distance from the stake to the yard line immediately behind the stake.) The distance is measured to the last foot passed and at a right angle to the throwing line.

Scoring. The item score is the best pass of the three trials.

50-Yard Dash with Football

Administration and Directions. While carrying the football, the performer runs as fast as possible for 50 yards. The starter shouts, "Go," and simultaneously swings a white cloth down. The timer starts the watch with the downward arm movement of the starter and stops it when the runner crosses the finish line. Two trials are administered, with a rest period in between.

Scoring. The score is the better time of the two trials to the nearest one-tenth second.

Forward Pass for Accuracy

Administration and Directions. A target is painted on an 8' × 11' canvas. The diameter is 2 feet for the center circle, 4 feet for the middle circle, and 6 feet for the outer circle. The bottom of the circle is 3 feet from the ground. The target is hung from the crossbar of the goalposts and tied to the goalposts so that it remains taut. A restraining line is placed 15 yards from the target. The test performer runs two or three small steps along the line in the direction of the dominant arm, turns, and throws the football at the target. The pass should be made with good speed. Ten trials are administered.

Scoring. The target values are three (inner circle), two (middle circle), and one (outer circle). Passes striking a line are given the higher value. The score is the point total for the ten trials.

Punt for Distance

Administration and Directions. The performer takes one or two steps within a 6-foot kicking zone and punts the ball as far as possible. The test is administered the same as the forward pass for distance.

Scoring. Same as forward pass for distance.

Ball-Changing Zigzag Run

Administration and Directions. Five chairs are placed in a line, with the first chair 10 yards from the starting line and the others 10 yards apart. The test performer stands behind the starting line, holding a football under the right arm. On the signal "Go," the performer runs to the right of the first chair, shifts the ball to the left arm, and runs to the left of the second chair. The run is continued in and out of the chairs (as shown in figure 18.18). The ball must be under the outside arm, and the inside arm must be extended (as in stiff-arming an opponent) each time a chair is passed. The runner is not permitted to touch the chairs. Two trials are administered.

Scoring. Each trial is timed to the nearest one-tenth of a second from the signal "Go" until the performer passes back over the starting line. The score is the better time of the two trials.

Catching the Forward Pass

Administration and Directions. Two end marks, located 9 feet to the right and left of the center, are placed on the scrimmage line. Turning points are placed 30 feet in front of the end marks (see figure 18.19). The test performer stands on the right end mark and faces straight ahead. On the signal "Go," the performer runs toward the turning point directly in front of him or her, makes a 90° right turn behind the turning point, and while continuing to run parallel to the scrimmage line prepares to receive a pass at the passing point. On the "Go" signal, the center snaps the ball to the passer. The passer then takes one backward step to be in position to pass the ball directly over the passing point, slightly above the head of the receiver. The same pattern is run from the left end mark, except the performer makes a left turn at the turning point. Ten trials are run around each turning point. Poorly thrown passes are repeated.

Scoring. One point is awarded for each pass caught. The score is the sum of the passes caught from both sides.

Pullout

Administration and Directions. The test performer assumes a 3-point stance midway between two goalposts. On the signal "Go," the performer turns to the right and runs parallel to the imaginary scrimmage line, makes a 90° turn around the goalpost, and races straight ahead across a finish line 30 feet away. Two time trials are administered, with the time starting on "Go" and stopping when the performer crosses the finish line.

Scoring. The score is the better time of the two trials, measured to the nearest one-tenth second.

Kickoff

Administration and Directions. A kicking tee is placed in the center of a yard line on the field. The football is placed on the tee so that it tilts slightly back toward the kicker. Taking as long

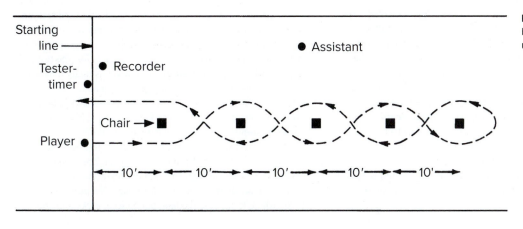

FIGURE 18.18 AAHPER ball-changing zigzag run test.

Starting line →
Tester-timer ●   ● Recorder   ● Assistant
Player ●
Chair → ■
←10'→ ←10'→ ←10'→ ←10'→ ←10'→

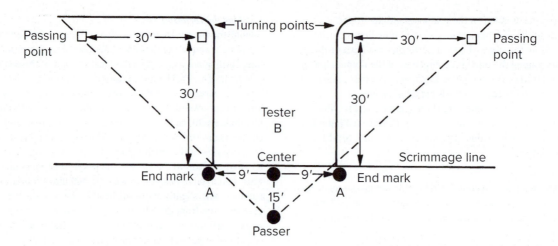

FIGURE 18.19 AAHPERD catching forward pass test.

a run as needed, the kicker attempts to kick the ball as far as possible. Three trials are administered.

Scoring. The score is determined in the same way as the forward pass and punt for distance tests.

Soccer

■ McDonald Soccer Test
(McDonald 1951)

Test Objective. To measure general soccer ability.
Age Level. High school through college-age.
Equipment. Three soccer balls and stopwatch.
Validity. A coefficient of .85 was found by correlating the test scores of fifty-three college soccer players from three varsity levels, with the subjective ratings of three coaches.
Reliability. Not reported.
Administration and Directions. A restraining line is marked 9 feet from a wall, 30 feet wide and 11½ feet high. A soccer ball is placed on the restraining line. On the signal "Go," the test performer kicks the ball against the wall as many times as possible in 30 seconds. Two soccer balls are placed 9 feet behind the restraining line in the center of the test area. In the event of a wild kick, the test performer may retrieve the original ball or use one of the two additional balls. The hands may be used to retrieve a ball. Any type of kick may be used, but all kicks must be kicked from the ground behind the restraining line. Four trials are administered.
Scoring. The number of legal kicks in each 30-second period is recorded. The test score is the highest total of any three trials.

■ Mitchell Soccer Test
(Mitchell 1963)

Test Objective. To measure general soccer ability.
Age Level. Originally designed for fifth- and sixth-grade boys but may be administered to girls and boys in grades 5 through 9.
Equipment. Soccer balls and stopwatch.
Validity. With fifth- and sixth-grade boys serving as subjects, coefficients of .84 and .76 were found.
Reliability. With the test-retest method, correlations of .93 and .89 were found.
Administration and Directions. A target 4 feet high from the base of the wall and 8 feet long is marked on a smooth, unobstructed wall. The total width of the kicking area on the wall should be at least 14 feet (3 feet on each side of the target). A restraining line is marked 6 feet from the wall, and a boundary line is marked 12 feet from the wall (6 feet behind the restraining line). A soccer ball is placed on the restraining line, and individuals who serve as ball retrievers are positioned around and behind the boundary line. On the signal "Go," the test performer kicks the ball against the wall target as many times as possible in 20 seconds. Any kicking technique may be used with either foot or leg, but the hands or arms may not be used. If the test performer miskicks or fails to block a kick, the retrievers stop the ball and place it back on the boundary line at the point where it rolled out. The performer retrieves the ball from that point (may not use hands), repositions it, and continues the test. The trial is given again for any action by the retrievers that causes an unnecessary time delay. The performer may go anywhere to retrieve the ball, but all legal kicks must be

made from behind the restraining line. Three consecutive trials are administered.

Scoring. The test score is the total number of legal kicks made in the three trials. Use of the hands or arms at any time results in a 1-point reduction.

Softball

■ AAHPERD Softball Skills Test
(AAHPERD 1991)

Test Objective. To measure the basic softball skills of batting, fielding, throwing, and baserunning.

Age Level. Grade 5 through college.

Equipment. Standard softball field, adjustable batting tee, bats, eight marking cones, lime, softballs, measuring tape, gloves, and stopwatch.

Validity. Concurrent coefficients ranging from .54 to .94 were found for the four items. The majority of the coefficients were above .70.

Reliability. Coefficients ranging from .69 to .97 were found for the four items.

Batting

Administration and Directions. Lines are placed on the field as shown in figure 18.20. Eight cones are used to mark the boundary areas. Two cones are placed at points 120 feet (grades 5–8) or 150 feet (grades 9–college) on diagonal lines drawn from home plate through points on the baseline 20 feet on each side of second base. Cones are also placed on these diagonal lines at points 180 feet (grades 5–8) or 240 feet (grades 9–college)

from home plate. Four other cones are placed at the respective distances on the outside fair-ball boundary lines. The cones and the chalked lines separate the field into three power zones and three placement areas. The batter assumes a batting stance at home plate and attempts to hit the ball off the batting tee as far as possible within the center field boundaries. The batting tee should be adjusted to approximately waist height and placed in the center of the strike zone, opposite the front hip of the batter. Two practice trials and six test trials are permitted.

Scoring. The batter's score is the sum of the values of the zones in which the ball stops rolling for the six test trials. A missed swing, balls hit into foul territory, and balls stopping within the infield score no points.

Fielding Ground Balls

Administration and Directions. A 20' × 60' area is marked off as shown in figure 18.21. The player being tested stands in ready position behind the restraining line (point A). A thrower (point B) stands behind the throwing line and throws two practice and six test balls to each player. Each throw must strike the ground before the 30-foot line and must stay within the sideline boundaries of the marked area. The throws should be sidearm, with sufficient velocity to carry an untouched ball a prescribed, age-adjusted distance beyond the end line: 65 feet (grades 5–6), 75 feet (grades 7–8), 90 feet (grades 9–12), and 100 feet (college). The prescribed distance beyond the end line is marked by a cone or similar object (point C). Of the six test trials, two balls (in varying order) should be thrown directly to the player, two to the right (between the player and the sideline), and two to the left side of the player. The player attempts

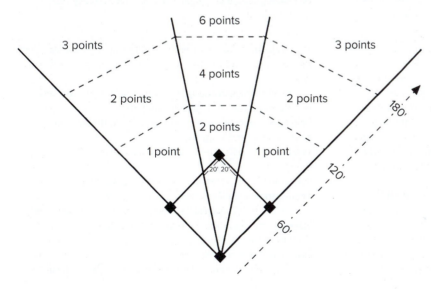

FIGURE 18.20 AAHPERD batting test for grades 5 through 8. Distances for grades 9 through college are 60 feet, 150 feet, and 240 feet.

FIGURE 18.21 AAPHERD fielding ground balls test.

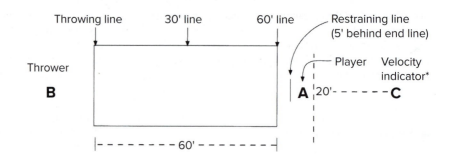

*Velocity indicator distances (past the 60' end line) are as follows:

65'–grades 5–6
75'–grades 7–8
90'–grades 9–12
100'–college

to field the ball cleanly and toss it back to the thrower. On each trial, the player starts behind the 5-foot restraining line but must move forward of the 60-foot line toward the approaching ground ball to obtain maximum points. Any throw not made as specified should be repeated. The thrower should periodically check the velocity of the throw by occasionally instructing the player to let the ball go by untouched. Throws should be within 5 to 8 feet of the velocity marker.

Scoring. Each ball cleanly fielded in front of the 60-foot line counts 4 points. A ball that is stopped, but bobbled, counts 2 points. Only the player's glove and the ball must be in front of the line. Balls fielded behind the 60-foot line receive one-half the points normally earned—that is, 2 points for cleanly fielded balls and 1 point for bobbled balls. Balls that get past the player score no points. The score is the sum of the six trials.

Overhand Throwing for Distance and Accuracy

Administration and Directions. A throwing line is marked off in feet down the center of a large open field area, with a restraining line marked at one end perpendicular to the throwing line as shown in figure 18.22. A back boundary line is marked off 10 feet behind the restraining line. After the proper warm-up, the player stands between the restraining line and the back boundary line, takes one or more steps, and throws as straight as possible down the throwing line. If a player steps over the restraining line before releasing the ball, the throw must be repeated. Two throws are attempted.

Scoring. The better of two throws is measured and recorded as the score. The score equals the throwing distance, measured at a point on the throwing line straight across from (perpendicular to) the spot where the ball landed, minus the number of feet the ball landed off target. Both error scores and distance scores are measured to the nearest foot. Figure 18.22 includes an example of scoring.

Baserunning

Administration and Directions. After a proper warm-up, the player takes a leadoff position in front of home plate with the back foot in contact with the front edge of the base. On the signal "Ready, Go," the player runs around first base to second base. The player is to run through second base, rather than slide into it or stop on it. Two trials, with a rest between, are attempted.

Scoring. Trials are timed to the nearest tenth of a second from the signal "Go" to the touching of second base. The score is the better of the two trials.

■ **Fielding Grounders—Agility, Speed, and Accuracy Test**
(Fringer 1961)

Test Objective. To measure the ability to field grounders, to run to a base, and to throw quickly and accurately to a target.

Age Level. Originally designed for high school girls but also may be administered to high school boys.

Equipment. Softball glove, several quality softballs, floor marking tape, and stopwatch.

Validity. For high school girls, a coefficient of .70 was found.

Reliability. A test-retest coefficient of .72 was found.

Administration and Directions. A floor space of 30' × 40' with a 20' × 20' wall is needed. A target is placed on the wall, and markings are placed on the floor (as indicated in figure 18.23). Dimensions for the base markings are the same as for a softball base. The test performer stands with a foot on the start mark with a softball and glove. On the signal "Go," the performer

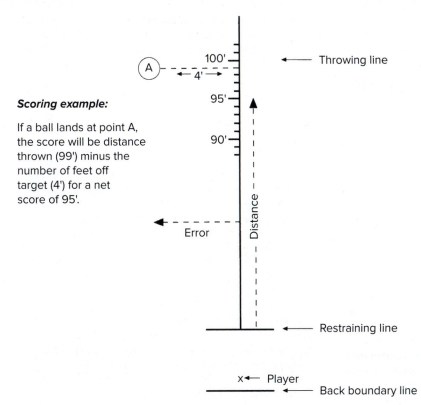

FIGURE 18.22 AAHPERD overhand throwing for distance and accuracy test.

100'

A

← 4' →

Throwing line

Scoring example:

If a ball lands at point A, the score will be distance thrown (99') minus the number of feet off target (4') for a net score of 95'.

95'

90'

Distance

Error

Restraining line

x← Player

Back boundary line

runs to either base, throws the ball at the target, rushes to field the ball, and quickly runs to the other base to make another throw at the target. The bases must be alternated for the throws, and a foot must be in contact with the base on each throw. Two

45-second trials are administered, with rest permitted between trials.

Scoring. Balls hitting on or in the target circle count. The test score is the sum of the target hits made in two trials.

FIGURE 18.23 Fringer fielding grounders—agility, speed, and accuracy test.

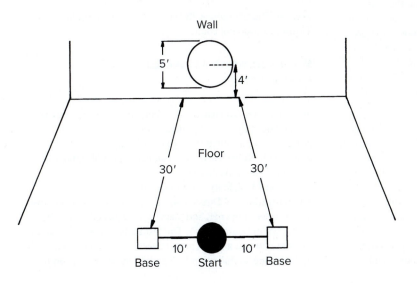

Wall

5'

4'

Floor

30' 30'

Base Start Base

10' 10'

■ Shick Softball Test Battery
(Shick 1970)

Test Objective. To measure defensive softball skills.
Age Level. Originally designed for college women, but the test may be administered to males and females in high school through college.
Equipment. Several softballs and stopwatch.
Validity. For two general softball classes of fifty-nine college females, a coefficient of .75 was found by correlating expert ratings with the test battery.
Reliability. A coefficient of .88 was found for the test battery.

Repeated Throws
Administration and Directions. A line is drawn on the wall 10 feet from and parallel to the floor. A restraining line is drawn on the floor 23 feet from and parallel to the wall. The test performer stands behind the restraining line, holding a softball. On the signal "Go," the student throws the ball against the wall above the 10-foot line (overhand or sidearm throw is required) and attempts to catch the rebound in the air or field it from the floor. This action is repeated as many times as possible in 30 seconds. If fielding errors occur, the performer must recover the ball. However, there is no penalty other than the loss of time. The test consists of four 30-second trials, and the performer is given one practice throw before each trial.
Scoring. A ball thrown with the test performer's stepping on or across the restraining line or a ball hitting below the wall line does not count. The test score is the sum of the legal hits for the four trials.

Fielding Test
Administration and Directions. A line is drawn on the wall 4 feet from and parallel to the floor. A line also is drawn on the floor 15 feet from and parallel to the wall. The procedures are the same as those for the repeated throws test, except any type throw may be used, and all throws are to hit below the wall line.
Scoring. The scoring method is identical to the repeated throws scoring, except no ball that hits above the wall line is counted.

Target Test
Administration and Directions. The dimensions of the wall and floor targets are shown in figure 18.24. The wall target is 66 inches square, and its center is 36 inches from the floor. The target value areas are color coded as follows: 5 = red, 4 = medium blue, 3 = bright yellow, 2 = pale aqua, and 1 = black. A restraining line is marked on the floor 40 feet from and parallel to the wall. The test performer stands behind the restraining line for all throws. Two trials of ten throws each are administered. Two practice throws are permitted.
Scoring. Each throw is given two scores: one for the wall hit and one for the hit of the first bounce on the floor. Any hit

outside the scoring areas of the wall and floor is recorded as 0. The test score is the sum of the two trials. The highest possible test score is 200 (50 per trial for the wall, and 50 per trial for the floor).

Volleyball

■ Brady Volley Test
(Brady 1945)

Test Objective. To measure general volleyball playing ability.
Age Level. College, but the test may also be appropriate for some high school groups. If administered to younger groups, it is suggested that the height of the target be lowered.
Equipment. Volleyballs, wall tape, tape measure, and stopwatch.
Validity. For college males, a coefficient of .86 was found for the correlation between test scores and the subjective ratings of four qualified judges.
Reliability. A test-retest coefficient of .93 was found.
Administration and Directions. A target consisting of a horizontal line 5 feet in length and 11½ feet from the floor is marked on a smooth wall. Vertical lines at the end of the horizontal line are extended toward the ceiling. The wall should be at least 15 feet high and 15 feet wide. No restraining line is used. The test performer begins the test by throwing the volleyball against the wall. On the rebound, and on all subsequent rebounds, the performer attempts to volley the ball within the boundaries of the target (balls landing on the target lines are counted). One 60-second trial is administered. Catching or losing control of the ball requires that the test performer rethrow the ball against the wall to continue the test.
Scoring. The test score is the number of legal hits in 60 seconds. Thrown balls do not count.

■ Brumbach Volleyball Service Test
(Brumbach 1967)

Test Objective. To measure the ability to serve the volleyball low and deep into the opponent's court.
Age Level. Junior high through college-age.
Equipment. Volleyballs, volleyball net, rope, tall standards, floor tape, and tape measure.
Validity and Reliability. Not reported.
Administration and Directions. A rope is placed 4 feet above and parallel to the net, and markings are placed on the floor (as shown in figure 18.25). The test performer stands behind the rear end line and attempts to serve the ball between the net and the rope so that it lands deep into the backcourt on the

FIGURE 18.24 Shick target test.

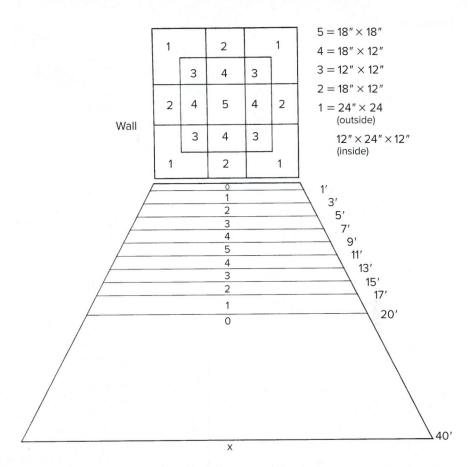

opposite side. Two sets of six trials are administered (total of twelve).

Scoring. A serve that passes between the net and the rope receives the higher value for the target area in which it lands. Serves going over the rope receive the lesser value for the target areas. Serves that hit the rope are repeated. Foot faults, serves hitting the net, and serves landing outside the target area are given a 0 score. The test score is the sum of the ten best trials.

■ **North Carolina State University Volleyball Skills Test Battery**
(Bartlett et al. 1991)

Test Objective. To measure and evaluate the three basic volleyball skills: serve, forearm pass, and set.

Age Level. High school through college-age.

Equipment. Volleyballs, volleyball net, floor tape, two 8-foot poles or standards, two 10-foot poles or standards, 30-foot rope, and 11-foot rope.

Validity. Because the ability to serve a ball, receive a ball with the forearm pass, and set a ball are basic volleyball skills, test items have content validity.

Reliability. Coefficients of .65 (serve), .73 (forearm pass), and .88 (set test) were found using the intraclass correlation technique.

Serve

Administration and Directions. The court is marked as shown in figure 18.26. Standing in the area indicated, the test performer serves ten times. The serves may be overhand or underhand.

Scoring. The point system was developed with the W formation of reception in mind. Therefore, test performers are rewarded according to their ability to direct the serve to the areas of the court with the least coverage. Serves landing on a line score the higher point value; serves contacting the net or antennae or landing out of bounds receive no score. The test item score is the total points, with a maximum score of 40 points.

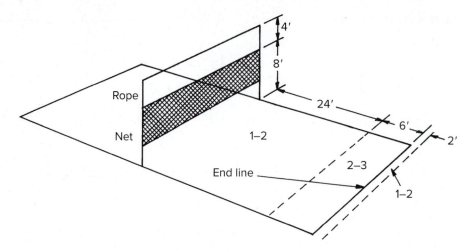

FIGURE 18.25 Brumbach volleyball service test.

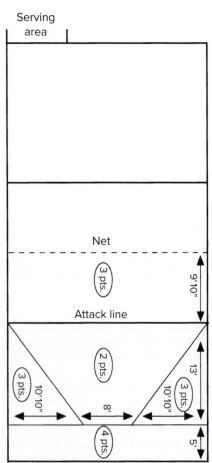

FIGURE 18.26 NCSU volleyball serve test.

Forearm Pass

Administration and Directions. The court is marked as shown in figure 18.27, and a rope is placed on the side of the test performer at a distance of 9'10" (attack line) from the net and 8 feet high. The test performer is given five trials from the right back position (10 feet from right sideline and 5 feet from the baseline) and five trials from the left back position (10 feet from left sideline and 5 feet from the baseline). The test performer receives 10 two-handed overhead-tossed balls from the tosser, who is positioned across the net at the attack line (14'9" from either sideline). The performer passes the tossed ball over the rope and into the target areas, which have values of 1 to 5 points.

Scoring. The point system rewards the test performer's ability to pass the ball high enough for a setter to easily get under the ball. In most offensive systems, the setter moves to the right center of the court. Therefore, the higher point values are given in the areas of the court where the setter can deliver a good set. Bad tosses may be repeated. Balls landing on a line score the higher point value. Zero points are awarded for (a)illegal contact by the test performer, (b)any ball that contacts or goes under the rope, and (c)any ball that contacts or goes under the net. The item score is the total points for the ten trials, with a maximum score of 50.

Set

Administration and Directions. The court is marked as indicated in figure 18.28, and a rope is placed perpendicular to the net at a distance of 11 feet from the left sideline and at a height of 10 feet. The rope should extend beyond the attack line. The test performer stands in the marked area (6 feet from right sideline and 5 feet from the net) and receives ten underhand-tossed balls from the tosser, who is positioned at midcourt (14'9" from either sideline and 10 feet in front of the baseline).

The performer sets the tossed ball over the rope and into the target area, which has values of 1 to 5 points.

Scoring. The point system rewards the test performer's ability to make a high, outside set, which is the most common form of setting for beginners. Therefore, the higher points are given for balls that have the appropriate height and proximity to the sideline and the fewer points are given to balls closest to the net and/or the center of the court. Bad tosses may be repeated. Balls landing on a line score the higher point value. Zero points are awarded for (a) illegal or double contacts, (b) any ball that contacts or goes under the rope, and (c) any ball that contacts or goes over the net. The item score is the total points for the ten trials, with a maximum score of 50.

■ **Russell-Lange Volleyball Test**
(Russell and Lange 1940)

Test Objective. To measure volleyball playing ability.
Age Level. Grades 7–12 girls, but the serve item is also appropriate for grades 7–12 boys.
Equipment. Volleyballs, floor and wall tape, and stopwatch.
Validity. Coefficients of .51 (volley) and .79 (serve) were found when test scores were correlated with ability ratings of seven judges.
Reliability. Coefficients of .89 (volley) and .84 (serve) were found.

Volley
Administration and Directions. A line, 2 inches wide and 12 feet long, is placed with the lower edge 7½ feet above the floor.

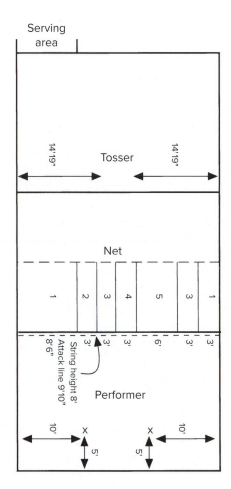

FIGURE 18.27 NCSU volleyball forearm pass test.

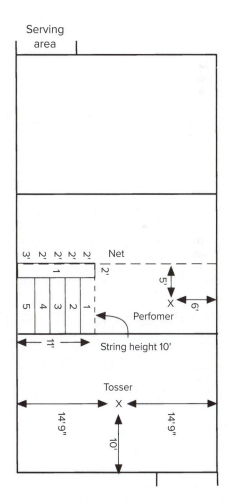

FIGURE 18.28 NCSU volleyball set test.

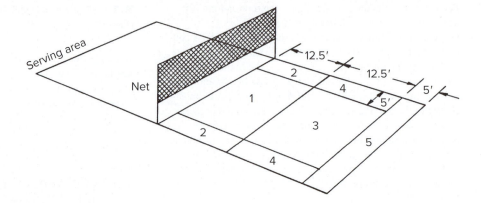

FIGURE 18.29 Russell-Lange volleyball serve test.

A restraining line is placed 6 feet from and parallel to the wall. Standing behind the restraining line, the test performer uses an underhand movement to toss the ball against the wall and then repeatedly volleys the ball on or above the wall line while remaining behind the restraining line. Three 30-second trials are administered.

Scoring. The legal volleys hit from behind the restraining line that hit on or above the wall line are recorded. The test score is the best score of three trials.

Serve

Administration and Directions. The court is marked as shown in figure 18.29. Standing behind the rear boundary line, the test performer attempts to serve the ball deep into the opponent's court. Two trials of ten legal serves are administered. Serves touching the net but landing in the opponent's court are repeated.

Scoring. Serves landing on a target line are given the highest target value, and serves in which foot faults occur

are given a 0 score. The test score is the total points of the best trial.

Review Problems

1. Administer one individual and one team sports skills test to several of your classmates. Ask them to provide constructive criticism of your test administration.

2. Additional sports skills tests are presented at the conclusion of this chapter. Review at least one test for each sport, noting the validity and practicability of the test.

3. Ask several physical education instructors of activity classes what sports skills tests they use and why they chose them.

Chapter Review Questions

1. Why would you measure sports skills in the school environment?

2. What is the difference between the use of a sports skills test and a rubric?

3. What influences your responsibilities after the measurement of sports skills? Why might you use local norms after testing rather than national norms?

Sources of Additional Sports Skills Tests

Archery

Hyde, E.I. 1937. An achievement scale in archery. *Research Quarterly* 8: 109–116.

Shifflett, B., and Schuman, B. 1982. A criterion-referenced test for archery. *Research Quarterly for Exercise and Sport* 53: 330–335.

Zabik, R.M., and Jackson, A.S. 1969. Reliability of archery achievement. *Research Quarterly* 40: 254-255.

Badminton

French, E., and Statler, E. 1949. Study of skill tests in badminton for college women. *Research Quarterly* 20: 257-272.

Lockhart, A., and McPherson, F.A. 1949. The development of a test of badminton playing ability. *Research Quarterly* 20: 402-405.

Miller, F.A. 1951. A badminton wall volley test. *Research Quarterly* 22: 208-213.

Thorpe, J., and West, C. 1969. A test of game sense in badminton. *Perceptual and Motor Skills* 28: 159-169.

Basketball

Boyd, C.A., MacCachren, J.R., and Waglow, L.F. 1955. Predictive ability of a selected basketball test. *Research Quarterly* 26: 364-365.

Broer, M.R. 1958. Reliability of certain skill tests for junior high school girls. *Research Quarterly* 29: 139-145.

Elbel, E.R., and Allen, F.C. 1941. Evaluating team and individual performance in basketball. *Research Quarterly* 5: 538-555.

Knox, R.D. 1947. Basketball ability tests. *Scholastic Coach* 17(3): 45.

Stroup, F. 1955. Game results as a criterion for validating a basketball skill test. *Research Quarterly* 26: 353-357.

Bowling

Martin, J., and Keogh, J. 1964. Bowling norms for college students in elective physical education classes. *Research Quarterly* 35: 325-327.

Olson, J., and Liba, M.R. 1967. A device for evaluating spot bowling ability. *Research Quarterly* 38: 193-201.

Philips, M., and Summers, D. 1950. Bowling norms and learning curves for college women. *Research Quarterly* 21: 377-385.

Field Hockey

Henry, M. E. 1970. Henry-Friedel field hockey test. In Collins, D. R., and Hodges, P. B. 2001. *A comprehensive guide to sports skills tests and measurement.* 2nd ed. Lanham, Maryland: The Scarecrow Press, Inc.

Football

Jacobson, T. V. 1960. Jacobson-Borleske touch football test. In Collins, D. R., and Hodges, P. B. 2001. *A comprehensive guide to sports skills tests and measurment.* 2nd ed. Lanham, Maryland: The Scarecrow Press, Inc.

Golf

Benson, D. W. 1960. Benson golf test. In Collins, D. R., and Hodges, P. B. 2001. *A comprehensive guide to sports skills tests and measurement.* 2nd ed. Lanham, Maryland: The Scarecrow Press, Inc.

Cotten, D.J., Thomas, J.R., and Plaster, T. 1972. A plastic ball test for golf iron skill. In Johnson, B.L., and Nelson, J.K. 1986. *Practical measurements for evaluation in physical education.* 4th ed. Edina, Minn.: Burgess Publishing.

Nelson, J. R. 1967. Nelson golf pitching test. In Collins, D. R., and Hodges, P. B. 2001. *A comprehensive guide to sports skills test and measurement.* 2nd ed. Lanham, Maryland: The Scarecrow Press, Inc.

Rowlands, D.J. 1974. Rowlands golf skills test battery. In Barrow, H.M., and McGee, R. 1989. *A practical approach to measurement in physical education.* 4th ed. Philadelphia: Lea & Febiger.

West, C., and Thorpe, J. 1968. Construction and validation of an eight-iron approach test. *Research Quarterly* 49: 1115-1120.

Handball

Cornish, C. 1949. A study of measurement of ability in handball. *Research Quarterly* 20: 215-222.

Montoye, H.J., and Brotzman, J. 1951. An investigation of the validity of using the results of a doubles tournament as a measurement of handball ability. *Research Quarterly* 22: 214-218.

Pennington, G.G., et al. 1967. A measure of handball ability. *Research Quarterly* 38: 247-253.

Sattler, T. 1973. Sattler handball battery. In Collins, D. R., and Hodges, P. B. 2001. *A comprehensive guide to sports skills tests and measurement.* 2nd ed. Lanham, Maryland: The Scarecrow Press, Inc.

Racquetball

Karpman, M., and Isaacs, I. 1979. An improved racquetball skills test. *Research Quarterly* 50: 526-527.

Soccer

Heath, M.L., and Rogers, E.G. 1932. A study in the use of knowledge and skill tests in soccer. *Research Quarterly* 3: 33-53.

Johnson, J.R. 1963. Johnson soccer test. In Collins, D. R., and Hodges, P. B. 2001. *A comprehensive guide to sports skills tests and measurement.* 2nd ed. Lanham, Maryland: The Scarecrow Press, Inc.

Mor, D., and Christian, V. 1979. Mor-Christian general soccer ability skill test battery. In Collins, D. R., and Hodges, P. B. 2001. *A comprehensive guide to sports skills tests and measurement.* 2nd ed. Lanham, Maryland: The Scarecrow Press, Inc.

Smith, G. 1947. Smith kick-up test. In Barrow, H.M., and McGee, R. 1979. *A practical approach to measurement in physical education.* 3d ed. Philadelphia: Lea & Febiger.

Vanderhoff, M. 1932. Soccer skills test. *Journal of Health and Physical Education* 3: 42.

Warner, G.F. 1950. Warner soccer test. *Newsletter of the National Soccer Coaches Association of America* 6: 13–22.

Yeagley, J. 1972. Yeagley soccer battery. In Collins, D. R., and Hodges, P. B. 2001. *A comprehensive guide to sports skills tests and measurement.* 2nd ed. Lanham, Maryland: The Scarecrow Press, Inc.

Softball

Broer, M.R. 1958. Reliability of certain skill tests for junior high school girls. *Research Quarterly* 29: 139–143.

Fox, M.G., and Young, O.G. 1954. A test of softball batting ability. *Research Quarterly* 25: 26–27.

Fringer, F. M. 1961. Fringer softball test. In Collins, D. R., and Hodges, P. B. 2001. *A comprehensive guide to sports skills tests and measurement.* 2nd ed. Lanham, Maryland: The Scarecrow Press, Inc.

O'Donnell, D.J. 1950. O'Donnell softball skill test. In Collins, D.R., and Hodges, P.B. 2001. *A comprehensive guide to sports skills tests and measurement.* 2nd ed. Lanham, Maryland: The Scarecrow Press, Inc.

Swimming

Fox, M.G. 1957. Swimming power test. *Research Quarterly* 28: 233–237.

Hewitt, J.E. 1948. Swimming achievement scales for college men. *Research Quarterly* 19: 282–289.

_____. 1949. Achievement scale scores for high school swimming. *Research Quarterly* 20: 170–179.

Resentswieg, J. 1968. A revision of the power swimming test. *Research Quarterly* 39: 818–819.

Wilson, C.T. 1934. Coordination tests in swimming. *Research Quarterly* 5: 81–88.

Tennis

Avery, C., Richardson, P., and Jackson, A. 1979. A practical tennis serve test: Measurement of skill under simulated game conditions. *Research Quarterly* 50: 554–564.

Broer, M.R., and Miller, D.M. 1950. Broer-Miller achievement test. In Collins, D. R., and Hodges, P. B. 2001. *A comprehensive guide to sports skills tests and measurement.* Lanham, Maryland: The Scarecrow Press, Inc.

DiGennaro, J. 1969. Construction of forehand drive, backhand drive, and service tennis tests. *Research Quarterly* 40: 496–501.

Edwards, J. 1965. Wisconsin wall test for serve. In Barrow, H.M., and McGee, R. 1989. *A practical approach to measurement in physical education.* 4th ed. Philadelphia: Lea & Febiger.

Fox, K. 1953. A study of the validity of the Dyer backboard test and the Miller forehand-backhand test for beginning tennis players. *Research Quarterly* 24: 1–7.

Hewitt, J.E. 1968. Classification tests in tennis. *Research Quarterly* 39: 552–555.

Johnson, J. 1957. Tennis serve of advanced women players. *Research Quarterly* 28: 123–131.

Kemp, J., and Vincent, M.F. 1968. Kemp-Vincent rally test of tennis skill. *Research Quarterly* 39: 1000–1004.

Purcell, K. 1981. A tennis forehand-backhand drive skill test which measures ball control and stroke firmness. *Research Quarterly* 52: 238–245.

Timmer, K. L. 1965. Timmer tennis skill test. In Collins, D. R., and Hodges, P. B. 2001. *A comprehensive guide to sports skills tests and measurement.* 2nd ed. Lanham, Maryland: The Scarecrow Press, Inc.

Volleyball

Brady, G.F. 1945. Preliminary investigation of volleyball playing ability. *Research Quarterly* 16: 14–17.

Clifton, M.A. 1962. Single hit volley test for women's volleyball. In Collins, D. R., and Hodges, P. B. 2001. *A comprehensive guide to sports skills tests and measurement.* 2nd ed. Lanham, Maryland: The Scarecrow Press, Inc.

Crogen, C. 1943. A simple volleyball classification test for high school girls. *The Physical Educator* 4: 34–37.

Cunningham, P., and Garrison, J. 1968. High wall volley test for women's volleyball. *Research Quarterly* 39: 486–490.

Kautz, E. M. 1976. Kautz volleyball passing test. In Collins, D. R., and Hodges, P. B. 2001. *A comprehensive guide to sports skills tests and measurement.* 2nd ed. Lanham, Maryland: The Scarecrow Press, Inc.

Kronquist, R.A., and Brumbach, W.B. 1968. A modification of the Brady volleyball test for high school boys. *Research Quarterly* 39: 116–120.

Liba, M.R., and Stauff, M.R. 1963. A test for the volleyball pass. *Research Quarterly* 34: 56–63.

Mohr, D.R., and Haverstick, M.V. 1955. Repeated volleys test for women's volleyball. *Research Quarterly* 26: 179–184.

Russell, N., and Lange, E. 1940. Achievement tests in volleyball for junior high school girls. *Research Quarterly* 11: 33–41.

Values of the Correlation Coefficient *(r)*

df	.05	.01	df	.05	.01
1	.9969	.9999	17	.456	.575
2	.950	.990	18	.444	.561
3	.878	.959	19	.433	.549
4	.811	.917	20	.423	.537
5	.754	.875	25	.381	.487
6	.707	.834	30	.349	.449
7	.666	.798	35	.325	.418
8	.632	.765	40	.304	.393
9	.602	.735	45	.288	.372
10	.576	.708	50	.273	.354
11	.553	.684	60	.250	.325
12	.532	.661	70	.232	.302
13	.514	.641	80	.217	.283
14	.497	.623	90	.205	.267
15	.482	.606	100	.195	.254
16	.468	.590			

Adapted from Table 13 of E. S. Pearson and H. O. Hartley, eds., *Biometrika tables for statisticians*, vol. 1 (3rd ed.), Cambridge University Press for the Biometrika Trustees, 1966.

B Critical Values of t (Two-Tailed Test)

df	.05	.01	df	.05	.01
1	12.706	63.657	18	2.101	2.878
2	4.303	9.925	19	2.093	2.861
3	3.182	5.841	20	2.086	2.845
4	2.776	4.604	21	2.080	2.831
5	2.571	4.032	22	2.074	2.819
6	2.447	3.707	23	2.069	2.807
7	2.365	3.499	24	2.064	2.797
8	2.306	3.355	25	2.060	2.787
9	2.262	3.250	26	2.056	2.779
10	2.228	3.169	27	2.052	2.771
11	2.201	3.106	28	2.048	2.763
12	2.179	3.055	29	2.045	2.756
13	2.160	3.012	30	2.042	2.750
14	2.145	2.977	40	2.021	2.704
15	2.131	2.947	60	2.000	2.660
16	2.120	2.921	120	1.980	2.617
17	2.110	2.898	∞	1.960	2.576

Adapted from Table 12 of E. S. Pearson and H. O. Hartley, eds., *Biometrika tables for statisticians*, vol. 1 (3rd ed.), Cambridge University Press for the Biometrika Trustees, 1966.

C

F-Distribution

p = .05 Values					F-Distribution				
Degrees of Freedom for the Denominator, v_2	Degrees of Freedom for the Numerator, v_1								
	1	2	3	4	5	6	7	8	9
1	161.4	199.5	215.7	224.6	230.2	234.0	236.8	238.9	240.5
2	18.51	19.00	19.16	19.25	19.30	19.33	19.35	19.37	19.38
3	10.13	9.55	9.28	9.12	9.01	8.94	8.89	8.85	8.81
4	7.71	6.94	6.59	6.39	6.26	6.16	6.09	6.04	6.00
5	6.61	5.79	5.41	5.19	5.05	4.95	4.88	4.82	4.77
6	5.99	5.14	4.76	4.53	4.39	4.28	4.21	4.15	4.10
7	5.59	4.74	4.35	4.12	3.97	3.87	3.79	3.73	3.68
8	5.32	4.46	4.07	3.84	3.69	3.58	3.50	3.44	3.39
9	5.12	4.26	3.86	3.63	3.48	3.37	3.29	3.23	3.18
10	4.96	4.10	3.71	3.48	3.33	3.22	3.14	3.07	3.02
11	4.84	3.98	3.59	3.36	3.20	3.09	3.01	2.95	2.90
12	4.75	3.89	3.49	3.26	3.11	3.00	2.91	2.85	2.80
13	4.67	3.81	3.41	3.18	3.03	2.92	2.83	2.77	2.71
14	4.60	3.74	3.34	3.11	2.96	2.85	2.76	2.70	2.65
15	4.54	3.68	3.29	3.06	2.90	2.79	2.71	2.64	2.59
16	4.49	3.63	3.24	3.01	2.85	2.74	2.66	2.59	2.54
17	4.45	3.59	3.20	2.96	2.81	2.70	2.61	2.55	2.49
18	4.41	3.55	3.16	2.93	2.77	2.66	2.58	2.51	2.46
19	4.38	3.52	3.13	2.90	2.74	2.63	2.54	2.48	2.42
20	4.35	3.49	3.10	2.87	2.71	2.60	2.51	2.45	2.39
21	4.32	3.47	3.07	2.84	2.68	2.57	2.49	2.42	2.37
22	4.30	3.44	3.05	2.82	2.66	2.55	2.46	2.40	2.34
23	4.28	3.42	3.03	2.80	2.64	2.53	2.44	2.37	2.32
24	4.26	3.40	3.01	2.78	2.62	2.51	2.42	2.36	2.30
30	4.17	3.32	2.92	2.69	2.53	2.42	2.33	2.27	2.21
40	4.08	3.23	2.84	2.61	2.45	2.34	2.25	2.18	2.12
60	4.00	3.15	2.76	2.53	2.37	2.25	2.17	2.10	2.04
120	3.92	3.07	2.68	2.45	2.29	2.17	2.09	2.02	1.96
∞	3.84	3.00	2.60	2.37	2.21	2.10	2.01	1.94	1.88

Adapted from Table 18 of E. S. Pearson and H. O. Hartley, eds., *Biometrika tables for statisticians*, vol. 1 (3rd ed.), Cambridge University Press for the Biometrika Trustees, 1966.

p = .05 Values	F-Distribution								
Degrees of Freedom for the Denominator, v_2	**Degrees of Freedom for the Numerator, v_1**								
	10	**12**	**15**	**20**	**30**	**40**	**60**	**120**	**∞**
1	241.9	243.9	245.9	248.0	250.1	251.1	252.2	253.3	254.3
2	19.40	19.41	19.43	19.45	19.46	19.47	19.48	19.49	19.50
3	8.79	8.74	8.70	8.66	8.62	8.59	8.57	8.55	8.53
4	5.96	5.91	5.86	5.80	5.75	5.72	5.69	5.66	5.63
5	4.74	4.68	4.62	4.56	4.50	4.46	4.43	4.40	4.36
6	4.06	4.00	3.94	3.87	3.81	3.77	3.74	3.70	3.67
7	3.64	3.57	3.51	3.44	3.38	3.34	3.30	3.27	3.23
8	3.35	3.28	3.22	3.15	3.08	3.04	3.01	2.97	2.93
9	3.14	3.07	3.01	2.94	2.86	2.83	2.79	2.75	2.71
10	2.98	2.91	2.85	2.77	2.70	2.66	2.62	2.58	2.54
11	2.85	2.79	2.72	2.65	2.57	2.53	2.49	2.45	2.40
12	2.75	2.69	2.62	2.54	2.47	2.43	2.38	2.34	2.30
13	2.67	2.60	2.53	2.46	2.38	2.34	2.30	2.25	2.21
14	2.60	2.53	2.46	2.39	2.31	2.27	2.22	2.18	2.13
15	2.54	2.48	2.40	2.33	2.25	2.20	2.16	2.11	2.07
16	2.49	2.42	2.35	2.28	2.19	2.15	2.11	2.06	2.01
17	2.45	2.38	2.31	2.23	2.15	2.10	2.06	2.01	1.96
18	2.41	2.34	2.27	2.19	2.11	2.06	2.02	1.97	1.92
19	2.38	2.31	2.23	2.16	2.07	2.03	1.98	1.93	1.88
20	2.35	2.28	2.20	2.12	2.04	1.99	1.95	1.90	1.84
21	2.32	2.25	2.18	2.10	2.01	1.96	1.92	1.87	1.81
22	2.30	2.23	2.15	2.07	1.98	1.94	1.89	1.84	1.78
23	2.27	2.20	2.13	2.05	1.96	1.91	1.86	1.81	1.76
24	2.25	2.18	2.11	2.03	1.94	1.89	1.84	1.79	1.73
30	2.16	2.09	2.01	1.93	1.84	1.79	1.74	1.68	1.62
40	2.08	2.00	1.92	1.84	1.74	1.69	1.64	1.58	1.51
60	1.99	1.92	1.84	1.75	1.65	1.59	1.53	1.47	1.39
120	1.91	1.83	1.75	1.66	1.55	1.50	1.43	1.35	1.25
∞	1.83	1.75	1.67	1.57	1.46	1.39	1.32	1.22	1.00

Degrees of Freedom for the Denominator, v_2	Degrees of Freedom for the Numerator, v_1								
	1	2	3	4	5	6	7	8	9
1	4,052	4,999.5	5,403	5,625	5,764	5,859	5,928	5,981	6,022
2	98.50	99.00	99.17	99.25	99.30	99.33	99.36	99.37	99.39
3	34.12	30.82	29.46	28.71	28.24	27.91	27.67	27.49	27.35
4	21.20	18.00	16.69	15.98	15.52	15.21	14.98	14.80	14.66
5	16.26	13.27	12.06	11.39	10.97	10.67	10.46	10.29	10.16
6	13.75	10.92	9.78	9.15	8.75	8.47	8.26	8.10	7.98
7	12.25	9.55	8.45	7.85	7.46	7.19	6.99	6.84	6.72
8	11.26	8.65	7.59	7.01	6.63	6.37	6.18	6.03	5.91
9	10.56	8.02	6.99	6.42	6.06	5.80	5.61	5.47	5.35
10	10.04	7.56	6.55	5.99	5.64	5.39	5.20	5.06	4.94
11	9.65	7.21	6.22	5.67	5.32	5.07	4.89	4.74	4.63
12	9.33	6.93	5.95	5.41	5.06	4.82	4.64	4.50	4.39
13	9.07	6.70	5.74	5.21	4.86	4.62	4.44	4.30	4.19
14	8.86	6.51	5.56	5.04	4.69	4.46	4.28	4.14	4.03
15	8.68	6.36	5.42	4.89	4.56	4.32	4.14	4.00	3.89
16	8.53	6.23	5.29	4.77	4.44	4.20	4.03	3.89	3.78
17	8.40	6.11	5.18	4.67	4.34	4.10	3.93	3.79	3.68
18	8.29	6.01	5.09	4.58	4.25	4.01	3.84	3.71	3.60
19	8.18	5.93	5.01	4.50	4.17	3.94	3.77	3.63	3.52
20	8.10	5.85	4.94	4.43	4.10	3.87	3.70	3.56	3.46
21	8.02	5.78	4.87	4.37	4.04	3.81	3.64	3.51	3.40
22	7.95	5.72	4.82	4.31	3.99	3.76	3.59	3.45	3.35
23	7.88	5.66	4.76	4.26	3.94	3.71	3.54	3.41	3.30
24	7.82	5.61	4.72	4.22	3.90	3.67	3.50	3.36	3.26
30	7.56	5.39	4.51	4.02	3.70	3.47	3.30	3.17	3.07
40	7.31	5.18	4.31	3.83	3.51	3.29	3.12	2.99	2.89
60	7.08	4.98	4.13	3.65	3.34	3.12	2.95	2.82	2.72
120	6.85	4.79	3.95	3.48	3.17	2.96	2.79	2.66	2.56
∞	6.63	4.61	3.78	3.32	3.02	2.80	2.64	2.51	2.41

F-Distribution

p = .01 Values	F-Distribution								
Degrees of Freedom for the Denominator, v_2	**Degrees of Freedom for the Numerator, v_1**								
	10	12	15	20	30	40	60	120	∞
1	6,056	6,106	6,157	6,209	6,261	6,287	6,313	6,339	6,366
2	99.40	99.42	99.43	99.45	99.47	99.47	99.48	99.49	99.50
3	27.23	27.05	26.87	26.69	26.50	26.41	26.32	26.22	26.13
4	14.55	14.37	14.20	14.02	13.84	13.75	13.65	13.56	13.46
5	10.05	9.89	9.72	9.55	9.38	9.29	9.20	9.11	9.02
6	7.87	7.72	7.56	7.40	7.23	7.14	7.06	6.97	6.88
7	6.62	6.47	6.31	6.16	5.99	5.91	5.82	5.74	5.65
8	5.81	5.67	5.52	5.36	5.20	5.12	5.03	4.95	4.86
9	5.26	5.11	4.96	4.81	4.65	4.57	4.48	4.40	4.31
10	4.85	4.71	4.56	4.41	4.25	4.17	4.08	4.00	3.91
11	4.54	4.40	4.25	4.10	3.94	3.86	3.78	3.69	3.60
12	4.30	4.16	4.01	3.86	3.70	3.62	3.54	3.45	3.36
13	4.10	3.96	3.82	3.66	3.51	3.43	3.34	3.25	3.17
14	3.94	3.80	3.66	3.51	3.35	3.27	3.18	3.09	3.00
15	3.80	3.67	3.52	3.37	3.21	3.13	3.05	2.96	2.87
16	3.69	3.55	3.41	3.26	3.10	3.02	2.93	2.84	2.75
17	3.59	3.46	3.31	3.16	3.00	2.92	2.83	2.75	2.65
18	3.51	3.37	3.23	3.08	2.92	2.84	2.75	2.66	2.57
19	3.43	3.30	3.15	3.00	2.84	2.76	2.67	2.58	2.49
20	3.37	3.23	3.09	2.94	2.78	2.69	2.61	2.52	2.42
21	3.31	3.17	3.03	2.88	2.72	2.64	2.55	2.46	2.36
22	3.26	3.12	2.98	2.83	2.67	2.58	2.50	2.40	2.31
23	3.21	3.07	2.93	2.78	2.62	2.54	2.45	2.35	2.26
24	3.17	3.03	2.89	2.74	2.58	2.49	2.40	2.31	2.21
30	2.98	2.84	2.70	2.55	2.39	2.30	2.21	2.11	2.01
40	2.80	2.66	2.52	2.37	2.20	2.11	2.02	1.92	1.80
60	2.63	2.50	2.35	2.20	2.03	1.94	1.84	1.73	1.60
120	2.47	2.34	2.19	2.03	1.86	1.76	1.66	1.53	1.38
∞	2.32	2.18	2.04	1.88	1.70	1.59	1.47	1.32	1.00

D

Values of the Studentized Range *(q)*

(p = .05) df for Denominator	Number of Groups (k)								
	2	3	4	5	6	7	8	9	10
1	18.0	27.0	32.8	37.1	40.4	43.1	45.4	47.4	49.1
2	6.09	8.3	9.8	10.9	11.7	12.4	13.0	13.5	14.0
3	4.50	5.91	6.82	7.50	8.04	8.48	8.85	9.18	9.46
4	3.93	5.04	5.76	6.29	6.71	7.05	7.35	7.60	7.83
5	3.64	4.60	5.22	5.67	6.03	6.33	6.58	6.80	6.99
6	3.46	4.34	4.90	5.31	5.63	5.89	6.12	6.32	6.49
7	3.34	4.16	4.68	5.06	5.36	5.61	5.82	6.00	6.16
8	3.26	4.04	4.53	4.89	5.17	5.40	5.60	5.77	5.92
9	3.20	3.95	4.42	4.76	5.02	5.24	5.43	5.60	5.74
10	3.15	3.88	4.33	4.65	4.91	5.12	5.30	5.46	5.60
11	3.11	3.82	4.26	4.57	4.82	5.03	5.20	5.35	5.49
12	3.08	3.77	4.20	4.51	4.75	4.95	5.12	5.27	5.40
13	3.06	3.73	4.15	4.45	4.69	4.88	5.05	5.19	5.32
14	3.03	3.70	4.11	4.41	4.64	4.83	4.99	5.13	5.25
15	3.01	3.67	4.08	4.37	4.60	4.78	4.94	5.08	5.20
16	3.00	3.65	4.05	4.33	4.56	4.74	4.90	5.03	5.15
17	2.98	3.63	4.02	4.30	4.52	4.71	4.86	4.99	5.11
18	2.97	3.61	4.00	4.29	4.49	4.67	4.82	4.96	5.07
19	2.96	3.59	3.98	4.25	4.47	4.65	4.79	4.92	5.04
20	2.95	3.58	3.96	4.23	4.45	4.62	4.77	4.90	5.01
24	2.92	3.53	3.90	4.17	4.37	4.54	4.68	4.81	4.92
30	2.89	3.49	3.84	4.10	4.30	4.46	4.60	4.72	4.83
40	2.86	3.44	3.79	4.04	4.23	4.39	4.54	4.63	4.74
60	2.83	3.40	3.74	3.98	4.16	4.31	4.44	4.55	4.65
120	2.80	3.36	3.69	3.92	4.10	4.24	4.36	4.48	4.56
∞	2.77	3.31	3.63	3.86	4.03	4.17	4.29	4.39	4.47

Adapted from Table 29 of E. S. Pearson and H. O. Hartley, eds., *Biometrika tables for statisticians*, vol. 1 (3rd ed.), Cambridge University Press for the Biometrika Trustees, 1966.

(p = .01) df for Denominator	Number of Groups (k)								
	2	3	4	5	6	7	8	9	10
1	90.0	135	164	186	202	216	227	237	246
2	14.0	19.0	22.3	24.7	26.6	28.2	29.5	30.7	31.7
3	8.26	10.6	12.2	13.3	14.2	15.0	15.6	16.2	16.7
4	6.51	8.12	9.17	9.96	10.6	11.1	11.5	11.9	12.3
5	5.70	6.97	7.80	8.42	8.91	9.32	9.67	9.97	10.2
6	5.24	6.33	7.03	7.56	7.97	8.32	8.61	8.87	9.10
7	4.95	5.92	6.54	7.01	7.37	7.68	7.94	8.17	8.37
8	4.74	5.63	6.20	6.63	6.96	7.24	7.47	7.68	7.87
9	4.60	5.43	5.96	6.35	6.66	6.91	7.13	7.32	7.49
10	4.48	5.27	5.77	6.14	6.43	6.67	6.87	7.05	7.21
11	4.39	5.14	5.62	5.97	6.25	6.48	6.67	6.84	6.99
12	4.32	5.04	5.50	5.84	6.10	6.32	6.51	6.67	6.81
13	4.26	4.96	5.40	5.73	5.98	6.19	6.37	6.53	6.67
14	4.21	4.89	5.32	5.63	5.88	6.08	6.26	6.41	6.54
15	4.17	4.83	5.25	5.56	5.80	5.99	6.16	6.31	6.44
16	4.13	4.78	5.19	5.49	5.72	5.92	6.08	6.22	6.35
17	4.10	4.74	5.14	5.43	5.66	5.85	6.01	6.15	6.27
18	4.07	4.70	5.09	5.38	5.60	5.79	5.94	6.08	6.20
19	4.05	4.67	5.05	5.33	5.55	5.73	5.89	6.02	6.14
20	4.02	4.64	5.02	5.29	5.51	5.69	5.84	5.97	6.09
24	3.96	4.54	4.91	5.17	5.37	5.54	5.69	5.81	5.92
30	3.89	4.45	4.80	5.05	5.24	5.40	5.54	5.65	5.76
40	3.82	4.37	4.70	4.93	5.11	5.27	5.39	5.50	5.60
60	3.76	4.28	4.60	4.82	4.99	5.13	5.25	5.36	5.45
120	3.70	4.20	4.50	4.71	4.87	5.01	5.12	5.21	5.30
∞	3.64	4.12	4.40	4.60	4.76	4.88	4.99	5.08	5.16

References and Additional Reading

Amateur Athletic Union. 1994. *AAU physical fitness program.* Bloomington, Ind.: Amateur Athletic Union.

American Alliance for Health, Physical Education, Recreation and Dance (AAHPERD). 1976a. *AAHPERD youth fitness test manual.* Reston, Va.: Author.

———. 1976b. *Special fitness test manual for mildly mentally retarded persons.* Reston, Va.: Author.

———. 1980a. *AAHPERD health-related physical fitness test manual.* Reston, Va.: Author.

———. 1980b. *Testing for impaired, disabled and handicapped individuals.* Reston, Va.: Author.

———. 1984. *Technical manual for health related physical fitness.* Reston, Va.: Author.

———. 1988. *Physical best.* Reston, Va.: Author.

———. 1989. *Tennis skills test manual.* Reston, Va.: Author.

———. 1991. *Softball skills test manual.* Reston, Va.: Author.

American Association for Health, Physical Education and Recreation (AAHPER). 1965. *Football: Skills test manual.* Washington, D.C.: Author.

———. 1967. *Archery for boys and girls: Skills test manuals.* Washington, D.C.: Author.

American College of Sports Medicine (ACSM). 1998. Position stand: Exercise and physical activity for older adults. *Medicine and Science in Sports and Exercise* 30: 992–1008.

———. 2003. *ACSM fitness book.* 3rd ed. Champaign, Ill.: Human Kinetics.

———. 2010a. *ACSM's guidelines for exercise testing and prescription.* 8th ed. Philadelphia: Wolters Kluwer Health.

———. 2010b. *ACSM's health-related physical fitness assessment manual.* Philadelphia: Wolters Kluwer Health.

———. 2018. *ACSM's health-related physical fitness assessment manual.* Philadelphia: Wolters Kluwer.

American Health and Fitness Foundation. 1986. *FTY program manual.* Austin, Tex.: American Health and Fitness Foundation.

Arnheim, D. D., and Sinclair, W. A. 1979. *The clumsy child: A program of motor therapy.* 2nd ed. St. Louis: C. V. Mosby.

———. 1985. *Physical education for special populations: A developmental, adapted, and remedial approach.* Englewood Cliffs, N.J.: Prentice Hall.

Baechle, T. R., and Earle, R. W. 2000. *Essentials of strength training and conditioning.* 2nd ed. Champaign, Ill.: Human Kinetics.

Barrow, H. M. 1954. Tests of motor ability for college men. *Research Quarterly* 25: 253–260.

Barrow, H. M., and McGee, R. 1979. *A practical approach to measurement in physical education.* 3rd ed. Philadelphia: Lea & Febiger.

Bartlett, J., et al. 1991. Development of a valid volleyball skills test battery. *Journal of Physical Education, Recreation and Dance* 62(2): 19–21.

Bass, R. I. 1939. An analysis of the components of tests of semi-circular canal function and of static and dynamic balance. *Research Quarterly* 10: 33–52.

Baumgartner, T. A., and Jackson, A. S. 1982. *Measurement for evaluation in physical education.* 2nd ed. Dubuque, Iowa: Wm. C. Brown.

Baumgartner, T. A., and Wood, S. S. 1984. Development of shoulder-girdle strength endurance in elementary children. *Research Quarterly for Exercise and Sport* 55: 169–171.

Baumgartner, T. A., et al. 1984. Equipment improvements and additional norms for the modified pull-ups test. *Research Quarterly for Exercise and Sport* 55: 64–68.

Baumgartner, T. A., et al. 2007. *Measurement for evaluation in physical education and exercise science.* 8th ed. New York: McGraw-Hill Higher Education.

Bennett, C. L. 1956. Relative contributions of modern dance, folk dance, basketball, and swimming to motor abilities of college women. *Research Quarterly* 27: 253–257.

Bloom, B., et al. 1956. *Taxonomy of educational objectives: The classification of educational goals: Handbook I. Cognitive domain.* New York: David McKay.

Bloom, S. B., Madaus, G. F., and Hastings, J. T. 1981. *Evaluation to improve learning.* New York: McGraw-Hill.

Body composition (a roundtable). 1986. *The Physician and Sportsmedicine* 14(3): 144–152, 157, 161, 162.

Bonci, C. M., Hensel, F. J., and Torg, J. S. 1986. A preliminary study on the measurements of static and dynamic motion at the glenohumeral joint. *American Journal of Sports Medicine* 14: 12–17.

Borg, G. A. V. 1973. Perceived exertion: A note on "history" and methods. *Medicine and Science in Sports* 5: 90-93.

———. 1982. Psychophysical bases of perceived exertion. *Medicine and Science in Sports* 14: 377-381.

Bosco, J. S., and Gustafson, W. F. 1983. *Measurement and evaluation in physical education, fitness, and sports.* Englewood Cliffs, N.J.: Prentice Hall.

Bowerman, W. J., and Harris, W. D. 1967. *Jogging.* New York: Grosset & Dunlap.

Brady, G. F. 1945. Preliminary investigations of volleyball playing ability. *Research Quarterly* 16: 14-17.

Broer, M. R. 1973. *Efficiency of human movement.* 3rd ed. Philadelphia: W. B. Saunders.

Brouha, L. 1943. The step test: A simple method of measuring physical fitness for muscular work in young men. *Research Quarterly* 14: 31-36.

Brouha, L., and Ball, M. V. 1952. *Canadian Red Cross Society's meal study.* Toronto: University of Toronto Press.

Brown, F. G. 1983. *Principles of educational and psychological testing.* 3rd ed. New York: Holt, Rinehart & Winston.

Brumbach, W. B. 1967. *Beginning volleyball, a syllabus for teachers.* Revised ed. Eugene, Oreg.: W. B. Brumbach. In Collins, D. R., and Hodges, P. B. 1978. *A comprehensive guide to sports skills tests and measurement.* Springfield, Ill.: Charles C. Thomas.

Bucher, C. A., and Prentice, W. E. 1985. *Fitness for college and life.* St. Louis: Times Mirror/Mosby.

Buell, C. E. 1982. *Physical education and recreation for the visually handicapped.* Reston, Va.: American Alliance for Health, Physical Education, Recreation and Dance.

Bunn, J. W. 1955. *Scientific principles of coaching.* Englewood Cliffs, N.J.: Prentice Hall.

Burton, B. T., and Foster, M. D. 1985. Health implications of obesity: An NIH consensus development conference. *Journal of the American Dietetic Association* 85: 1117-1121.

Canadian Society for Exercise Physiology. 2003. *The Canadian physical activity, fitness & lifestyle approach: CSEP–health & fitness program's health-related appraisal & counseling strategy.* 3rd ed. Ottawa: Canadian Society for Exercise Physiology.

———. 2013. *CSEP-physical activity training for health (CSEP-PATH).* Ottawa: Canadian Society for Exercise Physiology.

Chapman, N. L. 1982. Chapman ball control test—Field hockey. *Research Quarterly for Exercise and Sport* 53: 239-242.

Chase, C. I. 1978. *Measurement for educational evaluation.* 2nd ed. Reading, Mass.: Addison-Wesley.

Cirn, J. T. 1986. True/false versus short answer questions. *College Teaching* 34(4): 34-37.

Clark, H. H., ed. 1975. Exercise and fat reduction. *Physical fitness research digest.* Washington, D.C.: President's Council on Physical Fitness, Series 5, April.

———. 1979. Posture. *Physical fitness research digest.* Washington, D.C.: President's Council on Physical Fitness and Sports, Series 9, January.

Clark, H. H., and Clark, D. H. 1987. *Application of measurement to physical education.* 6th ed. Englewood Cliffs, N.J.: Prentice Hall.

Claxton, D., and Faribault, J. 1988. *Tennis.* Scottsdale, Ariz.: Gorsuch, Scarisbrick.

Clemmons, J. M., Campbell, B. C., and Jeansonne, C. 2010. Validity and reliability of a new test of upper body power. *Journal of Strength and Conditioning Research* 24(6): 1559-1565.

Clevett, M. A. 1931. An experiment in teaching methods of golf. *Research Quarterly* 2: 104-112.

Coleman, R., et al. 1987. Validation of 1-mile walk test for estimating VO2 max in 20-29 year olds. *Medicine and Science in Sports and Exercise* 19 (Suppl. 2): S29.

Collins, D. R., and Hodges, P. B. 2001. *A comprehensive guide to sports skills tests and measurement.* 2nd ed. Lanhan, Md.: Scarecrow Press.

Cooper, K. H. 1982. *The aerobics program for total well-being.* New York: M. Evans & Company.

Cooper Institute. 2004a. *Fitness specialist for older adults.* Dallas: Author.

Cooper Institute. 2004b. *Physical fitness assessment and norms.* Dallas: Author.

———. 2017. *FITNESSGRAM administration manual: The journey to myhealthy zone.* 5th ed. Champaign, Ill.: Human Kinetics.

Cooper Institute. 2007. *FITNESSGRAM/ACTIVITYGRAM test administration manual.* 4th ed. Champaign, Ill.: Human Kinetics.

Corbin, C. B. 1987. Physical fitness in the K-12 curriculum: Some defensible solutions to perennial problems. *Journal of Physical Education, Recreation and Dance* 58(7): 49-54.

Corbin, C. B., and Lindsey, R. 1985. *Concepts of physical fitness.* 5th ed. Dubuque, Iowa: Wm. C. Brown.

Corbin, C. B., and Noble, L. 1980. Flexibility: A major component of physical fitness. *Journal of Physical Education and Recreation* 51(6): 23-24, 57-60.

Cornelius, W. L., and Hinon, M. M. 1980. The relationship between isometric contractions of hip extensors and subsequent flexibility in males. *Journal of Sports Medicine and Physical Fitness* 20: 75-80.

Cratty, B. J. 1975. *Remedial motor activity for children.* Philadelphia: Lea & Febiger.

Cureton, K. J., and Warren, G. L. 1990. Criterion-referenced standards for youth health-related fitness tests: A tutorial. *Research Quarterly for Exercise and Sport* 61: 7-19.

Custer, S. J., and Chaloupka, V. A. 1977. Relationship between predicted maximal oxygen consumption and running performance of college females. *Research Quarterly* 48: 47–50.

Darling-Hammond, L. 1994. Setting standards for students: The case for authentic assessment. *The Educational Forum* 59(Fall): 14–20.

DiPietro, L. 1996. The epidemiology of physical activity and physical function in older people. *Medicine and Science in Sports and Exercise* 28: 596–600.

Doolittle, T. L., and Bigbee, R. 1968. The twelve-minute run-walk: A test of cardiorespiratory fitness of adolescent boys. *Research Quarterly* 39: 491–495.

Dotson, C. 1988. Health fitness standards: Aerobic endurance. *Journal of Physical Education, Recreation and Dance* 59(7): 26–31.

Dotson, C. O., and Kirkendall, D. R. 1974. *Statistics for physical education, health, and recreation.* New York: Harper & Row.

Downie, N. M., and Heath, R. W. 1974. *Basic statistical methods.* 4th ed. New York: Harper & Row.

Dunn, J. M., Morehouse, J. W., and Fredericks, H. D. 1986. *Physical education for the severely handicapped: A systematic approach to a data based gymnasium.* Austin, Tex.: Pro-Ed.

Ebel, R. L. 1979. *Essentials of educational measurement.* 3rd ed. Englewood Cliffs, N.J.: Prentice Hall.

Edgren, H. 1932. An experiment in the testing of ability and progress in basketball. *Research Quarterly* 3: 159–171.

Fait, H. F., and Dunn, J. M. 1984. *Special physical education: Adapted, individualized, and developmental.* 5th ed. Philadelphia: Saunders College Publishing.

Franks, B. D., and Deutsch, H. 1973. *Evaluating performance in physical education.* New York: Academic.

Franks, B. D., Morrow, J. R., and Plowman, S. A. 1988. Youth fitness testing: Validation, planning, and politics. *Quest* 40: 197–199.

French, R. W., and Jansma, P. 1982. *Special physical education.* Columbus: Charles E. Merrill.

Fringer, M. N. 1961. A battery of softball skill tests for senior high school girls. Master's thesis, University of Oregon, Eugene, Oregon. In Collins, D. R., and Hodges, P. B. 1978. *A comprehensive guide to sports skills tests and measurement.* Springfield, Ill.: Charles C. Thomas.

Fry, P. F. 1983. Measurement of psychosocial aspects of physical education. *Journal of Physical Education, Recreation and Dance* 54(8): 26–27.

Gabbard, C., et al. 1983. Effects of grip and forearm position on flexed-arm hang performance. *Research Quarterly for Exercise and Sport* 54: 198–199.

Gallagher, J. R., and Brouha, L. 1943. A simple method for testing the physical fitness of boys. *Research Quarterly* 14(1): 24–30.

Gates, D. P., and Sheffield, R. P. 1940. Tests of change of direction as measurement of different kinds of motor ability in boys of 7th, 8th, and 9th grades. *Research Quarterly* 11: 136–147.

Going, S., and Williams, D. 1989. Understanding fitness standards. *Journal of Physical Education, Recreation and Dance* 60(6): 34–38.

Golding, L. A., ed. 2000. *YMCA fitness testing and assessment manual.* 4th ed. Champaign Ill.: Human Kinetics.

Gould, D. 1985. *Tennis, anyone?* 4th ed. Palo Alto, Calif.: Mayfield.

Grady, J. B. 1994. Authentic assessment and tasks: Helping students demonstrate their abilities. *NASSP Bulletin* 78(566): 92–98.

Green, J. A. 1975. *Teacher-made tests.* 2nd ed. New York: Harper & Row.

Green, K. N., East, W. B., and Hensley, L. D. 1987. A golf skills test battery for college males and females. *Research Quarterly for Exercise and Sport* 58: 72–76.

Gribble, P. A., and Hertel, J. 2003. Considerations for normalizing measures of the Star Balance Test. *Measurement in Physical Education and Exercise Science* 7(2): 89–100.

Guralnik, J. M., et al. 1989. Physical performance measures in aging research. *Journal of Gerontology* 44: M141–146.

Harris, M. L. 1969. A factor analysis study of flexibility. *Research Quarterly* 40: 62–70.

Haskell, W. L., et al. 2007. Physical activity and public health: Updated recommendation for adults from the American College of Sports Medicine and the American Heart Association. *Medicine and Science in Sports and Exercise* 39: 1423–1434.

Hensley, L. D., East, W. B., and Stillwell, J. L. 1979. A racquetball skills test. *Research Quarterly* 50: 114–118.

Hensley, L. D., Morrow, J. R., and East, W. B. 1990. Practical measurement to solve practical problems. *Journal of Physical Education, Recreation and Dance* 6(3): 42–44.

Hewitt, J. E. 1965. Revision of the Dyer backboard tennis test. *Research Quarterly* 36: 153–157.

———. 1966. Hewitt's tennis achievement test. *Research Quarterly* 37: 231–237.

Heyward, V. H. 2002. *Advanced fitness assessment and exercise prescription.* 4th ed. Champaign, Ill.: Human Kinetics.

Hodgkins, J., and Skubic, V. 1963. Cardiovascular efficiency test scores for college women in the United States. *Research Quarterly* 34: 454–461.

Hoeger, W. W. K., and Hoeger, S. A. 2005. *Lifetime physical fitness and wellness: A personalized program.* 8th ed. Belmont, Calif.: Thomson Wadsworth.

Holcomb, Z. C. 2002. *Interpreting basic statistics.* 4th ed. Los Angeles: Pyrczak Publishing.

Holt, L. E., Travis, T. M., and Okita, T. 1970. A comparative study of three stretching techniques. *Perceptual and Motor Skills* 31: 611–616.

Hopkins, D. R., Shick, J., and Plack, J. J. 1984. *Basketball for boys and girls: Skills test manual.* Reston, Va.: American Alliance for Health, Physical Education, Recreation and Dance.

Humphrey, L. D. 1981. Flexibility. *Journal of Physical Education, Recreation and Dance* 52(7): 41–43.

Jackson, A., et al. 1982. Baumgartner's modified pull-up test for male and female elementary school aged children. *Research Quarterly for Exercise and Sport* 53: 163–164.

Jackson, A. S., and Coleman, E. 1976. Validation of distance run tests for elementary school children. *Research Quarterly* 47: 86–94.

Jackson, A. S., and Pollock, M. L. 1985. Practical assessment of body composition. *The Physician and Sportsmedicine* 13(5): 76–90.

Jackson, A. S., et al. 1995. Changes in aerobic power of men, ages 25–70 years. *Medicine and Science in Sports and Exercise* 27: 113–120.

Jansma, P., ed. 1988. *The psychomotor domain and the seriously handicapped.* 3rd ed. Lanham, Md.: University Press of America.

Jensen, C. R., and Hirst, C. C. 1980. *Measurement in physical education and athletics.* New York: Macmillan.

Jensen, C. R., Schultz, G. W., and Bangerter, B. L. 1983. *Applied kinesiology and biomechanics.* 3rd ed. New York: McGraw-Hill.

Jequier, E. 1987. Energy, obesity, and body weight standards. *American Journal of Clinical Nutrition* 45: 1035–1047.

Johnson, B. L., and Nelson, J. K. 1986. *Practical measurements for evaluation in physical education.* 4th ed. Edina, Minn.: Burgess.

Johnson, L., and Londeree, B. 1976. *Motor fitness testing manual for the moderately mentally retarded.* Reston, Va.: American Alliance for Health, Physical Education, Recreation and Dance.

Johnson, P. B., et al. 1975. *Sport, exercise and you.* New York: Holt, Rinehart & Winston.

Johnson, R., and Christian, V. 1982. *Laboratory experiences in measurement and evaluation: Theory to application.* Boone, N.C.: Appalachian State University.

Johnson, R. E., and Lavay, B. 1988. *Kansas adapted/special physical education test manual.* Topeka, Kans.: Kansas State Department of Education.

Kalakian, L. H., and Eichstaedt, C. B. 1982. *Developmental/adapted physical education: Making ability count.* Edina, Minn.: Burgess.

Katch, F. I., and McArdle, W. D. 1977. *Nutrition, weight control, and exercise.* Boston: Houghton Mifflin.

Kirby, R. F. 1971. A simple test of agility. *Coach and Athlete* (June): 30–31.

Kirkendall, D. R., Gruber, J. J., and Johnson, R. E. 1980. *Measurement and evaluation for physical educators.* Dubuque, Iowa: Wm. C. Brown.

Kline, G., et al. 1987. Estimation of VO2 max from a one-mile track walk, gender, age, and body weight. *Medicine and Science in Sports and Exercise* 19: 253–259.

Kryspin, W. J., and Feldusen, J. F. 1974. *Developing classroom tests: A guide for writing and evaluating test items.* Edina, Minn.: Burgess.

Lafuze, M. 1951. A study of the learning of fundamental skills by college freshman women of low motor ability. *Research Quarterly* 22: 149–157.

Logan, G. A., and McKinney, W. C. 1982. *Anatomic kinesiology.* 3rd ed. Dubuque, Iowa: Wm. C. Brown.

Lohman, G. A. 1982. Measurement of body composition in children. *Journal of Physical Education, Recreation and Dance* 53(8): 67–70.

Lohman, G. A., and Pollock, M. L. 1981. Which caliper? How much training? *Journal of Physical Education, Recreation and Dance* 52(1): 27–29.

Lohman, T. G. 1982. Body composition methodology in sports medicine. *The Physician and Sports Medicine* 10(12): 46–58.

Lund, J. 1992. Assessment and accountability in secondary physical education. *Quest* 44: 352–360.

Luttgens, K., and Wells, K. F. 1982. *Kinesiology: Scientific basis of human motion.* 7th ed. Philadelphia: Saunders College Publishing.

Lyman, H. B. 1963. *Test scores and what they mean.* Englewood Cliffs, N.J.: Prentice Hall.

Manitoba Education and Training. 1989. *Manitoba schools fitness.* Winnipeg: Manitoba Education and Training.

Masley, J. W., Hairabedian, A., and Donaldson, D. N. 1953. Weight training in relation to strength, speed, and coordination. *Research Quarterly* 24: 308–315.

Masters, L. F., Mori, A. A., and Lange, E. K. 1983. *Adapted physical education: A practitioner's guide.* Rockville, Md.: Aspen Publication.

Mattson, D. E. 1981. *Statistics: Difficult concepts, understandable explanations.* St. Louis: C. V. Mosby.

McArdle, W. D., et al. 1972. Reliability and interrelationships between maximal oxygen intake, physical work capacity, and step test scores in college women. *Medicine and Science in Sports* 4: 182–186.

McClenaghan, B. A., and Gallahue, D. L. 1978. *Fundamental movement: A developmental and remedial approach.* Philadelphia: W. B. Saunders.

McCloy, C. H., and Young, N. D. 1954. *Tests and measurements in health and physical education.* 3rd ed. New York: Appleton-Century-Crofts.

McDonald, L. G. 1951. The construction of a kicking test as an index of general soccer ability. Master's thesis, Springfield College, Springfield, Mass. In Collins, D. R., and Hodges, P. B. 1978. *A comprehensive guide to sports skills tests and measurement.* Springfield, Ill.: Charles C. Thomas.

McKeachie, W. J. 1969. *Teaching tips: A guidebook for the beginning college teacher.* Lexington, Mass.: D. C. Heath.

Melograno, V. J. 1994. Portfolio assessment: Documenting authentic student learning. *Journal of Physical Education, Recreation and Dance* 65(8): 50–55, 58–61.

Metheny, E. 1982. *Body mechanics.* New York: McGraw-Hill.

Metropolitan Life Insurance Company. 1983. *1983 height and weight tables announced.* New York: Metropolitan Life Insurance Company.

Miller, A. G., and Sullivan, J. V. 1982. *Teaching physical activities to impaired youth: An approach to mainstreaming.* New York: John Wiley & Sons.

Miller, D. K. 1970. A comparison of the effects of individual and team sports programs on the motor ability of male college freshmen. Unpublished doctoral dissertation, Florida State University.

———. 1983. *The well being–good health handbook.* New York: Leisure.

Miller, D. K., and Allen, T. E. 1990. *Fitness: A lifetime commitment.* 4th ed. New York: Macmillan.

Mitchell, J. R. 1963. The modification of the McDonald skill test for upper elementary school boys. Master's thesis, University of Oregon, Eugene, Oregon. In Collins, D. R., and Hodges, P. B. 1978. *A comprehensive guide to sports skills tests and measurement.* Springfield, Ill.: Charles C. Thomas.

Mood, D. P. 1980. *Numbers in motion: A balanced approach to measurement and evaluation in physical education.* Palo Alto, Calif.: Mayfield.

Moore, M. 1983. New height-weight tables gain pounds, lose status. *The Physician and Sportsmedicine* 11(5): 25.

Morehouse, C. A., and Stull, G. A. 1975. *Statistical principles and procedures with applications for physical education.* Philadelphia: Lea & Febiger.

Morrow, J. R., et al. 2005. *Measurement and evaluation in human performance.* 3rd ed. Champaign, Ill.: Human Kinetics.

Nichols, D. B., Arsenault, D. R., and Giuffre, D. L. 1980. *Motor activities for the underachiever.* Springfield, Ill.: Charles C. Thomas.

North Carolina Department of Public Instruction. 1977. *North Carolina motor fitness battery.* Raleigh, N.C.: North Carolina Department of Public Instruction.

Osness, W. H., et al. 1996. *Functional fitness assessment for adults over 60 years.* 2nd ed. Dubuque, Iowa: Kendall/Hunt Publishing.

Pate, R. R. 1985. *Norms for college students: Health-related physical fitness test.* Reston, Va.: American Alliance for Health, Physical Education, Recreation and Dance.

———. 1995. Physical activity and public health. *Journal of the American Medical Association* 273: 402–407.

Pate, R. R., et al. 1987. The modified pull-up. *Journal of Physical Education, Recreation and Dance* 58(10): 71–73.

Petray, C., et al. 1989. Designing the fitness testing environment. *Journal of Physical Education, Recreation and Dance* 60(1): 35–38.

Phillips, D. A., and Hornak, J. E. 1979. *Measurement and evaluation in physical education.* New York: John Wiley & Sons.

Physical fitness–motor ability test. 1973. Austin, Tex.: Texas Governor's Commission on Physical Fitness.

Piscopo, J., and Baley, J. A. 1981. *Kinesiology: The science of movement.* New York: John Wiley & Sons.

Pollock, M. L., Wilmore, J. H., and Fox, S. M. 1978. *Health and fitness through physical activity.* New York: John Wiley & Sons.

Poole, J., and Nelson, J. K. 1970. Construction of a badminton skills test battery. Unpublished study. In Johnson, B. L., and Nelson, J. K. 1986. *Practical measurements for evaluation in physical education.* 4th ed. Edina, Minn.: Burgess.

President's Council on Physical Fitness and Sports (PCPFS). 1986. *Presidential physical fitness award program.* Washington, D.C.: Author.

———. 1998. Physical activity and aging: Implications for health and quality of life in older persons. *Research Digest,* Series 3, no. 4 (December).

———. 1999a. Physical activity and fitness for persons with disabilities. *Research Digest,* Series 3, no. 5 (March).

———. 1999b. Physical activity promotion and school physical education. *Research Digest,* Series 3, no. 7 (September).

———. 2012. *The president's challenge physical fitness program.* Washington, D.C.: Author.

Pyrczak, F. 2003. *Making sense of statistics: A conceptual overview.* 3rd ed. Los Angeles: Pyrczak Publishing.

Radford, K. W., Schincariol, L., and Hughes, A. S. 1995. Enhance performance through assessment. *Strategies* 8(6): 5–9.

Rarick, G. L., Widdop, J. H., and Broadhead, G. D. 1970. The physical fitness and motor performance of educable mentally retarded children. *Exceptional Children* 36: 509–519.

Rikli, R. E., and Jones, C. J. 1997. Assessing physical performance in independent older adults: Issues and guidelines. *Journal of Aging and Physical Activity* 5: 244–261.

———. 1999a. Development and validation of a functional fitness test for community-residing older adults. *Journal of Aging and Physical Activity* 7: 129-161.

———. 1999b. Functional fitness normative scores for community-residing older adults, ages 60-94. *Journal of Aging and Physical Activity* 7: 162-182.

Rippe, J. M. 1991. *One mile walk test.* Marlboro, Mass.: Rockport.

Roach, E. G., and Kephart, N. C. 1966. *The Purdue perceptual-motor survey.* Columbus, Ohio: Charles E. Merrill.

Robbins, G., Powers, D., and Burgess, S. 1991. *A wellness way of life.* Dubuque, Iowa: Wm. C. Brown.

———. 1994. *A wellness way of life.* 2nd ed. Dubuque, Iowa: Brown & Benchmark.

Ross, R. M., and Jackson, A. S. 1990. *Understanding exercise: Concepts, calculations, and computers.* Houston: MacJr/CSI Publishing.

Rothstein, A. L. 1985. *Research design and statistics for physical education.* Englewood Cliffs, N.J.: Prentice Hall.

Russell, N., and Lange, E. 1940. Achievement tests in volleyball for junior high school girls. *Research Quarterly* 11: 33-41.

Safrit, M. J. 1981. *Evaluation in physical education.* 2nd ed. Englewood Cliffs, N.J.: Prentice Hall.

———. 1986. *Introduction to measurement in physical education and exercise science.* St. Louis: Times Mirror/Mosby College.

Safrit, M. J., and Wood, T. M. 1989. *Measurement concepts in physical education and exercise science.* Champaign, Ill.: Human Kinetics.

Sargent, D. A. 1921. The physical test of a man. *American Physical Education Review* 26(4): 188-194.

Scott, M. G., and French, E. 1959. *Measurement and evaluation in physical education.* Dubuque, Iowa: Wm. C. Brown.

Scott, M. G., et al. 1941. Achievement examination in badminton. *Research Quarterly* 12: 242-253.

Seashore, H. G. 1947. The development of a beam-walking test and its use in measuring development of balance in children. *Research Quarterly* 18: 246-258.

Seils, L. G. 1951. The relationship between measures of physical growth and gross motor performance of primary-grade school children. *Research Quarterly* 22: 244-260.

Semenick, D. 1990. Tests and measurements: The T-test. *National Strength and Conditioning Association Journal* 12(1): 36-37.

Sheehan, T. J. 1971. *An introduction to the evaluation of measurement data in physical education.* Reading, Mass.: Addison-Wesley.

Sheldon, W., Stevens, S. S., and Tucker, W. B. 1970. *The varieties of human physique.* Darien, Conn.: Hafner.

Shephard, R. J. 1993. Exercise and aging: Extending independence in older adults. *Geriatrics* 48: 61-64.

Sherrill, C. 1976. *Adapted physical education and recreation.* Dubuque, Iowa: Wm. C. Brown.

Shick, J. 1970. Battery of defensive softball skills tests for college women. *Research Quarterly* 41: 82-87.

Shick, J., and Berg, N. G. 1983. Indoor golf skill test for junior high school boys. *Research Quarterly for Exercise and Sport* 54: 75-78.

Skubic, V., and Hodgkins, J. 1963. Cardiovascular efficiency test scores for girls and women. *Research Quarterly* 34: 191-198.

———. 1964. Cardiovascular efficiency test scores for junior and senior high school girls in the United States. *Research Quarterly* 35: 184-192.

Smith, J. A. 1956. Relation of certain physical traits and abilities to motor learning in elementary school children. *Research Quarterly* 27: 220-228.

Society of Actuaries. 1959. *Build and blood pressure study.* New York: Metropolitan Life Insurance Company.

Society of Actuaries and Association of Life Insurance Medical Directors of America. 1980. *1979 build study.* New York: Metropolitan Life Insurance Company.

Society of Health and Physical Education (SHAPE America). 2014. *National standards for K-12 physical education.* Reston, Va.: Author.

Sparling, P. B. 1997. Field testing for abdominal muscular fitness: Speed versus cadence sit-ups. *ACSM's Health and Fitness Journal* 1: 30-33.

Spence, J. T., et al. 1968. *Elementary statistics.* 2nd ed. New York: Appleton-Century-Crofts.

Stamford, B. 1986. Somatotypes and sports selection. *The Physician and Sportsmedicine* 14(7): 176.

Sterner, T. G., and Burke, E. J. 1986. Body fat assessment: A comparison of visual estimation and skinfold techniques. *The Physician and Sportsmedicine* 14(4): 101-107.

Stodola, Q., and Stordahl, K. 1967. *Basic educational tests and measurements.* Chicago: Science Research Associates.

Strand, B. N., and Wilson, R. 1993. *Assessing sport skills.* Champaign, Ill.: Human Kinetics.

Thomas, J. R., Pierce, C., and Ridsale, S. 1977. Age differences in children's ability to model motor behavior. *Research Quarterly* 48: 592-597.

Torshen, K. P. 1977. *The mastery approach to competency-based education.* New York: Academic.

Tyson, K. W. 1970. A handball skill test for college men. Master's thesis, University of Texas, Austin. In Collins, D. R., and Hodges, P. B. 1978. *A comprehensive guide to sports skills tests and measurement.* Springfield, Ill.: Charles C. Thomas.

Ulrich, D. A. 2000. *Test of gross motor development–2 (TGMD-2)*. Austin, Tex.: PRO-ED, Inc.

U.S. Bureau of the Census. 2018. https://www.census.gov/library/visualizations/2018/comm/historic-first.html.

U.S. Department of Agriculture and U.S. Department of Health and Human Services. 1990. *Nutrition and your health: Dietary guidelines for Americans.* 3rd ed. Home Garden Bulletin No. 232. Washington, D.C.: U.S. Government Printing Office.

U.S. Public Health Service. 1996. *Physical activity and health: A report of the Surgeon General.* Washington, D.C.: U.S. Department of Health and Human Services.

University of the State of New York. 1966. *New York State physical fitness test.* Albany, N.Y.: State Education Department.

Vars, G. F. 1983. Missiles, marks, and the middle level student. *NASS Principal's Bulletin* 67(5): 72–77.

Veal, M. L. 1988a. Pupil assessment issues: A teacher educator's perspective. *Quest* 40: 151–161.

———. 1988b. Pupil assessment perceptions and practices of secondary teachers. *Journal of Teaching Physical Education* 7: 327–342.

———. 1992. The role of assessment in secondary physical education–A pedagogical view. *Journal of Physical Education, Recreation and Dance* 63(7): 88–92.

———. 1995. Assessment as an instructional tool. *Strategies* 8(6): 10–15.

Veal, M. L., and Taylor, M. 1995. A case for teaching about assessment. *Journal of Physical Education, Recreation and Dance* 66(1): 54–59.

Verducci, F. M. 1980. *Measurement concepts in physical education.* St. Louis: C. V. Mosby.

Vincent, W. J. 1976. *Elementary statistics in physical education.* Springfield, Ill.: Charles C. Thomas.

———. 1995. *Statistics in kinesiology.* Champaign, Ill.: Human Kinetics.

Wallin, D., et al. 1985. Improvement in muscle flexibility: A comparison between two techniques. *American Journal of Sports Medicine* 13: 263–268.

Weber, J. C., and Lamb, D. R. 1970. *Statistics and research in physical education.* St. Louis: C. V. Mosby.

Wessel, J. 1961. *Movement fundamentals.* 2nd ed. Englewood Cliffs, N.J.: Prentice Hall.

Wiggins, G. 1993. Assessment: Authenticity, context, and validity. *Delta Kappa* 75(3): 200–208, 210–214.

Williford, N. H. 1986. Evaluation of warm-up for improvement in flexibility. *American Journal of Sports Medicine* 14: 316–319.

Williford, N. H., and Smith, J. F. 1985. A comparison of proprioceptive neuromuscular facilitation and static stretching techniques. *American Corrective Therapy Journal* 39: 30–33.

Winnick, J. P. 1995. *Adapted physical education and sport.* 2nd ed. Champaign, Ill.: Human Kinetics.

Winnick, J. P., and Short, F. X. 1999. *The Brockport physical fitness test manual.* Champaign, Ill.: Human Kinetics.

Youjie, H., et al. 1998. Physical fitness, physical activity, and functional limitation in adults aged 40 and older. *Medicine and Science in Sports and Exercise* 30: 1430–1435.

INDEX

of criterion-referenced tests, 59
definition of, 4
determination of, 101
explantion of, 58–59
factors affecting, 62
of grades, 91
of norm-referenced tests, 59–60
predictive, 60
Validity coefficient, 59
Variability, 15. *See also* Measures of variability
Variable
criterion, 42
dependent, 42
explanation of, 5
independent, 42
Vertical jump, 177–178, 178t
Volleyball, 270–274, 271–274f
V-Sit, 122
V-Sit Reach tests, 152, 152t

W

Waist-to-hip circumference ratio, 202t
Waist-to-hip ratio, 201
Weight, of grades, 91
Weight-training equipment, 163–165, 164–165t
Wheelchair ramp test, 244

Y

YMCA 3-Minute Step Test, 141–142, 143t
YMCA Bench Press Test, 165, 165t
YMCA Physical Fitness Test, 195, 210–211, 211t

Z

Zigzag Run, 115
z-scores, 23–25, 26f